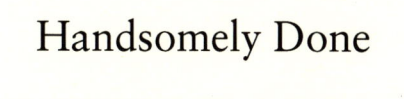

Handsomely Done

Handsomely Done

Aesthetics, Politics, and Media after Melville

✦

Edited by
Daniel Hoffman-Schwartz

NORTHWESTERN UNIVERSITY PRESS
EVANSTON, ILLINOIS

Northwestern University Press
www.nupress.northwestern.edu

Copyright © 2019 by Northwestern University Press.
Published 2019. All rights reserved.

Printed in the United States of America

10 9 8 7 6 5 4 3 2 1

Library of Congress Cataloging-in-Publication Data

Names: Hoffman-Schwartz, Daniel, editor.
Title: Handsomely done : aesthetics, politics, and media after Melville / edited by Daniel Hoffman-Schwartz.
Description: Evanston, Illinois : Northwestern University Press, 2019. | Includes index. | "The present book had its origin in a one-day workshop entitled 'Multimedia Melville' at Oxford's Ertegun House in 2013, organized by Denise Koller."
Identifiers: LCCN 2018049312| ISBN 9780810139732 (pbk. : alk. paper) | ISBN 9780810139749 (cloth : alk. paper) | ISBN 9780810139756 (ebook)
Subjects: LCSH: Melville, Herman, 1819–1891—Criticism and interpretation. | Melville, Herman, 1819–1891—Influence. | Melville, Herman, 1819–1891—Film adaptations—History and criticism.
Classification: LCC PS2387 .H33 2019 | DDC 813.3—dc23
LC record available at https://lccn.loc.gov/2018049312

CONTENTS

Acknowledgments — vii

Introduction — 3
   Daniel Hoffman-Schwartz

Part 1. Melville and the Limits of the Political

Moby-Dick and Perpetual War — 13
   Sorin Radu Cucu and Roland Végső

Bartleby Politics — 35
   Emily Apter

Land and See: The Theatricality of the Political in
   Schmitt and Melville — 55
   Walter A. Johnston

The Coward's Paradox: Pip's Weak Resistance — 89
   Barbara N. Nagel

From Lima to Attica: *Benito Cereno*, the Nixon Recordings,
   and the 1971 Prison Uprising — 113
   Paul Downes

Part 2. Audiovisual Melville

"A Sound Not Easily to Be Verbally Rendered":
   The Literary Acoustic of *Billy Budd* — 141
   David Copenhafer

Necrophilology — 159
   Jacques Lezra

Whaling in the Abyss between Melville and Zeppelin:
   Alex Itin's *Orson Whales*   *181*
   John T. Hamilton

The Confidence-Image (Melville, Godard, Deleuze)   *195*
   Peter Szendy

Belle Trouvaille: Between Aesthetics and Philology
   in *Billy Budd* (after *Beau Travail*)   *211*
   Daniel Hoffman-Schwartz

A-religion   *239*
   Jean-Luc Nancy

Contributors   *243*

Index   *245*

ACKNOWLEDGMENTS

The present book had its origin in a one-day workshop entitled "Multimedia Melville" at Oxford's Ertegun House in 2013, organized by Denise Koller. Thanks to Denise for that initial invitation, to Lloyd Pratt for moderation, and to Barbara Natalie Nagel and Jacques Lezra for their participation in this first iteration of the project. I would also like to recognize all of the contributors for their hard work, patience, and intellectual adventurousness. I learned a great deal about Melville from conversations with Sorin Radu Cucu, David Copenhafer, and Walter Johnston; shout-outs to all three of them for the sustenance of intellectual friendship. The volume improved greatly on account of two unusually thoughtful and learned reader's reports; whoever and wherever you are, thank you. Thanks are due to Gianna Mosser for finding such able readers, for seeing the project through to completion, and for taking the project on in the first place. For various forms of technical work on the manuscript, I offer humble appreciation to Anastasiya Osipova and S. C. Kaplan. Barbara Natalie Nagel offered inspired interlocution and crucial support at every stage of the process; and Lois Hoffman-Nagel arrived halfway through, bringing the best possible forms of distraction and motivation. To Barbara and Lois, I thus express my heartfelt gratitude.

—Daniel Hoffman-Schwartz

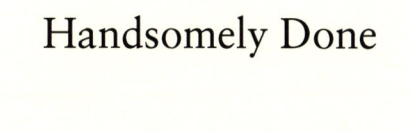

Handsomely Done

Introduction

Daniel Hoffman-Schwartz

"Handsomely done, my lad!" As any good reader of Melville is sure to recall, these lines ring out in a crucial scene of *Billy Budd*; the words come from the mouth of Billy's antagonist Claggart, the master-of-arms aboard the HMS *Bellipotent*, after the graceful Billy uncharacteristically stumbles, spilling his soup in Claggart's path. The stumble is in fact a dramatic pivot or peripeteia, a tragicomic moment foreshadowing the angelic Billy's subsequent downfall. Claggart's ironically mocking "Handsomely done" registers as a first manifestation of the envious antipathy that will lead him to frame Billy for conspiracy, the act that in turn leads to Billy's demise. Billy's lack of comprehension of the irony of these words signals the utter lack of guile that will make him so vulnerable to the guile of others.[1] But for our purposes the phrase "handsomely done" has an additional significance, one that perhaps overleaps that of its utterance in Melville's novella; it is this phrase that, by way of the detour of translation, yields the title of one of the most celebrated of Melville adaptations, namely Claire Denis's 1999 film *Beau Travail*, which transposes the story of *Billy Budd* to the French Foreign Legion in (post) colonial Djibouti. Though the film adaptation in fact excises the tragicomic soup-spill, it nonetheless borrows its title from Pierre Leyris's rendering of "Handsomely done" in his 1980 Gallimard translation *Billy Budd, marin (récit interne)*; "Handsomely done" becomes "Beau travail." But when *Beau travail* is transformed into a title, the irony of the exclamation is folded back onto the text itself; it thus comes to refer to the labor of adaptation and translation undertaken by the film. Billy's infelicitous stumble becomes that of the film *Beau Travail* in its attempt to carry out the impossible task of adaptation or translation; the title becomes an emblem for the film's own status as an impossible adaptation-translation. The *travail* in question thus recalls not only the famous "pains" or "pangs" (*Wehen*) that Walter Benjamin associates with the task of translation, but it also—more directly—recalls Jacques Derrida's post-Benjaminian concept-figure of the "en. tr.," which links precisely "*travail*" and "translation" (or *traduction*).[2] It should be clear that the "failure" of this *travail* is not simply negative; the infelicity or stumble is the very condition of possibility for the "success" of *Beau Travail*. Indeed, *Beau Travail is* handsomely done, and never more so than when it thematizes its own travails. It is thus with a nod and wink to this self-thematizing translation, poised ironically between felicity and infelicity, between the claims of freedom and the claims of fidelity, that the present volume assumes the title *Handsomely Done*, which now stands as a paradoxical translation of and tribute to Claire Denis's *Beau Travail*. In this spirit, the volume closes with "A-religion," Jean-Luc Nancy's brief meditation on the film, and includes one other contribution (by Daniel Hoffman-Schwartz) that takes up *Beau Travail*.

This volume's full title, *Handsomely Done: Aesthetics, Politics, and Media after Melville,* points to what we might think of, following Samuel Weber's pathbreaking work on Benjamin, as "Melville's-abilities"—that is, the "criticizability," "translatability," and "reproducibility" of Melville's writings.[3] The notion of "-ability" (*-barkeit*) allows for a capacious conceptualization of the *afterlife* of Melville's works, making it possible to read critical and philosophical appropriations of Melville alongside adaptations and translations; according to this distinctive Benjaminian logic, reception may retroactively disclose what will have been essential (if also virtual) features of "the works themselves" from the very beginning.

The concept of media at work in this collection is thus not limited to "mass" or "technological" media, though the various modern forms of image- and sound-recording figure prominently here, as do the "current events" that are inseparable from the media that present them. Rather, it is axiomatic for this anthology that Melville's works are characterized by an intensive engagement with the mediality of literature itself. Thus the pointed irony of the narrator's declaration in *Billy Budd* that Captain Vere exhibits "nothing of that literary taste which *less heeds the thing conveyed than the vehicle*."[4] In Melville's texts the "vehicle"—that is, the medium and its mediality—is inarguably part of "the thing conveyed." One thinks of Melville's syntactical extravagance, the virtuosic shifts of style and diction, the experiments with dialect and a plurality of "Englishes," the evident love of all manner of pun and wordplay. Moreover, in Melville the medium of language is not one: "speaking" to both eye and ear, Melville's writing is not simply a "medial" phenomenon but also a "multimedia" one.

It is this intense mediality that renders Melville's writings such a paradoxical object of translation and adaptation: at least according to the dominant, meaning-based conceptualization of translation, this medial, emphatically material character is precisely what ought to make Melville's works most resistant to translation, most untranslatable. And yet, turning again to the privileged example of *Beau Travail*, we might note the possibility of a disjunctive form of intensive translation, a translation of and by intensity: the unusual cinematic intensity of *Beau Travail*, irreducibly bound up with the very materiality of film, recalls and attests to Melville's distinctive literary-linguistic intensity. To take an object from a seemingly different cultural milieu, Led Zeppelin's sublimely wordless "Moby Dick" (also the topic of an essay in this anthology) similarly follows this path of intensive, disjunctive translation.

But the travails of Melville's afterlife are characterized by another tendency, one that is in some tension with that of materiality and intensive un-translatability—that of permanent contemporaneity or uncanny actuality. Whether we understand this as a matter of real prescience, as the effect of an ambiguous invitation to allegorization that inheres in Melville's texts, or indeed as the result of a peculiar "-ability" to be updated or put to work in new settings, Melville's writings have a way of flashing into relevance at every new cultural-political conjuncture. Here one could name most readily Edward Said's likening of the "War on Terror" to Ahab's pursuit of Moby Dick in a *London Observer* article in the immediate aftermath of the 9/11 attacks,[5] *Beau Travail*'s refashioning of *Billy Budd* as a story of the aftermath of French colonialism, or the Occupy movement's intermittent invocations of "Bartleby, the Scrivener: A Story of Wall Street." In keeping with this tendency, the Black Lives Matter movement emerges at several points in this anthology as Melville's uncanny or anachronic interlocutor;[6] similarly, we learn in what follows of the surprising invocations of Melville's name and works during the Attica Prison uprising and by the Red Army Faction.[7]

In this anthology, then, "aesthetics, politics, and media" does not name three discrete areas of interest or a merely eclectic juxtaposition of keywords, but points instead to a thinking of aesthetics and politics that is inseparable from questions of media, mediality, and mediation; one could go so far as to argue that the essays collected here are unified by the fact that they position "media"—paradigmatically, the medium of language—as the "common root" of aesthetics and politics. To some degree, this anthology can be situated within a recent second wave of theoretically oriented Melville scholarship that is not organized by the pseudo-opposition of "theory versus history." Much of this work has proceeded by recognizing common philosophical antecedents of Melville *and* theory, thus placing theory itself in history and dispelling any impression of a simple "application from without"; at the same time, this recent scholarship generally speaking dispenses with any historicist naivete, insisting on the necessity of speculation and the force of the latent or the unthought. Such work has focused to a large degree on Melville's relation to philosophical aesthetics and various (pre-, post-, anti-) Kantianisms; one thinks in particular of such works as Branka Arsić's *Passive Constitutions: or, 7½ Times Bartleby* (2007); Birgit Mara Kaiser's *Figures of Simplicity: Sensation and Thinking in Kleist and Melville* (2011); Paul Grimstad's *Experience and Experimental Writing: Literary Pragmatism from Emerson to the Jameses* (2013); Dominic Mastroianni's *Politics and Skepticism in Antebellum American Literature* (2014); and Paul Hurh's *American Terror: The Feeling of Thinking in Edwards, Poe, and Melville* (2015); as well as Samuel Otter and Geoffrey Sanborn's anthology *Melville and Aesthetics* (2011).[8] The present anthology offers a cognate mixing of theory and history, but differs somewhat from its predecessors in determining history as an afterlife rather than as a context of production and thus granting a certain privilege to figures of reception (translation, adaptation, appropriation). *Handsomely Done* thus rereads Melvillean politics and aesthetics by way of

Melville's anticipations of our media epoch *and* by way of this epoch's divergent appropriations of Melville. Here the specter of the mere "application" of theory is dispelled in two different ways: by foregrounding the productivity of Melville *for* theory, a productivity akin to and indeed inseparable from the productivity of Melville for the arts and culture at large; and by emphasizing the disruptive, anachronic force of Melville's "originals," texts that can never simply be located within a linear, homogeneous time.[9]

This volume is divided into two halves, with the first, "Melville and the Limits of the Political," foregrounding explicitly political questions and the second, "Audiovisual Melville," foregrounding questions of media. These divisions are meant to be suggestive and porous, rather than definitive or strict; thus media-theoretical questions recur with varying degrees of explicitness throughout the first half, and contributions in the second half return to many of the political questions raised in the first half of the volume.

"Melville and the Limits of the Political" reflects on borders and territoriality and the literally anomalous character of the sea (Johnston, Cucu/Végső), but also on figures that interrupt or trouble the political—namely the cowardice of Pip (Nagel) and the obstinacy of Bartleby (Apter); in the essay by Cucu/Végső, questions of media are front and center, whereas the essays by Johnston, Nagel, and Apter take a more oblique approach to these questions.

In "*Moby-Dick* and Perpetual War," Sorin Radu Cucu and Roland Végső argue that *Moby-Dick* has become part of the "aesthetic unconscious" of a modernity defined by perpetual war, citing appropriations of the novel as divergent as the Red Army Faction's use of the language of the novel in their encrypted internal communications during their incarceration and John Huston's 1956 *Moby-Dick* film, which includes an unmistakable allusion to the contemporary tests of nuclear weapons at Bikini Atoll. Approaching the figure of modernity as perpetual war through the question of the novel's status as a medium, they locate the conflict between singular materiality and allegorical substitution at the heart of the metaphysical concerns of *Moby-Dick* itself; on this account, the ontological negativity explored in "the whiteness of the whale" turns out not only to be the zero point where finite materiality "demands" its own mediation (or allegorical abstraction), but the very foundation of perpetual war itself.

Emily Apter's "Bartleby Politics" takes Bartleby as the emblem of obstinacy, understood as a political mode that encompasses phenomena as different from one another as Kim Davis's infamous stand against gay marriage, the dogged semantic vacuity of official political discourse, the alternately celebrated and reviled "demandlessness" of the Occupy movement, and the militant passivity of the "hands up" gesture associated with Black Lives Matter. Exploring the lexicon of obstinacy, Apter moves from the Greek *stasis* (at once peace and civil war) through Negt and Kluge's *Eigensinn* before turning to *ostinato* as the musical and ultimately literary figure for the obstinant, as exemplified by Louis-René des Forêt's Bartleby-esque experimental novel *Ostinato*.

Walter A. Johnston's "Land and See: The Theatricality of the Political in Schmitt and Melville" sets out from Carl Schmitt's evocations of *Benito Cereno* in *Ex Captivitate Salus* and his correspondence with Ernst Jünger, contextualizing these writings within the postwar spatial turn in Schmitt's theorization of sovereignty. Johnston demonstrates both the productivity and the limits of Schmitt's reading of Melville: while the Schmittian opposition of land and sea power illuminates certain aspects of Melville's story of a slave revolt in South America, Schmitt represses the vaporous theatricality that is so central to *Benito Cereno*, a theatricality that is ultimately democratic in character and which serves to undermine the ostensible fixity of Schmitt's sovereign spatial orders.

Barbara N. Nagel's "The Coward's Paradox: Pip's Weak Resistance" offers an intertextual reading of "The Castaway" chapter in *Moby-Dick*, building a literary and political counter-history of cowardice around the figure of Pip, the African American shipkeeper who jumps overboard in a moment of apparent madness. Nagel argues that Melville's seeming transvaluation of cowardice is central to his move beyond mere adventure fiction; it is, in other words, his very literary bravery (or what Hölderlin calls *Dichtermut*). The coward presents a paradox in that the already humiliated coward is immune to the humiliating punishments to which the law threatens to subject him; in this sense, the coward humiliates the law and thus stands as a figure of resistance to sovereign authority of all kinds. Reading the racialized violence of Pip's story alongside contemporary accounts of police violence against African Americans, Nagel's counter-history of cowardice opens onto a politics of escape.

Paul Downes's "From Lima to Attica: *Benito Cereno*, the Nixon Recordings, and the 1971 Prison Uprising" examines the citational politics of Melville's novella of slave revolt. Downes thus moves from Melville's literary reworking of historical sources and the protagonist Babo's theatrical repetition of his former enslavement to the broad recovery of *Benito Cereno* for black revolutionary and antiracist politics in the late 1960s and early 1970s in the circle around the African American writer and scholar Sterling Brown before turning to the specific case of the Attica uprising and the Nixon-Rockefeller tapes. Not only does the uprising itself manifest a certain connection to *Benito Cereno*—emblematized in the figure of the Attica activist Mad Bomber Melville (née Samuel Grossman)—but, as Downes demonstrates, Nixon's recorded conversations concerning Attica may entail a Cereno-esque subversion of sovereignty by citationality.

Part 2, "Audiovisual Melville," treats Melville's own writing as an "audiovisual" phenomenon itself (Copenhafer, Lezra), attends to transpositions of Melville's writing into audiovisual media traditionally conceived, that is, music and particularly film (Hamilton, Nancy), or alternates between these two approaches (Hoffman-Schwartz, Szendy).

David Copenhafer's "'A Sound Not Easily to Be Verbally Rendered': The Literary Acoustic of *Billy Budd*" contains this volume's most "focused" engagement with Melvillean audio and audition. Toggling between sounds of punishment (the whip, flogging) and discipline (the whistle), Billy's liberated nightingale-like song, and the musical historiography of the novella's concluding ballad "Billy in the Darbies," Copenhafer hones in upon the unexpected audio-politics of *Billy Budd*. The intensive time of listening, what Copenhafer calls "the time of the literary acoustic," is exemplified in the auditory atmosphere of Billy's execution, in which the human microphone-like "vocal current electric" of the assembled crew vies with the various inhuman sounds of sea and wind in an agonistic symphony that condenses and re-presents the famed ambiguity of the novella.

Jacques Lezra's "Necrophilology" uncovers a complex political economy of sound in Melville's story "Bartleby, the Scrivener," tying the poetics of rumor under equity capitalism to the story's narrative movement from the hustle and bustle of Wall Street to its closing invocations of silence—Bartleby's fate in "the Tombs," the notorious "dead letters" speeding to death, the implicit silenced copula of the story's famous final lines ("Ah, Bartleby! Ah, humanity!"). Lezra demonstrates that this movement from sound to silence via rumor in "Bartleby" encrypts the Marxian problem of general equivalence, as it is split between the analysis of capital and the production of political association. What is ultimately at issue in this "necrophilological" take on "Bartleby" is the sense in which the index governing these relations of equivalence might itself be said to be "contingent"; a comparison with Jorge Luis Borges's interestingly unfaithful translation of "Bartleby" reveals a tension in the story's very linguistic texture between the "contingent" index and its ontological substantialization, between "dead letters" and their reflexive animation as the voice of "humanity."

John T. Hamilton's "Whaling in the Abyss between Melville and Zeppelin: *Orson Whales*" explores Alex Itin's short animated video *Orson Whales*, which juxtaposes Orson Welles's reading of *Moby-Dick* with Led Zeppelin's instrumental "Moby Dick." Taking his cue from a Melvillean passage on Narcissus read aloud by Welles, Hamilton reads Itin's pairing of *Moby-Dick* and "Moby Dick" as an Ovidian meditation on mirroring, *mise en abyme*, and metamorphosis structured around the double sense of the verb "to whale"; the "whaling" Bonham thus metamorphoses into the "whaling" Ahab. Following this line of reading, Welles's varied engagements with Melville, many of which are cited in Itin's video, finally betray a thoroughly Ahabian "image" of shattered narcissism and abyssal reflection.

Peter Szendy's "The Confidence-Image (Melville, Godard, Deleuze)" reads *The Confidence-Man* alongside Jean-Luc Godard's 1964 adaptation of it, *Le Grand Escroc*, in pursuit of a Melvillean cinema. Szendy thus finds in Melville's writings aspects not only of a *proto-cinema*, but of an *archi-cinema*—that is, a conceptualization of subjectivity as itself structured (and de-structured) by moving images. Reading Melville and Godard through one another with the help of Deleuze and Derrida, Szendy argues that both archi-cinema and cinema as such are structures precisely of *confidence*—a belief strictly inseparable from non-belief. Szendy thus elaborates a theory of what he terms "the confidence-image"; images are intrinsically fiduciary, engaged in relations of credit and debt that yield endless de- and re-ferrals (or *renvois*), never arriving at a final guarantor of value that would transcend the structure of confidence. The relation Melville-Godard thus exemplifies a complex logic of seriality and serial referral that comprehends both (archi-) cinematic movement and intertextual allusion.

Daniel Hoffman-Schwartz's "*Belle Trouvaille*: Between Aesthetics and Philology in *Billy Budd* (after *Beau Travail*)" reads *Billy Budd* through the conflicting imperatives of *aisthesis* and *philia* and against the backdrop of *Beau Travail*. Set in the late 1790s, Melville's novella is a reflection on the aesthetic tradition as it is politicized in the wake of the French Revolution. The novella turns upon the very possibility of the disinterested apprehension of beautiful form—namely, the beautiful form of Billy—and the political uses of such an apprehension as an agent of an ideological "harmonization" aboard the man-of-war *Bellipotent*. At every turn, Melville's own literal "philology," his own "love of words" in their materiality, disrupts and complicates the thematic reflection on beautiful form. This tension between disinterested *aisthesis* and a passionately materialist *philia* is registered and arguably intensified in the highly "cinephilic" *Beau Travail*. Hoffman-Schwartz's essay thus at once follows *Beau Travail*'s "reading" of *Billy Budd* and outlines a reading of *Beau Travail*.

Jean-Luc Nancy's brief, dense "A-religion" meditates on the "*a*-religion" of beauty in *Beau Travail*; the post-Christian (or indeed "a-theist") Christology of *Billy Budd* is adapted as a meditation on art as the new immanent religion, with cinema in particular emblematizing a special iconic, self-sacralizing power that intensifies the post-theological "religion" of *Billy Budd*. For Nancy, then, "*a*-religion" names the pretended surpassing of religion in a secularized theology of the immanent work, but it names just as well the questioning of just such a theology of the work. Thus Nancy reads the title *Beau Travail* as the cipher of a "beauty that is worried for itself," a beauty that calls into question its own sacrality and sacralization. The privative "*a*-" thus points towards the immanent nonfigurative image as at once and undecidably a new modality of religion *and* the suspension of the religious as such.

Notes

1. On this point, see the justly celebrated reading of Barbara Johnson in "Melville's Fist: The Execution of *Billy Budd*," *Studies in Romanticism* 18, no. 4 (Winter 1979): 567–89, at 587.

2. Walter Benjamin, "The Task of the Translator," in Walter Benjamin, *Selected Writings, Vol. 1 (1913–1926)*, ed. Michael Jennings and Marcus Bullock (Cambridge, Mass.: Harvard University Press, 1996), 253–63, at 256. Jacques Derrida,

"What Is a 'Relevant' Translation?" trans. Lawrence Venuti, *Critical Inquiry* 27, no. 2 (Winter 2001): 174–200, at 176. Derrida's "en. *tr.*" also recalls the translational motif of the "*entre*," that is, the "between."

3. Samuel Weber, *Benjamin's–"abilities"* (Cambridge, Mass.: Harvard University Press, 2008). For a Benjamin-inspired account of "the after," see Gerhard Richter, *Afterness: Figures of Following in Modern Thought and Aesthetics* (New York: Columbia University Press, 2011).

4. Herman Melville, *Billy Budd, Sailor,* in *Melville's Short Novels*, ed. Dan McCall (New York: Norton, 2002), 103–70, at 118. Italics mine.

5. Edward Said, "'Islam' and 'the West' Are Inadequate Banners," *The Observer*, September 16, 2001.

6. See the contributions of Nagel and Apter in particular in this volume.

7. See the respective contributions of Downes and Cucu/Végső in this volume.

8. Branka Arsić, *Passive Constitutions: or, 7½ Times Bartleby* (Stanford, Calif.: Stanford University Press, 2007); Birgit Mara Kaiser, *Figures of Simplicity: Sensation and Thinking in Kleist and Melville* (Albany: State University of New York Press, 2011); Paul Grimstad, *Experience and Experimental Writing: Literary Pragmatism from Emerson to the Jameses* (Oxford: Oxford University Press, 2013); Dominic Mastroianni, *Politics and Skepticism in Antebellum American Literature* (Cambridge: Cambridge University Press, 2014); Paul Hurh, *American Terror: The Feeling of Thinking in Edwards, Poe, and Melville* (Stanford, Calif.: Stanford University Press, 2015); and Samuel Otter and Geoffrey Sanborn, *Melville and Aesthetics* (New York: Palgrave Macmillan, 2011). For an extremely informative history of Melville criticism, see Brian Yothers, *Melville's Mirrors: Literary Criticism and America's Most Elusive Author* (Rochester, N.Y.: Camden House, 2011).

9. In addition to the previously mentioned "aesthetically oriented" texts, *Handsomely Done* no doubt finds some common ground with the following recent works of Melville criticism: Cesare Casarino, *Modernity at Sea: Melville, Marx, Conrad in Crisis* (Minneapolis: University of Minnesota Press, 2002); Eyal Peretz, *Literature, Disaster, and the Enigma of Power: A Reading of "Moby-Dick"* (Stanford, Calif.: Stanford University Press, 2003); and Jason Franks, ed., *A Political Companion to Herman Melville* (Louisville: University Press of Kentucky, 2013). For a provocative and influential recent account of anachrony, see Alexander Nagel and Christopher Wood, *Anachronic Renaissance* (Brooklyn, N.Y.: Zone Books, 2010).

Part 1

✦

Melville and the Limits of the Political

Moby-Dick and Perpetual War

Sorin Radu Cucu and Roland Végső

> War is more than a true chameleon that slightly adapts its characteristics to the given case. As a total phenomenon its dominant tendencies always make it a paradoxical trinity—composed of primordial violence, hatred, and enmity, which are to be regarded as a blind natural force; of the play of chance and probability within which the creative spirit is free to roam; and of its element of subordination, as an instrument of policy, which makes it subject to reason alone.
> —Carl von Clausewitz, *On War*, trans.
> Michael Howard and Peter Paret

The World We Live in and the Militarization of *Moby-Dick*

The seemingly impossible task that our reading of Herman Melville's *Moby-Dick* sets for itself is to avoid producing yet another allegorical interpretation of the novel. Our goal, on the contrary, is to examine the common belief underlying allegorical readings of the text that the book is somehow relevant for the "world we live in."[1] This *world* that we live in is often defined in temporal rather than spatial terms, as an age with a beginning and an end, however blurred and inadequate these temporal limits or lines may be. According to these allegorical readings, *Moby-Dick* both parallels and intersects with the world that came into being long after the book's publication. Yet the foundations of these encounters between the fictional world Melville created and "the world we live in" are often interpretive acts that strip the elaborate and expansive text down to a unified and compact plot structure, reducing it to a cautionary or visionary tale about blind ambition's path to self-destruction. As Randy Kennedy notes in an article that calls on *Moby-Dick* to explain the Deepwater Horizon oil spill of 2010, "the novel has served over the years as a remarkably resilient metaphor for everything from atomic power, to the invasion of Iraq, to the decline of the white race (this from D. H. Lawrence, who helped revive Melville's reputation). Now, 50 miles off the Louisiana coast, its themes of hubris, destructiveness, and relentless pursuit are as telling as ever."[2]

Through these readings, Melville's narrative constitutes itself both as a mirror that can capture the world it does not directly know and as a lens through which events, situations, and belief systems can be observed as being rooted in the world. We use these optical metaphors here with some caution in order to provide a preliminary description of the system of mediations developed around *Moby-Dick*. What concerns us the most is the historical fact that the self-reproductive capacity of this system originated in the novel's reception during the Cold War. The history of these interpretations is a complex tale that includes both American and international readings of the novel presented in various texts of literary criticism, as well as in political commentary by intellectuals, journalists, and political activists.[3]

Of course, the significance of *Moby-Dick* for Cold War ideologies has been recognized for a long time.[4] F. O. Matthiessen's pre-Cold War interpretation of the novel in *American Renaissance: Art and Expression in the Age of Emerson and Whitman* (1941) inaugurated the allegorical puzzle that described in explicit political terms Ahab's obsessive quest and his ability to hold onto his power. From Richard Chase to R. W. B. Lewis and from C. L. R. James to Donald Pease, Cold War critics tended to believe that the challenge posed by this allegorical puzzle consisted of figuring out how to name Ahab's power and how to describe his relation to the crew as well as to Starbuck and Ishmael. On the one hand, these by-now canonical interpretations illustrate the generational shift from the antifascist politics of the 1930s (Matthiessen) to the anti-Stalinist liberalism of the 1950s (Chase), as well as to a defense of cosmopolitan populism (James). On the other hand, they reveal the capacity of Cold War discourse to absorb contradictory positions within its system of signification. For instance, Geraldine Murphy described these different available intepretations in the following terms: "Matthiessen and Chase recognized heroic qualities in Ahab, but for Matthiessen the ageing captain symbolized the dangers of Emersonian individualism, entrepreneurial capitalism, and spiritual isolation. To Chase, however, Ahab represented both versions of the false Prometheus; Stalin and 'Stalinist,' the captain was both a totalitarian despot and an evacuated mass man willing to sacrifice his individuality for an abstraction, to 'disappear into the whiteness of the whale.'"[5] To some extent, C. L. R. James appears to expand the same allegory by arguing that Ahab represents the "totalitarian type."[6] Yet his reading does offer some significant departures from the usual exclusive focus on the political symbolism of Ahab's power, including his power to deflect any mutiny in advance. He sees Ishmael, the young intellectual, as complicit in Ahab's totalitarian endeavor.[7] While C. L. R. James does not address Matthiessen's reading directly, his argument is the strongest rejection of the idea that Ishmael's hyperbolic narration, his freedom to digress—to go beyond the story of Ahab and the whale—represents *political* freedom.

As we see in this brief account, Cold War interpretations of the novel tend to concentrate on Western anticommunist readings of the text. We, on the other hand, would like to propose a different kind of *Moby-Dick*, a genuinely global *Moby-Dick*. The starting point for such a global reading is the recognition that the significance of *Moby-Dick* for the Cold War cannot be restricted to what is usually understood by Cold War discourse: Western anticommunist discourse. Of course, C. L. R. James's reading of the novel already showed us a way out of this interpretive pattern, since it proposed to interpret the crew's work and solidarity as the counterpoint "to this ultimate climax of individualism, this frenzy of subjectivity, megalomania and fatalistic despair."[8] *Moby-Dick* can thus support another translation of a key Cold War concept. The crew potentially symbolizes a Third World to come, that is, a resistance to the Cold War through nonalignment and the cosmopolitan populism of the Global South. Yet any interpretation that values the crew's dedication to work as the key aspect of their heroism must address why hard work on the *Pequod* factory fails to create an ethic that prevents the formation of a social bond of identification with the leader. On the second day of the chase, the narration describes the mythical and metaphorical vision, according to which the crew was not only united as one but also driven towards the white whale:

> They were one man, not thirty. For as the one ship that held them all; though it was put together of all contrasting things—oak, and maple, and pine wood; iron, and pitch, and hemp—yet all these ran into each other in one concrete hull . . . ; even so, all the individualities of the crew, this man's valor, that man's fear; guilt and guiltiness, all varieties were welded into oneness, and were all directed to that fatal goal which Ahab their one lord and keel did point to.[9]

While passages such as this point to the novel's effectiveness in capturing the politico-mythological imaginary that lies at the heart of collective social formations across historical ages, the surprising aspect of the novel is precisely that it turned out to be useful for what we would like to call the "global discourse of the Cold War"—a discourse that is "global" both in the ideological and the geographical sense. In other words, we want to argue that in order to understand the significance of the novel for the Cold War, we would have to investigate its role in a wider set of political and cultural discourses that includes all versions of communism and anticommunism, as well as various forms of nonalignment that emerged all over the globe.[10] No doubt, in such an extended context, the reception of *Moby-Dick* will appear to have been more complex, riddled with contradictions, and, in one word, overdetermined.

Take, for instance, the way that one version of Cold War political romanticism was articulated in the Red Army Faction's reading of *Moby-Dick* during their days in Stammheim Prison shortly before their collective suicide. Stefan Aust, the former editor-in-chief of *Der Spiegel*, called attention to the intellectual significance of Melville's novel for the terrorist group's efforts to represent themselves within the ideological and military struggles that emerged in West

Germany and on the global scene of modernity with the Cold War.[11] "What did the RAF have to do with Moby Dick?" Aust asks in a lecture delivered in 2008.[12] The answer matters for several reasons. Scholars of German and Cold War history discovered that *Moby-Dick* provided what we could call a "media channel" through which participation in the "highly efficient communication system from cell to cell in Stammheim prison" was ensured.[13] The literary work provided the Red Army Faction (RAF) members with code names that served as the prisoners' secret language, used perhaps to coordinate the suicide of the group, and, at the same time, with an opportunity to identify with the crew of the *Pequod* in order to come to terms with their own motivations and actions: Andreas Baader as Ahab, Gerhard Müller as Queequeg, Holger Meins as Starbuck, and Jan-Carl Raspe as the Carpenter. As readers-performers of *Moby-Dick*, "the group found the romantic apotheosis of their struggle in this novel: the idea of revolution as the hunt for the white whale as a fight against the state, which they called the 'machine.' "[14] A brief look at Melville's novel allows us to see what provided the foundation for the RAF's fascination with *Moby-Dick*: the isolation of the crew from the world and the anticapitalist message that they derived from Ahab's quest. According to Aust's analysis, "the story of Captain Ahab's fanatical hunt for the whale bears all the traits of a revolutionary anticapitalist parable. The murderous struggle of Baader and his crew against the Leviathan state bore the characteristics of a metaphysical final struggle much like the one that monomaniacal Captain Ahab was leading in his *war* against the whale."[15] The key word in this commentary is, of course, "war." But how does the novel become the mediator of this militarized perception of the world? How does one metaphor (as absurd as it may appear)—Ahab's *war* against the white whale—translate into another metaphor: that of war confused with revolutionary struggle, which is, in turn, confused with terror attacks, and confused, once more, with the fantasies and realities of the Cold War?

As we ask these questions, we are once again reminded of the fact that the book's mediating power has been activated by the cultural and political practices of the Cold War. To the RAF prisoners, *Moby-Dick* offered a mythical-symbolic framework through which the metaphysical fantasy of revolutionary struggle could provide an escape from the chaos of reality, as well as from their failure to shape this reality (the world we live in) according to their political will and ideological desires. In other words, the RAF's interpretation of the novel participated in the libidinal economy generated around revolutionary struggle, imperialism, anticapitalism, terrorism, and the Cold War, an economy that marks these rhetorical categories as *war*, in fact, a form of war that appears to have no end. As the RAF prisoners "had romantically imbued their struggle against reality," writes Aust, "they transformed themselves into icons, and became icons, with all the consequences that entailed, with all the severity and brutality against alleged opponents, innocent bystanders, against their comrades and, in the end, against themselves."[16]

The RAF's *Moby-Dick* effectively shows the fiction through which "revolutionary politics" are unavoidably riveted to a destructive fantasy. At the same time, the RAF's use of the novel also engages the global discourse of the Cold War organized around Melville's novel by depicting Ahab's pursuit of Moby Dick as a fiction involved in divergent cultural translations as well as contradictory political articulations. Within Cold War discourse, Ahab's figure is therefore not simply an ambiguous symbol open to conflicting interpretations, but an embodiment of the hyper-dialectical mode of that discourse, whereby Ahab simultaneously represents American individualism, and totalitarian passion, as well as revolutionary anarchism. The globality of this discourse is easy to miss precisely because the book is often read as a particular vision of the world, an American vision seeking universalization. The example of the RAF shows that the Cold War marked a significant moment in the reception of Melville's *Moby-Dick* not because it generated a complex "scene of persuasion" according to which "Ishmael proves his freedom by opposing Ahab's totalitarian will"[17] (in line with Matthiessen), nor because it created a "scene of seduction," in which Ishmael willingly and blindly follows Ahab (according to C. L. R. James's reading). We are not arguing at all that the RAF's reading transgresses the borders of Cold War discourse, but that it makes us question certain assumptions about the ways we think and write about the Cold War—particularly today, when its "history" is caught between the triumphalism of the 1990s and the contemporary geopolitics of fear in the new millennium.

In addition to providing the book with its "political unconscious," the discourse of the Cold War reduced the novel form as a medium to a mythical fable that presents an invaluable truth about the "world we live in," a truth that was later also confirmed by post-Cold War interpretations: in Ahab's self-destructive quest we find today the image of America's reckless "war on terror."[18] This Cold War discourse thus generated, in its expansive power, a system of mediations that could bring into relation *Moby-Dick*'s central aesthetic value for the American Renaissance with its disorienting political content. In *Moby-Dick*, mythical and religious materials as well as the medium-materiality of theatrical-rhetorical language become literary form. Cold War criticism discovered in this literary form the agonistic identity of political modernity, which allowed it to connect Melville's nineteenth-century imagination of power to the struggle between totalitarianism and liberal democracy in the middle of the twentieth century. By incorporating *Moby-Dick* into its philosophy of history, Cold War discourse instrumentalized the prophetic force of the novel. At the same time, it could appropriate the novel in order to create an aesthetic foundation for its political discourse. In other words, we claim that *Moby-Dick* provided one of the narratives that made up the "aesthetic unconscious" of Cold War discourse.[19] Thus, the fact that *Moby-Dick* became a privileged literary work for Cold War discourse was not simply an accidental occurrence. It was a result of the novel's peculiar imagination of a form of conflict that, contingent on the historical developments of war in the mid-twentieth century, began to expose the metaphysical underside of modern warfare.

Our goal is to show that *Moby-Dick* contains, in its rich textual and narrative fabric, the threads of the discursive networks that generate the textual-material conditions that allow for the book's mediation of its hunting expedition with modern warfare—both in the logistical sense of preparing for battle and in the sense of a reflection on war's "place" within the horizon of modern technological civilization. In other words, we will argue that Melville's similes and metaphors through which the crew appears as an army, the white whale is declared to be a foe, and the expedition is described as a battle, do not simply have an aesthetic and epistemological function, but orient the phenomenological language game of narration (the entire whaling expedition *appears* as a war against one fierce whale) towards an ontological displacement: *Moby Dick*'s fictional world is neither a world of whaling nor a world of war, but a peculiar synthesis of military strategy and economic production, that is, a peculiar military-industrial complex. There are, of course, several reasons why discussing war in *Moby-Dick* may seem absurd and only modestly persuasive. It is not entirely clear if humans can wage war against a creature belonging to another ontological region. More importantly, however, Ahab's actions are motivated by a desire for personal revenge rather than a clearly formulated politics. We thus need to clarify that we do not claim that Melville's novel is a war novel or that it prophesizes the Cold War. What we do claim is that *Moby Dick* captures something of the way war continues to play a fundamental role in modern technological civilization in spite of its proclaimed "dream of a modernity without violence."[20] Yet, if we avoid allegorical speculation, we find that Melville's war metaphors support our claim that the novel provides a critical response to the philosophy of liberalism, to its thesis that "wars and domestic conflicts necessarily appeared as the relics of a dying age that had not yet been illuminated by the dawn of the Enlightenment."[21] Melville, in effect, successfully mobilizes these ideas about modernity and war against each other. The *Pequod* benefits from the navigational technology of the age to move "around" the globe in search of the white whale. But for all his commitment to science, Ahab's passion finds a better expression in mysticism. He uses mystical symbolism and the blind belief in predestination to legitimate his quest as well as to construct his compelling scene of persuasion. Ahab, the strategic commander, is also a politico-mystical leader who fails to see the military limits of his political power.

C. L. R. James made it clear that in reading Melville's novel, we need to integrate the political-philosophical analysis within the dialectical process by which history connects *then* to *now*. He writes, "we shall show . . . how it was possible for an American writer to portray the totalitarian type as early as 1851."[22] Yet, if we learn something from the RAF's Moby Dick game, it is that the novel's relationship to the ideological and political fog of the Cold War goes further than the "portrayal" of totalitarianism or revolutionary anarchism. We thus also need to ask the question: How was it possible for an American writer to portray the Cold War as early as 1851? To answer this question, we would need to bracket for a moment the ideological framework of the conflict as well as the modus operandi of its discourse: "in totalizing the globe into a super opposition between the two superpowers the United States and the Soviet Union, the Cold War economizes on any opposition to it by relocating all options within its frame."[23] Instead, we should address the Cold War as a symbolic mutation in the sequence of the world wars of the twentieth century. In other words, as it concerns the reception of Melville's work, the Cold War is not simply the totalizing discourse through which Ahab's and Ishmael's positions can be grasped in terms of the totalitarianism/freedom opposition, but a paradoxical warfare, a deconstructed war that resonates with the novel's peculiar conflict. Isn't *Moby-Dick*, after all, staging a conflict where the distinction between war and peace no longer applies, in which a hidden enemy is localized in the wide-open space of the globe, and which involves the risk of total catastrophe? In his sophisticated genealogy of the concept of the Cold War, Anders Stephanson shows how polarity—a category already theorized by both Hegel and Clausewitz—is the metaphor that explained and illustrated the peculiarity of this global conflict. Yet the strangeness of the Cold War is not a matter of logical contradiction as much as a genuine paradox: "the cold war is war-like in every sense except the military. Its truth is 'war for unconditional surrender' but the reality is the kind of war one has when war itself is impossible."[24] This definition applies to *Moby-Dick* as well, albeit in a significantly different historical context. The structural similarity between the Cold War's deconstruction of warfare and *Moby-Dick*'s peculiar warlike hunt cannot be easily dismissed. It is this structural similarity, rather than the problematic of totalitarianism, that has secretly fueled the fascination with Melville's novel during the Cold War.[25]

Moby Dick Must Be Weaponized

In one of its crucial scenes, John Huston's 1956 film adaptation of Melville's *Moby-Dick* directly ties the classic story of the great white whale to the historical context of the 1950s. Deep in the captain's dark cabin, completely isolated from the noisy world of the crew, Ahab shows Starbuck his charts of the global movements of whales. To Starbuck's visible surprise and exhilaration, Ahab has designed a method of predicting the movements of whales with scientific thoroughness. We see a close-up of the two intent faces studying the map against an ominously dark and significantly empty background. Then we see Ahab's finger tracing with self-assured intensity the movements of whales across the oceans. But while Starbuck sees only future profits in these prophetic hieroglyphs of global circulations, Ahab's mind is set on only one problem, what he calls their "bigger business": how to intercept the seemingly unpredictable movements of Moby Dick. Starbuck is annoyed to discover that Ahab wants to use this magical device for one purpose only: to exact his own personal revenge. Triumphantly, Ahab dismisses Starbuck by exclaiming: "I shall be waiting for him *here!* At new moon in April." At this point, the camera once again zooms in on the map as Ahab's index finger vehemently pokes at a small group of islands in the Pacific Ocean. Our gaze lingers on this shot just long enough to let us know that something of importance was revealed to us. And we notice the name of the islands on Ahab's map: Bikini.

Even today, the reference is all but impossible to miss. For Huston's audience in 1956, it was presumably even more self-evident that this cinematic gesture directly ties the story of Ahab's hunt for the big white whale to the historical present of the Cold War. The scene was no doubt perceived as an all-too-obvious reference to the testing of atomic weapons at Bikini Atoll or, more concretely, as a reminder of the enormous thermonuclear explosion let loose by Operation Castle Bravo in 1954 (whose images still haunt our public imagination today). With this simple gesture, the film immediately establishes a direct link between Moby Dick and the hydrogen bomb. The catastrophic encounter with the white whale at the end of the narrative is now irrevocably inscribed in the context of the Cold War: Moby Dick is the agent of nuclear holocaust.

How was it possible for Moby Dick to become a hydrogen bomb? What is it in the novel and in the figure of the whale that makes this identification so easy and even self-evident? How malleable, plastic, or fluid must this figure be if its history is nothing but a series of transformations like this one? What really happens when the whale becomes a weapon of mass destruction? Could he have become something else? Even something that is the opposite of a powerful weapon? Was this metamorphosis nothing but a malicious misappropriation of the whale's elusive essence? Or was this transformation always part of its destiny?

To better understand this transfiguration of the whale into a weapon, we need to look to another significant appropriation of the story from the same period. The final novels of Ernest Hemingway are haunted by Melville's story in quite obvious ways. But Hemingway's adaptations break down the story into two of its fundamental constitutive forces, which now appear in alienated, albeit crystallized, forms. Two of Hemingway's late novels represent two paradigmatic readings of *Moby-Dick*. On the one hand, we have *The Old Man and the Sea* published in 1952. Here, the seemingly allegorical structure of the Melville novel is reduced to its bare minimum (like a fish without its flesh, reduced to a mere skeleton). It is enough to just put the two books next to each other and the contrast becomes clear: Melville's excessive encyclopedia of a world stands opposed to this meager minimalist existential allegory. But this is exactly what Hemingway got wrong about *Moby-Dick*: Melville's novel cannot be reduced to this simple allegorical skeleton. This is why we also have the other novel, the posthumously published *Islands in the Stream* that was written in 1950 and 1951. Among other things, the third part of the novel records in a fictionalized form Hemingway's experiences during World War II, when he used his fishing boat to hunt for German U-boats in the Caribbean.[26] Still under the historical spell of World War II, the big white whale appears to us here as a German U-boat rather than an atomic weapon. But the tendency is the same: Moby Dick must be weaponized.

Regardless of the merits of the individual novels, we can certainly say that they represent two possible and common interpretations of Melville's story: one metaphysical, the other political. The first would treat *Moby-Dick* as an existential allegory of the futility of human existence in a fundamentally hostile universe. The second tries to turn it into a reflection on the history of modern politics. As *The Old Man and the Sea* shows, there is a price to be paid for seeing nothing more than an existential metaphor in the text. In this reductive world, the enemy of man is either an abstract fate or the concrete universe in its pure indifference to human suffering. Either way, the enemy is metaphysical in proportion. According to the political reading, however, this elusive abstract enemy must always be replaced by concrete historical actors. For what is truly at stake in a reading of *Moby-Dick* is nothing less than a proof of Melville's prophetic power to anticipate our political present as the inherent outcome of the history of modernity. While the first interpretation finds that the truth of *Moby-Dick* is powerful because it is timeless and universal, the second holds that we ourselves, in our historical specificity today (whatever that today might be), are the truth of the novel.

So was this weaponization of Moby Dick and this militarization of *Moby-Dick* an ideological misappropriation of the novel that was characteristic of the Cold War? Or did this interpretation merely make something visible that was always inherently or even explicitly present in the text from the very beginning? To put the same question differently: is *Moby-Dick* a war novel? The most compelling evidence against reading *Moby-Dick* as a war novel appears to be the fact that right before *Moby-Dick*, Melville wrote *White-Jacket; or, The World in a Man-of-War* (1850), which is a direct exploration of military life on the sea. In contrast with this text, *Moby-Dick* is a novel of the whale trade—a novel of global capitalism rather than that of war. A more subtle reading could show, then, that it is imperialism which forms the historical foundation of the text, an imperialism in which global war and global capitalism function simply as the two sides of the same coin. Maybe, in this displaced sense, *Moby-Dick* is strangely enough a war novel after all, albeit a paradoxical one: a war novel in which war does not emerge as an explicit theme.

Arguably, then, there is a certain warlike structure to the very world that is disclosed to us in the novel, even if military battle is not the focus of the text. The figure of war thus appears in *Moby-Dick*'s plot as already under erasure, that is, as a displaced or dislocated figure. So, the question emerges if there can be an outside to war that is nonetheless still linked to warfare. The historical experience of the Cold War provides an affirmative answer to this question: even though *Moby-Dick* does not literally anticipate it, Cold War discourse is unsurprisingly (and unconsciously, perhaps) drawn by the novel's hyperbolic warlike structures. If war is in fact the unnamed mediator between the cultural-economic narrative of whaling and the mythic-poetic narrative of revenge, then traces of its defining categories (such as enmity and strategy) must be present in Melville's text. Furthermore, the novel's supposed reflection on global modernity can be reinterpreted in the framework provided by the modern struggle to contain war through legal means. C. L. R. James describes the "voyage of the Pequod" as "the voyage of modern civilization seeking its destiny."[27] In this interpretation, the whaler ship designates modernity itself understood as the combined systems of navigation technology, the science of whales, and the rational process of energy production (the production of oil that takes place on the ship). This modernity is the movement of globalization itself in which the Eurocentric age of discovery irreversibly gives way to the first global energy economy under U.S. hegemony.[28] Yet Melville reimagines this moment in the history of globalization. Instead of returning "home" with whale oil for the Nantucket market, the *Pequod* is fatally sailing towards a mythical-political confrontation with a symbolic enemy.[29]

But how is it possible that the *Pequod* resembles a military unit that nevertheless remains a whaler?

The answer lies in some of the more unusual implications of the novel's plot. The absurd premise of the story is not only that Ahab declares vengeance on a whale, hence reframing the *Pequod*'s global capitalist venture, but that Moby Dick—a singular entity within the particular class of whales—can be identified, located, and challenged to a final showdown. The point here is not simply that Moby Dick *is* an enemy that needs to be killed (and not just defeated), but that by including the white whale in the category of enemies, even on a metaphorical level, enmity becomes a dangerously porous concept that threatens to undermine traditional divisions between different orders of being.[30] Needless to say, the hunt for Moby Dick occurred long before the invention of radar and sonar technologies during the strategic operations of the world wars that would define the twentieth century. Following both military strategies of confrontation and political strategies of legitimation, Ahab is able to create this double identity of the *Pequod*, an identity that is constructed in the text by way of war metaphors as it gradually takes over both the economic task of the voyage and the crew's submission to the commander's will.[31] Focusing on the relation between Ishmael and Ahab as the leading narrative structure of the novel, Cold War critics failed to ask whether the absurd conflict willed by Ahab against Moby Dick illustrates an instance of modern war's increasingly confusing and confused syntax—the organizing logic that links combat to strategy and to enmity.[32]

The crucial point to keep in mind appears to be that the identification of the whale with the weaponized enemy is inherent in the novel itself. More precisely, the novel throws a net of metaphors around the white whale that are all explicitly militaristic in nature. These metaphors of war stick to everything in the novel. There is not one layer of the text that is left untouched by them. The novel gives in to this metaphorical seduction seemingly without any resistance: Ahab's hunt for the white whale is *like* a war. We cannot perceive any resistance to this appropriation here, perhaps because that is the point of the text: war has now reached a new global level, and in the process of this expansion it had to change its very essence.

To take one of the most obvious examples, Ahab himself describes his profession as a form of war: "Oh, Starbuck! it is a mild, mild wind, and a mild looking sky. On such a day—very much such a sweetness as this—I struck my first whale—a boy-harpooneer of eighteen! Forty—forty—forty years ago!—ago! Forty years of continual whaling! forty years of privation, and peril, and storm-time! forty years on the pitiless sea! for forty years has Ahab forsaken the peaceful land, for forty years to make war on the horrors of the deep!"[33] To make war on the horrors of the deep, however, appears to us here as a life story, as an autobiography (of a complete life) that is at least potentially still redeemable. After all, this life of war could be a heroic enterprise. In fact, in a similar vein, the crew of the ship is described by Ishmael as an army: "Now these three mates—Starbuck, Stubb, and Flask, were momentous men. They it was who by universal prescription commanded three of the Pequod's boats as headsmen. In that grand order of battle in which Captain Ahab would probably marshal his forces to descend on the whales, these three headsmen were as captains of companies. Or, being armed with their long keen whaling spears, they were as a picked trio of lancers; even as the harpooneers were flingers of javelins."[34] In spite of their significant differences, therefore, both Ahab and Ishmael see the world of the novel in militaristic terms: Ahab is waging a war on whales in general and on the big white whale in particular with his personal army.

Needless to say, however, no matter how instructive such a reading might be, it remains fundamentally quite banal. The mere presence of military metaphors would hardly make Melville's novel into the "prophetic" text that we all claim it to be. No doubt, there will be wars in the future of imperialism. The real prophetic force of the novel lies somewhere else. It might at first appear to be no more than a minor adjustment, a barely perceptible displacement of the original question, but it is crucial to see that what makes the novel into a genuinely modern text is that it discovers the problem of *perpetual war*. In *Moby-Dick*, Melville confronts not simply the problem of war, but the possibility of eternal war. And we need to go even further: the novel elevates perpetual war to the level of an ontological principle. While still tied to the global economy of whaling and to the narrative of modernity, the Melvillean conception of perpetual war projects a metaphysical and existential dimension that distinguishes it from both Hobbes's "war of all against all" as well as the historico-political discourse of war, which Michel Foucault traced to the work of the French historian Boulainvilliers, who "makes the relationship of war part of every social relationship . . . war [being] a sort of permanent state that exists between groups, fronts, and tactical units as they in some sense civilize one another, come into conflict with one another, or on the contrary, form alliances."[35] We will see that the novel's definition of eternal war is not the only mode, however, through which Melville's narrative touches on the structure of war; that is, on the specificity of combat, strategy, enmity, and the complex systems, technologies, and practices that evolved as modernity promised a containment of warfare by means of international legal norms.

This is how the global as well as imperial business of whaling becomes not merely a global war but "everlasting war":

> What wonder, then, that these Nantucketers, born on a beach, should take to the sea for a livelihood! They first caught crabs and quohogs in the sand; grown bolder, they waded out with nets for mackerel; more experienced, they pushed off in boats and captured cod; and at last, launching a navy of great ships on the sea, explored this watery world; put an incessant belt of circumnavigations round it; peeped in at Behring's Straits; and in all seasons and all oceans *declared everlasting war with the mightiest animated mass that has survived the flood; most monstrous and most mountainous!* That Himmalehan, salt-sea Mastodon, clothed with such portentousness of unconscious power, that his very panics are more to be dreaded than his most fearless and malicious assaults![36]

While it is no doubt significant that the imperial enterprise is depicted here as a perpetual war on the whale, the novel makes another more significant move in this direction. It is, of course, possible to argue that in the quoted passage the reference to "everlasting war" is nothing but an inspired figure that gives in to the excessive rhetoric of the whole passage. But the meaning of this allusion to perpetual war is significantly recontextualized by other passages in the text in such a way that its purport can no longer be reduced to a mere poetic simile. The moment when the merely "metaphorical" reference becomes an actual metaphysical argument occurs when the ocean itself becomes the symbol of "eternal war":

> Consider the subtleness of the sea; how its most dreaded creatures glide under water, unapparent for the most part, and treacherously hidden beneath the loveliest tints of azure. Consider also the devilish brilliance and beauty of many of its most remorseless tribes, as the

> dainty embellished shape of many species of sharks. Consider, once more, the universal cannibalism of the sea; all whose creatures prey upon each other, carrying on eternal war since the world began.[37]

We are now involved in a very different textual enterprise here. When the sea itself becomes the only setting for the narrative, it also appears to us as the pure background against which all human action must be measured. On the textual level, the sea appears as the condition of the narration itself; whereas on the level of the narrated world, it becomes the condition of life. So, the sea is not just an accidental setting in the novel, but the pure element of being itself: it is an ontological location. If we follow this argument, we now see that the plot of the novel unfolds against a metaphysical background which suggests that being is eternal war: from the dawn of time ("since the world began"), the sea (or more precisely "the universal cannibalism of the sea") makes something visible about the very world that contains this sea. The sea, as the very source of life, introduces the universal principle of negativity into being itself. This negativity, however, is not only essential (in that it belongs to the essence of life) and universal (in that it applies all over the globe), it is also radical in nature:

> But not only is the sea such a foe to man who is an alien to it, but it is also a fiend to its own off-spring; worse than the Persian host who murdered his own guests; sparing not the creatures which itself hath spawned. Like a savage tigress that tossing in the jungle overlays her own cubs, so the sea dashes even the mightiest whales against the rocks, and leaves them there side by side with the split wrecks of ships. No mercy, no power but its own controls it. Panting and snorting like a mad battle steed that has lost its rider, the masterless ocean overruns the globe.[38]

The sea is a formidable enemy. In fact, it is the extreme enemy that raises the intensity of enmity to unheard-of heights. Not only is the sea the enemy of man (who according to its nature is alien to the element of the sea), it is also its own enemy. The sea now appears as the pure element of war and enmity. It *is* pure enmity raised to a hyperbolic level: the sea is its own enemy and as such it is *the* absolute enemy. It becomes the womb or the matrix of all possible enmity. Within the world of the novel, we reach here the absolute maximum degree of enmity. The sea is the ur-element of radical negativity from which life itself emerged only to be negated by its very source. The sea is the medium or element of this fluid negativity.[39] It turns not only against its other (what is alien to it), but against itself, against its own "proper" or "same" as well. This self-consuming radical negativity, however, is the pure sovereignty that takes over the globe. It is the metaphysical condition of perpetual war.

Thus, what *Moby-Dick* proves is not that Melville was prophetic in foretelling the future, but that he grasped something about his own past and present. He discovered that perpetual war is the inherent condition of modernity. We recognize ourselves in the novel to the degree that we still live in the age of perpetual war today. We could, then, say that *Moby-Dick* does not immediately look like a war novel because it is a novel of *perpetual* war. And when war becomes perpetual, the priority of the battlefield recedes in favor of a total absorption of life in the logic of war. So what was inappropriate about the Cold War appropriation of the text? It was wrong in assuming that the novel foretold the Cold War as the unavoidable outcome of modernity. The Cold War wanted to see itself as the conclusion and even as the ultimate end of this history. But the real insight that the novel makes available for us is the exact opposite: not that modernity produced the Cold War in an unavoidable manner, but that modernity itself is a form of perpetual cold war.

Moby Dick as Medium

The conditions of the militarization of the discourse of the novel were, therefore, already present in the text itself. And the novel provides us with a very clear answer to the question as to what mechanisms make it possible to extend the logic of a simple metaphor to the construction of the whole of the text. This general militarization is made possible by the simple fact that, according to the novel itself, Moby Dick is a *medium*. In the novel, the whale is perceived *as something other than itself* and, therefore, literally introduces to the world of the text the possibility of these metaphorical substitutions. Following this line of reasoning, we should keep in mind that Ahab defines his relation to Moby Dick in terms of mediation. The whale itself functions here as a "medium" in the sense that it is a material agent communicating between two worlds, the visible and the invisible worlds. The whale becomes the material embodiment of an invisible agency:

> All visible objects, man, are but as pasteboard masks. But in each event—in the living act, the undoubted deed—there, some unknown but still reasoning thing puts forth the mouldings of its features from behind the unreasoning mask. If man will strike, strike through the mask! How can the prisoner reach outside except by thrusting through the wall? To me, the white whale is that wall, shoved near to me. Sometimes I think there's naught beyond. But 'tis enough. He tasks me; he heaps me; I see in him outrageous strength, with an inscrutable malice sinewing it. That inscrutable thing is chiefly what I hate; and be the white whale agent, or be the white whale principal, I will wreak that hate upon him.[40]

This well-known passage (which occurs in the context of the debate between Ahab and Starbuck, when the latter accuses the former of breaching their contract) could be interpreted as a direct reflection on mediation. Once again, the whale is a medium in the sense that it channels an otherworldly agency into the visible world. Ahab suggests that Moby Dick is not important in itself: the whale is merely a means of striking at an "inscrutable thing" that manifests itself through the whale. Consequently, if "*all* visible objects" are but mere masks that allow us to see vague contours of invisible yet reasonable entities, we find here the foundations of a genuine *ontology of mediation*: the objective world of our experiences is pure mediation in its very being.[41]

According to the demands of this ontology, then, Moby Dick ceases to be Moby Dick for Ahab. The whale in itself is not important, since it is a mere "unreasoning mask" that functions as the dent or impression made by a non-worldly agent within the visible world. In this regard, all objects including Moby Dick lose their immediate identities and are reduced to the status of mediums that communicate between the visible and invisible worlds. As Ahab puts it, the human being has no other means to get at the invisible other than through these masks: if he has to wage war on the "inscrutable thing," the only way for him to do so is to wage war on the visible object.

But, arguably, even Ishmael sees the whale as a medium. The famous chapter on "The Whiteness of the Whale" (chapter 42) concludes with the following metaphysical speculations that could be easily juxtaposed with the previous passage:

> Is it that by its indefiniteness it shadows forth the heartless voids and immensities of the universe, and thus stabs us from behind with the thought of annihilation, when beholding the white depths of the milky way? Or is it, that as in essence whiteness is not so much a colour as the visible absence of colour; and at the same time the concrete of all colours; is it for these reasons that there is such a dumb blankness, full of meaning, in a wide landscape of snows—a colourless, all-colour of atheism from which we shrink? And when we consider that other theory of the natural philosophers, that all other earthly hues—every stately or lovely emblazoning—the sweet tinges of sunset skies and woods; yea, and the gilded velvets of butterflies, and the butterfly cheeks of young girls; all these are but subtile deceits, not actually inherent in substances, but only laid on from without; so that all deified Nature absolutely paints like the harlot, whose allurements cover nothing but the charnel-house within; and when we proceed further, and consider that the mystical cosmetic which produces every one of her hues, the great principle of light, for ever remains white or colourless in itself, *and if operating without medium upon matter*, would touch all objects, even tulips and roses, with its own blank tinge—pondering all this, the palsied universe lies

before us a leper; and like wilful travellers in Lapland, who refuse to wear coloured and colouring glasses upon their eyes, so the wretched infidel gazes himself blind at the monumental white shroud that wraps all the prospect around him. And of all these things the Albino whale was the symbol. Wonder ye then at the fiery hunt?[42]

The last sentences seem to suggest that we find here a metaphysical justification of the "fiery hunt" for the albino whale and, as such, of the militarization of Moby Dick itself. Whiteness is not a color but the visible absence of color: it is the principle of negativity at work in the universe. As negation (absence of color), it is nevertheless universal as the very medium in which color as such becomes possible (as "the concrete of all colors"). But in a universe like this, color itself becomes the principle of a generalized deception, since it is not inherent in any substance. It is this theory of deceitful appearance (things are really not what they appear to be) that takes us back to the ontology of mediation and the metaphor of the mask. This time, however, the mask is that of the "harlot" Nature whose allurements hide an ugly reality. But if light were to hit objects "without medium," everything would appear universally white. To use a Hegelian quip, we could say that such a universe would be "the day in which all whales are white." Thus, reality is always mediated by light (itself invisible); but in the act of mediation, reality itself is distorted. This is why we need the secondary mediating force of colored glasses, to be able to bear the pure force of mediation. Therefore, we encounter here a model that is best described in terms of mediated mediations: the ontological mediation of beings (the fact that things exist in a mediated way) is complemented by a secondary phenomenological mediation (experience is a mediation of a reality that is already mediated in itself).

Moby Dick here becomes the symbol of the fact that there is no such thing as an unmediated reality. The white whale, the *one* whale among all the whales, is therefore the being that needs to be vanquished. At the same time, in Peter Sloterdijk's formulation, Moby Dick "symbolizes an exteriority that is otherwise neither in need nor capable of a manifestation."[43] Ahab, through Melville's fiction, does not focus therefore on the phenomenological problematic; the narrative frames his world in terms of ontological separation. War emerges as a horizon of meaning and practice only when the hunting and exploitation of whales is subordinated to the localization, search, and defeat of the Leviathan. Moby Dick—we learn from the narrative's ontological mediation—is a whale but also more than a whale; it appears as a "divine" or otherworldly creature. The condition for this singularization is the redrawing of the onto-theological matrix within which the determination of being according to difference and specificity occurs. Yet the moment Ahab begins to identify himself with the Lucifer position, as he prepares for the final battle with the white whale, Ahab and the white whale emerge as beings located on an equal onto-theological plane. From an ontological perspective, war—that is, the process through which Ahab manages to transform the sea of whalers into a theater of war against one whale—appears as a factor of stability, as the ground on which mediations are operating at their full potential. Yet, while war does not and cannot directly name the conflict between Ahab and Moby Dick, it remains recognizable even if the internalization of this conflict, the idea that the proper conflict is within Ahab (not between Ahab and the whale), masks how the *Pequod*'s whaling practices are subordinated to processes of mediation that presuppose a state of conflict and corresponding social structures that are warlike.

The metaphysical necessity of mediation, however, is never too far away from a direct reflection on the medium of the novel itself. For it appears that literature itself is a form of mediating reality:

> I do not know where I can find a better place than just here, to make mention of one or two other things, which to me seem important, as in printed form establishing in all respects the reasonableness of the whole story of the White Whale, more especially the catastrophe. For this is one of those disheartening instances where truth requires full as much bolstering as error. So ignorant are most landsmen of some of the plainest and most palpable wonders of the world, that without some hints touching the plain facts, historical and otherwise, of the fishery, they might scout at Moby Dick as a monstrous fable, or still worse and more detestable, a hideous and intolerable allegory.[44]

This passage shows that the novel is explicitly conscious of itself as a material medium. The medium of "printed form," however, is not without its inherent weaknesses: people can misunderstand it. While the narrative concerns "the plainest and most palpable wonders of the world," ignorance will lead people to allegorize the story rather than take it literally as mere material reality. The rejection of allegory here seems to move us in the direction of a literal reading of the materiality of the whale. But if the novel treats the whale as a medium (in the sense of a mediating agent) and is clearly aware of itself as a form of printed medium, we need to also consider the status of the novel itself as a medium. Two senses of the term "medium" are at work here. Without falling prey to equivocation, we could perhaps argue that in the expression "the materiality of the medium" both meanings have to be considered in this context: the whale is a material mediating agent between the visible and the invisible worlds; and the novel is a material mediating agent of mass communication. Hence the ambiguous identity between *Moby-Dick* and Moby Dick.[45]

At this point, however, we have arrived at an apparent contradiction. The two different lines of our argument that we have been following appear to say two very different things: on the one hand, Moby Dick as a medium is not to be taken for what it is in itself (since it is the material visibility of something invisible, something other than itself); on the other hand, we should not try to allegorize the story of the whale, and should take this whale in its literal materiality. Based on these two insights, we would have to conclude that what the novel insists on is that *the whale is a whale even if it is not a whale*. How can we make sense of this seemingly nonsensical proposition? As we have seen, the novel simultaneously asserts that the whale is the manifestation of something other than itself and that its identity is its material reality. The point is that the reality of mediation is its materiality ("the whale is a whale") but, as a mediator, the medium lacks an identity that is not contaminated by what it mediates ("the whale is not a whale"). In other words, negativity is mediation (and vice versa). The discovery of ontological negativity manifests itself in the text as the discovery of the need for perpetual mediation. Perpetual war and perpetual mediation emerge from the same ontological conditions.

The Ruin of the World

So what does this rejection of allegory in favor of the material reality of mediation really show us? How does it help us make sense of the Cold War appropriations of the novel? In order to answer these questions, we will have to return once again to the problem of the novel's relation to the world that we live in.

The temporal logic of the allegorical readings that discover in *Moby-Dick* prefigurations of the very worlds from which such allegorical readings become possible in the first place can be clearly described. The ideological fantasy that sustains these readings can be reduced to a simple formula: there is no world for us to live in unless the birth of this world was foretold, unless our world is the fulfillment of a prophecy. In fact, according to this same logic, we could go even further: we would not even exist if our possibility had not already been present in the (prophetic) past. We are the messianic or apocalyptic future of this past possibility. Allegory is the means of this double constitution of worlds: on the one hand, the past is constituted as a closed world unto itself only when it is declared to be the self-present location of the possibility of our present; on the other hand, the present becomes a completed world unto itself only as the future of this otherwise unfinished past that is still awaiting its completion in us. To put it differently, the present was already present in the past and the past is still present in the present. And the present in the past and the past in the present work together as mutually heteronomous moments of determination. As a result, in the fantasy of this fulfilled prophecy, two worlds come into being as each other's justifications. The "world" is historically constituted as the allegorical constellation of two incomplete worlds.[46]

So we can clearly see now that what is at stake in this resistance to allegory is nothing other than the ruin of the world itself. The perpetual negativity of mediation prevents the "world we live in" from coming into existence as the fulfilled prophecy of the novel. We should probably heed Peter Szendy's warning that it would be amiss to attribute the power of an "accomplished prophecy" to the novel: "It is, rather, a matter of thinking a kind of *propheticity*, which, in reading, remains to come like an open possibility, perhaps like the future itself. Like a promise, or better: a *prophecy of prophecy*."[47] The world that we live in is not a world after all. But what we are dealing with here is not the apocalyptic destruction of the world in the final war of human history (in a nuclear holocaust, as the Cold War would have liked us to believe), but a positive enabling condition that manifests itself in the form of the constitutive incompleteness of worlds. Moby Dick, therefore, does stand for the end of the world, but not in the sense of the destruction of our world by an enemy. On the contrary, the end of the world here simply means that there is no world that is not exposed to the pure materiality of mediation.

Notes

1. The phrase belongs to C. L. R. James, whose book *Mariners, Renegades, and Castaways* is a great example of the kind of reading practice that relies on literary fiction as the medium through which the world can be identified historically. See C. L. R. James, *Mariners, Renegades, and Castaways: The Story of Herman Melville and the World We Live In* (Hanover, N.H.: Dartmouth College Press, 2001).

2. Randy Kennedy, "The Ahab Parallax: *Moby-Dick* and the Spill," *New York Times*, July 12, 2010, http://www.nytimes.com/2010/06/13/weekinreview/13kennedy.html?_r=0.

3. For a useful sourcebook on Melville's global reception (especially during the early Cold War), see Leland R. Phelps and Kathleen McCullough, *Herman Melville's Foreign Reputation: A Research Guide* (Boston: G.K. Hall, 1983). For a more recent assessment of Melville's international reception, see Sanford E. Marovitz and A. C. Christodoulou, *Melville "Among the Nations": Proceedings of an International Conference, Volos, Greece, July 2–6, 1997* (Kent, Ohio: Kent State University Press, 2001).

4. For a brief overview of the role played by *Moby-Dick* in Cold War literary criticism, see Geraldine Murphy, "Ahab as Capitalist, Ahab as Communist: Revising *Moby-Dick* for the Cold War," *Surfaces* 4 (1994), http://www.pum.umontreal.ca/revues/surfaces/vol4/murphy.html. For two classic readings of *Moby-Dick*'s relation to the Cold War, see Donald Pease, "*Moby Dick* and the Cold War," in *The American Renaissance Reconsidered*, ed. Walter Benn Michaels and Donald E. Pease (Baltimore, Md.: Johns Hopkins University Press, 1985), 113–55; and William V. Spanos, *The Errant Art of "Moby-Dick": The Canon, the Cold War, and the Struggle for American Studies* (Durham, N.C.: Duke University Press, 1995). In fact, our title "*Moby-Dick* and Perpetual War" is intended to be a direct reference to Pease's essay "*Moby Dick* and the Cold War." The shift from the Cold War to "perpetual war" in our title, however, signals our intention to explore the conditions of Cold War appropriations of the novel in order to expand the scope of Pease's argument.

5. Murphy, "Ahab as Capitalist," 19–20.

6. James, *Mariners, Renegades, and Castaways*, 16. According to James, for Ahab, "the crew are not human beings but things, as he calls them, 'manufactured men.' For him their permanent condition is sordidness" (ibid.).

7. James writes: "when Ahab, the totalitarian, bribed the men with money and grog and whipped them to follow him on his monomaniacal quest, Ishmael, the man of good family and education, hammered and shouted with the rest. His submission to the totalitarian madness was complete" (ibid., 40).

8. Ibid., 62.

9. Herman Melville, *Moby-Dick, or the Whale* (New York: Penguin Books, 1992), 606.

10. In fact, we would also like to argue that there is an additional third temporal dimension to the "globality" of Cold War discourse that complements the ideological and geographical meanings. We cannot explore this problem here in more detail, but we would like to point out that the global discourse of the Cold War in a certain sense predates and survives the decades of the historical period of the Cold War.

11. Stefan Aust, *Baader-Meinhof: The Inside Story of the R.A.F.*, trans. Anthea Bell (Oxford: Oxford University Press, 2009), 191–94.

12. Stefan Aust, "Terrorism in Germany: The Baader-Meinhof Phenomenon," *GHI Bulletin*, no. 43 (Fall 2008): 45–57, at 46.

13. Ibid., 45.

14. Ibid., 45–46.

15. Ibid., 46. Emphasis added.

16. Ibid., 47.

17. Pease, "*Moby Dick* and the Cold War," 113.

18. For a brief set of journalistic examples regarding *Moby-Dick*'s relation to the war on terror, see Michael Brenner, "America's Moby Dick," *Huffington Post*, July 29, 2013, https://www.huffingtonpost.com/michael-brenner/americas-moby-dick_b_3670646.html; as well as Rick Salutin, "What *Moby-Dick* Can Teach Us about the War on Terror," *The Toronto Star*, May 30, 2015. In a completely different register that cannot be compared to the previous titles, the question of *Moby-Dick*'s relation to the "war on terror" does come up in Peter Szendy, *Prophecies of Leviathan: Reading Past Melville*, trans. Gil Anidjar (New York: Fordham University Press, 2010), 3–5.

19. For the concept of the "aesthetic unconscious" in relation to Cold War politics, see Roland Végső, *The Naked Communist: Cold War Modernism and the Politics of Popular Culture* (New York: Fordham University Press, 2013), 9–35. In addition, see also the way the concept of the "underside of politics" is used in Sorin Radu Cucu, *The Underside of Politics: Global Fictions in the Fog of the Cold War* (New York: Fordham University Press, 2013).

20. Hans Joas, *War and Modernity*, trans. by Rodney Livingstone (Malden, Mass.: Polity Press and Blackwell Publishing, 2003), 30.

21. Ibid., 30.

22. James, *Mariners, Renegades, and Castaways*, 16.

23. Pease, "*Moby Dick* and the Cold War," 114.

24. Anders Stephanson, "Fourteen Notes on the Very Concept of the Cold War," H-Diplo Essays, 1–21, https://issforum.org/essays/PDF/stephanson-14notes.pdf.

25. Stephanson's "definition" of Cold War is relevant here as well: "It is war as an ideological, political and economic claim to universality, taking place not in the two-dimensional space of traditional battles but mediated through other realms" (ibid., 20).

26. See Terry Mort, *The Hemingway Patrols: Ernest Hemingway and His Hunt for U-Boats* (New York: Scribner, 2010). The quintessential Cold War narrative that brings together the motif of the U-boat with nuclear catastrophe in the form of an underwater hunt is, of course, Tom Clancy's debut novel *The Hunt for Red October* (1984) and its popular 1990 film version.

27. James, *Mariners, Renegades, and Castaways*, 19.

28. One of the classic legitimating narratives of modernity refers to the containment of warfare both by the State and by international law. In the mindset of social contract theory, through Kant's well-known arguments, progress is equated with the creation of the foundations for durable (if not perpetual) peace. For a rigorous account of how international law is tied to these and others ideas of modernity, see Marti Koskenniemi, *The Gentle Civilizer of Nations: The Rise and Fall of International Law 1870–1960* (Cambridge: Cambridge University Press, 2004).

29. By imagining the *Pequod* as traveling towards a final disaster rather than back to Nantucket, Melville moves the focus from a spatial to a temporal narrative. The encounter with the whale is the end point of a regressive movement. As the modern technologies of navigation break down and Ahab embraces his harpoon as a sacred weapon, the global itinerary of the *Pequod* looks increasingly as a journey away from the present (the present of navigation technology) and towards the mythical power of the past.

30. For a useful discussion of how the logic of the hunt and the logic of warfare relate to each other under the historical conditions of the "global war against terror," see Grégoire Chamayou, *A Theory of the Drone*, trans. Janet Lloyd (New York: New, 2015), 52–59.

31. Cold War critics as well as their critics have used the term "totalitarianism" to explain the social reality of the *Pequod*. Ahab is authoritarian, for sure, but what is described by the term "totalitarian" is perhaps the consequence of the double identity of the ship: the warlike journey needs warlike social relations.

32. Would it be possible to read Ahab's mission through the lens of Deleuze and Guattari's "Treatise on Nomadology" (a text, let us mention in passing, that is not simply an inquiry into contemporary forms of combat, but an anxious reflection on the nature of the Cold War)? Deleuze and Guattari emphasize that we need to consider "two poles of the war machine": on the one hand, "the State appropriates the machine, even going so far as to project it as the horizon of the world"; on the other hand, "the machine does indeed encounter war, but as its supplementary or synthetic object, now directed against the State and against the worldwide axiomatic expressed by States." The issue is that the *Pequod* never fully becomes a war machine. It is simply arrested in the mimetic position, the position of a group reflecting onto itself the discipline of military strategy, its determination, and its heroism. At the same time, Melville's fiction does not explore the State's appropriation of war, but focuses on war as the horizon remotely shaping economic activity, social interaction, and cultural activity on the *Pequod*. See Gilles Deleuze and Félix Guattari, "1227: Treatise on Nomadology—The War

Machine," in *A Thousand Plateaus*, trans. by Brian Massumi (Minneapolis: University of Minnesota Press, 1987), 351–423.

33. Melville, *Moby-Dick*, 590.

34. Ibid., 130.

35. Michel Foucault, *"Society Must Be Defended": Lectures at the College de France 1975–1976*, trans. by David Macey (New York: Picador, 2003), 162.

36. Melville, *Moby-Dick*, 60. Emphasis added.

37. Ibid., 299.

38. Ibid.

39. For a classic discussion of the relationship of land and sea, see Carl Schmitt, *The Nomos of the Earth in the International Law of the Jus Publicum Europaeum,* trans. G. L. Ulmen (New York: Telos, 2006), 172–85.

40. Melville, *Moby-Dick*, 178.

41. We don't have the space here to go into further detail about this question, but it might be worth pointing out that the very idea of an "ontology of mediation" is fraught with ambiguities. Needless to say, the most compelling of these complications is that an ontology which imagines being itself as pure mediation threatens to undo the very possibility of an ontology. Against the background of this pure mediation, what we traditionally call "ontology" will always appear to be an attempt to bring to a halt the movement of mediation. Within the framework of this project, therefore, we would like to suggest that the ontology of "perpetual war" functions as such a concrete historical appropriation of the "ontology of mediation."

42. Melville, Moby-Dick, 178. 212. Emphasis added.

43. Peter Sloterdijk, *In the World Interior of Capital*, trans. Wieland Hoban (Cambridge: Polity, 2013), 114.

44. Ibid., 223.

45. See also Szendy, *Prophecies of Leviathan*, 41: "But what the narrator of the novel constantly affirms and reaffirms is that the whale is a book."

46. To be as clear as possible, we need to mention that what we find objectionable in this formula is not the mere fact that it locates the present in the past and the past in the present, but the nature of the link that it establishes between the two.

47. Szendy, *Prophecies of Leviathan*, 5.

Bartleby Politics

Emily Apter

Ostinato, the musical term for what continues, like a basso continuo, calls for an obstinate reading. In des Forêts's vocabulary, music is responsible for some of what he calls les temps forts—those stressed moments of intensity or exaltation that are often diminished, or lost altogether, upon reaching the paper as we try to inscribe or describe them. They are uncapturable. And yet the writer, reader, listener will persevere, stubbornly, obstinately. Like the aftercoming translator.
—Mary Ann Caws, "Translator's Preface" to *Ostinato* (by Louis-René des Forêts)

Then there is the purposeless obstinacy of the id, in its fixity and incorrigibility. It's hardwired to last. Structurally impervious to modification, indifferent to contradiction, the unconscious is the embodiment of motiveless intransigence in its pure form.
—Rebecca Comay, "Resistance and Repetition: Freud and Hegel"

The idea of lying flat before a tank, of "going limp" in the face of police power, involves a cultivated capacity to hold a certain position. The limp body may seem to have given up its agency, and yet, in becoming weight and obstruction, it persists in its pose. Aggression is not eradicated, but cultivated, and its cultivated form can be seen in the body as it stands, falls, gathers, stops, remains silent, takes on the support of other bodies that it itself supports. Supported and supporting, a certain notion of bodily interdependency is enacted that shows that nonviolent resistance should not be reduced to heroic individualism.
—Judith Butler, *Notes toward a Performative Theory of Assembly*

During the first week of September 2015, Kentucky county clerk Kim Davis, after defying a Supreme Court order to issue marriage licenses to gay couples on the grounds that it violated her Apostolic religious beliefs, retreated to her office and drew the blinds, communicating through her lawyers (as the

New York Times reported) that she would "*neither* resign *nor* relent." A gay couple, demanding that she confront them face to face, yelled through the closed door that they would continue the fight for their civil right to marry. Through an intermediary Davis replied: "I have *no animosity* toward anyone and harbor *no ill will*. To me this has *never* been a gay or lesbian issue." Casey Davis, her assistant, would also deploy the syntactic stonewall of the double negative: He had, he insisted, "'*not* tried to *prevent*' same-sex marriages but was only acting on his First Amendment rights."[1] Preterition, an affirmation secured through the subtractive logic of "not not" as in "not resigning," "no animosity, no ill-will," "not . . . preventing," recalls us to Bartleby's signature phrase, "I would prefer not to." Melville's canonical motto, invented in his story "Bartleby, the Scrivener," has played host to political resistance tactics ranging across civil disobedience, stop-work, interference, suspension, and obstruction to obstruction, as in micro-aggressive contestations of micro-aggression in the workplace; lie-ins and die-ins that refute legal indifference to violations of social justice; and delegitimations of the capitalist first principle of shareholder hegemony, which is itself predicated on the abrogated right to a living wage. "I would prefer not to" heralds notions of inoperative, non-instrumental community that expose the limits of existential politics, from Sartrean *engagement* to post-1968 theories of being and event. An incursion into the sphere of ordinary politics—lobbying, scandal-mongering, impeded legislation—the incantatory "formula" poses an alternative micropolitics under the gathering-term "*ostinato*," a term that I have borrowed from musical improvisation to underscore what is Bartlebyesque in forms of protest and mobilized postures of autoimmunity.

Negative articulations, offended meliorism, these are signal features of Bartleby politics in Melville's tale. Bartleby first employs the famous phrase in an unassuming way, but his employer immediately takes it as an offense to his self-regard as a benevolent and indulgent manager:

> "Bartleby! quick, I am waiting."
> I heard a slow scrape of his chair legs on the uncarpeted floor, and soon he appeared standing at the entrance of his hermitage.
> "What is wanted?" said he mildly.
> "The copies, the copies," said I hurriedly. "We are going to examine them. There"—and I held towards him the fourth quadruplicate.
> "I would prefer not to," he said, and gently disappeared behind the screen.
> For a few moments I was turned into a pillar of salt, standing at the head of my seated column of clerks. Recovering myself, I advanced towards the screen, and demanded the reason for such extraordinary conduct.
> "Why do you refuse?"

"I would prefer not to."

With any other man I should have flown outright into a dreadful passion, scorned all further words, and thrust him ignominiously from my presence. But there was something about Bartleby that not only strangely disarmed me, but in a wonderful manner touched and disconcerted me.[2]

The reference to the Old Testament character of Lot's wife, who was turned into a pillar of salt because she refused to obey God's prophylactic command to resist looking back on the city of Sodom in flames, is especially significant. Unprepared for Bartleby's noncompliance with basic commands, the lawyer is flummoxed. How can he respond to Bartleby's *pharmakon* of weak resistance, which works like a leeched toxin of incapacitation to effectuate sovereign disempowerment? ("Indeed it was his wonderful mildness chiefly, which not only disarmed me, but unmanned me, as it were.")[3] Derrida would identify this syndrome with sovereign-autoimmunity in relation to the condition of the United States after the 9/11 attacks, characterizing as autoimmune America's "War on Terror," in which a state of exception is diffused into all-over, unexceptional war. Bartleby personifies this exceptionalist defeat of sovereign exceptionalism; his weapon of choice is the phatic element of "preference" anomalously introduced into the restricted field of calculated perlocutionary interchange. As Giorgio Agamben notes, "I would prefer not to" "extinguishes the place of reason in the domain of will and potentiality."[4]

"Bartleby," said I, "Ginger Nut is away; just step round the Post Office, won't you? (it was but a three minute walk,) and see if there is any thing for me."

"I would prefer not to."

"You will not?"

"I prefer not."[5]

This is a speech-act that instead of misfiring, as Austin would say, is simply obstructed on its path by a change of channel. The language logic that produces meaningful communication is, as Deleuze famously argued, put out of action by another language logic:[6]

The usual formula would instead be *I had rather not*. But the strangeness of the formula goes beyond the word itself. Certainly it is grammatically correct, syntactically correct, but its abrupt termination, NOT TO, which leaves what it rejects undetermined, confers upon it the character of a radical, a kind of limit-function. Its repetition and its insistence render it all the more unusual, entirely so. Murmured in a soft, flat, and patient voice, it attains to the irremissible, by forming an inarticulate block, a single breath. In all these respects, it has the same force, the same role as an *agrammatical* formula.[7]

"Bartleby politics" relies on an agrammaticality that singularizes serial and limitless acts of resistance. It baffles the discursive struts and logical infrastructures of sovereign force and foregrounds a psychopolitics distinguished by gridlock, blockage, and a host of other symptoms associated with stasis. A key Greek term for both peace and civil war, predicated on the equilibrating standoff between equal factions, "stasis," as Rebecca Comay has analyzed it, retains its significance as the theoretical armature of theories of political resistance:[8]

> Stasis forces us to reconsider the opposition of motion and rest. It puts the very antithesis of stasis and kinesis into question. Too much stability can be destabilizing, while excessive mobility produces deadlock. In a medical register, stasis refers to digestive sluggishness, circulatory constriction, gastric blockage, constipation, the toxic coagulation or clogging of bodily humors, a stagnation that will eventually throw the whole organism into crisis. In a political register, stasis is a kind of hardening or rigidity that can precipitate upheaval precisely because in its obduracy, its one-sidedness, its refusal to adapt to circumstances, to go with the flow, it exposes the rigid armature sustaining the status quo, provoking violent counter-reactions and thus forcing latent antagonisms to the surface. We are *in a state* when our confinement, our stuckness, becomes explosive.[9]

"Bartleby politics" thus broadly construed, names the stasis of stuckness; whether in relation to reasons of state, defenestrated by recalcitrant willings affirmed outside institutional frameworks of political agency and decision; or to what Oskar Negt and Alexander Kluge, in their seminal work *History and Obstinacy* would imagine as a kind of civil war of the subject, riven between the drives of *Ent-eignung* (capitalized selfhood, the expropriated autonomy of the proletarianized laborer) and *Eigen-sinn* (willfulness, obstinacy); or to the vacuity of political speechifying, which normalizes self-sabotage, *horror vacui*, ruts of governance.[10]

In the heyday and aftermath of the Occupy Wall Street (OWS) movement of 2011, the very name "Bartleby," drafted directly from the gaunt and ghostly Melvillean character, singularized and made finite limitless and indeterminate micro-events. We were left with questions: What did OWS actually stand for? Is it over or not? Where did it lead or purposefully "prefer not to" lead? Did it allude to micro-practices involving care, unowned or unbranded efforts to reverse exploitation and destitution? To a metaphysics of divested *Eigentum* (Max Stirner's term for the ego's "ownness")?[11] To a paradigm of "the Political" other than the aporia of the state of exception? To resignation to opaque and pointless modes of political speech, including those that grant money the protected status of free speech? It has often been said that the very *disponibilité* of the name "Bartleby"—its amenability to being claimed by opposing factions on the political spectrum—accounts for its traction. It is hardly hyperbole to assert that Bartleby, the character, outlives all rivals in the long history of political literature (which includes Plato's Socrates, master of the annoying rejoinder), perhaps because Bartleby, the concept, is synonymous with the obstinacy of the concept at specific historical conjunctures.

"Bartleby, the Scrivener: A Story of Wall Street" originally appeared in 1853 in the November and December issues of *Putnam's* not long after *Moby-Dick* (1851) and was immediately tagged as a narrative enigma in Melville's corpus as well as in world literature. Among the ever-proliferating interpretations of the tale, several stand out. Critics have argued that "Bartleby, the Scrivener" channels Melville's abolitionism and antislavery journalism; that it echoes Henry David Thoreau's 1849 broadside "On the Duty of Civil Disobedience" (1849); that it recounts a messianic parable of survival and bare life; that it performs a how-to primer on squatting; that it functions as a case study of autism and locked-in syndrome; that it affirms the liberal doctrine of possessive individualism (Wyn Kelley maintains that Bartleby's "self-possession asserts such a primary claim that it has the force of actual proprietorship");[12] and that it documents New York's early history of borough politics, finance capitalism in the Wall Street district, and the monumental architecture of the law courts and debtor's prison (Bartleby is finally removed to the Tombs—an Egyptian-themed New York municipal jail located at Collect Pond and known as a debtor's prison).[13] It has been read as a document of the shift in the law from *equity* (based on "individual circumstances and peculiarities" and upheld in Chancery court) to *equality* (based on "deciding like and unlike cases by a single standard"), as well as a practical guide on how to survive in the cutthroat arena of politics and business (secure a "snug business among rich men's bonds and mortgages and title-deeds" by avoiding "juries and the public eye").[14]

Dubbed "the patron saint of Occupy," Bartleby resurfaced mightily during the Zuccotti Park protests in slogans, street signs, and an outpouring of articles; one hailing him as "America's first slacktavist" (*The New Yorker*), another as the hero of the movement against the 1 percent (*The Atlantic*).[15] Several essays took pains to link OWS to Bartleby's affront to American capitalism as defined in Melville's time. Russ Castronovo adumbrated Bartleby's anticapitalism: "his lack of interest in capitalist productivity, and his steadfast refusal to assent to charitable proposals that attempt to put a kind face on hierarchical wage labor."[16] Jonathan Poore, in "Bartleby's Occupation: 'Passive Resistance' Then and Now," drew out the story's prescient grasp of the collapse between the market and the state, anticipating contemporary neoliberalism:

One line of *Bartleby* criticism, beginning with a 1945 essay by Egbert Oliver and extending to contemporary critics like Michael Rogin and Brook Thomas, without claiming categorically that Melville had read Thoreau's "Resistance to Civil Government," nonetheless regards the short story as an extension of or, alternatively, a parody of the anti-authoritarian argument of the essay. What these (otherwise very different) critical interpretations have in common is that they ultimately regard Bartleby and Thoreau as resisting a version of the same thing, described variously as "society," "social institutions" or "the social system." In my view, however, these terms collapse an important distinction between two kinds of social "institution"—the market and the state—that is fundamental to understanding the nature of Bartleby's resistance and its difference from Thoreau's.[17]

"Bartleby politics" is consistently reduced to the idea of radical refusal, inclusive of and exceeding the gesture of dissent. Hester Blum, recounting an event on November 10, 2011, at which writers, booksellers, and OWS participants performed a public reading of "Bartleby, the Scrivener," stresses how they "invoked the long American history of refusal that informs and enlivens Occupy."[18] Bartleby, many note, endures as "Refusal" because he channels the refusal of others, from the slights and insults directed at him by his cohort of clerks, to his "refused" status in the physical space of the office, where he is subject to quarantine and invisibilization. (As Leo Marx observed, "the walls are controlling symbols of the story, and in fact it may be said that this is a parable of walls, the walls which hem in the meditative artist and for that matter every reflective man.")[19] Foregrounding the image of the protagonist's occupation of a corner hemmed in by folding doors, reinforced by a screen, "Bartleby politics," in this scenario at least, is synonymous with small acts of defensive micro-aggression and *ressentiment*, inflated by the threat of what Michael Jonck calls "permanent riotocracy."

Poore's observation that "Bartleby has arguably become the avatar for leftist political resistance—to both market *and* state—in recent years," has been more recently echoed in discussions related to the "Grexit" referendum, many of which affirmed Bartleby's relevance to the conflictual relation between markets and national-popular sovereignty. A blog post headed "Bartleby: A Story of Sophocleous Street," associates Bartleby's name with a street-space in Athens's Syntagma Square and the banner movement of the *Aganaktismenoi* (the "Outraged").[20] It is interpreted as a paradoxical space situated between "non-strategic strategy" and Rancière's notion of "non-entitled entitlement."[21] Such nonstrategic strategies or manifestations of non-entitled entitlement acquire concreteness in acts of physical occupation, interruption, civil disobedience, passive resistance, conscientious objection (redolent of the Bartleby of the Vietnam War protest movement), and dismissal of "the system," in the name of "real" democracy. Slavoj Žižek, in his characteristic mode of "cut off your nose to spite your face," would identify "Bartleby politics" with the gesture of "pure subtraction" embodied in the offense to political correctness:

> We can imagine the varieties of such a gesture in today's public space: not only the obvious "There are great chances of a new career here! Join us!—I would prefer not to"; or "Are you aware how our environment is endangered? Do something for ecology!"—"I would prefer not to"; or "What about all the racial and sexual injustices that we witness all around us? Isn't it time to do more?—"I would prefer not to." This is the gesture of subtraction at its purest, the reduction of all qualitative differences to a purely formal minimal difference.[22]

For Žižek, Bartleby's gesture of withdrawal is no mere "No" of resistance as such, nor a simple distance-taking from the "what is" of politics, but a parallax shift, aporetically manifest as "what remains of the supplement to the Law when its place is emptied of all its obscene superego content."[23] It is an assertion of resistance to the "*rumspringa* of resistance, all the forms of resisting which help the system to reproduce itself by ensuring our participation in it—today, 'I would prefer not to' is not to not participate in the market economy, in capitalist competition and profiteering," but—much more problematically for some—"I would prefer not to give to charity to support a Black orphan in Africa, engage in the struggle to prevent oil-drilling in a wildlife swamp . . ."[24] The opt-out on *bien pensant* liberalism, the adamant imperviousness to any form of "hegemonic interpellation," is read by Žižek as proof of the symbolic order's collapse; it has foundered on the "holophrastic" signifier-turned-object (embodied in "I would prefer not to") and thrives on the violence inhering in "immobile, inert, insistent, impassive *being*."[25] Žižek's three principles of "Bartleby politics"—subtraction, the aporia of the legal supplement, and the formal gesture of refusal as a symptom of the demise of the symbolic order—claim the empty formal gesture for a non-optimized, non-instrumentalized, unaccounted-for ontology. Living passively and resistantly, abstaining by withholding, waiting into worklessness, all these strategies are taken to undo neoliberal pieties and flush out the new hegemons lurking in the names for new activisms.

In the context of OWS, Bartleby's quixotic, uncooperative, phrase "I would prefer not to" became a rallying cry for groups practicing the micropolitics of civil disobedience; groups that categorically reject neoliberal models of "democracy" grounded in homogenized opinion and engineered consent, and which subscribe to forms of the political stipulating the "possibility of a rupture with what exists."[26] This rupture was often formulated as *the impossible demand*, expressed in the bodily assemblies of OWS, Podemos, Maidan, and Les Indigènes de la République;[27] in Arab Spring's rallying slogan *Ash-sha'b yurīd isqāṭ an-niẓām* ("People want to bring down the regime"), and the anti-austerity, anti-debt-slavery vote of "NO" ("Oxi") in the Greek referendum. The force of impossible demands resided in their being made vocally, again and again; and in the assertion of "a right to . . ." As Judith Butler, speaking in the heat of the OWS movement, would affirm:

> Perhaps to the skeptic the idea of making "impossible demands" is equivalent to vacating the field of the political itself. But that response should call our attention to the way that the field of the political has been constituted such that satisfiable demands become the hallmark of its intelligibility. In other words, why is it that we have come to accept that the only politics that makes sense is one in which a set of demands are made to existing authorities, and that the demands isolate instances of inequality and injustice from one another without seeing or drawing any links among them? . . . We might say the particular politics that defines practical and intelligible politics as the production and satisfaction of a list of discrete demands is committed in advance to the legitimacy of existing economic and political structures, and to a refusal of the systematic character of inequality.[28]

"Impossible demands" imply the rejection of the competition model of rival demands. They stake an activist claim to the act of claiming itself: the right to assembly, the right to a living wage, the right to education, the right to housing, the right to health and safe harbor, the right to a life unthreatened by racism, misogyny, and homophobia, and not least, the right to have rights, especially in the face of police brutality, compromised systems of legal punishment, carceral extradition, and extraordinary rendition.

In each of these cases Bartleby prevails as an aporetic figure of the political, of "inoperative power," compositing Jean-Luc Nancy's subject of "inoperative community," Roberto Esposito's *impolitico* (a construct of impossible political institution and self-annulling sovereignty), and Giorgio Agamben's "refugee," a figure of temporary power who "would prefer not to" be repatriated, in a reverse mirror of the inhospitable host nation, which would certainly "prefer not to" grant asylum or safe harbor.[29] But Bartleby is just as easily invoked as the premier self-managing agent of biopolitics dubbed by Wendy Brown "the miniature sovereign." For Brown, this Bartleby—recalled to his profession as a clerk who, as Michael Zakim observes, not only administered but embodied the circulation of property—personifies the residues of *homo politicus* lingering "in the subject's relation to itself" in the era of the waning state; a state which is autoimmune, walled off from community, and "receding as a destination for our equality, freedom, and orientation toward public life."[30] This wasted Bartleby, symbol of a dying demos, would be the neoliberal pendant to Deleuze's metaphysical Bartleby, a creature of "Being as Being and nothing more," and an "original" subject of American democracy.[31] Both Bartlebys make sense within a larger structure of political allegory, the former as a Lear of post-democracy, and the latter as *Dasein*'s gift to American exceptionalism.

Yet another kind of "Bartleby politics" emerges from Jean-Claude Milner's attempt to analyze the strange contentlessness of political speech; what he calls "le parler politique" (political talk, or talk-politics). For Milner, political speech is the filler that provides the primary substance of politicking. It "fills silences by asserting force and setting the relation between governors and governed."[32] "Talk politics" rests, he argues, on a "rhetoric of division that brandishes indifference to facts and collects the dirty run-off water."[33] Milner harks back to the discourses of praise and blame that were elevated to a high art during the French Revolutionary assemblies. The rhetoric of speeches encases politics in a fog of language, blunting perception of the exchange of deadly force between opponents. It was his keen appreciation of the power acquired through oral mastery, Milner argues, that led Saint-Just to propose a civic program (that included a kind of harassment code *avant la lettre*) enabling children to denounce the conduct of their elders and instructors. In this historical context, "talk politics" is distinguished by its instrumental motivation, its usefulness as a weaponized medium of revolutionary discourse.

But it is not of course this instrumental character which makes "talk politics" "Bartlebyesque," but rather its indifference to facts and its phatic dimension (typically associated with shaggy-dog stories). In testing the premise that politics is inseparable from "talk politics," Milner draws attention to the waste matter in political chatter. The banal, deadening, mimetic aspect of politics—heard in every canned speech and sound bite and reproduced by every blogger, on-air bloviator, shill, and professional pol—points to a basic conundrum posed by political speech: Why, to be effective, do politicians rely on vacuous formulae? On phrases riddled with redundancy and equivocation? Why is the episteme of political *ratio* so devoid of meaning? Bartleby, in this instance, becomes a tale of "talk politics," unmanned, as it were. In Episode Eight ("The Tangled Web") of *Yes, Prime Minister* (Series II, 1987–88), the specter of political vacuity looms large in the guise of absurdist circular locutions and didactic humbuggery. In this example, Prime Minister Hacker interrogates his aides on whether they have actually bugged the telephone of MP Hugh Halifax:

> Hacker: You mean we are bugging Hugh Halifax's telephones?
> Sir Humphrey: We were.
> Hacker: We *were*? When did we stop?
> Sir Humphrey: [*checks his watch*] Seventeen minutes ago.
> Bernard: The fact that you needed to know was not known at the time that the now known need to know was known, and therefore

those that needed to advise and inform the Home Secretary perhaps felt that the information that he needed as to whether to inform the highest authority of the known information was not yet known, and therefore there was no authority for the authority to be informed because the need to know was not, at that time, known or needed.[34]

This is "talk politics" at its most obstructionist; as a way of speaking that snakes its way in and out of so many mental cul-de-sacs that it performs epistemic failure as a speech-act even as it satirizes political failure meta-critically.

Written and produced by members of the clubby world of public school-trained civil servants, BBC writers, and public relations coaches, the show's portrayal of public choice politics (associated with James Buchanan's self-interest-based theory of public choice economics, which dismisses as romantic and illusory any theory of politics predicated on concern for others) has been denounced as a smokescreen for Thatcherism. The documentary filmmaker Adam Curtis deemed it "ideological propaganda for a political movement," citing, in his film *The Trap*, one of the show's writers, Sir Antony Jay:

> In *Yes Minister*, we showed that almost everything that the government has to decide is a conflict between two lots of private interest—that of the politicians and that of the civil servants trying to advance their own careers and improve their own lives. And that's why public choice economics, which explains why all this was going on, was at the root of almost every episode of *Yes Minister* and *Yes, Prime Minister*.[35]

Curtis rightly calls out a political philosophy that is powered exclusively by private interest and the cynical conviction that government—an engine of failure—is better off doing nothing than anything at all. The self-defeating prophecy of this philosophy was encapsulated by the famous "politician's syllogism," for which *Yes, Minister* was credited as the source. This is a non-following argument from a true premise that "commits the fallacy of the undistributed middle," as in:

1. "We must do something.
2. This is something.
3. Therefore, we must do this."[36]

What Curtis and his fellow critics fail to really appreciate, however, is the syllogism's reworking of "the formula"; for it brings to light the logic of sovereign autoimmunity, with the excluded middle acting pharmacologically as the defeat of individual interest. Bartleby in this case should not be read as the mouthpiece of public choice politics, but as an inhibitor of all "choice-ism"; a demotivator or disabling device of privatized willing and possessive individualism. To push further on this point, Bartleby is the individual subject dispossessed; he figures forth the bare life of heteronomy or action possessable by no one. Under such conditions, notions of free choice, consent, and self-determination give way to "inadequate causation," a state of subordination to material alterity. As Frédéric Lordon elaborates, drawing on Spinozist ethics: "All things are in the grip of inadequate causation; namely, they are partially determined to act by other, external things."[37]

Bartleby models the perplex of deactivated self-sovereignty conjugated with active stasis. We see how this works in Melville's tale when the lawyer describes Bartleby's reaction after being arrested as a vagrant and sent to prison: "As I afterwards learned, the poor scrivener, when told that he must be conducted to the Tombs, offered *not the slightest obstacle*, but in his pale *unmoving way*, silently *acquiesced*."[38] This acquiescence without compliance arguably converts "the formula" into "the position"; a position which, according to the lawyer, is "unaccountably eccentric" and "yet greatly to be compassionated," which is to say, the position of being *in* position to "front the dead-wall" of the Halls of Justice.[39] Bartleby baffles justice, not by directly obstructing it, but by foregrounding an attitude—*obstination*—that poses the very question of what justice is. As Judith Butler observes, when justice dissolves into the question of itself, politics tilts into philosophy:

> To demand justice is, of course, a strong thing to do—it also immediately involves every activist in a philosophical problem: What is justice, and what are the means through which the demand for justice can be made, understood, taken up? The reason it is sometimes said that there are "no demands" when bodies assemble in this way and for this purpose is that the list of demands would not exhaust the meaning of justice that is being demanded.[40]

To Žižek's Bartleby (a walking aporia or node of epistemological opacity), Agamben's Bartleby (an avatar of inoperative politics), Brown's Bartleby (a neoliberal champion of an eviscerated demos), Milner's Bartleby (the star of "talk politics"), Butler's Bartleby (a baffler of justice), we add Bartleby the obstinator, an ontologist of the curiously impactful effects of mutism, obduracy, and stubbornness.

The French writer Louis-René des Forêts, a founder in 1955 with Robert Anthelme, Dionys Mascolo, and Edgar Morin of the Action Committee of Intellectuals against the Algerian War, embarked on a path of traumatic literary withdrawal after his daughter died in an accident in 1965. Mutism became his refuge, untranslatable expressivity an abiding resource for living-on. John T. Naughton contends that his "entire oeuvre is concerned with the untranslatable dimension of our experience and with the inadequacy of human language to transmit the true nature of what we have lived and felt.... His work records the failure of writing, and given that his is so often a writing about not being able to write, his undertaking has been viewed by some as one of the truly exemplary projects of the postwar era." He also notes that "Raymond Queneau once compared des Forêts to Melville's Bartleby—the scrivener who 'would prefer not to.' "[41] Des Forêts's Bartleby, one could say, resembles Agamben's Bartleby, that "last, exhausted figure of what Avicenna refers to as complete or perfect potentiality that belongs to the scribe who is in full possession of the art of writing in the moment in which he does not write."[42]

Well before his vow of silence, in May 1968, amidst the clamor of joyful protest and demonstration, des Forêts discovered the political force of silence: "Our mutism—which has the meaning of a pathos-filled vigil—is the only form in our possession that will allow us to make present the arrival of a new force, one that is stormily hostile to anything that might come along and capture or enslave it, subordinate it to the sovereign movement that might carry it off ... it's the dream of rupture without return with the world of calculation."[43] Though he would in fact continue with sporadic worldly contact and professional assignments (as an editor, journalist, actor, and translator), in 1975 he began experimenting with a recessive form of autobiographical prose narrative that was published in 1997 under the title *Ostinato*. An unfinished and "unfinishable" work, the author insisted when he was interviewed in 1995 in *Le Nouvel Observateur* that while the work could be established as a manuscript, it could never be a book.[44] This book which was not a book adds something distinctive to the definition of "Bartleby politics." It highlights the valences of obstinacy as reserves of resistance. This is conveyed in des Forêts's writing through peculiar grammar: a language at once awkward, gnomic, limpid, and abstruse. In one instance, there is a remarkable rendering of the obstination of "without destination." The syntax deturns the paths of thought in run-on sentences that double back on themselves, and which toss and turn like a sailboat on waves. In this example, the sentence tacks to oblivion, jibs to abandon, and gets beached on the shoals of disabled decision and empowered forcelessness:

> Without destination, not wandering or distraught, not even avid to return to the heart of childhood to take back from oblivion [*l'oubli*] what was lost or to find again outside his own face and meaning [*par le dehors de sa propre figure et son propre sens*], nor to make himself anything other than what he was, but summoned, beckoned, seized, carried off by a movement having the force of an injunction to which he cedes in an ingenuous abandon [*un abandon ingénu*], like a legendary hero, his whole vigor of innocence letting him triumph over the obstacles set on his path by the evil angels of doubt powerless to turn him from it [*impuissants à l'en détourner*]. Too intimately linked to what he contests to be forced to any decisive test of confrontation

and perhaps drawing from this very impossibility itself the power to traverse in all candor these base and shadowy depths to the extreme end of the path, even having to skip a few steps or to fall from very high in a descent so terrifying that the furious appetite of destruction dwelling in him would not quench itself therein.[45]

In another instance, we are asked to parse the narrator's "astonishment" at his "state of being in life" ("Un si grand étonnement d'être en état de vie"), which opens onto a memory, that is occluded by a "thickness," that cannot be perforated: "So astonished at living that he tries as far back as his memory reaches for the obscure traces of his first death, but no thread leads back to the knot of the web. So many chimerical efforts to perforate the thickness of this indestructibly hard metal preventing any access to the enigmaless desert of immemorial night" ("Autant d'efforts chimériques pour perforer l'épaisseur de ce très dur minéral qui ne se laisse pas détruire et interdit tout accès au désert sans énigme de la nuit immémoriale").[46] Sentences like this one make impossible demands, posing the question of what something could "impossibly" mean as they take the reader through a welter of stoic abstractions and labored negations. Fronting the dead-wall of obtuseness, the reader is taught—through a rhythm of *ostinato* at the level of syntactic phrasing—to persevere in the face of recessionary aesthetics.[47]

When Deleuze observed that Bartleby does not outright refuse, but rather rejects both the preferred and the not-preferred, he opened a space for a something else that begs to be identified with *ostinato*. Though commonly used as a technical term for the repetition of a musical phrase that anchors a movement or an entire composition, as well as the fancy name for a hook or jazz riff played at the lower register and usually understood as the background to a main melody in the foreground (improvised or otherwise), des Forêt's *ostinato* is marked as a term of stylistic, philosophical abstention, with affinity to the styles of his better-known cohort: Bataille, Blanchot, Beckett, and Duras. (Little wonder that Derrida saw something philosophical in *ostinato*, a point raised when he interviewed Ornette Coleman on jazz.)[48] Des Forêts's syntax explores the perimeter of incommunicability, affirming the remoteness of a narrator who addresses himself by the third-person pronoun "he."

If Raymond Queneau nicknamed des Forêts "Bartleby the Scrivener," it was not just because his muteness approached that of Melville's clerk or that his narrator, in *Ostinato*, demonstrates a similar inclination to demur (as a captive member of the French Resistance, the narrator rehearses in his mind how he *will not* ask himself how he will remain silent when it is his turn to submit to torture), but also because he may have sensed a common psychic ground in explorations of the relation between obstination and humiliation.[49] Many fragments offer a window into the ways of a subject who discovers *ostinato* while quickening to the ordeals of domination, as in this instance of sexual hazing:

Little hairy squire, legs powdered with sand, struggling in the grip of bumpkins, his cheeks aflame and splattered with tears, hatefully turned over and undressed like a girl, his breath taken away by the riptide of the first spurt of semen that the huge leader of the pack brings to explosion in the sheath of his hand, holding him tight between his knees, but whose eyes stuck like cornflowers in the thicket of his hair soften the brutality of the gesture.

. . .

Solemnly brought before four haughty persons wearing doctors' caps, tightly encircled, interrogated, menaced with a whipping but wrapped in his pride as in his shirt unsewn at the shoulders, he utters not a word. *A silence cast like a long cry*, unholstered like a weapon to face up to iniquity and to put himself harshly to the trial of the purifying *vow to keep silent* that neither threats, insistence, cunning blackmail, nor the threat of punishment can alter.

The resolve to remain silent frustrates the satisfaction of the boy tormentor and outplays the equally sadistic hand of the school administrators who want to blame the victim not just for refusing to deliver the perpetrators, but for allowing himself to be already punished: "*The obstinate refusal* of any denunciation required by the rules of honor answers still more powerfully the repugnance of having to hear these masters garbed as inquisitors deflower, vilify what was a revelation of a stupefying intensity, although linked to fright and a feeling of extreme shame."[50] In these extracts the prose is relatively accessible, as is the dolorous, Christic mise-en-scène. But these features are props or hooks (like *ostinato* musical riffs) that advance the task of inculcation in the subtleties of obstination. Des Forêts provides a formation in subtracting from the imperium of others' wills; a training in the psychodynamics of winning by losing. *Ostinato* refines this instruction as the text proceeds across the narrator's life-line. It is cast as a questionably self-protective resistance to the love of a male soldier whose death will be a perpetual reproach: "Dumbness, obstinate, tyrannical dumbness, fruit of pride and fear. Everything is an obstacle to the heat of the exchange when losing even the strength to sustain the friendly blue of a glance."[51] Stresses and strengths must be redistributed over time, such that obstination may become powerfully astringent and metaphysically distilled as a condition of embodied negation:[52]

To persevere requires maintaining a sort of ingenuity exempt from intention, indifferent to the why and the how . . .[53]

Every wish of nothingness has limits that cannot be overstepped . . . A position all the less tenable in that it is incompatible with the use of language maintained toward and against everything—that is in fact the obstacle. Remain right there without saying anything and your wish will be in large part answered.[54]

...

Where is this sudden firmness coming from?
From fear. A fear like abulia, like that of a man who, knowing himself in mortal peril, would invoke the heavens without even moving his little finger.[55]

Throughout *Ostinato*, obstination is presented not so much as a moral value earned through survival in adverse circumstances, but as an experience of intransitivity within experience that dispatches one out to sea on an ontic journey. Historically speaking, this journey traces a line of continuity from the *ostinato* of 1960s jazz (where the politics of black empowerment was arguably aligned with the move to modal or free jazz), and the kind of extended meditative/exploratory improvisation that one finds in contemporary critical poetics, from the phrasings and musings on micro-aggression in Claudia Rankine's *Citizen: An American Lyric*, to scenes drawn from the visual archive of Black Lives Matter, which includes the riveting example of Titus Kaphar's *1968/2014* (2014), a diptych of two arms, one with clenched fist, the other with outspread palm.[56]

"He can no longer hold out his hand toward the others but sometimes contemplates the hand of his neighbor as a support."[57] This ambivalent image in *Ostinato* of the narrator's unhandedness alongside the fixated image of the neighbor's hand, invites the conjecture that there is a Bartleby connection (even if only a remote and tentative one) between the passive-aggressive, willfully inhibited, self-muting resistance of des Forêts's scrivener-like protagonist, and the striking images legated by the Black Lives Matter movement that include hands raised up in surrender or self-defense, curled into fists and defiant power grips ("gripping" for Kluge and Negt signifies essential labor powers and human capacities), folded across locked arms on protest days, and clasped in prayer for peace or open in outreach.[58]

Notes

Parts of this essay appeared previously in "Obstinacy" in *Unexceptional Politics: On Obstruction, Impasse, and the Impolitic* (New York: Verso, 2018).

1. Alan Blinder and Richard Pérez-Peña, "Kentucky Clerk Defies Justices on Marriages," *New York Times*, September 2, 2015.

2. Herman Melville, "Bartleby, The Scrivener: A Story of Wall Street," in *Benito Cereno, Bartleby The Scrivener, and the Encantadas* (Stilwell, Kans.: Digireads, 2005), 60.

3. Ibid., 64

4. Giorgio Agamben, *Potentialities*, trans. Daniel Heller-Roazen (Stanford, Calif.: Stanford University Press, 1999), 258.

5. Melville, "Bartleby," 63

6. Gilles Deleuze, *Critique et Clinique* (Paris: Seuil, 1993), 95.

7. Gilles Deleuze, "Bartleby; or, The Formula," in *Essays Critical and Clinical*, trans. Daniel W. Smith and Michael A. Greco (Minneapolis: University of Minnesota Press, 1997), 68.

8. See my discussion of "stasis" in relation to the concept "Peace" in *Against World Literature: On the Politics of Untranslatability* (New York: Verso, 2013), 131–37.

9. Rebecca Comay, "Resistance and Repetition: Hegel and Freud," *Research in Phenomenology* 45 (2015), 237–66, at 240.

10. In his introduction to the English edition of *History and Obstinacy*, Devin Fore provides the essential background on Negt and Kluge's notion of *Eigensinn*: "Whenever something is repressed, it becomes autonomous and intractable, Negt and Kluge observe. Capital's violent expropriation is countered by the subject with obstinacy, *Ent-eignung* with *Eigen-sinn*. Like Marx's old mole, a favorite image of Negt and Kluge, marginalized traits vanish from sight, but, exiled to the hinterlands of the psyche, they do not die. Instead, they mutate and enter into unexpected alliances with other capacities. . . . The word *Eigensinn*—rendered variously into English as 'autonomy,' 'willfulness,' 'self-will,' and, here, 'obstinacy'—implies a degree of stubborn obtuseness, an imperviousness to directives from above. Hegel, for example, famously defined *Eigensinn* as a 'freedom' that is 'enmeshed in servitude.' Kluge, in turn, describes *Eigensinn* as 'the guerilla warfare [*Partisanentum*] of the mind.' Obstinacy is the underside of history . . . for each luminous vista cleared by instrumental reason, a dense scotoma of stupidity emerges to blight the view; for every human trait that is singled out and capitalized, a resistant trait gathers force underground. 'It is not . . . some primal "self" that has *Eigensinn*, but rather a whole range of historically acquired and developed skills, drives, capacities, each of which makes its own "stubborn" demands and has its own distinct "meaning,"' writes Fredric Jameson about Negt and Kluge." See Devin Fore, "Introduction" to *History and Obstinacy*, by Alexander Kluge and Oskar Negt (New York: Zone Books, 2014), 35–36.

11. See Max Stirner, *The Ego and Its Own*, ed. David Leopold, trans. Steven Byington (Cambridge: Cambridge University Press, 1995).

12. Wyn Kelley, *Melville's City: Literary and Urban Form in Nineteenth-Century New York* (Cambridge: Cambridge University Press, 1996), 205–6. This reference came to my attention via Jane Desmarais's astute essay: "Preferring Not to: The Paradox of Passive Resistance in Herman Melville's *Bartleby*," *Journal of the Short Story in English* 36 (2001): 25–39.

13. Laurie Robertson-Laurent, *Melville: A Biography* (New York: Clarkson Potter, 1996), 335. Also cited by Desmarais, "Preferring Not to."

14. Naomi C. Reed, "The Specter of Wall Street: *Bartleby, the Scrivener* and the Language of Commodities," *American Literature* 76, no. 2 (2004): 247–73, at 261.

15. Jonathan D. Greenberg, "Occupy Wall Street's Debt to Melville," *The Atlantic*, April 30, 2012.

16. Russ Castronovo, "Occupy Bartleby," *The Journal of Nineteenth-Century Americanists* 2, no. 2 (Fall 2014): 253–72, at 253.

17. Jonathan Poore, "Bartleby's Occupation: 'Passive Resistance' Then and Now," Nonsite, http://nonsite.org/article/bartlebys-occupation-passive-resistance-then-and-now#foot_3_5576.

18. "Melville and Protest; Melville Occupies Wall Street," *Leviathan* 15, no. 1 (March 2013): 109–15.

19. Leo Marx, "Melville's Parable of the Walls," in *Bartleby the Inscrutable: A Collection of Commentary on Herman Melville's Tale "Bartleby the Scrivener,"* ed. M. Thomas Inge (Hamden, Conn.: Archon, 1979), 84–106.

20. Akis Gavrilidis and Sofia Lalopoulu, "Greek Referendum: Chaos," Interruption, https://interruptionint.wordpress.com/greek-referendum-chaos-par-akis-gavriilidis-sofia-lalopoulou/.

21. Ibid.

22. Slavoj Žižek, *The Parallax View* (Cambridge, Mass.: MIT Press, 2006), 382.

23. Ibid.

24. Ibid., 383.

25. Ibid., 385.

26. Alain Badiou, "Against 'Political Philosophy,'" in *Metapolitics*, trans. Jason Barker (London: Verso, 2005), 24.

27. "The Republic's Indigenous," a political party representing the neighborhoods and mostly immigrant populations of the French *banlieues*, who want to stress in their party name the relevance of French colonialism to a host of government-sanctioned operations that involve military intervention in national cities or communities on their outskirts. See Hacène Belmessous, *Opération Banlieues* (Paris: La Découverte, 2010).

28. Judith Butler, "So, What Are the Demands? And Where Do They Go from Here?" 2 *Tidal: Occupy Theory, Occupy Strategy* 8 (March 2012): 8–11, at 10.

29. Arne de Boever, "Overhearing Bartleby: Agamben, Melville, and Inoperative Power," *Parrhesia* 1 (2006): 142–62, at 142.

30. See Michael Zakim, "The Business Clerk as Social Revolutionary; or, a Labor History of the Nonproducing Classes," *Journal of the Early Republic* 26 (Winter 2006): 563–603, at 567. And see also Thomas Augst, *The Clerk's Tale: Young Men and Moral Life in Nineteenth-Century America* (Chicago: University of Chicago Press, 2003).

31. Deleuze, "Bartleby; or, The Formula," 71.

32. Jean-Claude Milner, *Pour une politique des êtres parlants: Court traité politique 2* (Paris: Verdier, 2011).

33. Ibid., 7 and 9.

34. "The Tangled Web," *Yes, Prime Minister*, series 2, episode 8, dir. Sydney Lotterby (London: BBC, 1988).

35. In a documentary titled *The Trap*, Adam Curtis characterized the series as "ideological propaganda for a political movement," namely, a Thatcherism that discredits public choice economics as hypocritical cover for the narrow self-interest of individual politicians. The documentary quotes Sir Antony Jay, one of the show's creators, on this view: "The fallacy that public choice economics took on was the fallacy that government is working entirely for the benefit of the citizen; and this was reflected by showing that in any [episode] in the programme, in *Yes Minister*, we showed that almost everything that the government has to decide is a conflict between two lots of private interest—that of the politicians and that of the civil servants trying to advance their own careers and improve their own lives. And that's why public choice economics, which explains why

all this was going on, was at the root of almost every episode of *Yes Minister* and *Yes, Prime Minister*." From Adam Curtis, *The Trap: What Happened to Our Dreams of Freedom, Part 1—F, You Buddy* (television production), BBC, quoted texts at 0:35:34 and 0:36:07 respectively.

36. "The politician's fallacy was identified in a 1988 episode of the BBC television political sitcom *Yes, Prime Minister* titled 'Power to the People,' and has taken added life on the Internet. The syllogism, invented by fictional British civil servants, has been quoted in the real British Parliament. The syllogism has also been quoted in American political discussion" (en.wikipedia.org/wiki/Politician %27s_syllogism). Entry citations include George Hayward Joyce, *Principles of Logic* (London: Longmans, 1908), 205; and Raymond Chen's "The Politician's Fallacy and the Politician's Apology," on his blog *The Old New Thing* (2011).

37. Frédéric Lordon, *Willing Slaves of Capital: Spinoza and Marx on Desire*, trans. Gabriel Ash (London: Verso, 2014), 75.

38. Melville, "Bartleby," 75, emphasis added.

39. Ibid., 75, 76.

40. Judith Butler, *Notes Toward a Performative Theory of Assembly* (Cambridge: Harvard University Press, 2015), 25–26.

41. John T. Naughton, "Louis-René des Forêts' *Ostinato*," in *Contemporary French Poetics*, ed. Michael Bishop and Christopher Elson (Amsterdam: Rodopi, 2002), 1–8, at 1.

42. Giorgio Agamben, "Bartleby, or On Contingency," in *Potentialities: Collected Essays in Philosophy*, trans. Daniel Heller-Roazen (Stanford, Calif.: Stanford University Press), 243–71, as cited by de Boever, "Overhearing Bartleby," 143.

43. Louis-René des Forêts, *L'Ephémère* no. 6 (Summer 1968), in *Oeuvres complètes*, ed. Dominique Rabaté (Paris: Gallimard, 2015), 79. Translation my own.

44. Interview with Jean-Louis Ezine, Louis-René des Forêts, *Le Nouvel Observateur*, February 16, 1995, as cited in *Oeuvres complètes*, ed. Rabaté, 133.

45. "Sans destination, non pas errant ni désemparé, pas même avide de faire retour au Coeur de l'enfance pour reprendre à l'oubli ce qui s'était perdu ou retrouver par le dehors sa propre figure et son propre sens, ni pour se rendre autre qu'il fut, mais mis en demeure, suscité, déssaisi, emporté par un movement qui a la force d'une injonction, auquel il cède dans un abandon ingénue, tel un héros de légende que toute sa vigueur d'être naïf fait triompher des embûches dressés sur son chemin par les mauvais anges du doute impuissants à l'en détourner. Trop intimement lié à ce qu'il conteste pour le soumettre à l'épreuve décisive de la contestation, et tirant peut-être de cette impossibilité même le pouvoir de traverser en toute candeur ce fond vaste et ténébreux jusqu'au point extrême du parcours, quitte à en brûler les étapes ou à retomber de très haut en une chute si foudroyante que le furieux appétit de destruction qui l'habite n'y trouverait pas à s'assouvir" (Louis-René des Forêts, *Ostinato*, in *Oeuvres complètes*, ed. Rabaté, 1055). *Ostinato*, trans. Mary Ann Caws (Lincoln: University of Nebraska Press, 2002) 18.

46. Des Forêts, *Ostinato*, 22; des Forêts, *L'Ephémère*, 106.

47. For a study in recessionary aesthetics linked to ecological quietism within Romantic lyrics, see Anne-Lise François, *Open Secrets: The Literature of Uncounted Experience* (Stanford, Calif.: Stanford University Press, 2008).

48. Jacques Derrida and Ornette Coleman, "The Other's Language: Jacques Derrida Interviews Ornette Coleman, 23 June 1997," trans. Timothy S. Murphy, http://jazzstudiesonline.org/files/TheOthersLanguage.pdf.

49. Des Forêts, *Ostinato*, 1093.

50. Louis-René des Forêts, *Ostinato*, trans. Mary Ann Caws (Lincoln: University of Nebraska Press, 2002), 20–21, emphasis added.

51. Ibid., 63.

52. *Ostinato* is possibly worthy of inclusion in the chain of terms for negation that Jane Bennett associates with the "*comprehending* materiality" or "thing-power" obliquely accessed in human being: "Because the human too is a materiality, it possesses a thing-power of its own. This thing-power sometimes makes itself known as an uneasy feeling of internal resistance, as an alien presence that is uncannily familiar. Perhaps this is what Socrates referred to as his *daemon* or nay-saying gadfly. Recent work in cultural theory has highlighted this force that is experience as in but not quite of oneself. This indeterminate and never fully determinable dimension of things has been called *difference* (Jacques Derrida), *the virtual* (Gilles Deleuze), *the invisible* (Maurice Merleau-Ponty), *the semiotic* (Julia Kristeva), and *nonidentity* (Theodor Adorno). Jean-François Lyotard describes this obstinate remainder, which hovers between the ontological and the epistemological registers, as 'that which exceeds every putting into form or object without being anywhere else but within them.' These various terms of art mark the fact that thing-power often first reveals itself as a negativity, a confounding or fouling up of an intention, desire schema, or concept. But, as many of the thinkers named above have noted, such negativity is also the same stuff out of which positive things emerge. It is a negativity that is profoundly productive: the materiality that resists us is also the protean source of being, the essentially vague matrix of things" (Jane Bennett, "The Force of Things: Steps towards an Ecology of Matter," *Political Theory* 32, no. 3 [June 2004]: 347–72, at 361).

53. Des Forêts, *Ostinato*, trans. Caws, 143.

54. Ibid., 143.

55. Ibid., 145.

56. The artist Brandon Coley Cox, whose oeuvre includes a complexly composed print of 2011 called *Hands Up*, followed the Bartleby formula of negative preference when asked by Antwaun Sargent whether "black artists should specifically respond to the historic, recent and continued killing of innocent black men and women in this country": "I found it very difficult to create anything at all after the nearly simultaneous indecisions happened around the murders of Eric Garner and Michael Brown . . . I want[ed] to act, and not to react, but to pro-act, but I wasn't sure how" (Antwaun Sargent, "Black Lives Matter," http://www.theaesthete.com/art/black-lives-matter).

57. Des Forêts, *Ostinato*, trans. Caws, 21.

58. Kluge and Negt write of "gripping" in their "Obstinacy" entry in the "Atlas of Concepts," an appendix of *History and Obstinacy*, "A fundamental current observable throughout human history. It develops out of a resistance to primitive expropriation" (*History and Obstinacy*, 390).

Land and See: The Theatricality of the Political in Schmitt and Melville

Walter A. Johnston

Let me only say that it fared with him as with the storm-tossed ship, that miserably drives along the leeward land. The port would fain give succor; the port is pitiful; in the port is safety, comfort, hearthstone, supper, warm blankets, friends, all that's kind to our mortalities. But in that gale, the port, the land, is that ship's direst jeopardy; she must fly all hospitality; one touch of land, though it but graze the keel, would make her shudder through and through. With all her might she crowds all sail off shore; in so doing, fights 'gainst the very winds that fain would blow her homeward; seeks all the lashed sea's landlessness again; for refuge's sake forlornly rushing into peril; her only friend her bitterest foe!
. . .
Glimpses do ye seem to see of that mortally intolerable truth; that all deep, earnest thinking is but the intrepid effort of the soul to keep the open independence of her sea . . . the highest truth, shoreless, indefinite as God.

—Melville, *Moby-Dick*

O place and greatness! millions of false eyes
Are stuck upon thee: volumes of report
Run with these false and most contrarious quests
Upon thy doings: thousand escapes of wit
Make thee the father of their idle dreams
And rack thee in their fancies.
. . . make haste;
The vaporous night approaches.

—Shakespeare, *Measure for Measure*

"A very current topic." These are the enigmatic words with which Carl Schmitt refers to Melville's 1855 text *Benito Cereno* in a letter to Ernst Jünger dated July 4, 1941.[1] The German jurist's reference to Melville's story, which tells the tale of an American ship captain's encounter with a Spanish slaver whose African "freight" has risen up and overthrown its European handlers, takes place six years after his own deposition as crown jurist under Hitler, five months after the United States' passage of the Lend-Lease Act, and one month after the first deployment of U.S. Marines in support of Allied forces. Melville's story, published serially in *Putnam's* from October to November 1855 and included as the third of five collected stories that together comprised the *Piazza Tales* of 1856, is based on the *Tryal* slave ship rebellion of 1805, as recounted in chapter 18 of the American ship captain Amasa Delano's memoir *Narrative of Voyages and Travels in the Northern and Southern Hemispheres*, published in New England in 1817.[2] Delano's story, the basic premises of which Melville does not alter, recounts the experiences of the putatively enlightened Northern republican and forebear of Franklin Delano Roosevelt as he boarded an apparently distressed "Spanish merchantman," in fact a slave ship upon which the slaves, unbeknownst to the American, have killed their owner, Alexandro Aranda, and subordinated their ship's captain, Benito Cereno, along with a few surviving crew members. Upon Delano's arrival, the slaves successfully deceive the American into thinking that the Spaniards are still in control of their vessel by staging an impromptu play based on the ship's former, European-led condition. The story is that of Delano's gradual undeception, upon which his crew attacks the Spanish vessel, kills or reenslaves its African inhabitants, and subjects the remaining putative leaders of the revolt to trial ending in their legally mandated torture and execution.

As the editors of Schmitt's correspondence note, references to literary works allowed German intellectuals writing between 1933 and 1945 to comment on wartime historical developments obliquely, thus mitigating the risks entailed in more direct discussion of current affairs. For Schmitt, who had already been deposed from government service for failing to adequately assimilate his published views to Nazi Party doctrine, pressure to avoid such risks would have been particularly pronounced. The jurist's cryptic references to Melville are thus of great importance in discussions of his works, particularly as they pertain to his relationship to National Socialism.[3] And yet the meaning of Schmitt's allusion to Melville has remained controversial, to say the least.[4] In what follows, I will suggest that this is in part the result of many scholars' equation of meaning with historical reference, and in this case with a narrowly construed range of proximate historical referents whose significance within Schmitt's larger theory of history remains largely unappreciated. The rush to establish historical reference, which has characterized studies of Melville's story as well, has led to a neglect of the formal differences between the two authors' works, and of the important philosophical differences that, I will suggest, they imply. Though it would be pointless to deny the significance of specific historical allusions in both authors' works, attention to their works' form does not lead one away from their historicity. Indeed, what is surprising about the not-so-new historicism that has characterized interpretations of the historical nexus marked by Schmitt's allusion to Melville is its neglect of the profound ways in which Schmitt and Melville's works erode the distinction between what one might provisionally call representational form and the historical content that, one is often encouraged to imagine, lies waiting beneath or behind it.[5]

Just what make Melville's "topic" so "current" for Schmitt? Though reticent with regard to historical reference, Schmitt is far more forthcoming regarding Melville's place within the larger theory of history he begins to develop in the early 1940s. In the course of his correspondence with Jünger, Schmitt identifies Melville's writing as central to his understanding of an idea that will become increasingly important to his work beginning in 1941: that of the world-historical significance of the sea as an element mediating human existence. This association is highly suggestive, since in the years leading up to and following Schmitt's first mention of Melville, the jurist had identified the sea as one among two elements whose difference could explain nothing less than "world-history" in its entirety, which he defined as in its essence "a history of wars waged by land-powers against sea-powers and sea-powers against land-powers."[6] In his correspondence with Jünger, he identifies Melville as the single, unparalleled authority regarding the nature of this element. "The sea as an element can only be grasped through Melville," he writes.[7]

While Schmitt's reading of Melville is of central importance to an understanding of the theory of world history that preoccupied him from the early 1940s until his death in 1985, Melville's text does not itself fit easily in the role that Schmitt assigns it. While Schmitt reads *Benito Cereno* as a representation of the world-historical conflict between the two elemental powers of land, as represented by the Continental European Cereno, and sea, as represented by the Anglo-American Delano, Melville's tale clearly distinguishes a third power besides—that of *theater*, as represented by the African slave revolt leader Babo.[8] Schmitt's neglect of this third power is all the more remarkable given that, upon scrutiny, this neglected power may be seen to collapse the distinction between the two forms of power that do interest him, flooding the firmness of land with the fluidity of sea to produce a historico-political brew of truly world-historical consistency. In what follows, I will argue that the illegibility of this form of power for Schmitt derives from the jurist's disavowal of a dimension of history that threatens to undermine the interrelated concepts of the political and of sovereign power he had developed prior to the war. This dimension is that of an immediate liquidation of historical identities, including those identities recognized by their relation to firm land or fluid sea, by the mediating power of the spectatorial gaze. As we shall see, without the immediate mediation of the onlooking masses that Schmitt feared to the point of repression, history as the jurist himself defines it could never emerge to begin with. And yet with it, the categorical function of the decision in politics reveals its debt to a primordial indecision, because of which the sovereign organization of the body politic resists monopolization by any of its members, and can accordingly never be said to have definitively come to pass. Melville's "topic" may thus have been and continue to be "current," but only because its current does not conform to the topoi that Schmitt imagined, since the u-topic condition of possibility of his text's historically determined topicality, as Schmitt might well have known, breaches the banks of this and every topography according to which one might direct its flow.

The Space of History

Schmitt's intra-war reading of Melville belongs to the period in which he develops the theory of global space that will preoccupy him throughout the postwar period. Contrary to much scholarship, this turn toward space does not mark a break with the concepts of sovereignty and the political for which Schmitt is best known. The theory of space is rather the basis of a theory of history that builds upon those earlier concepts.

The opening dictum of Schmitt's 1922 work *Political Theology*, "sovereign is he who decides on the state of exception," defines sovereignty as the capacity to join two seemingly opposed attributes: those of suspending and legitimating law, which are reconciled by the sovereign decision as an empirically underived, self-grounding act that secularizes the event of divine creativity. In his 1927 work *The Concept of the Political*, Schmitt argues that the essence of the political is the decisive distinction between friend and enemy, which expresses the existential tension between contrasting "forms of life."[9] Schmitt's postwar theory of space is a historicization of the concept of decision that unites these earlier works.

For Schmitt, historical dynamics are produced by the differences between politically foundational decisions, which give rise to distinct historical powers, or "forms of life." In *Land and Sea*, Schmitt suggests that such powers emerge from decisions for different concrete media or "elements"—different kinds of space in and through which different powers carry out their distinctive life processes. For Schmitt, space is accordingly not an abstract universal. It is not a historically neutral container in which life transpires. Spaces are rather the products of historically significant groups within particular historical periods. Such groups' decisions for particular elements produce the distinctive spaces in which they dwell by traversing them *as this or that kind* of space. The specific differences between powers thus derived structure the historical unfolding of politics.[10]

The shift from politics to history marked by Schmitt's theory of space is clearer in the German original, which includes the subtitle *A World-Historical Observation*. The odd use of the word "observation" is characteristic of Schmitt's style, which exudes the disinterested neutrality of the scholarly expert. The term's connotations of empirical verifiability ought not to distract one, however, from the nature of Schmitt's "observation" and the kind of concreteness to which it may legitimately lay claim. Just as the world Schmitt constructs has no unified space, it can also have no unified empirical objectivity, but is rather a world of competing objectivities based on competing models of space.

Space Revolution

Of the four elements distinguished by the pre-Socratics—earth, water, air, and fire—Schmitt's world-historical observations emphasize two, land (earth) and sea (water), whose conflict, according to Schmitt, determines the unfolding of history from antiquity to his present. Interestingly, Schmitt locates the decisive moment in this unfolding not in the ascendance of a particular land power over a particular sea power or vice versa, but rather in the transition from one kind of sea power to another. Drawing categories from Ernst Kapp's 1845 *Comparative General Geography*, Schmitt argues that the transition from a "thalassic" epoch, in which sea power is held by "cultures of the closed seas," to an epoch of "oceanic civilization," inaugurated by Europe's circumnavigation of the globe and discovery of a "new world," marks not only the beginning of an ascendance of sea over land power but, far more importantly, the transformative intensification of humanity's relationship to the sea.[11] For Schmitt, this transformation marks nothing less than a revolution of global scale, which, he argues, could be carried out by only one among the world's many nations.

> So it was that England became the heir, the universal heir of that great rupture in the existence of European nations. How was this possible? The phenomenon cannot be explained by drawing sweeping comparisons with earlier historical examples of maritime supremacy, whether one thinks of Athens, Carthage, Rome, Byzantium, or Venice. Here appears a case that is unique in its essence. Its specificity, its incomparability lies in the fact that England consummated its elemental metamorphosis at a moment in history that was unlike any other, and in a way that was shared by none of the earlier maritime powers. It truly displaced its collective existence from land onto sea. This enabled it to win not only countless wars and naval battles, but also something else and in fact infinitely more, namely a revolution, and a revolution of the greatest kind, a planetary space-revolution.[12]

However striking Schmitt's attribution of a revolution of global significance to a single island nation may be, it is important to note that the theory of revolution he develops here is one in which no familiar notion of national identity plays an essential role. Nor is the space-revolution Schmitt identifies to be understood as the result of naval prowess, which, he notes, many other historical sea powers also possessed. The uniqueness of the case of England lies rather in the element in which it consummated its maritime metamorphosis: the open ocean. England's uniqueness is accordingly the uniqueness of an elemental space that Schmitt elsewhere calls "categorical."[13] The greatness of the "revolution of the greatest kind," in other words, lies in the categorical nature of transformation it brings about. It is in these terms, moreover, that one must understand the concept of "space" that underlies Schmitt's concept of "space-revolution." Yet here Schmitt's "world-historical observation" would seem to encounter difficulty; how can one found a theory of history on the category of space, when such a category, within the Kantian philosophical tradition from which Schmitt draws this term, is by definition not only pre-empirical or transcendental but, for this very reason, by definition unobservable and ahistorical?

Schmitt expands upon the historico-categorical nature of the elements in a chapter devoted to the concept of space-revolution, linking it to the concept of the individual human being's quotidian "environment" (*Umwelt*):

> What is a space-revolution?
>
> Humanity has a determinate awareness of its "space," which is subject to great historical metamorphoses. Its various ways of life correspond to equally various spaces. Even within one and the same period of time, the environment [*Umwelt*] in which individual human beings carry out their day-to-day lives is differently determined according to their vocations. The urbanite has a different image of the world than the farmer; the whale hunter has a different vital space than the opera singer, and both world and life appear to the pilot not only in a different light, but with a different scale, depth, and horizon. Still greater and deeper are the differences between spatial images [*Raumvorstellungen*] when one looks to different nations and to different epochs in the history of humankind.
>
> Scientific theories of space tell us a lot and very little at once . . . If you ask a learned person, they will tell you that mathematical space is something totally different from the space of an electro-magnetic field, and that this is once again totally different from space in the psychological or biological senses of the word. Here one finds no unity, but risks fragmenting and dissolving a great problem through the irrelevant serialization of various different concepts.
>
> But the forces [*Kräfte*] and powers [*Mächte*] that forge history wait for science as little as Christopher Columbus and Copernicus did. Each time that, through a new outburst of historical forces or an unbinding of new energies, new lands and new seas enter human consciousness's field of vision, the spaces of historical existence undergo a change as well. From this emerge new criteria and dimensions for politico-historical activity, new sciences, new forms of order, a new life, or new, reborn peoples. This development can be so sudden and so profound that it alters . . . the concept of space itself. Then one

Land and See 61

can speak of a space revolution. In reality most great historical transformations are bound up with a changed image of space [*Raumbild*]. That is the true core of the thoroughgoing political, economic, and cultural change that subsequently transpires.¹⁴

Schmitt's provocative coupling of Copernicus and Columbus serves as a synecdoche for the historicization of Kantian *categoriality* that his theory of spatial revolution entails. In Schmitt's iteration, the "Copernican revolution" that Kant positions as the origin of both modern science and of his own critical epistemology represents, not the final turn toward the phenomenological elucidation of the categories that structure all human cognition a priori, but one among many revolutionary transformations of the categorical structure of historical life. Though Schmitt does not say so explicitly, this historicization of judgment entails a liquidation of the Kantian distinction between theoretical philosophy (or philosophy of knowledge) and practical philosophy (or philosophy of action), which sets the categorical structure of cognition into historical motion.

It is not insignificant, moreover, that this liquidation involves the categorialization of space. Kant differentiates space, as the form of outer sense, from the categories of pure reason and from time as the form of inner sense. It is this differentiation, moreover, that safeguards the "transcendental unity of apperception," thus guaranteeing the ahistorical, universal validity of the results of phenomenological science.¹⁵ By making space categorical, Schmitt undoes this guarantee. By bringing the outside of Kantian subjectivity in, as it were, he compromises the autonomy of the subject by abrogating the purity of primary auto-affection, thus rendering the subject heteronomous and exposing it to alteration. The various elements are modifications of this originary contamination. They are different ways in which the historical subject is constitutively outside of itself in the world in which it dwells.

Concrete Imaginings

The "powers that forge history" are thus neither empirical nor purely transcendental, neither efficiently causal nor ahistorically formal. What, then, is their nature? The answer to this question becomes explicit in *Nomos of the Earth in the International Law of the Jus Publicum Europaeum*, in which Schmitt identifies them as the powers of the "image" (*Bild*).¹⁶ Though Schmitt does not say so directly, and for reasons that will become clear, the "powers [*Kräfte*] that forge history" are neither empirical nor purely transcendental for a surprisingly simple reason: they are those of the *Einbildungskraft* or "power of imagination," through whose secondary sight the extrinsic is made part of the invisible world of thought, and thought is made part of the sensible world of experience, such that a priori and a posteriori worlds interpenetrate.

Once one has grasped the significance of the image in the forging of history, one can better understand why, despite his stylistic pretensions to an objectivity redolent of positive science, Schmitt would look to an imaginative writer to reveal the "objective, elementary and concrete *situation*" of sea power in its oceanic phase.[17] And though it is Melville's *Moby-Dick* that Schmitt names as the oceanic equivalent of Homer's *Odyssey*, it is *Benito Cereno* that earns the American writer the title of undisputed authority on the "epoch of the sea," and it is the "underlying symbolism" of this text that draws Schmitt's sustained attention. Indeed, Schmitt's *Ex Captivitate Salus: Experiences of the Years 1945–47* opens with a direct reference to Melville's story: "Every situation has its secret, and every science carries its *arcanum* within it. I am the last, conscious representative of the *jus publicum europaeum*, its last teacher and researcher in an existential sense, and experience its end as Benito Cereno experienced the journey of the pirate ship."[18]

This direct identification with Cereno is not unique. During the war, Schmitt had signed two letters to Jünger with Cereno's name in place of his own,[19] insinuating a parallel between Cereno's position as deposed captain of the slave ship and that of German intellectual elites under the "mass-system" of National Socialism.[20] By establishing continuity with his analysis of the *jus publicum europaeum*, however, Schmitt's published reference to *Benito Cereno* situates his reading of Melville within a historical field that extends beyond the immediate postwar period, returning one's attention to the meaning of his designation of Melville as the superlative writer of the sea. But what exactly is the significance of this designation, for Schmitt, and what might that tell us about his understanding of Melville's text?

The Terrestrial Telos of Right

Answering these questions requires further study of the transition from *Land and Sea* to *Nomos of the Earth*, which contains Schmitt's analysis of the *jus publicum europaeum*. Schmitt describes this shift as a transition from "elemental-mythological observations" to fundamentally "jurisprudential" concerns. The "jurisprudential orientation" (*rechtswißenschafliche Grundgedanke*) of Schmitt's later work, however, brings with it an unmarked and yet fundamental change in the story he tells regarding the world-historical conflict of land and sea powers. Whereas Schmitt's earlier work represents the influence of the two world-historical elements as equiprimordial, his reconstruction of this conflict as it pertains to the history of jurisprudence argues for the primacy of land over sea.[21] The shift in perspective is explained by the special relationship Schmitt posits between land and *Recht*, which he claims to find immanent in the language of myth.[22] The "jurisprudential orientation" (*rechtswissenshaftliche Grundgedanke*) of Schmitt's later work thus allows him to surreptitiously close the "open question" of *Land and Sea* at

Land and See 63

the outset of *Nomos of the Earth*, such that the apparently decisive victory of Anglo-American oceanic power over Continental-European terrestrial power he was forced to confront in the earlier work may be situated within a longer historical trajectory whose telos is discernible in the original unity of *Recht* and firm land.

The essential bond between land and *Recht* derives, for Schmitt, from the particular type of element that earth is and the particular spatial order that it reflects. What makes earth special is the way it rewards and reflects human labor, providing for the stable externalization of inward intentions via the sensible forms of agriculture, distributive marking, and architecture.[23] In contrast to earth, what one takes from the sea does not appear as the just reward of one's labor. Since the fisherman does not sow what he reaps, no "inner measure," no earthly "justice" bridging the visible and the invisible, the ideal and the real, emerges from this relation. And since its surface is ever-changing, the sea does not support the notions of "property" and "sanctity," and accordingly fails to support the separation of "different types of human activity," remaining "indifferently open [to] fishing, peaceful transport, and war" alike.[24]

For Schmitt, it is the sea's indifference to the various types of human activity that transpire upon it that is historically decisive. What the firm land supports and the open sea does not is the ability to bracket lethal violence—to displace war, the possibility of which is the essence of the friend/enemy relation and accordingly of the political as Schmitt has defined it, from one place to another. What the decisive, existential transition from land to sea accomplished by the British during the age of discovery threatens is accordingly the political as such and the history to which it gives rise. Without the political interruption of the war of each against all that Schmitt, following Hobbes, posits as the prehistoric origin of all sociopolitical institutions, no history, which is to say, nothing that transcends the mere struggle for existence common to all animal life, would emerge.

Catastrophic Confusion

For Schmitt, the threat to world history posed by the English turn to sea is not immediately realized. Rather, in the period stretching from Columbus to the end of the Second World War, the annihilation of land-based by sea-based forms of life is staved off by the displacement of the unbracketed violence characteristic of sea life to the colonial scene, which allows for a "bracketing of war" (*Hegung des Krieges*) in the European-metropolitan domain. According to Schmitt, this displacement institutes a new "line of amity" that synthesizes the functions of the political and sovereign decisions by distinguishing between friend and enemy and norm and exception at once, separating the space of Europe from that of the rest of the world and, in so doing, giving shape to the spatial order of the *jus publicum europeaum*.

64 Walter A. Johnston

Schmitt conceives of the *jus publicum europeam* as a secularization of the medieval Christian *katechon*, which hinders the apocalyptic arrival of the Antichrist. It is thus no mistake that Schmitt uses the word "confusion" (*Verwirrung*) to indicate the threat posed by Anglo-American power, echoing the biblical notion of a confusion preceding apocalypse, nor that he associates this confusion with the cacophonous intermixing of peoples and tongues at Babel. Nor is it surprising that Schmitt insinuates Melville's tale as the allegorical prefiguration of the threat whose fulfillment he believes he witnesses, or that he would identify himself with Cereno's position in this tale. Melville's story is, above all, the story of a great and indeed world-historical confusion. This confusion is embodied by the American ship captain Amaso Delano, the putatively enlightened New Englander whose dim wit threatens not only Cereno's life, but more importantly from Schmitt's perspective, the clear distinction between European and non-European peoples that subtends the colonialist's way of living. That this threat would be represented by an American rather than a British character poses no problem for Schmitt's reading, since the jurist had long viewed the rise of American power as a stage in the globalization of British oceanic civilization.[25] Indeed, Schmitt seems almost to paraphrase Melville's depiction of then President Roosevelt's progenitor Amaso Delano when, in a 1942 text addressing German pessimism induced by the United States' entry into war, he refers to the United States as a nation whose characteristic irresolution portends "the fate of those who, lacking all inner determination, glide with their ship into the maelstrom of history."[26]

In Melville's tale, Amaso Delano is indeed a character of great contradictions, and one can certainly see how Schmitt would perceive the world-historical confusion that interests him aptly represented by the New Englander's inability to grasp the nature of the conflict with which he is confronted aboard the European slave ship. The sea captain's oft-remarked, absurd musings regarding the organic social hierarchy he sees represented in the relationship between the (in fact deposed) Cereno and the (in fact rebelled) slave Babo—and indeed at the very moment that the latter holds the blade of existential hostility to the throat of the trembling Cereno under the guise, donned for Delano's benefit, of the deposed slave ship captain's barber and valet—would clearly represent, from Schmitt's perspective, the result of an epochal imperviousness to the clear line of amity separating European from non-European space, friendship from enmity, politics from economy, and the space of bracketed from that of unbracketed violence, as a world-historical effect of the rise of Anglo-American oceanic civilization more broadly.[27] For Schmitt, at the core of this confusion lies a tendency toward moral universalism—aptly reflected in the "republican impartiality" Delano displays when he distributes water to blacks and whites alike—that is inappropriate to political situations, in which all judgments must be subordinated to the fundamental distinction between friend and enemy, such

Land and See 65

that those who rely upon universal categories ("humanity" is Schmitt's primary example) are doomed either to hypocrisy, political blindness, or some ideological mixture of two.[28] As many scholars have noted, Delano's mixture of good will and racial prejudice does likely reflect Melville's awareness of the limitations of even some of his most admired abolitionist compatriots.[29] Delano thus represents the benighted condition of Northern progressives whose political commitments rely upon moral universals that render them powerless to comprehend the irreducible hostilities that divide the concrete sociohistorical spaces they traverse.[30]

Delano's bipolar vacillation between benighted credulity and absolute suspicion of the multicolored hosts who greet him aboard Cereno's slave ship is eminently legible in these terms. In the opening lines of Melville's story, the unnamed narrator introduces Delano as "a person of singularly undistrustful good nature, not liable, except on extraordinary and repeated incentives, and hardly then, to indulge in personal alarms, any way involving the imputation of malign evil in man." As in the classical tragedy with which Melville frequently associates his own worldview, the entire unfolding of Benito Cereno's narrative is prefigured in this presentation of Delano's fundamental flaw, with the difference that Melville does not delay appending the following rhetorical question, which in its directness tips this latter-day tragedy in the direction of farce: "Whether, in view of what humanity is capable, such a trait implies, along with a benevolent heart, more than ordinary quickness and accuracy of intellectual perception, may be left to the wise to determine."[31]

With this, the stage is set, and in terms that Schmitt could no doubt well understand. Melville's tale announces itself as the tragicomedy of the American progressive's slow wit, born of a singularly undistrustful disposition, itself derivative of the uninterrupted supposition of the fundamental benevolence of humankind, which blinds him to the existence of "malign evil in man," thus leaving him vulnerable to the machinations of his enemies. Melville, moreover, positions Delano's less than average quickness of wit in relation to precisely the geospatial phenomena whose judgment the American moral-universalist, from Schmitt's perspective, remains constitutively incapable of comprehending in its specificity, namely "the lawlessness and loneliness of the spot" in which he finds himself.[32]

It is Delano's failure to comprehend the nature and consequences of this oceanic lawlessness that leads to his surprise regarding a departure from custom: the approaching ship's failure to fly its flag. Melville's full passage reads:

> To captain Delano's surprise, the stranger, viewed through the glass, showed no colors; though to do so upon entering a haven, however uninhabited in its shores, where but a single other ship might be lying, was the custom among peaceful seamen of all nations. Considering the lawlessness and loneliness of the spot, and the sort of

stories, at that day, associated with those seas, Captain Delano's surprise might have deepened into some uneasiness had he not been a person of a singularly undistrustful good nature, not liable, except on extraordinary and repeated incentives, and hardly then, to indulge in personal alarms, any way involving the imputation of malign evil in man. Whether, in view of what humanity is capable, such a trait implies, along with a benevolent heart, more than ordinary quickness and accuracy of intellectual perception, may be left to the wise to determine.[33]

Melville identifies Delano with the faith in custom characteristic of Anglo-American, common law-based juridical history, insinuating this faith as the ground of the American captain's failure to access the uneasiness that might have befit a more accurate consideration of the lawlessness and loneliness of the spot in which he finds himself. The lawlessness in question, moreover, may easily be read, from a Schmittian perspective, as the product of the United States' "official absence and factual presence" in the Western Hemisphere, codified by the Monroe Doctrine, which succinctly characterizes the fundamentally inchoate nature of American power for the German jurist.[34] That Melville's story immediately juxtaposes the juridical ambiguity of the oceanic locale to the "plain . . . true character of the approaching vessel . . . a Spanish merchantman of the first class, carrying negro slaves, amongst other valuable freight, from one colonial port to another," could not fail to have escaped Schmitt's notice.[35] The Schmittian tension between European thalassocratic colonialism and Anglo-American oceanic imperialism is further reflected in Melville's contrast of the sociopolitical orders aboard the two vessels, which juxtaposes the clear hierarchy of negro slaves and Spanish sailors with Delano's more ambiguous rule over the former convicts in his employ. And yet, as we shall see, Melville's meditation on the vagaries of the South American spot he reimagines also contains much that undermines the framework that Schmitt offers.

The Coastal Image

Though Melville's description of Delano's predicament does indeed reflect many of the attributes that Schmitt assigns to oceanic cultures, it is far less certain that his tale as a whole can be persuasively read as a "primordial image" (*Urbild*) of the oceanic element in Schmitt's sense. This is so not only because the main action of Melville's tale does not transpire upon the open ocean but rather in the decidedly thalassic "haven" of Santa Maria, but because of the far more striking attributes of the image with which Melville introduces the reader to his chosen scene, which isolates and intensifies the layering of land and sea he finds immanent in its coastal topic. Melville writes:

Land and See

> The morning was one peculiar to that coast. Everything was mute and calm; everything gray. The sea, though undulated into long roods of swells, seemed fixed, and was sleeked at the surface like waved lead that has cooled and set in the smelter's mould. The sky seemed a gray *surtout*. Flights of troubled gray fowl, kith and kin with flights of troubled gray vapors among which they were mixed, skimmed low and fitfully over the waters, as swallows over meadows before storms. Shadows present, foreshadowing deeper shadows to come.[36]

Melville's opening image does not depict the sea as a space of universal, undifferentiated flow, but rather a coast whose peculiarity it is, of a morning, to merge the attributes of land and sea, water and meadow, fixity and flow, in an arrestingly portentous manner. Thus while, as Eric Sundquist demonstrates, Melville's text is certainly colored by his awareness of the South American coast as the site of conflict between "old world" colonialism and "new world" imperialism, his elemental allegorization of this conflict suggests an understanding of its nature that differs markedly from Schmitt's.[37] The stakes are no lower: Melville's image, like Schmitt's, is an image of world-historical suddenness. Its strictly unimaginable conjunction of undulation and stillness models the lightning-like blacking-out of the "light of sense" that, since Wordsworth's ode to the sublime, self-wounding "power" of the "imagination," marks access to the "invisible world" of transcendental form.[38] Yet while, for Schmitt, the punctual power of the primordial image is that of a decisive, polemical, and world-historical transition from one spatial order or mode of cognition to another, the opening scenes of *Benito Cereno* dwell instead upon an "infinite" suspension of knowing, gesturing toward that essential "landlessness" that, in Ishmael's words, is at once the "only friend and bitterest foe" of "all deep, earnest thinking," in which nevertheless resides "the highest truth, shapeless, indefinite as God."[39]

Like Turner's 1835 painting *Waves Breaking on a Lee Shore*, which likely inspired the "stoneless" monument to one of *Moby-Dick*'s many mariners (chapter 23, "The Lee Shore") from which I quote above, *Benito Cereno*'s conjunction of classical representation and proto-modern abstraction overlays well-delineated objects and the amorphous environment from which they emerge. *Benito Cereno*'s opening image is one in which vision is at once halted by and sustained in relation to the medium that enables it, doubling back upon itself, as it were, so as to see not only what is in front of it but also the sudden, simultaneously blinding and illuminating, revealing and concealing influence of visibility itself.[40] The tension this produces is not Schmitt's antinomy of clearly delineated land and catastrophically inchoate sea, but belongs to a space in which the fluid transposability of form and the apparent solidity of determinate content interpenetrate. In *Benito Cereno*, Melville explores this space thematically via an emphasis on a thickening of atmosphere within the representational space of his narrative, which is permeated by a substance in which earth and water intermix: the "vapors" that, "troubled" and "grey," "skim . . . low and fitfully over the waters, as swallows over meadows before storms."[41]

Troubled Vapors

In a recent book on Melville's story "Bartleby, the Scrivener," Branka Arsić traces Melville's interest in atmospheric phenomena back to his study of Descartes's meteorology, the second discourse of which is devoted to the analysis of "vapors and exhalations."[42] Descartes defines vapor as a mixture of earth and water particles that have been excited by the sun.[43] Vapors become visible, according to him, when their degree of excitation varies from that of surrounding particles, as when the "breath and sweat" of an "overheated horse" passes into the cold air of a winter's day. Importantly, however, the condition of vapor's visibility is not that of its existence, nor does its invisibility denote its absence. Rather, according to Descartes, when vaporized particles "move at the same speed and with the same oscillation as the subtle material that surrounds them, they cannot prevent this material from receiving the action of the luminous bodies,"[44] and so become as invisible as the breath of horses on a hot summer's day.

The thesis regarding the presence of invisible vapor is not a matter of passing interest for Descartes. Indeed, regarding the presence of such vapors, the philosopher of radical doubt evinces uncharacteristic certainty: "we must not doubt that the atmosphere often contains as many or more vapors when they are unseen as when they are seen," he inveighs, "for how would it happen, short of a miracle, that in warm weather and in the middle of the day, the sun, shining on the lake or a swamp, would fail to raise many vapors from it, seeing that we notice that in that sort of weather the waters dry up and recede more than in cold and cloudy weather?"[45] It is perhaps no surprise, then, that the philosopher's injunction would have made an impression on Melville, whose story hinges on the apparent dispersals and returns of the vapor of visibility. Although Melville's narrative establishes itself as a story of revelation at its outset, and although the "shadows present" that cloud both the reader's and Delano's "long benighted mind[s]" will indeed eventually withdraw before "the negro" Babo, leader of the slave revolt, this rebel's unmasking and consequent defeat will only cast new "shadow[s]" upon the fatally disconsolate Cereno till the story's end.[46]

Melville packs much of what is at stake in this deferral of revelation into his story's opening tableau, which establishes an expectation of progressive enlightenment through the deployment of a trope no less reliable than that of the rising sun. But although the rising sun promises a passage from darkness to light, as through blackness to white, this particular morning takes the stage costumed in textiles woven to resist such passage, since to the narrator

Land and See

69

its very "sky seem[s] a grey *surtout*."[47] The incursion of the French word for "overcoat," more literally translated as "over-all," like the equally capacious categories of *liberté* and *egalité* that inspire the San Domingo revolution with which Melville associates *Benito Cereno*'s slave revolt, threatens the clear foresight of its European inventors by encompassing more than they had intended.[48] Melville's tale calls our attention not so much to the disabling abstractness of such categories, as Schmitt is frequently wont to do, but rather to the concrete ungovernability and capacity for world-historical drift that is reflected in their atmospheric circulation. Melville's text meditates on the implications of this ungovernable "creep" of French fashion. As we read, the Gallic cloak morphs into the vaporous "mantle" through which the light of the rising sun shines only "equivocally," making the strange approaching vessel, from whose cabin window a similar light streams as would a mirror through a lamp, appear ready to reverse its trip northwestward for the enticingly veiled "Lima intriguante" it might otherwise leave in her "Indian . . . dusk." Such is the truly confusing composition of the strange seagoing vessel that, "in navigating into the harbor, was drawing too near the land." Melville writes:

> With no small interest, Captain Delano continued to watch her—a proceeding not much facilitated by the vapors partly mantling the hull, through which the far matin light from her cabin streamed equivocally enough; much like the sun—by this time hemisphered on the rim of the horizon, and apparently, in company with the strange ship, entering the harbor—which, wimpled by the same low, creeping clouds, showed not unlike a Lima intriguante's one sinister eye peering across the plaza from the Indian loop-hole of her dusk *saya-y-manta*.[49]

Here, the misty veil that insinuates itself as the object and limit of enlightenment, extending the dusky Indian attributes of the *saya-y-manta* to the most westerly reaches of Spanish colonial America, positions the costume as the backslidingly Catholic accompaniment to the vapors that pervade the scene. Like those vapors, the intriguante's partially veiled visage literalizes the indistinction of blindness and insight that follows from vision's reflective turn. That the shift from natural to cultural forms of obfuscation takes place by way of this costume is, moreover, surely no mistake, since the ever-deepening shadow "the negro" will cast in the remainder of Melville's tale will be associated less with his "dusk[y]" complexion than with his unsettling ability to pirate the products of the increasingly less buoyant stage of European colonial power as the means-without-ends of an insurgent theater adrift. Babo's story thus extends the metaphor of the ship of state, which subtends Melville's association of the Haitian revolution and the *Tryal* slave revolt from the outset, to a consideration of the specific dimension of the political that, since Plato, has been so frequently to blame for the fragility of governance and the social hierarchy that subtends it: its precarious relationship to theater.[50]

The Politics of Theater

For Plato, theater threatens the organic integrity of the body politic because, like Melville's Cartesian vapors, it is that strange, shifting medium which erodes the clear boundaries between classes of people and things, disrupting the body politic by confusing its organs as to their proper place and role. Theater does so, as is well known, because the power of mimetic abstraction allows mere appearance to pass for the practically grounded identity of persons and things, breaking the union of doing and knowing that is characteristic of a vocationally organized society. Like the *surtout* that spans the horizon of Melville's opening scene, the theatrical mask threatens the social organism because it can be donned by anyone. By making theater the means of captaining a vessel he cannot navigate, Babo seems to embody the worst fear of Plato's *Republic*.

Like Shakespeare's Caliban, who makes an appearance as the hermit Oberlus in Sketch Nine of Melville's "Encantadas,"[51] Babo's piratical power is that of the theatrical mimicry of the social forms that hold sway in the culture that has enslaved him.[52] The story that *Benito Cereno* tells is, at its most basic level, simply the narrative of Delano's gradual recognition of this theater as theater, and therewith the revelation that the Spanish slave ship upon which he finds himself has been under the dramaturgical control of its ostensible "freight" from the start. The removal of the many veils that proliferate at the beginning of *Benito Cereno* would thus take place through a proto-Brechtian revelation of theatrical illusion as such—that "these our actors," in Prospero's prophetic words, "were all spirits and / Are melted into air, into thin air."[53] Yet Prospero's words disproportionately precede the actual end of Shakespeare's play, and serve the narrative function not of ending his production but rather of preparing a mere change of scene, together with a change of costume, which in turn provides the eminently theatrical means of the magus's promotion to yet another position of power. Like that of Descartes, Shakespeare's "thin air" thus proves imperceptibly thickened. Similarly, Delano, though "in time undeceived" regarding the nature of his empirical surroundings, will remain subject to another, higher-order mystification, which Melville associates with his faith.[54]

Delano's faith is thematized in the course of a conversation between the Catholic Cereno and his Protestant rescuer regarding the meaning of the events they've lived through together. At stake in their discussion is nothing less than the relationship between the sensible and the supersensible, the temporal and the eternal, the transience of appearance and the meaning that underlies it, as refracted in the question of the hermeneutic status of good works in the knowledge of salvation. When Delano, thinking that the Spaniard congratulates himself unjustly for keeping the two whites alive aboard the revolted slave ship, subtly rejoins "true, true . . . you saved my life, Don Benito, more than I yours; saved it, too, against my knowledge and will," the Spaniard responds by insisting upon the value of the American's deeds.[55] "'Nay my friend,' rejoined the Spaniard, courteous even to the point of religion, 'God charmed your life, but you saved mine.'" Delano, however, remains unmoved, and expresses this in exceedingly illuminating terms. He answers:

> Yes, all is owing to Providence, I know; but the temper of my mind that morning was more than commonly pleasant, while the sight of so much suffering, more apparent than real, added to my good nature, compassion, and charity, happily interweaving the three. Had it been otherwise, doubtless, as you hint, some of my interferences might have ended unhappily enough. Besides that, those feelings I spoke of enabled me to get the better of my momentary distrust, at a time when acuteness might have cost me my life, without saving another's. Only at the end did my suspicions get the better of me, and you know how wide of the mark they proved.

The story of Delano's undeception would thus end with an encomium to the practical benefits of his former benightedness, which he unwittingly places parallel to those of that particular type of Othello-murdering theatergoer whose suspension of disbelief is so total that they take the "sight of so much suffering" as real and act accordingly. Yet the story's opening question, whether Delano's "singularly undistrustful good nature" betrays "more than ordinary quickness and accuracy of intellectual perception," is not hereby answered in the negative, for Delano's rejoinder introduces a perspective that is fundamentally incompatible with that of "the wise": blind faith in providence.

Notwithstanding, the position Delano describes may still "remain for the wise" to judge, if not to unconditionally laud, since it finds its pagan precursor in the work of that preeminent wisdom-lover who, as we have seen, identifies the philosopher-king's rule with the existence of a particular type of citizen: one whose virtue it is to believe lies, and most of all the noble one which founds that eminently believable theater-of-state, the ideal republic. Like that Platonic credulity, the virtue of Delano's blind faith is practical, rather than theoretical. It consists in the ability to act well in the absence of knowledge, or in the presence of only that highly circumscribed knowledge which accrues to one by virtue of one's vocation. Yet this virtue is not evenly distributed in Platonic society. It is rather the virtue of those subordinate subjects whose role is to do and not to question, to work and not to wonder why. In addition to such people, there must always be some others who know that

72 Walter A. Johnston

social order depends upon the plebeian behaving *as if* his or her role were naturally given. There must always be some who know the lie as lie, since it is to them that the task of caring for and maintaining the mechanisms of the theater of state falls.

In Melville's tale, this role devolves upon the fallen aristocrat Cereno, who knows theater as theater from the start. Yet, as fallen, the one-time philosopher-king's knowledge is one that has outlived its concrete utility, since Cereno is no longer king but rather enslaved within his own theatrical mechanism. The horror of his position is that of one who knows the baselessness of the power to which he is nevertheless effectively subjected. His position is the monstrous one of the philosopher-slave, whose appearance as a form of life the entire structure of the Platonic state is designed to forestall, and whose similarity to Schmitt's own position in intra-war Germany the jurist at once could, and could not fully, comprehend.

By the time Delano meets him, Cereno is a ghost of himself, having witnessed the theatrical evisceration of the way of life that defines him. The most traumatic aspect of Cereno's tale, the part of his story about which he cannot bring himself to speak, is not the memory of the murderous physical violence he has witnessed, but rather that of the piratical appropriation of the theatrical means of his ship of state. It is this terror that is dramatized in the "play of the barber," which Sundquist identifies as Melville's greatest invention, noting that it is among the few scenes entirely absent from the historical Delano's narrative.[56] In this scene, we are introduced to the captain's dressing chamber, which is unmistakably likened to the backstage area of a theatrical performance. It is here that Babo holds the blade to Cereno's throat, playfully reproducing the role of barber and valet that was likely once his unwilling lot, thus preparing Cereno to perform the empty shell of his un-rule upon the tattered stage of his former vessel. The theatrical tools of a European master, up to and including the flag that signifies his sovereign state, in which Babo wraps Cereno during the performance of his toilet, are thus used, not to dismantle the master's proverbial house, but rather to expose it in its existentially terrifying symbolic emptiness, to the memory of which Melville returns us at the story's end. He writes:

> But if the Spaniard's melancholy sometimes ended in muteness upon topics like the above, there were others upon which he never spoke at all . . . The dress so precise and costly, worn by him on the day whose events have been narrated, had not willingly been put on. And the silver mounted sword, apparent symbol of despotic command, was not, indeed, a sword, but the ghost of one. The scabbard, artificially stiffened, was empty.

One can well imagine how Schmitt must have read these lines, in which a knowing but tragically destined representative of European colonial power gives way to American universalism, in all its unwitting, and therefore catastrophic, self-contradiction. This reading would only be strengthened by the fact that, in the ensuing narrative, Delano motivates his men to brutally reenslave the Africans with the promise of half the *San Dominick*'s value as booty, driving home the suspicion that Melville's renaming of the American ship after a famous freebooter would already have signaled to an attentive reader.[57] From Schmitt's perspective, the crucial insight to be derived from these clues would not be that Delano's is perhaps a pirate ship, but rather that the American operates in an oceanic space in which there is no clear distinction between the economic and the political, nor between public and private interests, and where there is accordingly no way of distinguishing between the legitimate and illegitimate deployment of lethal violence.

What this reading of Melville's tale misses is that Cereno is not in fact undone by the American ship captain, but rather by the African dramaturge. For although many scholars have seen a critical reference to the role of the German masses in the rise of National Socialism in Schmitt's 1942 claim regarding the relevance of *Benito Cereno*'s slave revolt, such a reading has no life in the rest of Schmitt's writings from that period or thereafter. The slaves may nevertheless be plausibly positioned as the colonial other in relation to whom Schmitt triangulates Anglo-American/European-Continental conflict, to be sure, but it is the latter that is, for him, historically decisive, such that this perspective adds little to one's ability to read Babo from Schmitt's perspective. This difficulty calls one's attention to one of the most remarkable aspects of Schmitt's analysis of the rise and fall of the *jus publicum europaeum*: that it is a story of competing European colonialisms in which the colonized play almost no positive role, though the question of their treatment as the indifferent, passive objects of European power and the worldview that this treatment reflects is decisive for Schmitt's analysis.

Political Romanticism

Schmitt develops no elemental category reflecting the political space characteristic of any of the non-European peoples that enter into his world-historical analysis. His blindness to the question of Babo's world-historical agency, however, reflects a broader repression of the theatricality of the political that has its roots in his early critique of political Romanticism. In his 1925 text *Political Romanticism*, Schmitt defines the latter as the effect of a subjective occasionalism that is antithetical to the political, and thereby as nonexistent.[58] By transforming the world into the indifferent occasion for an in-principle infinite number of individual subjective experiences, Romanticism "dissolves" the objectivity of the phenomenal world as such.[59] This dissolution of phenomena "negates . . . the mechanical calculability of the causal"—a departure from a Newtonian worldview fomented by the expansive application of

Kant's theory of aesthetic reflective judgment to the phenomenal world in general—which Schmitt finds expressed in the "tumultuous ... bewildering colorfulness of Romantic scenery."[60] Schmitt's prima facie odd use of the word "colorfulness" (*Buntheit*), which the standard translation consistently circumvents with the inaccurate but less perplexing term "disorder," is in fact quite apropos here, since for Schmitt, whose critique of Romanticism is very close to the Platonic critique of theater in this regard, the disordering of the natural world evident in Romantic landscapes is directly linked to the dissolution of the not infrequently color-coded "hierarchical ... distribution" of the "different functions of the social order," which follows from the joint evacuation of unified divine authority and the belief in empirical objectivity that rests thereupon.[61] In the context of Romanticism, empirical and moral clarity, the "mechanical calculability of the causal" and "every binding norm," are dissolved by the "flow" of one and the same "river," which finds its own a-causal "source" in the aestheticizing movement through which "the church is replaced by the theater, and the religious is treated as material for a drama or an opera."[62] Since, pursuant to such "universal aestheticization," the Romantic subject can recognize no external authority on the basis of which any particular organization of society could be legitimated, he lacks the criterion for genuine political decision-making.[63]

Schmitt's dismissal of political Romanticism presupposes a theory of political representation that, although not explicitly put forth in *Political Romanticism*, may nevertheless be negatively derived from what he says there.[64] There can be no political Romanticism because the Romantic subject is "no longer capable of representation," and the Romantic subject is incapable of representation because he can produce no works that possess a stable, "concrete reality" or "form" that transcends their subjective investment and reconstruction by a reader or viewer.[65] This is what it means for Romantic objects to be mere "occasions" of subjective experience; like the theatrical work, the Romantic object has no meaningful existence apart from the spectatorship that brings it into being each time anew and sustains it in unavoidably multiple and fragmented ways. Romantic knowledge of the world is thus not knowledge of a world at all, but rather aesthetic reflection on the subjective experience of it.

For Schmitt, such world-aestheticization is intimately related to Anglo-American global economism. The same term—"elastic"—which takes on a strangely technical meaning in Schmitt's works, characterizes both the condition of Romantic phenomena and the condition of the globe under Anglo-American economic hegemony.[66] In his "Age of Neutralization and Depoliticization," Schmitt makes this connection explicit. Though "aesthetic-Romantic" and "economic-technical" tendencies are seemingly opposed, he argues, Romantic aestheticization is in fact the surest path from the metaphysical and moral commitments of the eighteenth century to the economism of the nineteenth century, since under the aesthetic regime of Romanticism all that might have resisted purely techno-utilitarian treatment melts into thin air, making way for "a state of mind which finds the core categories of human existence in production and consumption."[67] In this way, the aesthetic liquidation of transcendent authority paves the way for the deposition of political decision-making by the calculations of Anglo-American global imperial economics and the hollow moral universalism that sustains its undifferentiating reach.

From Schmitt's perspective, Melville's *Benito Cereno* could not but represent this economic repression of the political in the willfully dim-witted Delano, whose obliviousness to the historical and political structure of the situation in which he intervenes does not prevent him from capitalizing upon the losses it entails. Cereno is the story's unquestioned hero because the European colonialist sees, however impotently, what the American will not, thus reflecting Schmitt's own tragic historical position after the Second World War.[68] Yet Schmitt's blindness to Babo's historical significance reveals his own repression of a dimension of the political that is prior to the existential hostility that Cereno apprehends: the originary, politicizing force of theatrical dissolution, without which history as Schmitt understands it could never emerge to begin with.

An Unfilled Part

Schmitt's neglect of Babo is perhaps understandable given Melville's peculiar treatment of his character. As many scholars have noted, Babo's perspective is never focalized throughout Melville's tale, even though his story's extension to the period of Babo's trial, sentencing, and punishment provide ample opportunity for this. This fact, to which Melville himself calls our attention when he refers to Babo's "end" as "voiceless," has led most readers of Melville's tale to steer clear of C. L. R. James's remarkable identification of Babo as "the most heroic character in Melville's fiction."[69] This tendency has not only characterized those not-so-early readers who saw in Babo a figure of pure evil representative of the primitive savagery of man, but also more recent readers who interpret Melville's tale as a tract revealing the horrors of slavery and the contradictions of Northern abolitionism.[70] Yet while it is true that Melville never lets us hear Babo out of character, as it were, limiting his speech to the masquerade aboard Cereno's vessel, and while the effect of this certainly is to refuse us access to the African leader's subjectivity via his speech, this avoidance of Babo's interiority need not foment our interpretive neglect of his significance as a character, especially in light of the sustained questioning of representation and of the reliability of points of view that characterizes Melville's exploration of the theatrical construction of identity throughout his tale. With the latter in mind, Babo's voicelessness becomes legible as a pregnant pause that measures the absence of any but theatrically produced subjects. And yet the originary negation made present by this absence is not absolute. Although Babo's end is indeed voiceless, it is not altogether effaced. What survives of him are not his words but rather his visage, which, after his arrest, torture, and execution, is "placed upon a spike . . . overlooking the plaza."[71]

A strange monument indeed, and one no less ambiguously heroic than the odd "hive of subtlety" Melville chooses for its epithet. Yet Melville's seemingly cold nomination may appear less so when one considers a hitherto unremarked fact about the ghastly image of Babo's demise. Like most of his story, Melville's account of Babo's end remains faithful to the record regarding the punishment of the surviving slaves contained in the historical Delano's memoir, but it departs from that text in two crucial and interrelated ways. In the historical record, the place of the survivors' impalement is described as "a square in the port of Talcahuano."[72] Melville, on the other hand, describes the dead man's gaze looking out across a "plaza" in the city of Lima.[73] This change links Babo's gaze to an earlier one in Melville's story, that of the imaginary "Lima intriguante" whose piercing gaze "across the plaza" characterizes the quality of the light that "stream[s] equivocally enough" from the glass of the approaching slave ship's cabin. The dead Babo's gaze is thus associated with his living one, at a time when, as effective captain of the vessel on which he rode, he may well be imagined looking out along with the light that streamed from that ship's cabin. Yet Babo's gaze is thus reanimated only through further fragmentation and multiplication, his dismembered figure reintegrated only via the misrecognition of yet another spectator, making the meaning of the light this casts upon Babo's strangely opaque character no less "equivocal" than the voicelessness it would replace. Melville's substitution of Lima's "plaza" for Talcahuano's "square," however, suggests still more, since it recalls as well the title of the book in which he published *Benito Cereno*: *The Piazza Tales*. Though Melville had envisioned titling his book *Benito Cereno & Other Sketches*, with the titular story placed first among five tales, he eventually decided to add a sixth story, which he refers to in letters as "some . . . prefatory matter," from which the book took its new title.[74] This sixth, prefatory tale is called "The Piazza," and the book is thus named, as Melville reveals in its titular story, after a portion of his home that he himself had added—its covered porch or piazza—from which the author looked out over Pittsfield at that very Mount Greylock whose shape, according to him, inspired the description of the whale in *Moby-Dick*. Melville wrote *Benito Cereno*, as well, while seated at the second-story window positioned directly above his piazza. In his letters, moreover, he compares the view from his second-story windows—which are neither large nor small and placed low upon the wall, so that one can more easily see through them from a sitting, or writing position—to the view out the window of a ship.[75] Melville was indeed fond of comparing the whole of his Arrowhead house, so named because of the remains of native peoples he found embedded in the land there, to a ship: a metaphor no less apt given the fact that Melville considered his home under constant threat of liquidation due to his financial insolvency, which seemed to advance in worryingly direct proportion to the flow of dark liquid from his quill.[76] In a particularly memorable moment from a letter to his publisher penned in the winter of 1850, Melville writes:

> I have a sort of sea-feeling here in the country, now that the ground is all covered with snow. I look out of my window in the morning when I rise as I would out of a port-hole of a ship in the Atlantic. My room seems a ship's cabin; and at nights when I wake up and hear the wind shrieking, I almost fancy there is too much sail on the house, and I had better go on the roof and rig in the chimney.[77]

In "The Piazza," Melville casts further light upon his land-bound house's ship-like morphology. It is not only the second-story rooms that are ship cabin-like. The piazza that his writing window overlooks also often seems the "sleety deck . . . [that] once more, with frosted beard, I pace . . . weathering Cape Horn."[78] Having thus prefatorily transported his Massachusetts home to the southernmost tip of Chile, as Melville's story develops, the landscape viewed across the piazza becomes nearly indistinguishable from the seascape with which *Benito Cereno* opens, the "long roods and swells" of ocean water becoming the "long ground-swells" that "roll the slanting grain," and the "strange sail" that appears in *Benito Cereno*'s opening lines finding its echo in the "first peep" of a "strange house" whose appearance is as foreboding as that of an "unknown sail" in waters thick with pirates. Melville's full passage reads:

> In summer, too . . . sitting there, one is often reminded of the sea. For not only do long ground-swells roll the slanting grain, and little wavelets of the grass ripple over upon the low piazza, as their beach, and the blown down of dandelions is wafted like the spray, and the purple of the mountains is just the purple of the billows, and a still August noon broods upon the deep meadows, as a calm upon the Line; but the vastness and the lonesomeness are so oceanic, and the silence and sameness, too, that the first peep of a strange house, rising beyond the trees, is for all the world like spying, on the Barbary coast, an unknown sail.

Despite this opening, "The Piazza," like *Benito Cereno*, is not really a story of the sea,[79] but rather what Melville calls an "inland voyage to fairy-land"—an exploration of the power of imagination as it is revealed in the theatricality of the phenomenal world, in which the firmness of land and the fluidity of sea, the solidity of the actual and the transience of the fictive, interpenetrate.[80] His will be "a true voyage," Melville writes, "but, take it all in all, interesting as if invented."[81] The characters that populate the landscape through which Melville's narrator travels accentuate the theatricality of the space in which he moves; Titania, Oberon, and the fairies themselves are all drawn directly from Shakespeare's *A Midsummer Night's Dream*, while the story's central character is *Measure for Measure*'s jilted fiancé Mariana, "sister of Frederick / the great soldier who miscarried at sea" together with her dowry, who "at the moated / grange resides," and who doubles Melville's autobiographical narrator.[82]

The narrator discovers Marianna sitting in a hut that, perched halfway up the mountain opposite his, quite literally mirrors his own. Like *Benito Cereno*'s slave ship, Marianna's hut emerges from the midst of vapors. The narrator discovers it when "a little shower islanded in misty seas of sunshine" produces a "rainbow's medium," at the end of which he spies a "sparkle of that vividness [that] seemed as if it could only come from glass."[83] The metaphor of nature as looking glass, together with the vaporous visibility of the medium of light itself in the refracted form of the rainbow, echoes the parallel Melville draws between the light of the rising sun and the light that streams "equivocally enough" from Babo's cabin window in *Benito Cereno*'s opening scene, but the link between "The Piazza's" autobiographical narrator and the inhabitant of this other cabin is far more directly drawn than that between the one who looks out from the piazza and he who looks out across the plaza.

Behind the glass, the solitary Marianna sits and weaves, her inconsummate textilic productivity evidently reflecting the author's own textual profligacy; and like the author, the things Marianna sees appear strangely intermixed with the vapors through which she sees them, as with the shadows that—like the "dusk *saya-y-manta*" through whose "Indian loophole" the Lima intriguante's "one sinister eye peer[s] . . . across the plaza"—also "dusk" this seamstress's "work."[84] Melville's narrator feigns perplexity, for Marianna, seeing thusly, seems capable of describing objects at which she does not look:

> Have you, then, so long sat at this mountain-window, where but clouds and vapors pass, that, to you, shadows are as things, though you speak of them as of phantoms; that, by familiar knowledge, working like a second sight, you can, without looking for them, tell just where they are, though, as having mice-like feet, they creep about, and come and go; that, to you, these lifeless shadows are as living friends, who, though out of sight, are not out of mind, even in their faces—is it so?[85]

The narrator's question is quite evidently self-directed, for the "truth" of his own story will shortly be revealed as that which "comes in with darkness . . . when the curtain falls," "no light shows from the mountain," and "I walk the piazza deck [to and fro], haunted by Marianna's face, and many as real a story."[86] But the question might as well be put to Babo, who "casts such a shadow" upon Cereno until the story's end that the European colonialist finds himself incapable, at Delano's inducement, of perceiving "the bright sun . . . yon" that "has forgotten it all, and the blue sea, and the blue sky," which, the American exhorts with palpable enthusiasm, "have turned over new leaves." For Melville's text suggests that one may only travel by way of such untroubled skies and such transparent waters only if one can in truth bring about Babo's voicelessness, which, like the clear day's vaporlessness, can only ever be an illusion.

It would seem that Schmitt's hero's dying words, which refer one so enigmatically to "the negro" as he who "casts such a shadow upon" him, may contain more than the jurist could allow. In the "silence" that follows them, there emerges the "aspect" of one who, "some months after," is "carried to Lima," where he is "dragged to the gibbet at the tail of a mule," there to "me[et] his" only apparently "voiceless end." For although Babo's "slight frame" is "burned to ashes," his "head," which, Melville does not fail to remind us, "had schemed and led the revolt, with the plot" through strength of "brain" and not of "body," and which furthermore, like the bobble-headed Melville's own, sits atop a frame that is "inadequate to that which it h[olds]," is "fixed upon a pole in the Plaza," from which it "me[ets], unabashed, the gaze of the whites; and across the Plaza look[s] toward St. Bartholemew's church, in whose vaults sle[ep] . . . the recovered bones of Aranda."[87]

The plaza across which Babo peers at the canonized bones of his former master, mapped onto the piazza across which Melville gazes during the writing of *Benito Cereno*, is also the "amphitheater over which," Melville tells us in the dedication to *Pierre*, "my own more immediate sovereign lord and king" the "Imperial Purple Majesty" of "royal born mount . . . Greylock . . . presides."[88] The gaze that traverses this space is thus immediately political. The question it silently poses is whether this "immediate sovereign lord," before whom the author "kneel[s]" and "render[s] up [his] gratitude," will "benignantly incline his hoary crown or no." The politics of this gaze is accordingly a politics of authorship, for in both Melville's and Babo's cases it pertains to the relationship between a writer and the canon from which he draws the tools of his trade. But it is just as well a politics of spectatorship, not only because its space is that of an "amphitheater," nor merely because the texts our authors read are those of theater written or performed, but more importantly because the "voiceless" historical agency they jointly exemplify is one in which spontaneity and receptivity palpably interpenetrate.

The question posed by these authors' spectatorial gazes, in both cases, would thus seem to be whether and how the power of a heteronomous means of existence may be appropriated and redeployed as the support for another way of living. The impossible answer that Schmitt would give to this question is resoundingly negative. This is the meaning of his silencing of Babo, *Benito Cereno*'s autobiographical hero. And Melville's text would indeed seem to contemplate this fate when its narrator describes Babo's silent "aspect," once returned to European chains, as one that "seeing all was over . . . utter[s] no sound . . . and [can] not be forced to . . . seem[ing] to say, since I cannot do deeds, I will not speak words."[89] And yet the pregnant silence with which Melville's text leaves us would seem to suggest the opposite, for it positions us within a space in which originary displacement and heteronomy, and the passivity that these bespeak, are the conditions of possibility for historical subjectivity. By marking the originary absence of an autochthonous form of life and thus holding open the non-place of this constitutive heteronomy, Babo points us to the empty core of this strangely "equivocal" way of living.

And Schmitt might have too, had he not feared the implications of his own insights and retreated behind the mythic walls of an essentializing decisionism. For in his *Land and Sea*, the jurist glimpses the condition of possibility of history in a state of indecision that the decisiveness of the political must always presuppose:

> One cannot imagine the "Elements" of land and sea, of which I shall speak, as mere natural-scientific categories. For when one does so, one dissolves them straightaway into mere chemical materials, and thereby into historical nothingness. The determinations that proceed from them, in particular maritime and terrestrial forms of historical existence, do not emerge in a mechanical or compulsory way. Were man naught but a living being wholly determined by its environment [*ein von seiner Umwelt restlos bestimmtes Lebewesen*], he would be, accordingly, a land animal, a fish, a bird, or some fantastic mixture of these elemental determinations. The pure types associated with the four elements, in particular the purely terrestrial and purely maritime peoples, would have little to do with one another; they would coexist without relation, and would become the more isolated in proportion to their elemental purity. Mixing them would produce good or bad types and give rise to affinities and hostilities in the manner of chemical reactions. The existence and destiny of man would be naturally determined, like that of an animal or a plant. There would be no human history in the form of human deed and decision.
>
> But man is a creature who does not arise together with his element [*nicht in seiner Umwelt aufgeht*]. He rather has the capacity to historically overcome his given existence and consciousness. He knows not only birth, but also the possibility of rebirth. In conditions of need or danger, in which animal and plant perish helplessly, he can save himself . . . through a decision for a new form of existence. He has a space [*Spielraum*] in which his power and historical formativity [*Geschichtsmächtigkeit*] can play. He can choose, and at particular historical moments he can indeed choose an element, to which he attaches himself as a new form of historical existence through his own act and accomplishment, and according to which he reorganizes himself. In this sense he has, as the poet would say, "the freedom to depart wheresoever he will."[90]

If we take Schmitt at his word, then we might expect him to have seen that it is Babo, and not Cereno, who represents the possibility of historical existence in its purest form. While the sea-change that Cereno endures can signify nothing but the end of his way of living, the freed slave transforms the literal chains that bind him into the theatrical props of his precarious emancipation, converting the peculiar passive power derived from an originary homelessness, an originary lack of any proper element, and a persistent decoupling of the subject from any simply given form of life into its own irreducibly equivocal way of living. It is the ambivalent power of this withholding, which Melville makes manifest in the vaporous visibility of a medium through which one fails or refuses to pass, that makes manifest the difference and distance from itself of every form of life capable of historicizing its own existence. And in the passage quoted above, Schmitt too sees that it can only be this fundamental ambivalence that first multiplies the spaces into which individuals may be reborn.

If Schmitt allows himself to forget this, it is not without good reason, for its implications undermine the theory of sovereignty that his theory of space sets out merely to historicize. One will recall that, for Schmitt, a form of life is comprised of an element and the existential decision for it, which together give rise to a new historical power ex nihilo. But as we see above, this *prima facie ex nihilo* creation in fact presupposes a prior dehiscence, an originary separation of human being from any particular way in which it might live, which can only transpire in a space whose categoriality is not the fait accompli of any unilateral decision. Forms of life can attain the mythic unity of character Schmitt lends them only by disavowing this primordial indecision that their very existence presupposes. Yet if this disavowal were absolute in its effects, the human history in the name of which it is performed would come to a close, for human life would in no respect differ from the elemental determinacy that is characteristic of all sentience.

While Schmitt's mythic essentialization of the decision and of the monolithic life forms to which it gives rise works to eclipse history in the name of history, the world into which Melville invites his reader brings the historicizing indecisiveness of the decision to the fore as the spectatorial overdetermination of the space in which his story unfolds and the vaporousness through which this plurality of vision manifests itself to each viewer. This difference implies a deeper one regarding the politics of the categorical. Schmitt's theory of history understands the categorical mutation of life as an intermittent crisis that is each time resolved by the autonomous force of a sovereign act, which creates a new form of life that is bound to a new way of knowing. Melville's world is by contrast one in which categorical instability never fully recedes from view, but rather lingers in and as the vaporousness of vision itself. While Schmitt's understanding of history as the repeated, differential repression of the indeterminacy that makes it possible limits historical possibility by presupposing the political normativity of cognitive over reflective ways of being in the world, Melville's text suggests that one ignores the shadow vision that reflective judgment reveals only at one's peril, since its instability and flux reflect the irreducibly plural and nonlinear way in which the world may in truth be. To the clear-cut categoriality of Schmitt's sovereign decision Melville thus counterposes the disintegrating power of the light that suffuses the space in which his narrative unfolds—a light that streams "equivocally enough" that one could reduce the conflicts reflected in its rainbow colors to the "mild trades" that Delano's clear blue skies bespeak only by accomplishing one truly impossible task: to have read in advance each and every one of the gazes that may greet one, unabashed, from across the p(i)laz(z)a.

Notes

1. The Lend-Lease Act, which committed the United States to material support to the Allied forces, and above all Britain, marked the first step toward full American involvement in war. For a detailed account of Schmitt's deposition and the accusations that led to it, see Joseph W. Bendersky, *Carl Schmitt, Theorist for the Reich* (Princeton, N.J.: Princeton University Press, 1983). See also Gopal Balakrishnan, *The Enemy: An Intellectual Portrait of Carl Schmitt* (London: Verso, 2000); and Jan-Werner Müller, *A Dangerous Mind: Carl Schmitt in Post-War European Thought* (New Haven, Conn.: Yale University Press, 2003).

2. Enrst Jünger and Carl Schmitt, *Briefwechsel, 1930–1983* (Stuttgart: Klett-Cotta, 2012), 121; Herman Melville, *The Piazza Tales,* in *Pierre, or, The Ambiguities; Israel Potter: His Fifty Years of Exile; The Piazza Tales; The Confidence-Man: His Masquerade; Uncollected Prose; Billy Budd, Sailor: (An Inside Narrative)*, ed. Harrison Hayford (New York: Literary Classics of the United States, 1984), 617–834; Amasa Delano, *Narrative of Voyages and Travels, in the Northern and Southern Hemispheres: Comprising Three Voyages round the World; Together with a Voyage of Survey and Discovery, in the Pacific Ocean and Oriental Islands* (New York: Praeger, 1970). All subsequent references to Melville's stories draw page numbers from the Hayford edition cited above.

3. The latter has been of particular concern given Schmitt's influence on works across the political spectrum. See, for example, the essays collected in Chantal Mouffe, *The Challenge of Carl Schmitt* (London: Verso, 1999). See also Giorgio Agamben, *Homo Sacer*, trans. Daniel Heller-Roazen (Stanford, Calif.: Stanford University Press, 1998); and Daniel Heller-Roazen, *The Enemy of All: Piracy and the Law of Nations* (New York: Zone Books, 2009).

4. For a useful summary of competing interpretations, see Thomas O. Beebee, "Carl Schmitt's Myth of Benito Cereno," *Seminar: A Journal of Germanic Studies* 42, no. 2 (2006): 114–44.

5. Two notable exceptions to this rule are Geoffrey Sanborn's excellent chapter "Walking Shadows: 'Benito Cereno' and the Colonial Stage," in *The Sign of the Cannibal: Melville and the Making of a Postcolonial Reader* (Durham, N.C.: Duke University Press, 1998), 171–200; and Eric Sundquist's chapter "Melville, Delany, and New World Slavery," in *To Wake the Nations: Race in the Making of American Literature* (Cambridge, Mass.: Belknap Press of Harvard University Press, 1993), 135–224, to which I return below.

6. Carl Schmitt, *Land und Meer: Eine Weltgeschichtliche Betrachtung* (Köln-Lövenich: Hohenheim, 1981), 16; translated as *Land and Sea*, trans. Simona Draghici (Washington, D.C.: Plutarch, 1997). All English translations of material cited in German are my own. Where English translations are available, I have included them in the notes.

7. Jünger and Schmitt, *Briefwechsel*, 121.

8. Melville follows the historical record in representing Babo himself as Senegalese and others among the slave ship's cargo as native Ashanti. For an illuminating consideration of the ethnic, linguistic, and sociopolitical backgrounds of the *Tryal* slaves in the historical record and in Melville's story, see Sundquist, "Melville, Delany," 168.

9. Carl Schmitt, *Politische Theologie: Vier Kapitel zur Lehre von der Souveränität* (Munich: Duncker & Humblot, 1934); Carl Schmitt, *Political Theology: Four Chapters on the Concept of Sovereignty*, trans. George Schwab (Cambridge, Mass.: MIT Press, 1985); Carl Schmitt, *Der Begriff des Politischen: Text von 1932 mit einem Vorwort und drei Corollarien* (Berlin: Duncker & Humblot, 1932); Carl Schmitt, *The Concept of the Political*, trans. George Schwab (Chicago: University of Chicago Press, 1999).

10. Schmitt, *Land und Meer*, 12–15.

11. Ernst Kapp, *Philosophische oder Vergleichende allgemeine Erdkunde als Wissenschaftliche darstellung der Erdverhältnisse und des Menschenlebens nach ihrem innern Zusammenhang* (Braunschweig: Verlag Von George Westermann, 1845).

12. Ibid., 54–55.

13. Schmitt, *Nomos der Erde*, 17.

14. Schmitt, *Land und Meer*, 56–57.

15. See Immanuel Kant's "Transcendental Aesthetic," in *Critique of Pure Reason*, trans. Norman Kemp Smith (New York: St. Martin's, 1965) 65-82; Immanuel Kant, *Kants Gessamelte Schriften*, vol. 4 (Berlin: de Gruyter, 1902–), 29–46.

16. Jünger and Schmitt, *Briefwechsel*, 23–24, 40–41. This is anticipated by Schmitt's earlier use of the term "Raumbild" (Schmitt, *Land und Meer*, 57).

17. Ibid., 121.

18. Carl Schmitt, *Ex Captivitate Salus: Erfahrungen der Zeit 1945/47* (Berlin: Duncker & Humblot, 2010), 75.

19. Jünger and Schmitt, *Briefwechsel*, 159, 193.

20. These letters have largely determined intepretations of Schmitt's references to Melville, which tend to identify the "symbolism" to which Schmitt refers in terms of the immediate postwar context. See, for example, Müller's *A Dangerous Mind*, Balakrishnan's *The Enemy*, and Bendersky's *Theorist for the Reich*. These readings are plausible given the explicit historicism of Schmitt's own published readings of literary works. See, for example, Carl Schmitt, *Hamlet oder Hekuba; Der Einbruch der Zeit in das Spiel* (Düsseldorf: E. Diederichs, 1956). Yet this approach also poses difficulties. Schmitt's references to Melville's text have proven capable of supporting a great number of often irreconcilable historical-allegorical interpretations, which one finds usefully outlined in Beebee's "Carl Schmitt's Myth of Benito Cereno," while the neglect of Schmitt's larger theory of history obscures what is at stake in deciding, or not being able to decide, between these.

21. In *Land and Sea*, Schmitt writes, "one is consistently led to question, what is our element? Are we the children of the land or of the sea? The question isn't answerable as simple either-or. Myths immemorial, modern natural-scientific hypotheses, and the results of research into ancient cultures leave both alternatives open" (*Land und Meer*, 10–11). In *Nomos of the Earth,* by contrast, one reads that "the originally terrestrial world underwent a change in the age of discovery . . . [as] England dared to take a step from a terrestrial to a maritime existence" (Schmitt, *Nomos der Erde*, 19).

22. The first sentence of *Nomos of the Earth* reads: "In the language of myth, the earth is called the mother of law [*Recht*]."

23. Schmitt, Land and See, 6.

24. Ibid., 14.

25. Carl Schmitt, *Staat, Großraum, Nomos: Arbeiten aus den Jahren 1916–1969*, ed. Günter Maschke (Berlin: Duncker & Humblot, 1995), 431–32.

26. Ibid., 436. Schmitt's use of the term "maelstrom" recalls his discussion of *Benito Cereno* with Jünger in 1941–42, in which Poe's maritime tale "A Descent into the Maelstrom" figures as a point of direct comparison, with Schmitt insisting that "next to Melville even Poe strikes one as merely anecdotal" (Schmitt, *Briefwechsel*, 121).

27. Melville, *Benito Cereno*, 705–16.

28. Ibid., 712.

29. See, for example, Sundquist, "Melville, Delany," 152.

30. In "Auflösung der eurpäischen Ordnung im 'International Law,'" Schmitt identifies the first sign of the ascendancy of such universalism in none other than the American recognition of the flag representing a territory produced by a European colonial enterprise on the continent of Africa, which he argues demonstrates that the "dissolving of a specifically European international law in an undifferentiated universal world-law" and of a "concrete order rooted in determinate presuppositions" in "an empty normativism . . . could no longer be held back" (Schmitt, *Staat, Großraum*, 374).

31. Melville, *Benito Cereno*, 673.

32. Ibid.

33. Ibid.

34. Schmitt, *Staat, Großraum*, 430–37.

35. Melville, *Benito Cereno*, 675.

36. Ibid., 673.

37. Sundquist, "Melville, Delany." See also Greg Grandin, *The Empire of Necessity: Slavery, Freedom, and Deception in the New World* (New York: Metropolitan Books, 2014).

38. From *The Prelude* (book 6) in William Wordsworth and Stephen Gill, *William Wordsworth: The Major Works* (Oxford: Oxford University Press, 2000), 463. Melville owned a carefully annotated edition of Wordsworth's poems, but may have been first exposed to the posthumous *Prelude* as late as 1850. See Hershel Parker, *Herman Melville: A Biography* (Baltimore, Md.: Johns Hopkins University Press, 1996), 742.

39. Herman Melville, *Moby-Dick, Billy Budd, and Other Writings*, ed. Thomas Tanselle (New York: Library of America, 2000), 906.

Land and See 85

40. For an annotated collection of the works by Turner that Melville possessed, see Robert K. Wallace, *Melville's Prints and Engravings at the Berkshire Athenaeum* (West Haven, Conn.: University of New Haven Press, 1986).

41. Melville, *Benito Cereno*, 673.

42. Branka Arsić, *Passive Constitutions: or, 7½ Times Bartleby* (Stanford, Calif.: Stanford University Press, 2007), 156–66.

43. Rene Descartes, *Discourse on Method, Optics, Geometry and Meteorology*, trans. Paul J. Olscamp (Indianapolis, Ind.: Bobbs-Merrill, 1965), 269–74.

44. Ibid., 273.

45. Ibid.

46. Melville, *Benito Cereno*, 673, 754.

47. Ibid.

48. Melville renames the historical slave ship *Tryal* the *San Dominick* and backdates the events that transpire upon it from 1805 to 1799, both establishing reference to the Haitian revolution.

49. Melville, *Benito Cereno*, 674.

50. In her recent book *The Art of Freedom: Toward a Dialectic of Democratic Existence*, Juliane Rebentisch compellingly demonstrates the continuity of Schmitt's concept of the political and Plato's famous exclusion of theater from his ideal republic. Juliane Rebentisch. *Die Kunst der Freiheit: Zur Dialektik Demokratischer Existenz* (Berlin: Suhrkamp, 2011). We shall see that it is this dimension of Schmitt's thought that limits his reading of *Benito Cereno*.

51. Melville published this tale in *Putnam's* just prior to *Benito Cereno* and again together with it in the 1856 edition of *The Piazza Tales*.

52. See Sanborn, "Walking Shadows." Sanborn's excellent exploration of the interpenetration of theater and history in the colonial scene of *Benito Cereno* is illuminating in many regards. Drawing on Homi Bhabha's theory of mimicry, Lacanian psychoanalysis, and (tacitly) Paul de Man's reading of the tension between "sign" and "symbol" in Hegel's *Aesthetics*, Sanborn shows how the performative power of the sign erodes the representational power of the symbol in *Benito Cereno*, leading to a generalized crisis of identity, authority, and well-grounded meaning that structures the unfolding of Melville's narrative. For Sanborn, the ethico-political moral of the story bears on the response to this crisis. Against Delano's dim-witted repression and Cereno's more discerning yet ultimately disabling traumatic knowledge, Melville suggests that his reader "learn to live in a world where meaning is the product of ungrounded decisions, and where acts of illumination are always shadowed by the darkness they displace" ("Walking Shadows," 175). The conclusion is recognizably therapeutic. The "transition from the fully constituted symbol of racial otherness to its destitute sign" is "traumatic" for the "racist vision" (185) that Melville's story works to dismantle, and the "melancholy" this trauma produces in Cereno—the story's would-be "subject-who-knows" (193)—is a "dead-end" (175) that must be overcome through a work of mourning. "In encouraging us to share Cereno's recognition of the significance of 'the negro,' Melville is not encouraging us to fall, like Cereno, into a suicidal depression. Instead, he is asking his 'white' readers to make a pair of related choices: to choose Cereno's open, empty realm of mind over Delano's closed, complete realm of Discourse, and then to choose against Cereno's

conduct: to learn how to live with the loss that he has so narcissistically refused" (194). The difficulty with this reading is that, in the name of setting the subject in (progressive) historical motion, it unwittingly naturalizes the psychoanalytically derived, quasi-categorical structure of the subject as an ahistorical constant. Thus, while we are disabused of an understanding of anticolonial "struggle . . . as an encounter of essences" and encouraged to view such struggle, instead, as "a mutual masquerade" (184), the truth that underlies this and indeed all struggle (for Sanborn, following Robert Young, "it is hard to see why Bhabha's theory of the colonial encounter cannot be said to encompass every kind of encounter in which power is unequally distributed" [186]) will always be the same: lack as the universal essence of the masquerading subject. This difficulty is in fact already reflected in Sanborn's suggestion that Melville's text presents us with a "world where meaning is the product of ungrounded decisions." To suggest that one is always-already on the far side of such decisions is one way of ensuring that the structures that decisions institute are not subject to radical revision in the struggles that they frame. This reading, accordingly, would dovetail with Schmitt's historical decisionism, although from a monistic and thus ultimately de-historicizing perspective. In pitting Melville against Schmitt's decisionism, by contrast, I aim to show how his work brings the historicizing indecisiveness of the decision to the fore as the concrete spectatorial overdetermination of the space in which his story unfolds. Such categorical instability comes to the fore not as a traumatic loss that must be mourned, nor a state of exception upon which one must decide, but rather as the immediate mediation of the present that allows for the historical transformation of life. And though within the scope of this interpretive essay I can do no more than gesture toward the broader theoretical insight this reading suggests, it should be said here that the historical force this event presents us with may not be understood as "performative," but is rather "afformative" in the sense Werner Hamacher gives this term in his reading of the divine violence of the general strike in the work of Walter Benjamin. See Werner Hamacher, "Afformative, Strike," *Cardozo Law Review* 13, no. 4 (December 1991): 1133–57.

53. William Shakespeare, *The Tempest* (New Haven, Conn.: Yale University Press, 2006), 4.1.1880–86.

54. For an extended consideration of the role of religion in *Benito Cereno*, see Jenny Franchot, *The Roads to Rome: Antibellum Protestant Encounters with Catholicism* (Berkeley: University of California Press, 1994).

55. Melville, *Benito Cereno*, 754.

56. Sundquist, "Melville, Delany," 155–63.

57. Melville changes the ship's name from the historically accurate *Perseverance* to *Bachelor's Delight*, a famous pirate ship active in the Caribbean in the 1680s, and invents rumors according to which the leader of the recovery mission was a one-time pirate.

58. The subjective posture characteristic of Romanticism comes about through a secularization of Malebrancheian occasionalism, according to which the phenomenal world is the indifferent occasion of divine intervention. Romanticism replaces Malebranche's divinity with human creative genius, transforming the world from a phenomenon devolving upon the authority of one God to the occasion for a multiplicity of subjective experiences.

59. Carl Schmitt, *Politische Romantik*, 6th ed. (Munich: Duncker & Humblot, 1998), 18; Carl Schmitt, *Political Romanticism*, trans. Guy Oakes (Cambridge, Mass.: MIT Press, 1986).

60. Schmitt, *Politische Romantik*, 16–17; Schmitt, *Political Romanticism*, 16.

61. Schmitt, *Politische Romantik*, 20.

62. Ibid., 16.

63. Ibid., 17.

64. The theory of political representation that subtends Schmitt's critique is contained in his roughly contemporary *Römischer Katholizismus und politische Form* (Stuttgart: Klett-Cotta, 1984); Carl Schmitt, *Roman Catholicism and Political Form*, trans. Gary L. Ulman (London: Greenwood, 1996). For a consideration of this work in the context of Schmitt's larger project, see Samuel Weber's chapter "'The Principle of Representation': Carl Schmitt's Roman Catholicism and Political Form," in *Targets of Opportunity: On the Militarization of Thinking* (New York: Fordham University Press, 2005), 22–41.

65. Schmitt, *Politische Romantik*, 16–17, 20.

66. Schmitt, *Politische Romantik*, 98; Schmitt, *Staat, Großraum*, 421; Schmitt, *Nomos der Erde*, 164, 219.

67. Schmitt, *Begriff des Politischen*, 79–95.

68. See Geoffrey Sanborn, *The Sign of the Cannibal* (Durham: Duke University Press, 1998), 193. For a consideration of Schmitt's self-understanding as tragic, see the final section of Victoria Kahn, "Hamlet or Hecuba: Carl Schmitt's Decision," *Representations* 83, no. 1 (Summer 2003): 67–96.

69. C. L. R. James, *Mariners, Renegades, and Castaways: The Story of Herman Melville and the World We Live In: The Complete Text* (Hanover, N.H.: Dartmouth College Press, 2001), 112.

70. See, for example, in Jason A. Frank, ed., *A Political Companion to Herman Melville* (Lexington: University of Kentucky Press, 2013): Lawrie Balfour, "What Babo Saw: *Benito Cereno* and 'the World We Live In,'" 1–20; Tracy B. Strong, "'Follow Your Leader': Melville's *Benito Cereno* and the Case of Two Ships," 259–80; and Jason Frank, "American Tragedy: The Political Thought of Herman Melville," 281–309. See also the selection of critical works in Herman Melville, *Melville's Short Novels: Authoritative Texts, Contexts, Criticism*, ed. Dan McCall (New York: Norton, 2002).

71. Melville, *Benito Cereno*, 755.

72. Delano, *Voyages*, 347.

73. Melville, *Benito Cereno*, 755.

74. Herman Melville, *Correspondence*, ed. Lynn Horth (Evanston, Ill.: Northwestern University Press, 1993), 284.

75. Ibid., 173. Melville's Arrowhead house is now a museum where one can sample the views from the piazza and writing room windows at one's leisure.

76. Ibid., 291–93.

77. Ibid., 173.

78. Melville, *The Piazza Tales*, 623–24.

79. In a letter to *Duyckinck* in February 1851, Melville apparently refuses the assignment of a sea-story for Holden's magazine by writing, "'A dash of salt-spray'!—where am I to get salt spray here in inland Pittsfield? I shall have to

import it from foreign parts. All I now have to do with salt, is when I salt my horse and cow" (Melville, *Correspondence*, 179).

80. *Benito Cereno* contains the inverse projection of the sea "inland," at a moment when Delano, "trying to break one charm," finds himself "but becharmed anew. Though upon the wide sea, he seemed in some far inland country; prisoner of some deserted château, left to stare at empty grounds, and peer out at vague roads, where never wagon or wayfarer passed" (Melville, *The Piazza Tales*, 705).

81. Ibid., 624.

82. Shakespeare, *Measure for Measure* (New York: Oxford World Classics, 1991), 163.

83. Melville, *The Piazza Tales*, 625.

84. Ibid., 632.

85. Ibid.

86. Ibid., 634.

87. Melville, *Benito Cereno*, 755.

88. Melville, *Pierre, or the Ambiguities*, 3.

89. Melville, *Benito Cereno*, 755.

90. Schmitt, *Land and Sea*, 13–15. Schmitt quotes the final stanza of Hölderlin's poem "Lebenslauf" without attribution.

The Coward's Paradox: Pip's Weak Resistance

Barbara N. Nagel

The painful question: "Am I a coward?"[1] A coward for not acting more courageously, for not trying harder, for instance, to change a political situation that I despise? Or, taking another recent example: Is someone a coward for running away from the police? Moving closer to Melville: Would you call someone a coward for jumping off a ship that he believes to be sinking, or one that is being pulled away by a big whale? One thing is certain: nobody likes to think of him- or herself as a coward. And yet, capitalism and neoliberalism have produced ample forms of violence from which we would like to run away or at least to distance ourselves: exploitation, corruption, racism, torture, and other forms of structural violence—with all of which one feels too ashamed to identify, even though (or precisely because) our society rests upon them. Reflections such as these concern the relation between cowardice and resistance. There is no author better suited than Melville to thinking through this relation and asking the following question: Is cowardice opposed to resistance? Or can cowardice itself become a peculiar form of resistance?

In the current situation in the United States, moderate forms of political agency, such as demonstrations, appear to be ineffective. We can go on the streets, get charged with disorderly conduct or refusal to disperse, but nothing much changes because those in power do not see a reason to alter their (economic) priorities. Certainly, there is no lack of critique, especially in academia—but this critique does not seem to have the power to change a situation that is so fraught. Towards the end of her book *Economies of Abandonment*, Elizabeth Povinelli channels skeptical voices like this one: "What good does immanent critique do for a practical politics if, after stripping social life bare—exposing the brutality of social injustice—it provides it with no alternative closing?"[2] In the end, we are left with no more than two alternatives for how to judge our current situation: either we are cowards or we are living in an unfree society. Which of these two alternatives requires more courage to admit?

Though Melville is not from this time, he is never simply untimely. "To read Melville, and *Moby-Dick* in particular . . . is *to read what reading means*. This is why reading Melville is an abyssal enterprise, which . . . demands *re-reading*."[3] Peter Szendy's reflections allude to the curious fact that Melville,

89

more than other authors, offers himself for reading contemporary events through his "prophecies," that is, through the potential of his texts to connect past to present. In this specific sense, Melville's untimeliness—even his anachrony—is indeed timely; Melville is timely and untimely because anachrony is precisely what is needed to disrupt the complacency of the present. The first to tap Melville's anachronic potential was, of course, C. L. R. James, who was himself some sort of a castaway when he wrote *Mariners, Renegades, and Castaways: The Story of Herman Melville and the World We Live In* while he was interned on Ellis Island.[4] Taking up James and Szendy's bold claims, I want to test how Melville's texts can help us today to look at our own political situation from a different perspective, namely that of the castaway, and to immerse ourselves in Melville's literary scenarios, which encompass phenomena of cowardice, agency, and resistance. Our trajectory is as follows: I will first delve into Melville's novels to see how he employs the notion of "cowardice." We will then resurface from this with an extended reading of the ninety-second chapter of *Moby-Dick*,[5] "The Castaway," in which the black shipkeeper Pip is called on to replace an injured whaleboat oarsman. Once the whale-chase begins, Pip is so scared that he jumps from the boat into the ocean, with the result that the crew has to cut the harpoon rope in order to save "the coward." Pip is warned that should he ever jump again, he would be deserted in the sea. When Pip jumps a second time, the crew abandons the coward and then forgets about him. When the *Pequod* finally picks up Pip he has already lost his mind. "The Castaway" is so insightful as a reflection on cowardice because instead of treating the cowardice as a mere matter of representation, Melville shows us how a coward is produced, that is, how the "coward" is a reaction-formation to a mode of being that threatens or even *frightens* the system. In order to develop these thoughts, I will have other, untimely authors enter the dialogue with Melville: Dante, Montaigne, and Shakespeare, whose echoes we can still hear in "The Castaway," but also voices like those of Conrad's *Lord Jim* or Claudia Rankine's *Citizen*, who will later join Melville's community of the excluded.

"Cowards!"—An Insult Becomes a Question

"cowards!"[6]
"I am no coward."[7]
"You took me for a non-combatant did you?—thought, seedy coward that you are."[8]
"you are a coward—just the man to be a parson, and pray."[9]
"a cannibal and a coward,"[10]
"traitor, or coward!"[11]
"but, really, no coward's bed, for me, however comfortable."[12]
"A coward friend, he makes a valiant foe."[13]

"Ho, cowards, guards, turn about! charge upon them! Away with your grievances! Drive them out, I say, drive them out!"[14]—"Croak on, cowards! . . . and fly before the hideous phantoms that pursue ye."[15]

One just has to take but a few of the earlier texts by Melville—*Omoo, Redburn, Mardi, Moby-Dick, The Confidence-Man*—to assemble a strangely self-inquisitive coward-collage. In all of these quotes, taken mostly from Melville's adventure stories, "coward" is used as a pejorative term in argumentative dialogue; the only narrative voice ever to deliver the verdict (however, in negative form) is Ishmael, who records his terror upon seeing Queequeg for the first time: "I am no coward."[16] As we know, Melville descended from a family of proud Revolutionary War heroes and consequently in these quotes, too, being a coward is presented as something of which one ought to be ashamed. At the same time, the rare use of the term "coward" by Melville's narrators could perhaps be taken as a hint that Melville himself might have had certain reservations against the pejorative use of the word. Be that as it may, from a certain point in Melville's work, it becomes obvious that a shift has taken place in his perspective on cowardice. With *White-Jacket* and *Moby-Dick*, the question of cowardice—though still peripheral—starts to take up more space in his writing and even turns into a philosophical question: what is cowardice?

The philosophical question of how to define cowardice also brings up the more practical, juridical problem of how the law should treat cowards, that is, of how best to punish a coward and of how to use the threat of punishment to prevent other cowards from acting cowardly. In his recent study *Cowardice: A Brief History*, Chris Walsh writes that "cowardice seems to be severely attenuated in its archetypal setting, war."[17] Accordingly, punishments prescribed by military and naval law for cowardice were, for the longest time, very harsh: "humiliating punishments," "shaming punishments," even capital punishment.[18] The punishment was justified in that it was supposed to elicit "the fear of the shame of cowardice"[19] and thus to deter others from deserting their "duty." It is at this point of total restriction that the possibility for resistance emerges in Melville. For those in power will ask: "How do we discourage people from abandoning their courage? How do we increase people's fear to the degree that they are too afraid of being afraid to actually be afraid?" But the coward's potential for resistance—one could even say *the coward's paradox*—consists in the fact that terror has no means other than terror and that terror thus proves (almost comically) useless when it is directed at people who are already terrorized by anxiety. It is in this nonheroic sense that cowardice in Melville becomes an event of weak resistance. Like Deleuze's masochist, the coward "is insolent in his obsequiousness, rebellious in his submission."[20] The coward, like the masochist, humiliates the law as someone who has already humiliated himself and thus cannot be humiliated *by* the law. Rather, both figures bring out the absurdity of the law by taking the law in its strictest, most literal sense. And if the masochist and the coward might appear, at times, idiotic in their literal application of the law, then this does not contradict the courageousness of their seemingly stupid gesture.

Good Cowards and Bad Cowards

Admittedly, not every coward in Melville's texts is a figure of resistance. It seems as if Melville here follows a distinction made earlier by Michel de Montaigne, whom he brings up from time to time. In his various essays on the quality of cowardice, Montaigne formulates parameters for differentiating between bad cowards and not-so-bad ones. One can identify two groups of cowards in Montaigne: those who are in power and those who are subjected to power. In his aphorism "Cowardice is the Mother of Cruelty," Montaigne records that "some of the most cruel are subject to weeping easily and for frivolous reasons."[21] This characterization fits a figure such as Melville's Captain Paul in *Israel Potter* (1854–55), a coward who introduces himself with the words: "I—bloodthirsty, coward dog that I am—flogged a sailor . . . to death."[22] Melville supposedly bought a copy of Montaigne's essays in 1848,[23] which is two years before the publication of *White-Jacket* and three years before *Moby-Dick*. In both novels the French philosopher appears, and before already in *Mardi* as well as later in *Billy Budd*.[24] In *White-Jacket* and *Moby-Dick* Melville indeed introduces a second sort of coward, who bears a certain resemblance to the type of cowards addressed in Montaigne's essay on the punishment of cowardice. Montaigne lends his voice to "a very great captain" who demands that cowardice, or weakness of the heart ("lâcheté de coeur")[25] not be punished with death but "only" with public debasement. Montaigne's narrator justifies this demand by saying that in certain cases cowardice is an effect of weakness, not of malice—thus, "nature is our warrant, because it has left us in such imperfection and defect."[26] This cowardice out of weakness is a quality that could affect anyone, for it bears a transcendental or ontological character.

White-Jacket

A similar thought comes up in *White-Jacket,* where the narrator criticizes that cruel and degrading punishment of so-called cowards as an insult to their creator:

> But even in cases where no deep-seated dissatisfaction was presumed to prevail among the crew, and where a seaman, in time of action,

impelled by pure fear, "shirked away from his gun"; it seems but flying in the face of Him who made such a seaman what he constitutionally was, to sew *coward* upon his back, and degrade and agonize the already trembling wretch in numberless other ways.[27]

White-Jacket and *Moby-Dick* appeared in consecutive years, and both explore the question of how to deal with cowards. *White-Jacket; or, The World in a Man-of-War* bears autobiographical traces from the time Melville served as a common seaman aboard the frigate USS *United States* (1843–44). At the time the book appeared, the punishment for cowardice was still *"flogging through the fleet."*[28] The horrific description in *White-Jacket* of the procedure as well as of the effects later became instrumental in abolishing flogging in the U.S. Navy. Melville's narrator deconstructs the idea of cowardice by deconstructing the idea of courage: because courage, the narrator states, presupposes the possibility of free will, to act courageously is impossible within a system of oppression: "Thus, with death before his face from the foe, and death behind his back from his countrymen, the best valour of a man-of-war's-man can never assume the merit of a noble spontaneousness."[29] If a situation is such that it does not allow for courage, then how could one accuse someone within this situation of cowardice? If it is impossible to be a hero, then it must be equally impossible to be a coward. And yet the scene that precedes the flogging in *White-Jacket* is said to describe an act of cowardice in the Navy:

> Some years ago a fire broke out near the powder magazine in an American national ship, one of the squadron at anchor in the Bay of Naples. The utmost alarm prevailed. A cry went fore and aft that the ship was about to blow up. One of the seamen sprang overboard in affright. At length the fire was got under, and the man was picked up. He was tried before a court-martial, found guilty of cowardice, and condemned to be flogged through the fleet.[30]

The act that will lead to torture: "One of the seamen sprang overboard in affright." In Melville's description of the flogging, the entire fleet must watch the spectacle—"the leading idea is to strike terror into the beholders,"[31] Melville's narrator White-Jacket explains. If torture has the function of enabling the sovereign's revenge as well as that of eliciting fear in the beholders, then likewise in the case of the flogging of cowards, the flogging shall prevent cowardice through terror. This use of torture is based upon the assumption that one can shut off anxiety by creating another anxiety on top of it that thus silences the (first, original) anxiety. The questions would be the following: Which is the bigger fear? Am I more afraid of dying on an exploding boat, or am I more terrified at the thought of being tortured to death by my countrymen? But then again: Is this really how anxiety works? Is anxiety really a matter of degree? Can I weigh one anxiety against another? We know the coward's reaction to these kinds of reflections: "the seamen sprang overboard in affright." I would argue that this jump, indeed, is the last trace of that "noble spontaneousness" mourned by Melville's narrator.

One often finds parallel scenes in Melville, as if his books were engaged in an ongoing dialogue with each other; figures, scenes, and affective constellations reappear. If, for example, you zoom into the crowd which witnesses the flogging in *White-Jacket,* your eyes might meet a spectator who is only mentioned in passing, hardly noticeable because of his smallness:

> However much you may desire to absent yourself from the scene that ensues, yet behold it you must; or at least, stand near it you must; for the regulations enjoin the attendance of almost the entire ship's company, from the corpulent captain himself to the smallest boy striking the bell. "*All hands witness punishment, ahoy!*"[32]

A character from elsewhere in Melville who bears noticeable resemblance to this "smallest boy striking the bell," is Pip, or Pippin, from *Moby-Dick.* This boy in fact will be the next to spring "overboard in affright"—another coward daring the jump—even after having witnessed the torture of his fellow coward, as one might speculate in intertextual delirium.

The Castaway

Pip, or Pippin, is the black bell-boy and shipkeeper of the *Pequod*, to whom *Moby-Dick* devotes the chapter "The Castaway" (Pip reappears in other chapters, but I will limit myself here to "The Castaway"). The story that Melville narrates is exceptional because the shame resulting from cowardice usually silences all stories of the latter. In Dante's *Inferno* Virgil explicitly demands a *damnatio memoriae* for cowards: "Let us not speak of them, but look and go."[33] And yet, Melville does speak of them. We read at the beginning of "The Castaway" chapter that "a most significant event befell the most insignificant of the Pequod's crew; an event most lamentable" (319). The notion of the "event" makes clear that Melville, unlike Montaigne, will desubstantialize the idea of cowardice, treating cowardice less in terms of some substance, character, or psychology, and more as a need and as a singular event. "The Castaway" tells the story of Pip being left alone out in the ocean, an experience that leaves him "an idiot" (321).

To the reader of *Moby-Dick*, Pip is described in this chapter as "an unduly slender, clumsy, or timorous wight" (380). Because of his timid nature, Pip is put temporarily in the position of an after-oarsman in the boat of the second mate Stubb who is described as "an easy-going, unfearing man," who "presided over his whale-boat as if the most deadly encounter were but a dinner, and his crew all invited guests" (104). Pip foresees the threat that Stubb poses him: "Oh, thou big white God aloft there somewhere in yon darkness, have mercy on this small black boy down here; preserve him from all men that have no bowels to feel fear!" (151). Pip understands courage as a *lack* of fear, that is, as a deficit of some kind, an amputation. Pip would have been better off in the boat of Starbuck, who represents the dialectical antithesis to Stubb; just as Starbuck's name contains the letters of Stubb's, his courage, too, goes beyond that of the second mate in that it is of a more complex, deliberate nature: "'I will have no man in my boat,' said Starbuck, 'who is not afraid of a whale.' By this, he seemed to mean, not only that the most reliable and useful courage was that which arises from the fair estimation of the encountered peril, but that an utterly fearless man is a far more dangerous comrade than a coward" (102). In Starbuck's case, courage has a synthetic nature, in that it also implies anxiety. Courage thus touches upon wisdom, just as Melville's text implicitly touches upon Plato's *Laches*, the dialogue on how to educate men to be courageous in war: to know when to be afraid, and when to be confident. But in the (non-)conclusion of Plato's dialogue, Socrates criticizes this very definition of courage because it is not distinct: "Then courage is knowledge not merely of what is to be dreaded and what dared, for it comprehends goods and evils not merely in the future, but also in the present and the past and in any stage, like the other kinds of knowledge."[34] Courage no longer is only *one* aspect of virtue but becomes a megalomaniacal concept: a synthetic meta-virtue, including knowledge of future goods and evils. If courage, in this sense, is paradoxically restricted to a wide-scope perspective, then cowardice, on the contrary, stays a "small concept" in that it sticks with particulars. Courage is sublated cowardice, but cowardice is not the sublation of courage—rather, it is its reversal.

There are only a few critical texts that stick with the particular, minor character of Pip. Usually these texts concentrate on the (later) metaphysical scene where Pip is abandoned in the ocean; few other scholars investigate Pip's reading of the doubloon in the ninety-ninth chapter; more again examine the subsequent dialectical friendship that unfolds between Pip and Ahab.[35] But I would like, for once, to investigate an earlier event: Pip's jump, more exactly the two instances in which Pip jumps from the whaleboat into the sea.[36] So how does it happen that Pip jumps into the ocean? And why does he jump twice? After Pip is put in Stubb's boat, upon the second lowering the whale gives the boat a sudden rap and Pip, out of fear, jumps off the boat and gets caught by the whale line. While "Pip's blue, choked face plainly looked" (320), the others discuss whether or not to save the coward. They finally decide to cut the line, thus losing the whale. Stubb permits the crew to punish the "poltroon" by "yells and execrations" (320), with the aim of making him more courageous. But how do you make a coward courageous? Already after the first lowering, Stubb exhorted Pip to cherish his courageousness by affirmation. As this strategy failed, Stubb gives Pip "much wholesome advice":

The substance was, Never jump from a boat, Pip, except—but all the rest was indefinite, as the soundest advice ever is. Now, in general, *Stick to the boat*, is your true motto in whaling; but cases will sometimes happen when *Leap from the boat*, is still better. Moreover, as if perceiving at last that if he should give undiluted conscientious advice to Pip, he would be leaving him too wide a margin to jump in for the future; Stubb suddenly dropped all advice, and concluded with a peremptory command, "Stick to the boat, Pip, or by the Lord, I won't pick you up if you jump; mind that. We can't afford to lose whales by the likes of you; a whale would sell for thirty times what you would, Pip, in Alabama. Bear that in mind, and don't jump any more." (320–21)

Of course, Stubb's advice is useless and is so on purpose. Although the "rules" that Stubb lays out for Pip ("Now, in general, *Stick to the boat*, is your true motto in whaling; but cases will sometimes happen when *Leap from the boat*, is still better") maintain the logical form of "if . . . then" clauses, these rules are ineffective because they are not distinct. Already in our discussion of Plato's *Laches* we pointed out that courage is not limited as a virtue—in Melville it is also entirely dependent on its context. Even though this goes for any "context" of communication, as Derrida pointed out,[37] the infinity of the context becomes especially graspable here in that it is the ungraspable ocean. The ocean as the limitless context endangers what Pip fears for—his life ("But Pip loved life," 319). Now, Pip was born in Connecticut, and since no one on the ship owns him, he must have signed on, in Massachusetts, himself. Yet, this freedom becomes volatile in the moment when Stubb threatens to sell Pip as a slave in Alabama; for it becomes clear that Pip has nothing to lose or to win *but* his life.

The epistemological function embodied by the coward in this way allows for an alternative perspective on the world, the perspective of anxiety; the coward helps us to see something which we otherwise would not see; he becomes a medium for a certain kind of otherwise bracketed knowledge. In this sense, Pip the coward serves as a placeholder that can channel certain anxieties and affects that would otherwise remain obscure. More precisely, Melville makes us see the world through the eyes of someone who has lost all trust in the smooth functioning of rules. After all, rules as such are always directed at the general, and their abstractness must therefore overlook the individual. Likewise, the rules of whaling that Stubb cites to Pip prove to be useless for the singular case—even more: these rules *singularize* in the sense that they exclude the one who does not fit the general rule. We could also say: the language of rules *produces* cowards, it creates anxiety, understood in the Heideggerian sense that "anxiety singularizes and discloses being as 'solus ipse.'"[38]

Coming back to Stubb's catalog of (non-)rules, the narrator Ishmael admits that Stubb does not want Pip to be able to move from the general rule to the singular case. Rather, Stubb is concerned that "he would be leaving (Pip) too wide a margin to jump in for the future"—a silent avowal of the fact that in whaling practically any situation is dangerous enough for jumping to be the sound thing to do. Stubb concludes his speech by enacting a sovereign ban on leaping from the boat; this ban entails a possible punishment: if Pip jumps again, they will desert him in the water.[39] Stubb thus posits a threat in order to frighten Pip out of his fear.

Pip Jumps Again

"But we are all in the hands of the Gods; and Pip jumped again" (321). The comical shock of this sentence arises from its very center, from the semicolon and the succeeding "and." Together, the word and the mark string together two autonomous sentences: one establishing a total determinism ("But we are all in the hands of the Gods"), and the other satisfying the idea of free will ("Pip jumped again"), featuring the leap as *the* classical metaphor for free will, the act par excellence. This aporia comes up again—albeit in a less comical and less empathetic tone—in Joseph Conrad's *Lord Jim*, which tells the story of a first officer (whose real name like Pip's remains unknown) who leapt from what he believed to be a sinking ship, thereby abandoning its passengers: "'I had jumped . . .' He checked himself, averted his gaze . . . 'It seems,' he added."[40] Just as for Jim the question of agency remains up in the air, so for Pip the two statements "But we are all in the hands of the Gods; and Pip jumped again" seem to suspend each other reciprocally. Moreover, the adverb "again" suggests that Pip's jump is not so much an act of self-determination as an instance of the compulsion to repeat. This jumble of activity and passivity is intensified by the fact that Pip's "performance" is described alternately as an active "jump" as well as a passive "plumping into the water" (321).

The scene of Pip's jump unsettles the idea of agency to the extent that it does not make a difference whether Pip *jumps* or *plumps* into anxiety. This is even more the case because of the fact that Pip is framed by Stubb as always already a potential slave. Ishmael famously asks at the beginning of the novel "Who aint a slave?"—and Ishmael's fate indeed ends up running parallel to Pip's in the end when Ishmael is cast away on the ocean in Queequeg's coffin. One could also read Melville's use of the word "slave" here in terms of Hamlet's utterance "Give me that man / That is not passion's slave" (3.2.66–67), even if in this case that "passion" is fear. But then, using the position of the slave metaphorically, as Melville does, in the well-meant attempt to turn exclusion into inclusion still runs the risk of downplaying the traumatic experience of being a slave in the strict or literal sense. In fact, we cannot read Pip's jump independently from the long tradition of racialized songs involving coerced or compelled jumps, unfolded by Aisha Harris.[41] "Jumping songs" were often sung by slaves, such as the tune "Pick a Bale of Cotton" from the nineteenth century, which describes the slaves' grueling daily routine with the words "You gotta jump down, turn around / Pick a bale of cotton." In the beginning of "The Castaway," Pip is characterized by Ishmael in a racialized manner praising the "jolly brightness peculiar to his tribe; a tribe, which ever enjoy all holidays and festivities with finer, freer relish than any other race" (319). This depiction of Pip, however, contradicts an earlier appearance of his, at the midnight party given to the last arrived harpooners because instead of enjoying the festivity, Pip is terrified by the sailors who command him to be merry, to make music and to jump:

> French Sailor: Pip! little Pip! hurrah with your tambourine!—PIP (Sulky and sleepy) Don't know where it is. . . . FRENCH SAILOR Beat thy belly, then, and wag thy ears. Jig it, men, I say; merry's the word; hurrah! Damn me, won't you dance? . . . Throw yourselves! Legs! legs! . . . AZORE SAILOR (Dancing) Go it, Pip! Bang it, bellboy! Rig it, dig it, stig it, quig it, bell-boy! Make fire-flies; break the jinglers! . . . FRENCH SAILOR Merry-mad! Hold up thy hoop, Pip, till I jump through it! Split jibs! tear yourself! TASHTEGO (Quietly smoking) That's a white man; he calls that fun. (146–48)

The slave is supposed to dance naturally. But can you tell the dancer from the dance? Does the concept of agency pertain to the racialized subject as slave?

The aspect of enslavement thus radicalizes the already difficult question: are you acting freely or courageously when you follow an order and do your "duty"?[42] The problem with voluntarism is that one never knows whether a given act was free or not. This aporia structurally resembles the one that makes Pip jump: the line of the harpoon hitting the whale, and the whale abruptly pulling the boat forth. When holding the line of the whale, are you moving freely or are you part of a bigger structure? Are you holding the line of the whale or is the whale holding you? It is this very line, in which Pip gets "entrapped" after his first jump, the line that almost chokes him—one may call it: the fine line between freedom/autonomy and determination/coercion.[43] In jumping—that is, in an act of more or less liberatory flight[44]—Pip, the coward, at once escapes this aporia and mirrors it.

To Be a Coward or Not to Be a Coward?

After Pip jumps off the boat a second time, Stubb leaves him in the water. The boat is quickly pulled away by the harpooned whale.

> In three minutes, a whole mile of shoreless ocean was between Pip and Stubb. Out from the centre of the sea, poor Pip turned his crisp, curling, black head to the sun, another lonely castaway, though the

The Coward's Paradox 99

loftiest and the brightest. Now, in calm weather, to swim in the open ocean is as easy to the practiced swimmer as to ride in a spring-carriage ashore. But the awful lonesomeness is intolerable. The intense concentration of self in the middle of such a heartless immensity, my God! who can tell it? (321)

The narrator comments upon Stubb's abandonment of Pip: "Alas! Stubb was but too true to his word" (321). Yet, how can you be "too true"? There is an air of absurdity about this intensification because the mere expression of more or less truth hollows out the idea that anything could be true. The effect of Melville's impossible hyperboles is an increasing degree of anxiety because there is nothing more to hold on to—no rules, no laws, no justice, especially no truth. "In this world of lies, Truth is forced to fly like a scared white doe in the woodlands," Melville writes in "Hawthorne and His Mosses."[45] With truth taking flight like a scared bird (an animal-coward, so to speak), what is left of truth is no more than the mere sound of the word: "too true to." By means of this sound installation, the text seems to perform an additional shift away from truth (or substance) to mimesis—in this case, the mere imitation of sound as well as visual patterns—with mimesis (in a Platonic sense) presenting a threat to truth.

The strangely symmetrical formulation of "too true to" (321) reveals itself to be a larger, structuring pattern. It phonetically re-sounds and visually mirrors P-i-P's name as well as the sailors' mocking calls "Pip! little Pip!" (146), and it also echoes the sound of his bell, "ding, dong, ding" (392, 400). What seems at first like a purely formal joke of symmetry becomes more meaningful in two instances: once when Ahab explains his strange affection for Pip by referring to their unlikely *likeness* by means of the same symmetrical pattern: "like-cures-like" (399). The other time is when the sound-image turns entirely visual: "Out from the centre of the sea, poor Pip turned his crisp, curling, black head to the sun, another lonely castaway, though the loftiest and brightest" (321). In a first move, "Pip's ebon head" performs a literalization of the melancholic metaphor of the *soleil noir*, which appears even lonelier than the incomparable, singular metaphor of the heliotrope.[46] So there is the white sun in the sky, Pip's black head on the water surface: "Like a head of cloves," Pip head lies on top of the sea, which is "flatly stretching away" like a mirror-axis. But this horizontal image undergoes a vertical pull in the moment when Pip's soul is drowned and "carried down alive" (321). What is up with this peculiar pattern? We could visualize the pattern as two dots separated by a line, *dot line dot*. On what does this pattern insist? Bear in mind that the pattern itself represents repetition: what appears before and after the line is the same, only mirrored; which makes the line of decision in the middle a line of indecision as well. This is an apt illustration of how cowardice works, for as cowards we are always driven by the same anxiety—anxiety is always anxiety of being-towards-death.

The narrator explains Pip's abandonment by commenting that "oarsmen jeopardized through their own timidity" would often be forsaken; "in the fishery, a coward, so called, is marked with the same ruthless detestation peculiar to military navies and armies" (321). The effect of the oceanic feeling on Pip is described as follows: "The sea had jeeringly kept his finite body up, but drowned the infinite of his soul. Not drowned entirely, though. Rather carried down alive" (321). Pip drowns without drowning, dies without dying—a limbo that resembles the liminal position that cowards inhabit in the *Divina Commedia*.[47]

The madness of the moment of drowning and the horrible loneliness cause waves that traverse centuries. If we listen closely, perhaps approaching a kind of hallucinatory hearing, we can perceive another voice coming from the water, the voice of "another lonely castaway" (321): that of Shakespeare's equally "cast away" Ophelia (4.5.190). Both Pip and Ophelia experience death by water, and both characters can be read as "document(s) in madness" (4.5.171) in their mourning rituals. The mad Pip's eerie singing mourning his own death resonates with Ophelia's singing for her dead father. This is because Pip and Ophelia's words show the same uncanny repetitions, the same singsong style and intensified orality, which breaks with grammatical reason: "You must sing 'a-down a-down, and you call him a-down-a'" (4.5.165). Note that Ophelia's use of "a-down-a" even prefigures Pip's symmetrical formulations. If one were to compose a song of Pip's lines that joined in Ophelia's singing, it could sound like this:

OPHELIA (*Sings.*)	PIP
And will 'a not come again?	Pip! Pip! Pip! Reward for Pip!
And will 'a not come again?	Who's seen Pip the coward?
No, no, he is dead,	No, no! shame upon all cowards—
Go to they deathbed.	shame upon them!
He will never come again.	Let'em go drown like Pip, that
	jumped from a whale boat.
	Shame! shame!
His beard was as white as snow,	a little negro lad, five feet high,
Flaxen was his poll.	hang-dog look, and cowardly!
He is gone, he is gone,	he's missing
And we cast away moan.	
Go a' mercy on his soul.	Oh! thou big white God aloft ...
And of all Christians' souls. God buy you.	have mercy on this small black boy down here
(4.5.182–92)	(pp. 392, 400, 151)

Thanks to Charles Olson, and more recently, Julian Markel, we are well informed about the connection that exists between Shakespeare's plays and Melville's writing of *Moby-Dick*. In 1849, Melville acquired a seven-volume edition of Shakespeare's plays and studied them intensively just before and during the composition of *Moby-Dick* in 1850–51.[48] But whenever a literary scholar compares Pip to a character from Shakespeare, it is the fool from *King Lear* (with Lear modeling Ahab).[49] However, *Moby-Dick* equally holds references from various other plays by Shakespeare, for instance from *Hamlet*.[50] When Olson cites Melville's rough notes on Shakespeare—"Madness is undefinable"—he reads this statement in the context not only of *Lear* and *Hamlet*, but he also argues that both plays were influential for the development of Pip's character. And yet Olson thinks exclusively of Hamlet, never mentioning Ophelia.[51]

The obvious reason why the strange resemblance between Pip and Ophelia has gone unnoticed is that the two characters are of different genders from one another. This opposition is complicated, however, by the fact that one form of the punishment of cowardice entails the public "shaming" through feminization.[52] Montaigne, for instance, reports that in ancient Greece, someone who deserts the battlefield "should be placed in the public square for three days, dressed in women's clothes."[53] Melville picks up on this practice of the coward's feminization, though not in a shaming or exclusionary manner. On the contrary, in a moment of weak resistance or *Queer Optimism*,[54] to borrow Michael Snediker's pointed formulation, Melville invites us to indulge in queer eroticism and thus to reverse the logic of punishment. The transfixed Ahab approaches Pip with the words "Who art thou, boy?" and invites him to come "down" to his cabin (or wherever "down" may be): "Here, boy; Ahab's cabin shall be Pip's home henceforth, while Ahab lives. Thou touchest my inmost centre, boy; thou art tied to me by cords woven by my heart-strings. Come, let's down" (392). We hence owe one of the most romantic passages in *Moby-Dick* to the coward's capacity to be transgender; Ahab seems to be aware that Pip is initiating an even more general transvaluation of values. This transvaluation already commences in Pip's jump, in the sense that Pip embraces his anxiety; he is faithful to his fear, stubbornly affirming what is negated by society, thus transgressing taboos along the vector of desire. In exploring the erotic potential of cowardice, Melville—and not just his characters—becomes a precursor to other literary-criminal perverts.[55]

But there is a second reason why the character of Hamlet—rather than that of Ophelia—is associated with Pip: Ophelia is not a cowardly figure. Ophelia might be shy and react timidly to Hamlet's outrageous sexual puns—but a coward? Instead, the question "Am I a coward?" (2.5.506) haunts Hamlet. Before staging the mouse trap, Hamlet thought he "toughened up" ("Why, what an ass am I: this is most brave," 2.2.517). But a little later he accuses himself of being a "coward" for not having taken revenge for his parents already ("How stand I then / That have a father killed, a mother stained," 4.4.42 and 4.4.62). Only after his death will Hamlet be buried as a hero in a military funeral ceremony. In conclusion, Hamlet carries traits both of Pip and Ahab, a coward and a hero.[56]

Ophelia and Pip, on the other hand, share their relation to Hamlet/Ahab in that they both fall victim to their protagonist's paranoia. What is the nature of this paranoia? It is the fear of being a coward that drives Hamlet and Ahab to disastrous actions, and it is fear that produces cowards by violently excluding fear from the community. Pip himself is not scared of his fear; Ishmael even translates Pip's "fear" into more positive terms: "But Pip loved life" (319). This makes clear that cowardice is not least a matter of perspective: Does Pip leap *from the whale-boat* out of cowardice? Or could one just as well say that he is brave to jump twice over *into the open sea*?[57] Is Ophelia's suicide a sign that she is scared of life or that she is not scared of death? Could the coward be the truly brave one because—other than the courageous—she is constantly subjected to fear in the sense in which Shakespeare's Caesar suggests: "Cowards die many times before their deaths, / The valiant never taste of death but once"?[58]

Pity and Sadism

Why do we only now consider giving credit to the coward? Pip's punishment is usually thought of exclusively as his being abandoned in the sea. But there is an additional, latent mode of punishment that is at work, and that is the ambivalent tone of Ishmael's description. Melville's readers easily get entrapped in Ishmael's melancholic, pitiful description, just as Pip got "entrapped" (319) in the whaling line.[59] Throughout *Moby-Dick*, Pip is either called "Poor Pip!" (6 times), "poor little Pip" (once), "poor lad" (once), "poor me" (once), "poor little negro" (twice), or "poor Alabama boy" (once).[60] We can never be sure whether sadism is the pretext for pity, or pity the pretext for sadism. The half-pitiful, half-comical tone can be taken as an attempt to ignore, and even break the coward's resistance. After all, the coward is always a source of aggression—Ishmael tells us that Tashtego "hated Pip for a poltroon" (320). It is by being frightened that the coward threatens to destabilize the system of whaling. The coward is a form of provocation: an aggression that calls forth punishment, a transgression of the codes of masculinity. As always, one has to threaten to punish the weakest because one perceives their weakness as aggression.

In "The Castaway," we are consequently not dealing with pity *or* sadism but with both of them, that is, with layers of emotions.[61] Since we cannot decide what is pain and what is pleasure in Melville's narration of the coward's abandonment, what remains is irony. Interestingly, in *The Concept of Irony* Kierkegaard criticizes Romantic irony as "infinitely cowardly."[62] If cowardice, according to Montaigne, is the mother of all cruelty, and irony, according to Kierkegaard, is cowardly—could one then say that irony is the mother of cruelty? It is noteworthy that the book in which cowardice becomes an event is *Moby-Dick*. The novel often is taken to mark the rupture of Melville's turning from mere adventure story to the adventure of profound literariness. Melville's becoming literary thus is tied to the coward, just as Ahab is tied to Pip, to the fool, the romantic figure of the poetical par excellence, and just as Melville himself remains tied to Friedrich Hölderlin, in this regard, and the latter's shift in his poetry from the poet's courage ("Dichtermut") to stupidity ("Blödigkeit").

One last stylistic feature of "The Castaway" that is related and in a way answers to the perplexing ambiguity of pity and sadism in relation to the coward is the strange frequency of the conjunctions "now" and "but." A general rule is introduced with the conjunction "now"; but only a little later this rule has to be corrected as the contrasting conjunction "but":

> "In outer aspect . . . But while . . ."; "So, though in the clear air of the day . . . ; yet . . ."; "Now . . . As a general thing, . . . ship-keepers are . . . hardy fellows. . . . But if there happen to be an unduly slender, clumsy, or timorous wight in the ship, that wight is certain to be made a ship-keeper. It was so in the Pequod with . . . Pip . . . Poor Pip!" (319)
>
> "Now, in calm weather, to swim in the open ocean is as easy to the practiced swimmer as to ride in a spring-carriage ashore. But the awful lonesomeness is intolerable." (321)

What happens here has to do with the logical question of rule and exception. Normally, the logic of law proceeds from the general rule to the exception to it. In "The Castaway," the *now*-sentence introduces the rule, whereas the *but*-sentence presents the actual—which every time turns out to be an exception. One could also say: the law that Pip is subjected to is Murphy's Law. The effect of this juxtaposition is a tragicomic one, if we accept Kierkegaard's definition of the comic: "wherever there is life there is contradiction, and where there is contradiction the comic is present."[63] Pip floating alone in the ocean would hence be an instance of "suffering contradiction." As a consequence, when scholarly pieces engage with "The Castaway," they usually lament the fate of "poor Pip" whereby the latter is sublated from a coward into something like an idiot-hero,[64] or even a representation of "the ethical."[65] But these kinds of readings tend both to recuperate the violence of the scene and to ignore the violently comical quality of Melville's prose. This comic quality arises from the use of contradiction as well as from the dehumanization of the human as illuminated in Bergson's essay *Le Rire*, in which laughter is said to have the social function of indicating and "correcting" a person's lack, so as to assimilate him to society.[66] This lack of assimilation manifests itself in unconscious, mechanical moments, such as the repetition of words and logical-semantic structures (*now . . . but*), phonetic and graphic patterns, and of slapstick-like actions. If for Bergson, comedy deals not with individuals but with types,[67] then Melville's "Pip the coward" is an example of how someone who was first excluded on account of his singularity is then treated as a dehumanized type.

"As He Was Running"

In his brief history of cowardice, Walsh defines cowardice as a concept belonging to war. But towards the end of his book, he asks, "can cowardice figure with any clarity and power in everyday moral discourse?"[68] In everyday life, many people—due to the color of their skin (black) and often additionally due to their gender (male)[69]—are precisely forced to live in a militarized atmosphere, that is, in an atmosphere in which the notion of the "coward" could be employed. Whenever a police officer kills a black man, the situation is presented as a state of exception and the public is therefore expected to approve of the killings as a logical consequence of martial law. A recurring phrase in the police reports is that the victim "ran away from the police." Recall the case of Walter Scott, in which the video "shows the officer firing eight times as the man, Walter L. Scott, 50, fled."[70] In regard to the police killing of Freddie Gray, the news reads: "Authorities can't say if there was a particularly good reason why police arrested Gray. According to the city, an officer made eye contact with Gray, and he took off running, so they pursued him."[71] For Michael Brown, too, there were witnesses who claim that the policeman was "firing at Brown's back as he was running."[72] The fact that a person was shot while running away should only matter insofar as this means that the victim was shot in the back and that the officer who shot him most likely acted illegally.[73] But if police reports emphasize that the person who was shot was running away, then this can also be interpreted as a perverse attempt at justification, insofar as it enables the framing of the victim as a coward or even as an admission of guilt—so much so that in fall 2016 the Massachusetts Supreme Judicial Court felt compelled to clarify that men of color when approached by the police have "a reason for flight totally unrelated to consciousness of guilt."[74] When running away—or in Melville, jumping off a boat—is cited as a reason for why a life has been taken away, then the one who runs is treated as a deserter.

What would be the alternative to the attempt to escape? To stay where you are and possibly to sacrifice your life to ensure the smooth functioning of the state? The real threat does not consist in the fact that anyone runs away from the police, for whatever reason.[75] The real danger is that running away, jumping off a boat, trying to escape tells us something about just how bad the situation is.[76] The person who takes flight demonstrates that he is neither in a position to trust the state nor to believe that justice is served.[77] In this way, the attempt to escape functions as a form of indictment—and it is this cowardly resistance that the state is too afraid to acknowledge.

In Ta-Nehisi Coates's *Between the World and Me* the word "escape" pervades the autobiographical letter to his son like an Ariadne-thread: "you may feel the need for escape even more than I did. You have seen all the wonderful life up above the tree-line, yet you may understand that there is no real distance between you and Trayvon Martin."[78] The word "escape" stands in for the smallest of all hope: the hope of opening a way out of a deadly labyrinth, in which an unconscionable monster devours the children of the enslaved neighbor-city. Escape thus is also a positive, dynamic need, as Emmanuel Levinas emphasizes: "with escape we aspire only to get out [*sortir*]. It is this category of getting out, assimilable neither to renovation nor to creation, that we must grasp in all its purity."[79] Whereas Levinas approaches escape as an entryway to philosophy, Wai Chee Dimock compares "the art of authorship" in Melville's literary oeuvre to "the art of escape."[80] In coward-figures such as Pip we are confronted with what Dimock calls "metaphors of powerlessness," or with "the specters of those for whom powerlessness is anything but metaphor."[81] Melville shows us how difficult it is to bear powerlessness, to take this punch of weakness, and how it gives birth to the need to escape. In Melville's fantasies of cowardly resistance, Pip who takes the jump into the ocean meets Claudia Rankine's *Citizen*, together with other castaways on the run:

> Some years there exits a wanting to escape—
> you, floating above your certain ache—
> still the ache coexists.
> Call that the immanent you—[82]

Notes

1. William Shakespeare, *Hamlet*, in *The Norton Shakespeare: Based on the Oxford Edition*, ed. Stephen Greenblatt et al. (New York: Norton, 1997), 2.5.506. Further references to this edition will be cited parenthetically within the text.

2. Elizabeth A. Povinelli, *Economies of Abandonment: Social Belonging and Endurance in Late Liberalism* (Durham, N.C.: Duke University Press, 2011), 189.

3. Peter Szendy, *Prophecies of Leviathan: Reading Past Melville*, trans. and intro. Gil Anidjar (New York: Fordham University Press, 2010), ix.

4. C. L. R. James, *Mariners, Renegades, and Castaways: The Story of Herman Melville and the World We Live In* (New York: University Press of New England, 1953).

5. Herman Melville, *Moby-Dick: Norton Critical Edition*, ed. Hershel Parker and Harrison Hayford (New York: Norton, 2002). Further references to this edition will be cited parenthetically within the text.

6. Herman Melville, *Omoo: A Narrative of Adventures in the South Seas*, in *Typee, Omoo, Mardi*, ed. G. Thomas Tanselle (New York: Library of America, 1982), 317–646, at 420.

7. Melville, *Moby-Dick*, 34.

8. Herman Melville, *The Confidence-Man: His Masquerade*, in *Pierre, Israel Potter, The Piazza Tales, The Confidence-Man, Uncollected Prose, Billy Budd,*

Sailor, ed. Harrison Hayford (New York: Library of America, 1984), 841–1112, at 854.

9. Herman Melville, *Redburn: His First Voyage*, in *Redburn, White-Jacket, Moby-Dick*, ed. G. Thomas Tanselle (New York: Library of America, 1983), 7–340, at 317.

10. Melville, *Omoo*, 417.

11. Herman Melville, *Israel Potter*, in *Pierre, Israel Potter, The Piazza Tales, The Confidence Man, Uncollected Prose, Billy Budd, Sailor*, ed. Harrison Hayford (New York: Library of America, 1984), 429–615, at 540.

12. Melville, *The Confidence-Man*, 1006.

13. Ibid., 1000.

14. Herman Melville, *Mardi: and a Voyage Thither*, in *Typee, Omoo, Mardi*, ed. G. Thomas Tanselle (New York: Library of America, 1982), 647–1316, at 1268.

15. Ibid., 1283.

16. Melville, *Moby-Dick*, 34.

17. Chris Walsh, *Cowardice: A Brief History* (Princeton, N.J.: Princeton University Press, 2014), 167.

18. Ibid., 104. In chapter 5, Walsh argues that the notion of cowardice has vanished over the last century due to a therapeutic shift, especially the treatment of shell shock or war neurosis, and later of post-traumatic stress disorder.

19. Ibid., 168.

20. Gilles Deleuze, *Masochism: Coldness and Cruelty & Venus in Furs*, trans. Jean McNeil (New York: Zone Books, 1991), 87–89, at 89.

21. Michel de Montaigne, "Cowardice, Mother of Cruelty," in *The Complete Essays of Montaigne*, ed. and trans. Donald M. Frame (Stanford, Calif.: Stanford University Press, 1965), 523–24, at 523; Michel de Montaigne, "Couardise, Mère de cruauté," in *Essais*, vol. 2 (Paris: Chez Abel L'Angelier, 1588), XXVII, 295–98.

22. Melville, *Israel Potter*, 528.

23. Robert Shulman, "Montaigne and the Techniques and Tragedy of *Billy Budd*," *Comparative Literature* 14, no. 4 (Fall1964): 322–30, at 322, n. 1.

24. Melville, *Moby-Dick*, 9; Herman Melville, *White-Jacket*, in *Redburn, White-Jacket, Moby-Dick*, ed. G. Thomas Tanselle (New York: Library of America, 1983), at 401; Melville, *Mardi*, 1022; Melville, *Billy Budd*, 843; see also Shulman, "Montaigne and the Techniques and Tragedy of *Billy Budd*."

25. Michel de Montaigne, "De la punition de la couardise," in *Essais*, vol. 1 (Paris: Chez Abel L'Angelier, 1588), XVI, 24–25, at 24.

26. Michel de Montaigne, "Of the Punishment of Cowardice," in *The Complete Essays of Montaigne*, ed. and trans. Donald M. Frame (Stanford, Calif.: Stanford University Press, 1965), 48–49.

27. Melville, *White-Jacket*, 680.

28. Ibid., 738.

29. Ibid., 680.

30. Ibid., 740.

31. Ibid., 739.

32. Ibid., 488.

33. Dante Alighieri, *Inferno*, trans. Michael Palma (New York: Norton, 2003), III.51. See also Walsh, *Cowardice*, 14: "It may be the most common and

profound human failing, but cowardice remains strikingly underreported and underanalyzed."

34. Plato, *Plato in Twelve Volumes*, trans. W. R. M. Lamb, vol. 8 (Cambridge, Mass: Harvard University Press, 1955), 199b–d.

35. See John Bryant, "Pip: Castaway and Cosmopolite," in *Melville and Repose: The Rhetoric of Humor in the American Renaissance* (New York: Oxford University Press, 1993), 223–29; Sharon Cameron, "Ahab and Pip: Those Are Pearls That Were His Eyes," in *The Corporeal Self: Allegories of the Body in Melville and Hawthorne* (Baltimore, Md.: John Hopkins University Press, 1981), 20–35; Tim Deines, "Re-Marking the Ultra-Transcendental in *Moby-Dick*," *symplokē* 18, no. 1–2 (2010): 261–79; James, *Mariners, Renegades, and Castaways*, 64–65; Samuel Otter, *Melville's Anatomies* (Berkeley: University of California Press, 1999), 92–171; Donald Pease, "Pip, *Moby-Dick*, Melville's Governmentality," *Novel: A Forum on Fiction* 45, no. 3 (2012): 327–42; Gabriele Schwab, "Aesthetics of Blankness in *Moby-Dick*," in *Subjects without Selves: Transitional Texts in Modern Fiction* (Cambridge, Mass.: Harvard University Press, 1994), 49–71, at 54–55.

36. Szendy's *Prophecies of Leviathan* presents an exception in this regard in that Szendy indeed examines Pip's being caught in the whaling-line.

37. Jacques Derrida, "Signature Event Context," trans. Alan Bass, in *Margins of Philosophy, Jacques Derrida* (Chicago: University of Chicago Press, 1982), 309–30.

38. "Die Angst vereinzelt und erschließt so das Dasein als 'solus ipse' " (Martin Heidegger, *Sein und Zeit* [Tübingen: Niemeyer, 1967], 188).

39. On Stubb's interdiction as an act of sovereignty, see Deines, "Re-Marking the Ultra-Transcendental," 269.

40. Joseph Conrad, *Lord Jim*, ed. Susan Jones (London: Wordsworth Classics, 2002), 70. In *Lord Jim* as well as in Ruben Östlund's movie *Force Majeure* (2014), the catastrophe is that there is no catastrophe. The one who deserted not only has to live with the shame of having jumped off a boat instead of helping the passengers (*Lord Jim*), or the shame of having run away from his family when he should have protected it from a potential avalanche (*Force Majeure*)—but he also has to come to terms with the irony that his action of cowardice was superfluous.

41. Aisha Harris, "The Complicated History of Jumping Songs," Slate.com, May 2, 2013, http://www.slate.com/blogs/browbeat/2013/05/02/chris_kelly_of_kris_kross_dies_contributed_to_long_history_of_jumping_songs.html.

42. "Capital punishment for failure of duty both invests duty with supreme importance and makes a mockery of the idea that duty should be performed 'apart . . . from any external compulsion.' " Walsh, *Cowardice*, 105.

43. Szendy's *Prophecies of Leviathan* calls this the "simultaneous counterpoint of attachment and ultimate detachment" (58).

44. See Joseph Ledoux, "For the Anxious, Avoidance Can Have an Upside," *New York Times*, April 7, 2013, http://opinionator.blogs.nytimes.com/2013/04/07/for-the-anxious-avoidance-can-have-an-upside/.

45. Melville, *Moby-Dick*, 541–42.

46. Jacques Derrida, "La Mythologie blanche," in *Marges: de la philosophie* (Paris: Éditions de Minuit, 1972), 247–324.

47. Dante, *Inferno*, canto III. Whereas one might consider Dante himself a coward-like figure (there is no page in the *Inferno* where the character would not

hide behind Virgil), Dante's anxiety is redeemed as *pietas*, that is, a pious fear of God. In comparison, "real" cowardice in the *Commedia* is punished as a form of indecision. Therefore, cowards are located at the gate to hell: "Here all your doubt is to be left behind, / here all your cowardice is to fall dead." They are neither allowed into heaven nor into hell.

48. Julian Markels, *Melville and the Politics of Identity: From King Lear to Moby-Dick* (Urbana: University of Illinois Press, 1993), 132.

49. See Charles Olson's "*Lear* and *Moby-Dick*," *Twice a Year: A Semi-Annual Journal of Literaure, the Arts, and Civil Liberties* 1 (1938): 165–89, as well as his *Call Me Ishmael* (New York: Grove, 1947), 63; Markels, *Melville and the Politics of Identity*, 62–69. In Carl Rollyson and Lisa Paddock, *Herman Melville A to Z: The Essential Reference to His Life and Work* (New York: Facts on File, 2001), 209, the authors see Vee Vee, a minor character in *Mardi*, as being modeled on the Fool in *King Lear* and as prefiguring Pip.

50. Julian Markel, "*King Lear* and *Moby-Dick*: The Cultural Connection," *The Massachusetts Review* 9, no. 1 (Winter 1968): 169–76, at 169.

51. Olson, *Call Me Ishmael*, 54–55.

52. See Walsh, *Cowardice*, 35.

53. Montaigne, "Of the Punishment of Cowardice," 48.

54. Michael D. Snediker, *Queer Optimism: Lyric Personhood and Other Felicitous Persuasions* (Minneapolis: University of Minnesota Press, 2009).

55. For instance, Jean Genet's libidinal fixation on betrayal, or the teasing pleasures that Robert Walser's characters experience in acts of quotidian disobedience.

56. Olson, *Call Me Ishmael*, 54.

57. James goes even further, claiming that "Pip learned even greater wisdom. He lost fear. Alone of the crew he now spoke to the terrible Ahab as one human being to another" (*Mariners, Renegades, and Castaways*, 64).

58. William Shakespeare, *The Tragedy of Julius Caesar*, in *The Norton Shakespeare, Based on the Oxford Edition*, ed. Stephen Greenblatt et al. (New York: Norton, 1997), 2.2.32–37.

59. An example is Pease's otherwise excellent reading of the chapter "The Castaway" in "Pip, *Moby-Dick*, Melville's Governmentality"; Pease takes both Ahab as well as Ishmael's approach to Pip to be sincerely melancholic.

60. Some readers might be familiar with such inflations of "poorness" from the work of Henry James: take a short novel like Henry James's *Washington Square* (1880), in *Novels 1881–1886*, ed. William T. Stafford (New York: Library of America, 1985), and the adjective "poor" appears, in variations, no less than 67 times; most often used for the (anti-)heroine who is described as the "poor child" (3 times), the "poor girl" (22 times), or alternatively as "poor Catherine" (17 times). Even if this comparison appears counterintuitive—the anatomist of late Victorian bourgeois culture meets up with the metaphysical seafarer—in Melville the excess of pity has the same effect as in James.

61. Tilottama Rajan very pointedly observes in her reading of Foucault's accounts of torture in *Deconstruction and the Remainders of Phenomenology: Sartre, Derrida, Foucault, Baudrillard* (Stanford, Calif.: Stanford University Press, 2002) that the "fate of writing is connected to an aestheticization of suffering … One is never sure whether its analyst is a victim or a collaborator, whether the

disfiguration of the body is a source of pain or aesthetic pleasure, or even whether that choice has any meaning" (225).

62. Søren Kierkegaard, *The Concept of Irony: With Continual Reference to Socrates: Notes of Schelling's Berlin Lectures*, in *Kierkegaard's Writings*, ed. and trans. Howard V. Hong and Edna H. Hong, vol. 2 (Princeton, N.J.: Princeton University Press, 1989), 298.

63. Søren Kierkegaard, *Concluding Unscientific Postscript to Philosophical Fragments*, ed. Alastair Hannay (Cambridge: Cambridge University Press, 2013), 431.

64. "It is Pip who in the end will be hailed as the greatest hero of all" (James, *Mariners, Renegades, and Castaways*, 18).

65. Paul Brodtkorb, Jr., *Ishmael's White World: A Phenomenological Reading of "Moby-Dick"* (New Haven, Conn.: Yale University Press, 1965), reads Pip and Starbuck as "the ethical," "away from heroism" (75).

66. "Les attitudes, gestes et mouvements du corps humain sont risibles dans l'exacte mesure où ce corps nous fait penser à une simple mécanique" (Henri Bergson, *Le Rire: Essai sur la signification du comique* [Paris: Presses Universitaires de France, 1995], 22–23; see also 53). Indeed, Pip's repetitive jumping bears a certain resemblance to that of Buster Keaton's *Navigator*.

67. Bergson, Le Rire, 123.

68. Walsh, *Cowardice*, 167.

69. I am focusing here on the police killings of young black men because of the comparison with the character of Pip, but also because women and girls are still "missing from the narrative," as a recent article by Dani McClain shows. Dani McClain, "#SayHerName Shows Black Women Face Police Violence, Too—and Pregnancy and Motherhood Are No Refuge," *The Nation*, May 21, 2015, http://www.thenation.com/blog/207905-sayhername-shows-black-women-face-police-violence-too-and-pregnancy-and-motherhood-are-n.

70. "A white police officer in North Charleston, S.C., was charged with murder on Tuesday after a video surfaced showing him shooting in the back and killing an apparently unarmed black man while the man ran away. The officer, Michael T. Slager, 33, said he had feared for his life because the man had taken his stun gun in a scuffle after a traffic stop on Saturday. A video, however, shows the officer firing eight times as the man, Walter L. Scott, 50, fled" (Michael S. Schmidt and Matt Apuzzo, "South Carolina Officer Is Charged with Murder of Walter Scott," *New York Times*, April 7, 2015, http://www.nytimes.com/2015/04/08/us/south-carolina-officer-is-charged-with-murder-in-black-mans-death.html?_r=0).

71. David A. Graham, "The Mysterious Death of Freddie Gray," *The Atlantic*, April 22, 2015, http://www.theatlantic.com/politics/archive/2015/04/the-mysterious-death-of-freddie-gray/391119/.

72. "McCulloch again says witness statements were inconsistent, with claims ranging from Wilson firing from the car, firing at Brown's back as he was running, and others saying Wilson didn't fire until Brown turned around and came back toward Wilson" (Jaeah Lee and AJ Vicens, "5 Key Inconsistencies in What Happened during the Michael Brown Shooting," *Mother Jones*, November 27, 2014, http://www.motherjones.com/politics/2014/11/inconsistencies-what-happened-during-michael-brown-shooting/).

73. "Can a police officer legally shoot a fleeing suspect in the back? That simple question—being asked around the country after a video of a white police officer in North Charleston, South Carolina, shooting and killing an unarmed black man as he ran away from the officer provoked widespread shock and condemnation—has a not-so-simple answer: It depends. In the legal test of whether an officer is justified in shooting a fleeing person, certain factors must be present, including a belief by the officer that the suspect committed or was about to commit a dangerous and serious felony such as an assault, legal experts said. . . . Law professors, former prosecutors and police officers who watched the North Charleston video said . . . that based on what they saw in the video, the officer was not legally justified in opening fire" (Manny Fernandez, "North Charleston Police Shooting Not Justified, Experts Say," *New York Times*, April 9, 2015, http://www.nytimes.com/2015/04/10/us/north-charleston-police-shooting-not-justified-experts-say.html).

74. "Flight is not necessarily probative of a suspect's state of mind or consciousness of guilt. Rather, the finding that black males in Boston are disproportionately and repeatedly targeted for FIO [Field Interrogation and Observation] encounters suggests a reason for flight totally unrelated to consciousness of guilt. Such an individual, when approached by the police, might just as easily be motivated by the desire to avoid the recurring indignity of being racially profiled as by the desire to hide criminal activity" (Zeninjor Enwemeka, "Mass. High Court Says Black Men May Have Legitimate Reason to Flee Police," *WBUR News*, September 20, 2016, http://www.wbur.org/news/2016/09/20/mass-high-court-black-men-may-have-legitimate-reason-to-flee-police).

75. "Some do it because there are warrants for their arrest. Others because they possess drugs, are seeking a thrill, or are just plain scared. Sometimes people do it even when they have done nothing wrong" (John Eligon, "Running from Police Is the Norm, Some in Baltimore Say," *New York Times*, May 10, 2015, https://www.nytimes.com/2015/05/11/us/running-from-police-is-the-norm-some-in-baltimore-say.html?_r=0).

76. In her much-discussed sociological study *On the Run: Fugitive Life in an American City* (Chicago: University of Chicago Press, 2014), Alice Goffman writes, "On the one hand, young men are quite literally running from the police, who chase them on foot or in cars, through houses and over fences. They are also running from the information in the police database that designates them as arrestable on sight" (see beginning of chap. 2). In his review, "On America's Front Lines," in *the New York Review of Books*, October 9, 2014, Christopher Jencks presents educational discrimination against young black men as an effect of punitive policing on crime.

77. An alternative reading of the series of deadly shots in the back by the police could be ventured, following Adorno: "But if someone is shouted at to 'run' . . . the prisoner ordered by his escort to flee so that they have a pretext for murdering him, the archaic power makes itself heard that otherwise inaudibly guides our every step" (*Minima Moralia: Reflections on a Damaged Life*, trans. E. F. N. Jephcott [London: Verso, 2005], aphorism 102).

78. Ta-Nehisi Coates, *Between the World and Me* (New York: Spiegel and Grau, 2015), 24, and later (129): "That was the same summer that the killer of Trayvon Martin was acquitted, the summer I realized that I accepted that there is no velocity of escape."

79. Emmanuel Levinas, *On Escape*, intro. Jacques Rolland, trans. Bettina Bergo (Stanford, Calif.: Stanford University Press, 2003), 54.

80. Wai Chee Dimock, *Empire for Liberty: Melville and the Poetics of Individualism* (Princeton, N.J.: Princeton University Press, 1989), 7. Dimock refers in this passage to the already quoted line from Melville's "Hawthorne and His Mosses": "in this world of lies, Truth is forced to fly like a scared white doe in the woodlands."

81. Ibid., 78.

82. Claudia Rankine, *Citizen: An American Lyric* (Minneapolis, Minn.: Graywolf, 2014), 139.

From Lima to Attica: *Benito Cereno*, the Nixon Recordings, and the 1971 Prison Uprising

Paul Downes

> It is as if prison were an inevitable fact of life, like birth and death.
> —Angela Davis, *Are Prisons Obsolete?*

> Apropos: in what sense did Nixon pretend to be Nixon, President of the United States up to a certain date? Who will ever know this, in all rigor? He himself?
> —Jacques Derrida, *Limited Inc*

"Early on the eve of Laylat al-Qadr," writes Greg Grandin in *The Empire of Necessity*, "three hours before sunrise and five days after setting sail from Valparaiso on December 22 [1804], the West Africans rose up and took control of the *Tryal*."[1] This slave uprising would become the basis for Herman Melville's novella *Benito Cereno*, but only after it had first been represented in the *Narrative* of Amasa Delano, the American captain who stumbled upon the revolt and helped to ensure its collapse.[2] The events on the *Tryal*, that is to say, passed through at least two rounds of formal translation before most of us encountered them, and Greg Grandin's detailed return to the historical circumstances surrounding the story has, in a sense, only enriched our appreciation of Melville's subtle mediation. But the slave revolt was not merely waiting to be cited in these literary and historiographical adaptations. The uprising itself deployed an uncannily citational force; the Africans fought their enslavement (in part) by performing (as fiction or theater) the structures and rituals of their own exploitation. This African (and, in a proleptic sense, American) revolt also took the form of a media event—an exploitation of the volatility of iteration—that fascinated Melville and continues to absorb readers over 150 years later. The slave-trading Spaniard whom Babo manipulates from behind the scenes is traumatized not only by the force of black resistance, but by an encounter with the unstable citational structure of his personal and political identity. He becomes a puppet of himself, and his exposure to this possibility unravels him. His final mournful refrain, "the Negro,"[3] might be read to inscribe a correspondence between the shock of revolutionary egalitarianism (signified here by black resistance) and the epistemological disturbance announced by deconstructive models of mediated being.

Benito Cereno follows the lead of its African protagonists by augmenting its condemnation of slavery with a formal interest in aspects of perception and mediation. Melville's carefully calibrated third-person adaptation of Amasa Delano's first-person memoir highlights the self-difference that all autobiographical writing performs, and thereby exposes Delano, in a literary sense, to some of the same effects of self-undoing that Babo forces upon Benito Cereno. Delano's racialized investment in gradations of human value is thereby brought to the surface along with what Toni Morrison calls his "willful blindness."[4] Resistance to democratic egalitarianism, for Delano and Cereno, coincides with a fantasy of immunity with regard to the supplemented structure of the self and the sign.[5] When Cereno is made to act out his absolute authority over the slaves or when Delano's own phrases are transcribed into the free indirect discourse of Melville's narration, language itself—the iterability of the sign—appears to participate in the work of revolution. Power does not like to have to repeat itself. When Melville writes, as he does of Captain Vere in *Billy Budd*, that like "every serious mind of superior order occupying any active post of authority" Vere had "nothing of that literary taste which less heeds the thing conveyed than the vehicle,"[6] he seems to confirm this analysis. Vere pays little heed to the "vehicle" of communication because to do so would be to nurse the kind of mutinous (proto-deconstructive) inclinations that, on a British naval ship, threaten the prevailing order. As he tells his subordinate officers at the trial of Billy Budd, he and they are charged with a vehicular irresponsibility that functions just as long as it does not stop to see itself (or "recoil upon itself" in the manner of the doomed Claggart). Aboard the *Bellipotent*, Vere reminds the officers, they are not "actual men" but conduits of English power: "Would it be so much we ourselves that would condemn as it would be martial law operating through us? For that law and the rigor of it, we are not responsible."[7] If Billy is "a goldfinch popped into a cage,"[8] Vere and his officers are that cage, and their efficacy depends upon a determined refusal to reflect upon their formal role. Vere's refusal to contemplate the "vehicle" of literary and political communication coincides with a conviction with regard to "the thing conveyed" that, on a political level, equates with a conviction about the righteousness of the English social order. His logocentric preoccupation with the "thing conveyed," in other words, coincides with his resistance to "mutinous" and "anarchic" democratization. Justice has arrived (in England), and whatever formal system of inequality might be required to protect and convey that justice through history can be more or less ignored. The law operates "through" Vere and his officers, and insofar as their lives coincide with that mediation, they are urged not to look upon the vehicle that they have become. Babo's strategy, in *Benito Cereno*, is to force such reflection upon the Spanish colonial conduit of Euro-American capitalism. By breaking the spell between the "mediating" signifiers of power and the signified content of that power (white superiority), Babo and his fellow Africans protect their revolution and cripple Cereno.

To a certain extent, Melville's preoccupation with the relationship between forms of mediation and particular expressions of power and inequality becomes diluted by the passage of time. The historical specificity of *Benito Cereno* and the temporal distance that separates us from its events and its composition threaten to defuse some of its critical formal power. Melville's narrative dexterity, as we have noted, went a long way towards drawing nineteenth- and twentieth-century readers into the orbit of Delano's prejudice, but beginning with African American literary critics as early as 1937 and continuing in post-1960s studies of the novella, readers have had very little difficulty distinguishing their own politically "progressive" perspective from that of the "benevolent" New Englander.[9] *Benito Cereno* has produced a host of invaluable interpretations grounded in this change of perspectival allegiance, but the depth and sophistication of such historically informed criticism can have the paradoxical effect of reinforcing a perceptual confidence on the part of the reader that Melville's story originally strained to put in question. Historical contextualization is in some degree of tension with the critical immediacy effected by Melville's original formal achievement.

In order to activate the full conceptual and political force of *Benito Cereno*'s mediatory achievement, then, contemporary readers have to find some way to collapse the safe historical distance that has opened up between the present moment and the moment(s) of Melville's story (the Haitian Revolution of 1799, the revolt on the *Tryal* in 1801, the publication of the story in 1855). This ought not to be so difficult. "More than two centuries have passed since the events on Benito Cereno's ship took place," Toni Morrison writes, "but the deception of racial inferiority as an excuse for theft of resources and labor is worldwide and in important ways contemporary."[10] How might a contemporary rereading or adaptation of *Benito Cereno*, one that pays attention to the disturbing contemporaneity of its concerns, reactivate the story's formal and political power? One possible approach, as I hope to show, would be to draw on the work of the many activists and intellectuals who are currently fighting to expose the racialized violence perpetrated by the American prison-industrial complex; these activists have charted the steady expansion of the prison system as a decoy for a capitalist system every bit as desperate in its pursuit of economic and ideological power as Delano and his fellow fur-hunters were in their pursuit of dwindling seal populations in the early nineteenth century. In other words, if we were to look for a contemporary equivalent of the slave rebellion on the *San Dominick*, it might take the form of a prison uprising, and in pursuing this equivalence I want to consider an example from the earliest years of the racialized expansion of the prison system—the Attica uprising of 1971. Delano's "humanitarian" blindness, so relatively easy for us to see now, has to be seen again in the form of the contemporary difficulty we have seeing the prison as anything other than a container of some determined "thing"—namely, "criminals." "We have set forth demands," wrote the Attica prisoners in the statement they released after their takeover on September 9, "that will bring closer to reality the demise of these prisons, institutions that serve no useful purpose to the People of America but to those who would enslave and exploit the people of America."[11] To *see* the prison is to expose the illusion of its substantive *content* and to focus attention on the ideological, political, and economic work of its formal structure. But this requires us to supplement our easy condemnation of Amasa Delano's complicity with slavery with a contemporary commitment to ending the prison system as we know it. This commitment, exemplified by the work of Angela Davis, is inseparable from what it means to "read" *Benito Cereno* in the twenty-first century.[12] Adapting *Benito Cereno* for our time, however, also requires us to ignore certain borders between genres (political, literary, documentary) and to pursue hints and correlations that may not always coalesce with the elegance of a story by Melville or Morrison. "What might be required," writes Samuel Weber, "in order *not* to take the past for granted?"

> First and foremost, it might require the present to rediscover its own heterogeneity by becoming more sensitive to the way in which the past exists not merely as a derived form of the present, as a present which "is" no more, as a *past present*. The past might be approached not simply as a weak or deficient mode of the present, but rather as a dimension and function of that iterability which belongs as much to the future as to what we commonly think of as the present.[13]

To this end, then, I want to try to shuttle back and forth between the coast of South America in 1801 and upstate New York in 1971, between what the colonial Spanish court in Lima referred to as the "insurrection" of the enslaved Africans to what Hoover's FBI called the "mutinous" actions of the prisoners at Attica.[14] But I want to begin in Washington with one of the architects of what Michelle Alexander has so memorably called the "new Jim Crow": Richard Nixon.

On September 13, 1971, the White House recording devices captured a telephone conversation between President Nixon and Governor Nelson Rockefeller of New York: "I know you've had a hard day," says the president, "but I want you to know that I just back you to the hilt." Rockefeller might have had a hard day, but it had been a nightmare for the inmates of the Attica State Correctional Facility in upstate New York, whose unprecedented uprising had just been violently defeated. Constructed in the 1930s to be New York State's most secure prison, Attica was built to accommodate 1,600 inmates. On the eve of the uprising, it housed 2,243 inmates, 54 percent of whom were black, 9 percent Puerto Rican, and 37 percent white. There were no black correctional officers and only one Puerto Rican officer among the prison's 398 uniformed correctional staff.[15] The emphasis in the prison, as the official report on the uprising later put it, "was on confinement and security": "Despite brave talk about rehabilitation as a prime objective of detention, the shortage of trained personnel and the inadequacy of facilities made rehabilitation an impossible dream. In fact, it is not even clear that it was then, or is now, a real objective of the American prison system."[16]

In response to deteriorating conditions and the deep culture of racism at the prison, inmates began educating each other, and a group calling themselves the Attica Liberation Front produced a manifesto calling for a series of moderate reforms and expressing a commitment to nonviolence.[17] This draft set of demands was discovered during a surprise cell search in June 1971 and was promptly handed over to the New York State commissioner of prisons, Russell G. Oswald. Oswald, recognizing aspects of the demands issued at Folsom Prison in California under the leadership of the Black Panther Party, became convinced that "Black Muslims were involved."[18] Meanwhile, officials at Attica decided to "clamp down even harder" on the prison population, and, in response to rumors suggesting that organized prisoners intended to rise up on July 4, the administration kept the yards closed and under tight security throughout the day.[19] On July 7, Oswald replied to the authors of what came to be known as the July Manifesto, assuring them that he would "give careful consideration to [their] entire list," but, needless to say, little changed. In the aftermath of George Jackson's killing at San Quentin on August 21, tensions mounted, and on Thursday, September 9, 1,281 inmates, in possession of 43 hostages, took over control of the central square ("Times Square") of the prison, and for the next four days attempted to issue a series of demands and to engage in negotiations with the commissioner and with a select group of intermediaries. On September 13, New York State troopers, accompanied by corrections officers from Attica, dropped tear gas on the square and, over the course of six minutes, stormed the prison, fired over 4,500 rounds of ammunition, shot dead 29 inmates and 10 hostages, and injured at least 88.[20] "It really was a beautiful operation," said Governor Rockefeller into the ear of President Nixon and the microphone of his White House recording machines.[21]

On recently rediscovered presidential tapes from 1971, Nixon can be heard praising Rockefeller for refusing to grant amnesty to any of the inmates and for putting down the uprising so decisively.[22] "If you would have granted amnesty in this case," Nixon tells the governor, "you would have had prisons in an uproar all over this country ... You did the right thing." Rockefeller, here and throughout the conversation, is painfully obsequious. "Well, aren't you great, Mr. President," he replies. "Four days of negotiating," says Rockefeller, "everybody had a chance." In a second call, Rockefeller explains what was not initially clear, namely, that the hostages (all but one corrections officer, who later died of wounds suffered during the initial uprising) were killed not by the inmates, but by the state troopers. "We got a little problem . . . you can't have sharpshooters picking off the prisoners . . . at a distance . . . without having a few accidents . . . but that's life."[23] But Nixon is insistent. It was all good; it was all "worth it." And anyway, Nixon knows who is really at the center of all this:

> Nixon: "Tell me this, is this a . . . are these primarily blacks that you're dealing with?"
> Rockefeller: "Oh yes. The whole thing was led by the blacks."[24]

Nixon and his Republican allies came to power on the back of a pointedly racialized displacement of the nation's attention away from questions of political economy (the work of capitalist ideological consolidation) and onto the figure of the urban black criminal.[25] That figure protected American capitalism from its own contradictions and from the critical gaze of democratic expansion; and it propelled a new conservative political class into a position of power that it continues to occupy forty-five years later. Nixon knew exactly what he was doing because, from the 1968 presidential campaign on, he was one of the primary architects and beneficiaries of what came to be known as the "Southern Strategy." The pioneers of this strategy, as Cory Robin writes, "understood that after the rights revolutions of the sixties they could no longer make simple appeals to white racism. From now on they would have to speak in code, preferably one palatable to the new dispensation of color blindness."[26] As one of Nixon's closest advisors, the White House chief of staff H. R. Haldeman later recalled: "[Nixon] emphasized that you have to face the fact that the whole problem is really the blacks. The key is to devise a system that recognized this while not appearing to."[27] That system drew on the "dog-whistle" politics of "states' rights" and "law and order" in order to win over working-class white southerners and suburban northerners who might otherwise be in danger of recognizing the extent to which their interests clashed with the principles and practices of free-market capitalism.[28] Nixon's 1968 presidential campaign produced an advertisement that the candidate particularly liked: "it is time for an honest look at the problem of order in the United States," the ad quoted Nixon saying; "I pledge to you, we will have order in the United States." "[That] hits it right on the nose," said Nixon to his team; "it's all about those damn Negro-Puerto Rican groups out there."[29] Looking back on this strategy in 1981, the Republican strategist Lee Atwater spelled out its elements more clearly:

> You start out in 1954 by saying, "Nigger, nigger, nigger." By 1968 you can't say "nigger"—that hurts you. Backfires. So you say stuff

like forced busing, states' rights and all that stuff. You're getting so abstract now you're talking about cutting taxes, and all these things you're talking about are totally economic things and a by-product of them is blacks get hurt worse than whites. And subconsciously maybe that is part of it.[30]

Atwater's suggestion that racialized exploitation might have been a "by-product" of a certain Republican strategy performs its own act of deception by refusing to acknowledge the centrality of this violence to over 300 years of capitalist expansion. As Melville's story reminds us (particularly when supplemented by the work of the historian Greg Grandin), white European and American traders and merchants repeatedly sought enrichment (and emergency bailouts) from an international trade in, and deployment of, the stolen labor of Africans. Racism has not been a "by-product" of "totally economic things" in the West: the economy, we might be tempted to say, has been a by-product of racialized exploitation.[31] Race often comes into view, in other words, wherever and whenever capitalism's status as a vehicle of class enrichment (rather than as the mere carrier of "wealth" for all) risks exposure. Part of Melville's achievement in *Benito Cereno* lay in his ability to demonstrate the role that a liberal moral certainty played in this pernicious substitution of racial for economic exploitation: Delano was "lost in pity,"[32] but so was any modicum of his critical political perception. It's hard to know at what point it still makes sense to call this dynamic, as Atwater does, "subconscious."[33]

In the context of a prison system that has inherited the violence and racism of slavery (and that of the post-slavery regime of lynching), Delano's liberal preoccupation with philanthropy throughout his *Narrative* (and in Melville's retelling) has been replaced by a liberal faith in the objective reality of an ontologically simple criminality. The calcified figure of the criminal helped to ensure that the judicial system would take over where institutionalized slavery left off after 1865, and by 1970, the politically and economically motivated investment in "crime" as a force of nature was ripe for exploitation. "Although actual crime vastly exceeds that which is reported [?]," wrote the authors of the New York State report on the Attica uprising, "the amount of crime officially reported is depressing enough."[34] The report goes on to document the 175 percent increase in "crimes known to police" between 1960 and 1970 without ever stopping to consider the possibility that the widespread political preoccupation with this "depressing" phenomenon might have any relation to the expansion of black civil rights and black political consciousness. Instead, the language of the report works to reinforce the sense that the criminal is a species of being that has always been with us even if his numbers are increasing. The criminal, in 1970 (and still today), seems to be a direct descendent of that phantasmatic figure who occupied a crucial role in one of the founding documents of liberal political philosophy, John Locke's *Second Treatise of Government*:

> And thus it is that every Man in the State of Nature, has a power to kill a Murderer, both to deter others from doing the like Injury . . . and also to secure Men from the attempts of a Criminal, who having renounced Reason, the common Rule and Measure, God hath given to Mankind, hath by the unjust Violence and Slaughter he hath committed upon one, declared War against all Mankind, and therefore may be destroyed as a Lyon or a Tyger, one of those wild Savage Beasts, with whom Men can have no Society nor Security.[35]

On Melville's fictionalized slave ship, the good American, Amasa Delano, is lulled by "naked nature"—the sight, for example, of an African woman who sleeps like "a doe in the shade of a woodland rock" while nursing her infant "fawn."[36] But how far do we need to travel to get from this "philanthropic" screen-image to the figures conjured by white literary critics in the early days of Melville's academic recognition for whom Babo was, as Stanley Williams wrote in 1947, "just an animal, a mutinous baboon."[37] And these bestial phantasms return in our present era of carceral racism to ensure that we recognize the "thing" that prisons were made to contain. "WE are MEN. We are not beasts and do not intend to be driven or beaten as such," wrote the Attica prisoners in the preface to the list of demands drawn up on the first day of the uprising.[38] But doctors treating wounded prisoners in the aftermath of the uprising were confronted by guards who had every intention of treating them as such: "Why do it?" one doctor recalls being asked as he treated a prisoner; "They're not people, they're animals."[39] Surviving prisoners at Attica were told to strip naked and then forced first to crawl "snakelike" through the mud of the open yard before passing through a gauntlet of guards on the way back to their cells. As Tom Wicker describes the scene in *A Time to Die*, numerous corrections officers stationed themselves on either side of the tunnel leading to A-block:

> They all had clubs, banging them on brick walls and concrete floors and steel bars. As each inmate ran or stumbled by, with his hands behind his head, the corrections officers, public employees of the state of New York, agents of law enforcement, hit him with their clubs. If he fell, they took turns hitting him while he was down. Shouts of "Nigger" and "motherfucker" rang through the echoing corridor.[40]

The horrific aftermath of the police assault on Attica recalls the scene on the *Tryal* after Delano's men and the surviving Spaniards had retaken their ship. The American captain waited until the next morning to go on deck, but what he found, in addition to the remains of Babo and six other West Africans, were the tortured bodies of many others, chained to the deck, disemboweled or with the skin shaved off their backs and thighs. "Their wounds," Melville wrote (once again drawing on Delano's *Narrative*), were "mostly inflicted by the long-edged sealing spears—resembling those shaven ones of the English at Preston Pans, made by the poled scythes of the Highlanders."[41] But Delano would also have recognized something particular in the gauntlet that the Attica prisoners were made to run, because it resembles the manner in which he and his men clubbed seals to death on the islands of the South Pacific. "The method practiced to take them," Delano explained, "was to . . . make a lane of men, two abreast, forming three or four couples, and then drive the seal through this lane; each man furnished with a club, between five and six feet long; and as they passed, he knocked down such of them as he chose; which are commonly the half grown, or what are called young seals."[42] Indeed, Delano himself (as imagined by Melville) had been subjected to the hint of such violence during his time on the Spanish ship. Invited to pass between two of the African "hatchet polishers" as he follows Cereno to the poop deck, Delano hesitates: "Gingerly enough stepped good Captain Delano between them, and in the instant of leaving them behind, like one running the gauntlet, he felt an apprehensive twitch in the calves of his leg."[43]

As Melville's repeated references to the "good" Captain Delano ought to remind us, the liberal Lockean invention and demonization of the "criminal" as a "beast" from whom "Mankind" must be protected comes into ideological focus alongside the liberal humanitarian "creature" of Delano's sympathetic gaze. Both discourses of alienation work to contain or quarantine a fundamental commonality that threatens the inegalitarian distribution of power and wealth. This, too, is why, as Angela Davis has noted, the discourse of prison "reform," despite all the ways in which it might continue to describe necessary work, has actually accompanied the rise of the prison system in its worst forms from the beginning of the modern penal system. "Incarceration within a penitentiary," she reminds us, "was assumed to be humane—at least far more humane than the capital and corporal punishment inherited from England and other European countries."[44] And the continued need for real improvements in the treatment of and conditions suffered by the imprisoned is increasingly vulnerable to exploitation by those invested in maintaining the prison system per se (including all those with a direct monetary investment in the business of incarceration).[45] "Debates about strategies of decarceration, which should be the focal point of our conversations on the prison crisis," writes Davis, "tend to be marginalized when reform takes the center stage."[46] Locke's monstrous criminal who must be isolated from "mankind" (and who is repeatedly figured as nonwhite in the American tradition) needs to be seen as the counterpart of the liberal prison reformer's idealized subject of "penitential" rehabilitation in more or less solitary confinement. Substituting the "humane" discipline of social isolation for the spectacularly public punishment of another era, the designers of the modern prison system also participated in the atrophying of social and egalitarian belonging that has consistently characterized liberal capitalist ideology. The modern prison, as Angela Davis has noted, emerged as the form of punishment most suited to the individualized, rights-bearing subject of the liberal imaginary. Locke's distinction between "Mankind" and those "Savage beasts" whom all "men" have a right to kill announced, in advance, a fantastic rupture in the very category of the human that racialized subjects would help to effect and conceal.[47]

As an obscenely material—indeed, *concrete* bearer of a profoundly antisocial political philosophy, the prison operates for us in something like the way that the slave ship functioned for Amasa Delano as he boarded it in the waters off the coast of Chile in 1801: both the prison and the ship, "the one by its walls and blinds, the other by its high bulwarks like ramparts, hoard from view their interiors till the last moment."[48] But the ship, Melville continues, has this added peculiarity: "that the living spectacle it contains, upon its sudden and complete disclosure, has, in contrast with the blank ocean which zones it, something of the effect of enchantment. The ship seems unreal; these strange costumes, gestures, and faces, but a shadowy tableau just emerged from the deep, which directly must receive back what it gave."[49] In the contemporary United States, it is the "living spectacle" of the prison population that provokes a sense of enchantment; but it is those of us who tend to remain on the outside, who, like Delano, have been enchanted by the steady and systematic emergence of a shadowy and horrific tableau: "When I first became involved in antiprison activism during the late 1960s," writes Angela Davis in *Are Prisons Obsolete?* "I was astounded to learn that there were close to two hundred thousand people in prison. Had anyone told me that in three decades ten times as many people would be locked away in cages, I would have been absolutely incredulous."[50] "Short of major wars," Elliott Currie writes, "mass incarceration has been the most thoroughly implemented governmental social program of our time."[51] And we could go on, piling up the evidence of the enchantment that has overcome us:

> As of June 2001, there were nearly 20,000 more black men in the Illinois state prison system than enrolled in the state's public universities . . . The young men who go to prison rather than college face a lifetime of closed doors, discrimination, and ostracism. Their plight is not what we hear about on the evening news, however. Sadly, like the racial caste systems that preceded it, the system of mass incarceration now seems normal and natural to most, a regrettable necessity.[52]

Those of us who are fortunate enough to proceed as if we were not likely to end up behind bars are all contemporary Amasa Delanos, walking the honeycombed deck of a prison-industrial complex that can barely conceal the violence it effects and the resistance it must provoke. To read Melville's novella today is to work to re-create this difficult identification. It should not be too easy to see ourselves seeing what the good American fails to perceive.

From Lima to Attica

Given that he was instrumental in the initiation of the systematic escalation of black incarceration, it is all the more peculiar—if not nauseating—to listen, once again, to Richard Nixon asking Governor Nelson Rockefeller, in the hours after the Attica uprising, who was "responsible":

> Nixon: "Tell me this, is this a . . . are these primarily blacks that you're dealing with?"
> Rockefeller: "Oh yes. The whole thing was led by the blacks."
> Nixon: "I'll be darned! And all the prisoners that were killed were blacks or were there any whites?"
> Rockefeller: "Er, I haven't got that report but I would say, just offhand, yes."[53]

"I'll be darned!" says Nixon, and we know he would be; but at this precise moment, in the context of this conversation, it's not immediately apparent how we should read that exclamation. Surely he has anticipated Rockefeller's answer? He just wants to hear the governor say it: "Oh yes. The whole thing was led by the blacks." The intimacy of this private conversation between power and wealth (Rockefeller was also one of the richest men in the world) is charged and sealed by the invocation of race: Nixon hesitates for a second before saying what he's been dying to say: "is this a . . . are these primarily blacks that you're dealing with?" We might even wonder if something of the revolutionary power of the prison uprising fills Nixon with a kind of sublime fear or awe: "I'll be darned!" he says, but is it presidential power or black power that has Nixon anticipating his own death?

> "You are saved," cried Captain Delano, more and more astonished and pained; "you are saved; what has cast such a shadow upon you?"
> "The negro."
> There was silence, while the moody man sat, slowly and unconsciously gathering his mantle about him, as if it were a pall.[54]

Nixon's recording machine captures what was perhaps only barely concealed from the public: the racism—and the racialized terror—haunting the Oval Office and the almost immediate association of revolutionary violence in America with black, African American (and Puerto Rican) violence. In secret, but while being recorded, the American president whispers to the governor about race war and the violence of rebelling black men. At this precise moment, Nixon's self-undoing via the *pharmakon* of the recording machine crosses paths with the violence of black revolution in a moment that perhaps only a Herman Melville could have imagined. "The negro!" says a traumatized Benito Cereno, as he fades out of history and out of Melville's novella. "I'll be darned," says Richard Nixon, "I'll be darned."[55]

If there is a faint intimation of Benito Cereno to be heard in Nixon's sinister preoccupation with "the blacks," there is perhaps an equally shadowy echo of Amasa Delano in Governor Nelson Rockefeller. The *Official Report of the New York State Special Commission on Attica* contains the transcript of an interview with Rockefeller conducted as part of the commission's work. "I'm just curious," asks Amos Henix, "is there anything which you could see that took place on those days [at Attica] if you had it to do again, you would have done differently?"

> Governor Rockefeller: . . . if I could go back 14 years instead of six months . . . I would have to say to you that one of the things I regret most is my own lack of perception of the tremendous need which existed in this area, which our society—I'm not blaming anything on society—I say this is a big area that I did not fully understand and perceive and that had I done then 12 years ago, 14 years ago, what I was doing now, I'm sure this wouldn't have happened.[56]

Rockefeller continues to be remembered in some circles as a "moderate" Republican, a decent, well-intentioned American who prided himself on his family's generosity towards black causes. "Spelman College," as Clarence Jones recalls, "was funded by the family and christened with Nelson's mother's maiden name," and the Rockefellers gave money to bail Martin Luther King and hundreds of others out of the Birmingham city jail in the spring of 1963.[57] But, like Delano, he was also ambitious and quite willing to sacrifice any goodwill he felt towards African Americans in his desire for higher recognition. Delano, as we know, pursued gratitude and a financial reward from the king of Spain after helping to deliver the West Africans over to slavery and execution, and Rockefeller, with one eye on the White House himself, betrays a fawning desire in the taped conversations to please Nixon and to confirm his racist assumptions. "Oh yes! The whole thing was led by the blacks." Unlike Melville's Delano, however, the governor seems to have at least some slight sense of his own limitations: "I would have to say to you that one of the things I regret most is my own lack of perception of the tremendous need which existed in this area," he tells the commission. And he goes on to suggest that reform efforts were underway: "Primarily what we are now working on, namely the rebuilding of prisons, [is] a whole different approach to the concept of prisons as such, rehabilitation instead of custodial care, both physical and in terms of program." But two years later, Rockefeller had helped to gut the only independent ombudsman organization for New York prisons and, as Tom Wicker reported in 1973, "little had improved" in Attica or throughout the prison system.[58] By 1974, Vice President Nelson Rockefeller had followed his leader into the executive branch and the American carceral nightmare rolled on. As of 2013, the United States had 4.4 percent of the world's population and 22 percent of its incarcerated human beings.[59]

One of the striking things about the list of demands issued as "15 Practical Proposals" by the inmates who rose up at Attica in 1971 is how many of them focus on aspects of pedagogical or political communication:

2. Allow all New York State prisoners to be politically active, without intimidation or reprisals.
3. Give us true religious freedom.
4. End all censorship of newspapers, magazines, letters, and other publications coming from the publisher.
5. Allow all inmates, at their own expense, to communicate with anyone they please.
8. Institute realistic rehabilitation programs for all inmates according to their offense and personal needs.
9. Educate all correctional officers to the needs of the inmates, i.e., understanding rather than punishment.
11. Modernize the inmate education system.
13. Have an institutional delegation comprised of one inmate from each company authorized to speak to the institution administration concerning grievances (QUARTERLY).[60]

This emphasis on communication had been a crucial component of the Attica Liberation Front (ALF) from the start. The five founders of the ALF were Frank Lott, Donald Noble, Carl Jones-EL, Herbert X. Blyden, and Peter Butler; and as Carl Jones-EL later explained, the ALF was founded "to try to bring about some change in the conditions of Attica." Their work began with a course of education: "We started teaching political ideology to ourselves. We read Marx, Lenin, Trotsky, Malcolm X, du Bois, Frederick Douglass and a lot of others."[61] In a galvanizing speech to the inmates, witnessed by Tom Wicker, Brother Flip (Charles Horatio Crowley) reminded everyone that the men were not "advocating violence": "we want to be treated as human beings," he said, "we are advocating communications and understanding."[62]

The public, declaratory manner in which the Attica inmates proceeded to collectively draft and share their demands for "communication and understanding" contrasts strikingly with President Nixon's peculiar obsession with secret communication.[63] If his presidency deserves to be remembered for its systematic escalation and exploitation of populist racism, it has also come to be associated with a new regime of paranoia and concealment centered around the technology of voice recording. And this feature of his presidency began long before the illegal wiretapping of the Democratic National Committee's headquarters in the Watergate complex in 1972. The idea of keeping a scrupulous, word-by-word record of presidential interactions began with the Nixon administration in January 1969 when a program called "Memos for the President's File" was initiated ("someone sat in on every meeting, even meetings with his own staff people . . . in there taking notes").[64] But this program soon became more sophisticated. Between February 16, 1971, and July 12, 1973, President Nixon secretly recorded all his meetings and conversations in the White House, the Old Executive Office Building, and the presidential retreat at Camp David, Maryland.[65] Multiple microphones were installed in an attempt to capture every official conversation that took place, in person or on the phone, and the system was designed to operate without Nixon himself having to do anything to start or stop the recording. "Haldeman and Butterfield decided that the best solution was to install a voice-activated recording system [because] they felt that Nixon would forget to turn a manually controlled system on and off." The president, they suspected, was "far too inept with machinery ever to make a success of a switch system.'"[66] Whenever Nixon entered one of the designated recording areas, the electronic device he wore to let the Secret Service know his location at all times would signal to the devices to go into record/pause mode. A voice-operated relay then turned the recorders on as soon as the microphones picked up any sound.[67] Nixon's microphones eventually yielded over 3,700 hours of recorded conversation.[68]

Nixon may have been "inept with machinery," but he knew something about power. He agreed to the installation of the recording devices despite the fact that he "abhorred the idea of taping" his conversations and meetings.[69] Something about this perpetual doubling must have felt, to Nixon, like a violation, a vulnerability, or even an embarrassment. He was notorious for preferring to conduct consequential meetings with no aides or secretaries present, and he referred to presidential note-takers as "scribbling intruders" who inhibited the important conversations he was trying to conduct.[70] The presence of any kind of recording device, human or otherwise, threw Nixon off, and so Haldeman and Butterfield constructed a system so automatic that it could operate without having to remind Nixon of its spectral presence. Even in the one location, the Cabinet Room, where an on/off switch had to be installed, Nixon did not activate the system himself; "rather, he had Butterfield activate the system using the switch on his desk."[71] In other words, Nixon recognized the political value of having an exact record of all his conversations (and he was, from the start, acutely aware of their prospective value for producing his presidential memoirs), but he did not want to have to be aware of the recording as it was taking place. Asked if he thought that Nixon ever forgot he was being recorded, Butterfield recalled, in 2003: "Absolutely. Yes. Yeah. We, we marveled at his ability to, uh, seemingly be oblivious to the tapes. I mean, even I was sitting there uncomfortably sometimes saying, 'He's not really going to say this, is he?'"[72] Years later, Butterfield discussed the now-public tapes and admitted that "it gives me a pain in the pit of my stomach" to recall how Nixon "was so sure" the tapes would never be revealed. On July 30, 1974, Nixon complied with a unanimous Supreme Court order to release the tapes to the special prosecutor. The claims of executive privilege over the recordings, the court declared, were void. Has any president ever been so undone by his own recordings and his own obsession with recording others?

From a literary perspective, we might say that Nixon's relationship to his recording devices shares something with any author's relationship to the unmasterable language upon which they must depend to tell their stories or relate their experiences. The autobiographer, in particular, might want to believe that he or she is using language not to invent a self or expose that self to deconstructive undoing, but to archive a life for posterity. The historical Captain Amasa Delano certainly cannot have anticipated all the ways in which his 1817 narrative of *Voyages and Travels in the Northern and Southern Hemispheres* (written as part of one more desperate attempt to recoup financial losses) would morph into, and be received as, a multilayered record of liberal American racism and a source of insight into the complexities of humanitarian blindness and disavowal.[73] The history of Nixon's tapes, and his relationship to them, hyperbolize a more general ambivalence with regard to our irreducibly mediated identity even as they also display the intensity of power's determination to command the ways and means of signification. Nixon's vexed relationship to the recording of his own conversations recalls something of power's more general ambivalence with regard to what Derrida calls (following Plato's account in the *Phaedrus*) the "poisoned present" of writing.[74] Recording technology holds out a promise and a threat to the president: he might be empowered, as a politician and as a memoirist, by possession of the technology's *super-memory*; but Nixon also seems to have a premonition about the threat concealed in any event of transcription. The recording devices promise to keep the past for the future according to a fantasy of temporal mastery that also collapses both into a permanent present: writing as I live, doubling every word, I also inscribe the future of my remembering into the present. It is a sovereign fantasy that Nixon detects in the recording technology, a sovereign command not just of time's endless deferrals, but of the *différance* that undoes any present: the living note-takers that Nixon initially used not only inhibited the parties to the conversation (thereby helping to compose what they also only recorded), but they often muddied their notes with their own misinterpretations of the conversations they had witnessed: "the quality of prose," Nixon himself wrote in his *Memoirs*, "varied as much as the quality of perception."[75] The voice-activated, invisible, and highly secretive recording machines materialized a fantasy of idealized writing—a writing uncontaminated by the living, and even by the material. Hence, the important proviso that neither Nixon nor his interlocutors be aware of the presence of the machines. The very idea of the reproducibility of his conversations might, for Nixon, have ruined those conversations in advance. Nixon (like all of us?) dreamed of repeating the unrepeatable; of remembering without the technical supplement of memory: "what Plato dreams of," Derrida writes, "is a memory with no sign. That is, with no supplement. A *mneme* with no *hypomnesis*, no *pharmakon*."[76]

Nixon's "inept" relationship to machinery thus recalls the king who does not want to learn to write ("God the King does not know how to write, but that ignorance or incapacity only testifies to his sovereign independence. He has no need to write. He speaks, he says, he dictates, and his word suffices").[77]

Nixon's investment in a hyperbolically secret mode of communications technology (he even wants to keep it secret from himself!) betrays another form of the desire to appropriate socially generated value for private accumulation. The recording device's promise of temporal, political, and personal mastery over the irreducibly social and historical vagaries of language mirrors capital's promise to turn socially generated value into privately appropriated wealth. Similarly, Nixon's desire not to see the recording technology at work figures capital's investment in the social, political, and economic invisibility of a class of people who can generate surplus value without intruding their own desires, their own material difference upon the scene of private accumulation. But there is no recording without revolution, and that is why the recorder, human or not, spoils power's view. Babo also turns Cereno into the repeating machine he always was, and Delano cannot tell the difference. And then again, like the decapitated head of Babo, gazing across the square in Lima, out of his head of subtlety, and looking through the narrative eyes of Melville's *Benito Cereno*, Nixon's recording machines seem always to have been preparing to speak against him and (as with Cereno on the San Dominick) damn him in his own voice, via a repetition that cannot even be said to belong to the machine, or the decapitated head, that nevertheless testifies and condemns.[78]

"Looking back," said Hillary Clinton on the campaign trail in 2016, "I shouldn't have used those words, and I wouldn't use them today."[79] She was referring to her reference, twenty years earlier, to a new kind of juvenile criminal: "the kinds of kids that are called 'super-predators.' No conscience, no empathy. We can talk about how they ended up that way but first we have to bring them to heel."[80] Clinton used those words while speaking in support of the Violent Crime Control and Law Enforcement Act of 1994. The act provided for 100,000 new police officers, expanded the federal death penalty, authorized "adult prosecution of those 13 and older charged with certain serious violent crimes," introduced "mandatory life imprisonment without possibility of parole for Federal offenders with three or more convictions for serious felonies or drug trafficking crimes," and provided $9.7 billion in funding for prisons.[81] The bill was originally written by Senator Joe Biden of Delaware and was signed into law by President Bill Clinton on September 13, 1994. As James Forman Jr. has so effectively explained, the approach to crime that reached something of an apogee in the 1994 act emerged out of a complex set of historical circumstances, including the desperate desire on the part of African American urban politicians and ministers to protect their constituencies from a massively disproportionate vulnerability to violence, theft, and inadequate policing.[82] But what Forman and Black Lives Matter and so many others have also tried to underscore is the systematic and overwhelming way in which the ontologizing of the criminal has performed the work of racial exclusion, subordination, and exploitation that was once carried out by institutionalized slavery and Jim Crow.[83] Melville's American, Amasa Delano, was "lost in pity" upon seeing the inhabitants of the plague-stricken slave ship off the coast of Chile, but he was also entranced by a racially encoded tendency to view the Africans he encountered as one or another kind of innocent animal (a Newfoundland dog, a doe and her fawns, etc.).[84] In response to the gradual realization of black American civil rights in the second half of the twentieth century, liberal racism began to mesmerize us with another kind of beast (a "superpredator"; a kid with "no conscience, no empathy"). We may now be prepared to understand how Delano's humanitarian idealism coincided, in 1805, with his racism and his economic self-interest, but we still need to come to terms with the ways in which an uncritical ontologization of "the criminal" feeds and is driven by racist and capitalist imperatives. For those of us for whom this work might not come easily, it means learning to see ourselves seeing "the criminal." This would be to try occupying an out-of-joint perspective (something Melville was peculiarly adept at manipulating) such that we might, for example, see ourselves seeing from the perspective of the incarcerated and criminalized (and not just from the perspective of the "nonviolent criminal," as James Forman Jr. so adroitly reminds us).[85] Critical political reading and literary reading converge here at the sight of an exposure to originary mediation that promises a democratic undoing of persistent discrimination.

The administration of prisons in America has always depended upon exploiting the tension between racially distinct groups, and this is why the administration at Attica in the summer of 1971 became particularly nervous when factions within the prison gave way to new forms of solidarity.[86] "I can't tell you what a change has come over t[he] brothers in Attica," wrote inmate No. 26124 in August 1971 to a former inmate:

> So much more awareness & growing, consciousness of themselves as potential revolutionaries, reading, questioning, rapping all t time. Still bigotry & racism, black, white & brown, but one can feel it beginning to crumble in t knowledge so many are gaining that we must build solidarity against our common oppressor—t system of exploitation of each other & alienation from each other.[87]

Inmate 26124 was born Sam Grossman in the Bronx in 1935, but his radical opposition to the Vietnam War and to the inequality and poverty that accompanied capitalist expansion prompted him to engage in a series of (Weather Underground) bombings at banks and federal military offices in downtown Manhattan in the late 1960s.[88] His arrest in 1970 led to a short spell in the Tombs where, according to John Cohen, he became involved in black revolutionary politics and more aware of his own racism.[89] By then he had also long ago abandoned his birth name and had taken on the name of his favorite writer. It was as Sam Melville that he was transferred to Attica in early 1971, where he became known as "Mad Bomber Melville" and where, on September 13, he was shot to death by New York State troopers who claimed, falsely, that he had charged towards them holding four Molotov cocktails.[90] According to John Cohen, Melville was instrumental in the effort to bridge the divide between white radicals and black radicals in Attica. He was one of the few white prisoners to develop a close relationship with members of both the Black Panthers and the Young Lords. He was involved in the drafting of the first list of demands and strenuously advocated for presenting them collectively, not divided by race.[91] The Attica Liberation Front that formed in June 1971 was a multiracial coalition, and Sam was the head of the white faction of A-block.[92] There is some evidence to believe that the authorities thought of Melville as one of the prime instigators of the uprising and singled him out for execution.

Sam Melville's nominal tribute to the author of *Benito Cereno* might stand in for a largely undocumented reappropriation of Herman Melville in certain underground circles in the 1960s. Greg Grandin has recently reminded us that "in the wake of the civil-rights movement of the 1950s and the black power protests of the 1960s, African American writers and activists started to celebrate Babo as an 'underground hero' and to read *Benito Cereno* as subversive, seeming to take the side of the whites while skewering their idiocy."[93] As students of Sterling Brown, Grandin continues, such diversely influential African American writers and activists as Toni Morrison, Stokely Carmichael, Ossie Davis, and Amiri Baraka may well have been introduced to another version of *Benito Cereno*. What this also means is that Sterling Brown and his students read Melville's story again for the first time.[94]

There were 2,200 prisoner reports of abuse at Attica between 2010 and 2014. In 2014, three guards pled guilty to a horrifically violent attack on inmate George Williams and were convicted of misconduct. They left their jobs but retained their pensions. This was the first time a prison guard had ever pled guilty to, and been convicted of, a violent act against a prisoner at Attica.[95] "I mean, it's just—it's such a gruesome story," *New York Times* journalist Tom Robbins told an interviewer for *Democracy Now*. "And yet, what really struck me in the time that I spent in Attica getting this story was that it's not surprising to the inmates there. They said it happens all the time." "But you know," added former Attica inmate Antonio Yarbough, "you can only be scared for a certain amount of time before the pipes burst." He continued: "And what I thought was going to happen, was that a riot is going to come, and this one is going to be much worse than the last one, because you can only take so much, when you think no one on the outside actually gives a damn about what's going on."[96]

Notes

1. Greg Grandin, *The Empire of Necessity: Slavery, Freedom, and Deception in the New World* (New York: Metropolitan Books and Henry Holt, 2014), 173.

2. Herman Melville's *Benito Cereno* is a fictional adaptation of chapter 18 of Amasa Delano's *Narrative of Voyages and Travels in the Northern and Southern Hemispheres* (Boston: E.G. House, 1817). Delano's *Narrative* also contains the court transcripts from the trial of the Africans that took place in Spanish colonial Lima shortly after the uprising was put down. All further references to Melville's novella refer to the Northwestern-Newberry edition of *Benito Cereno* in *The Piazza Tales and Other Prose Pieces, 1839–1860*, ed. Harrison Hayford et al. (Evanston, Ill: Northwestern University Press, 1987), 47–117.

3. Melville, *Benito Cereno*, 257.

4. Toni Morrison, "Melville and the Language of Denial," *The Nation*, January 7, 2014.

5. The correlation of an antiracism with the deconstruction of logocentric models of writing can perhaps be approached via Derrida's personification of writing in *Dissemination*: "If writing, according to the king and under the sun, produces the opposite effect from what is expected, if the *pharmakon* is pernicious, it is because, like the one in the *Timaeus*, it doesn't come from around here. It comes from afar, it is external or alien: to the living, which is the right-here of the inside, to *logos* as the *zoon* it claims to assist or relieve." Jacques Derrida, *Dissemination*, trans. Barbara Johnson (Chicago: University of Chicago Press, 1981), 104.

6. Herman Melville, *Billy Budd, Sailor*, in *Billy Budd and Other Stories* (New York: Penguin, 1986), 287–385, at 311.

7. Ibid., 362.

8. Ibid., 292.

9. Grandin points out that Sterling Brown, in his 1937 book *The Negro in American Fiction* (repr. New York: Arno, 1969), broke with the tendency to bestialize Babo and his comrades: "Brown, a professor of literature at Howard, himself the son of a slave who trained a generation of writers, poets, activists, and actors . . . wrote that he wasn't troubled by the portrayal of the West Africans as 'bloodthirsty and cruel.' They weren't villains, Brown wrote, much less incantatory exclamations of cosmic evil. They were human men and they 'revolt as mankind has always revolted'" (Grandin, *Empire of Necessity*, 92).

10. Morrison, "Melville and the Language of Denial."

11. Like the Africans on the *Tryal*, the inmates who took part in the Attica uprising at first sought "speedy and safe transportation out of confinement to a non-imperialistic country." See the September 9 "Declaration to the People of America" as reproduced in Mariame Kaba's "Attica Prison Uprising 101: A Short Primer," with Lewis Wallace (September 2011), https://niastories.files.wordpress.com/2011/08/attica_primerfinal.pdf.

12. I have been particularly influenced in this approach by Angela Davis's *Are Prisons Obsolete?* (New York: Seven Stories, 2003) and Michelle Alexander's *The New Jim Crow: Mass Incarceration in the Age of Colorblindness* (New York: New, 2010). But there is a large and growing bibliography of critical works on the expansion of the prison system in America and the rise of a racialized prison-industrial complex. See, among others, Mumia Abu-Jamal's *Live from Death*

Row (New York: Perennial, 2002); Robert Perkinson, *Texas Tough: The Rise of America's Prison Empire* (New York: Metropolitan, 2009); and Elliott Currie, *Crime and Punishment in America* (New York: Picador, 2013).

13. Samuel Weber, *Mass Mediauras: Form, Technics, Media* (Stanford, Calif.: Stanford University Press, 1996), 148.

14. FBI Domestic Intelligence Division, "Informative Note, September 10, 1971," quoted in Heather Ann Thompson's indispensable *Blood in the Water: The Attica Prison Uprising of 1971 and Its Legacy* (New York: Pantheon, 2016), 82.

15. Chairman Robert B. McKay, *Attica: The Official Report of the New York State Special Commission on Attica* (New York: Bantam, 1972), 24, 28.

16. Ibid., xiv–xv.

17. Ibid., 107. See the comprehensive list of demands made in the July 2, 1971, manifesto in Kaba, "A Short Primer." See also Thompson's account of the protests and demands made by prisoners at the Auburn Correctional Facility in November 1970 in *Blood in the Water*, 22–23. In the same book, Thompson explains the evolution of the Attica prisoners' demands between July and September 1971 (31–32, 74–79).

18. Qtd. in Thompson, *Blood in the Water*, 32. "Probably not all of Aranda's captives were Muslim," writes Grandin. "But their extreme experience might have allowed those among them, like Babo and Mori, who could make prophetic sense of their journey, who could use the moon and the stars not just to explain their movements but to promise deliverance from their sufferings, to rise as leaders" (*Empire of Necessity*, 172).

19. See Thompson, *Blood in the Water*, 33; and Tom Wicker, *A Time to Die* (New York: Quadrangle and New York Times Book Co., 1975), 6.

20. Kathleen E. Slade, "Attica State Correctional Facility: The Causes and Fallout of the Riot of 1971," *The Exposition* 1, no. 1 (2012), http://digitalcommons.buffalostate.edu/exposition/vol1/iss1/3. Thompson notes the incredible extent of the federal preoccupation with Attica. Her painstaking research among previously unaccessed or deliberately concealed files reveals the expansive intelligence-gathering efforts of the FBI with regard to the Attica rebels and their sympathizers throughout the country. "Whatever intelligence the FBI gathered, credible or not," she writes, "was then relayed to authorities at the highest levels of the United States government, including President Richard Nixon, Vice President Spiro Agnew, and U.S. Attorney General John Mitchell, as well as the Defense Intelligence Agency, the Department of the Army, the Department of the Air Force, the Naval Investigative Service, the Secret Service, and the National Security Agency" (Thompson, *Blood in the Water*, 81).

21. The final death toll from the Attica uprising was 43: 9 hostages and 26 inmates were killed by gunfire on September 13; 1 hostage and 3 inmates died later of gunshot wounds; 1 corrections officer died of injuries during the initial uprising and 3 inmates' deaths could not be definitively dated. No hostages were killed by the prisoners, nor was there any evidence of mutilation despite horrific reports to the contrary. Officers attacking the prison had come to believe, with telling ease, the lie that inmates had castrated one of the hostages (Wicker, *A Time to Die*, 291). The relatives of one corrections officer were told that he had died of a slash to the throat. But when they viewed the body they found only a

bullet wound, a bullet that, in the words of one relative, "had the name Rockefeller on it" (ibid., 301).

22. The Miller Center at the University of Virginia has a collection of the recordings, along with many other taped conversations between Nixon and others: https://millercenter.org/president/nixon. See also the holdings of the recordings at https://archive.org/details/AtticaUprisingTheRockefeller-nixonTapes. Theresa Lynch, an adjunct history professor at the University of New Hampshire at Manchester, found the tapes in the National Archives in 2004 and wrote about them in her dissertation, "Attica: A Monstrous Credibility Gap" (Ph.D. diss., University of New Hampshire, 2006), before sharing them with Scott Christianson in 2011, who then made them available to the *New York Times* (Sam Roberts, "Rockefeller on the Attica Raid, from Boastful to Subdued," *New York Times*, September 12, 2011, https://www.nytimes.com/2011/09/13/nyregion/rockefeller-initially-boasted-to-nixon-about-attica-raid.html?pagewanted=all).

23. In fact, as later autopsies and reports explained, the inmates who held knives at the throats of their hostages did not use those knives to kill the officers, even after the troops started shooting. No hostages were killed by inmates, despite initial reports to the contrary. All were killed by bullets from the rifles of state troopers. Wicker concludes his book by returning to what he calls "one essential contradiction": "All the state officials, all the observers—so far as he knew—had believed explicitly that the inmates would kill the hostages if D-yard was attacked. But the inmates *had not done it* . . . In the long run, the power of the state had not believed it possible that the men of D-yard could behave with decency and humanity. But . . . many of these despised inmates finally had not believed that the state . . . would shoot them down. The hard truth was that the Attica brothers had more faith in the state than the state had in them. Both had been wrong" (Wicker, *A Time to Die*, 309). "'We did it [shot at the prisoners],' said Rockefeller to Nixon, 'only when they were in the process of murdering the guards or when they were attacking our people.' 'I have great admiration for . . . that operation' says Nixon, 'Well, that's wonderful of you,' replies Rockefeller; 'We're not going to have any . . . we just . . . not tolerate this kind of anarchy.'"

24. "Attica Uprising: The Rockefeller-Nixon Tapes," Internet Archive, https://archive.org/details/AtticaUprisingTheRockefeller-nixonTapes.

25. The specter of the black criminal began to expand in the early 1960s, fueled, as Eddie S. Glaude Jr. explains, by would-be Republican presidents like Barry Goldwater and Southern segregationists like Strom Thurmond: "Senator Strom Thurmond suggested that calls for integration would result in 'a wave of terror, crime, and juvenile delinquency'" (Glaude, *Democracy in Black: How Race Still Enslaves the American Soul* [New York: Crown, 2016], 77). Thompson suggests that the politicization of urban crime really took off under the Johnson regime. In 1965 Johnson created the Office of Law Enforcement Assistance (OLEA), "not only granting a wholly new level of funding to law enforcement and prisons, but also creating the bureaucracy necessary to wage a historically unprecedented War on Crime" (*Blood in the Water*, 18–19). "In 1954, the year of Brown v. Board of Education," writes James Forman Jr., "about one-third of the nation's prisoners were black. By 1994 . . . the number was approaching 50 per cent" (*Locking Up Our Own: Crime and Punishment in Black America* [New York: Farrar, Straus

and Giroux, 2017], 8). "Crime has polarized us," Forman concludes, "far more effectively than Jim Crow ever did" (ibid., 48).

26. Corey Robin, *The Reactionary Mind: Conservatism from Edmund Burke to Sarah Palin* (Oxford: Oxford University Press, 2011), 50.

27. Haldeman's remarks are cited in Perkinson, *Texas Tough*, 297.

28. "The late 1960s and early 1970s marked the dramatic erosion in the belief among working-class whites that the condition of the poor, or those who fail to prosper, was the result of a faulty economic system that needed to be challenged . . . Just as race had been used at the turn of the century by Southern elites to rupture class solidarity at the bottom of the income ladder, race as a national issue had broken up the Democratic New Deal 'bottom-up' coalition dependent on substantial support from all voters, white and black, at or below the median income" (Alexander, *The New Jim Crow*, 47). See note 82 (below) for Forman Jr.'s nuanced account of the motivations behind support for aspects of the "law and order" initiative among sectors of the black community.

29. In Alexander, *The New Jim Crow*, 47, quoting from Philip A. Klinker and Rogers M. Smith, *The Unsteady March: The Rise and Decline of Racial Equality in America* (Chicago: University of Chicago Press, 1999), 292.

30. Atwater in Robin, *The Reactionary Mind*, 50–51.

31. See Edward E. Baptist, *The Half Has Never Been Told: Slavery and the Making of American Capitalism* (New York: Basic Books, 2014).

32. Melville, *Benito Cereno*, 51.

33. Delano's *Narrative* recorded his experiences and thoughts on three trading voyages that took place between 1790 and 1807. His immediate motive for writing the narrative was pecuniary. He had not made a success of trade, and he was in desperate need of funds to repay some of the debts he had accumulated. In this sense, too, the dramatic episode with the *Tryal* promised one more chance for Delano to cash in on what Naomi Klein has referred to as "disaster capitalism." See Naomi Klein, *The Shock Doctrine: The Rise of Disaster Capitalism* (New York: Henry Holt, 2007).

34. McKay, *Attica: The Official Report*, xiv.

35. John Locke, *Two Treatises on Government*, ed. Peter Laslett (Cambridge: Cambridge University Press, 1988), 274.

36. Melville, *Benito Cereno*, 73.

37. Quoted in Grandin, *Empire of Necessity*, 92.

38. See Wicker, *A Time to Die*, for the list of demands. The initial list of five demands was eventually expanded to "15 Practical Proposals."

39. Ibid., 296.

40. Ibid., 289–90. After the uprising had been put down, the police went around beating, kicking, and cursing the surviving inmates. "A National Guardsman helping to carry a wounded man was unable to stop several troopers from hitting the inmate with their clubs while he lay on a stretcher. The inmate screamed, and a trooper shouted, 'Fuck you, nigger, you should have gotten it in the head!' " (ibid., 288, citing McKay, *Attica: The Official Report*, 430). "The corrections officers with their clubs had a special preoccupation with the inmates' watches. Some they smashed on the inmates' wrists; some they tossed up in the air and hit like fungoes [practice balls for flyballs in baseball]; some they threw on the ground and stomped" (Wicker, *A Time to Die*, 288).

41. Melville, *Benito Cereno*, 102.
42. Ibid., 306.
43. Ibid., 59. I discuss this passage in a little more detail in "Melville's *Benito Cereno* and the Politics of Humanitarian Intervention," *South Atlantic Quarterly* 103, no. 2–3 (Spring/Summer 2004): 465–88, at 477.
44. Davis, *Are Prisons Obsolete?* 40.
45. Thompson's book would also allow us to see traces of Amasa Delano's dangerous humanitarianism in the figure of Russell G. Oswald, the New York State commissioner of prisons: "Oswald, a squat, portly man who always looked harried and slightly unkempt, came across as kind-hearted. He considered his new job an opportunity to improve the lives of prisoners and parolees. By renaming prisons, jails, and reformatories 'correctional facilities,' redubbing prison guards as 'corrections officers,' and calling prisoners 'inmates,' Oswald felt that he was sending a message about his intention to professionalize and humanize prisons" (Thompson, *Blood in the Water*, 20).
46. Davis, *Are Prisons Obsolete?* 20.
47. Needless to say, and as Davis notes, Foucault's *Discipline and Punish* is an essential document for any study of the rise of the modern prison system.
48. Melville, *Benito Cereno*, 50.
49. Ibid. Attica, with its massive grey walls—"Each thirty-foot slab was cemented twelve feet deep into the ground and on each corner perched a gun tower from which guards could scan the fifty-five acre penal complex"—conveys its own peculiar sense of terrifying unreality. See Thompson's description of the prison and its disjunctive relationship to the "wildflower-sprinkled pasture" that surrounds it and the "quaint" little town that shares its name (*Blood in the Water*, 5–6).
50. Davis, *Are Prisons Obsolete?* 11. "If we hope to return to the rate of incarceration of the 1970s," writes Alexander, "—a time when many civil rights activists believed rates of imprisonment were egregiously high—*we would need to release approximately four out of five people currently behind bars today*" (*The New Jim Crow*, 230).
51. Quoted in Davis, *Are Prisons Obsolete?* 11.
52. Alexander, *The New Jim Crow*, 190.
53. "The Rockefeller-Nixon Tapes."
54. Melville, *Benito Cereno*, 116.
55. Perhaps we should think of the revolutionary violence feared by the president and his people as the political force of *the American Revolution to come*, which is also to say, the transformative force of the revolution within the revolution that every American celebrates on July 4. The manifesto of the Attica Liberation Faction would be one of the founding documents of this (democratic) revolution.
56. Wicker, *A Time to Die*, 306–7, quoting McKay.
57. Clarence B. Jones and Stuart Connelly, *Uprising: Understanding Attica, Revolution and the Incarceration State* (Amazon Digital Services, 2011). In other words, rereading *Benito Cereno* in the context of the Attica uprising might mean finding the essential characteristics of Amasa Delano distributed among a number of actors, including Rockefeller and (as I suggested earlier) Commissioner Oswald.

58. Wicker, *A Time to Die*, 308. Asked about the racial makeup of the attacking officers by the post-uprising commission, Rockefeller became agitated: "I would like to say, seeing you have raised this question, I don't think there is anyone who is more conscious or concerned about the problem of equality of opportunity, of representation of government at all levels and in all activities and that I take second place to no one on the record in our government in this field" (ibid., 306).

59. Roy Walmsley, *World Prison Population List*, 10th ed. (International Centre for Prison Studies, 2015), http://www.prisonstudies.org/sites/prisonstudies.org/files/resources/downloads/wppl_10.pdf.

60. See the website of the Zinn Education Project for the prisoners' demands and other invaluable resources for teaching and understanding the Attica riot: https://zinnedproject.org/materials/attica-prison-uprising/, as well as Kaba, "A Short Primer."

61. See Kaba, "A Short Primer."

62. Wicker, *A Time to Die*, 96. Compare the inmates' investment in education, communication, and improved access to various forms of media publication with Forman Jr.'s recommended alternatives to incarceration in *Locking Up Our Own*. His list includes "funding public defenders adequately" as well as "building quality schools inside juvenile and adult prisons, restoring voting rights to people who have served their sentences (or, better yet, allowing people to vote while incarcerated), and welcoming . . . those who are returning from prison" (236).

63. See Thompson, *Blood in the Water*, for invaluable details concerning the inmates' procedures for democratizing their deliberations and for drafting, communicating, and revising their statements.

64. See "Alexander Butterfield Explains the Nixon Taping System," the transcript of an interview conducted by John W. Carlin at the John F. Kennedy Library conference on Presidential Tapes, February 16, 2003, online at the website of the Miller Center at the University of Virginia: http://millercenter.org/presidentialrecordings/nixon/about#Alexander_Butterfield_Explains_the_Nixon_Taping_System.

65. See "A History of the White House Tapes," Nixon Presidential Materials Project (NLNP), National Archives and Records Administration (NARA), March 1995. Quoted in "The Richard M. Nixon White House Recordings: Overview," at http://millercenter.org.

66. H. R. Haldeman, "The Nixon White House Tapes: The Decision to Record Presidential Conversations," *Prologue Magazine* 30, no. 2 (Summer 1988): 83 (quoted in "Alexander Butterfield").

67. "White House Tapes Scope and Content Note," 3 NLNP, NARA, undated, as quoted in "Alexander Butterfield."

68. The Attica prisoners, on the other hand, were systematically and insistently invested in the use of media technology to open up, expose, and broadcast. Hence, the Attica uprising is also significant as an event in media history. As a result of the prisoners' repeated call for national media presence, journalists were eventually joined at Attica by cameramen from NBC and ABC. "For the first time ever," Thompson writes, "Americans could get an inside look at a prison rebellion and watch it unfold" (*Blood in the Water*, 77). But does an "inside look" always allow you to see what's going on? That was Melville's question in 1855.

69. Haldeman, "The Decision to Record," 80.

70. Quoted ibid., 81.

71. John Powers, "The History of Presidential Audio Recordings and the Archival Issues Surrounding Their Use," CIDS Paper, National Archives and Records Administration, July 12, 1996, excerpted in "Nixon Secret White House Recordings: Collection Specifications" on the website of the Miller Centre at the University of Virginia, https://millercenter.org/nixon-secret-white-house-recordings-collection-specifications.

72. "Alexander Butterfield."

73. What I am tentatively trying to suggest here is that Nixon's self-undoing relationship to his recordings bears comparison with both Cereno's forced repetition of himself during the uprising and Delano's undoing via his memoirs. Melville's literary achievement, in part, has to do with the way in which *Benito Cereno* activates the internal *différance* of a discourse that Melville sometimes appears simply to repeat.

74. Derrida, *Dissemination*, 77.

75. Richard Nixon, *RN: The Memoirs of Richard Nixon* (New York: Grosset and Dunlap, 1978), 501.

76. Derrida, *Dissemination*, 109.

77. Ibid., 76.

78. It is the very particular way in which Melville took Delano's own words and subtly rehearsed them (as well as his direct reproduction of the actual recorded transcripts of the ensuing trial) that prompts my reflection on the Nixon tapes and their relationship to Attica and racialized criminalization in the United States more generally.

79. See Nathan J. Robinson, *Superpredator: Bill Clinton's Use and Abuse of Black America* (W. Somerville, Mass.: Current Affairs, 2016), 16. Clinton was forced to revisit the phrase by Black Lives Matter activists (and in particular Ashley Williams) who confronted her and Bill Clinton at rallies and fund-raising events during the 2016 presidential campaign.

80. Qtd. ibid., 14.

81. U.S. Department of Justice, "Violent Crime Control and Law Enforcement Act of 1994, U.S. Department of Justice Fact Sheet," October 24, 1994, https://www.ncjrs.gov/txtfiles/billfs.txt.

82. "We must start with a profound social fact," writes Forman Jr.: "In the years preceding and during our punishment binge, black communities were devastated by historically unprecedented levels of crime and violence" (*Locking Up Our Own*, 10). Forman Jr.'s book goes on to document the complex racist dynamics that have been responsible for both the high levels of crime in black neighborhoods and the increasing criminalization and incarceration of black men and women. For a powerful documentary account of the relationship between slavery and incarceration, see Ava DuVernay's 2016 film *13th*.

83. Needless to say, the election of Donald Trump has done nothing to alleviate this situation. While Hillary Clinton was apologizing for her earlier remarks, Trump was rehearsing familiar scripts: "Trump revived the 'law and order' mantra that Republicans such as Goldwater, Nixon and Reagan had once used to great effect, portraying America's black neighborhoods as killing fields whose only hope lay in aggressive policing" (Forman Jr., *Locking Up Our Own*, 12). Stock prices for the private prison companies CCA and GEO Group surged in the wake of Trump's

election victory, and the new attorney general Jeff Sessions promptly overturned the Obama administration's 2016 decision to stop using private prisons at the federal level. See Roque Planas, "Private Prison Stocks Surge after Donald Trump Victory," *Huffington Post*, November 9, 2016, http://www.huffingtonpost.ca/entry/private-prison-stocks-trump_us_582336c5e4b0e80b02ce3287.

84. Melville, *Benito Cereno*, 51.

85. See Forman Jr.'s discussion of the inconsistency of President Obama's position on "violent" crime in *Locking Up Our Own*, 229–31. "The label 'violent offender,' tossed out to describe a shadowy group for whom we are supposed to have no sympathy, encourages us to overlook their individual stories . . . And it ensures that we will never get close to resolving the human rights crisis that is 2.2 million Americans behind bars" (ibid., 231). Forman also reminds us that black males are the leading victims of homicide in the United States. "The Department of Justice would later estimate that in the mid-1990s, a black American male faced a 1-in-35 chance of being murdered over his lifetime—a risk that was eight times higher than a white man's, whose chances were 1 in 251.36" (ibid., 161–62).

86. Wicker, *A Time to Die*, 7.

87. Sam Melville quoted in Wicker, *A Time to Die*, 8. Melville's letters were collected after his death and published with prefatorial essays by John Cohen, William Kunstler, and Jane Alpert. See Samuel Melville, *Letters from Attica* (New York: William Morrow, 1972).

88. Jane Alpert, "Profile of Sam Melville," in Samuel Melville, *Letters from Attica* (New York: William Morrow, 1972), 3–43.

89. John Cohen, "Introduction," in Melville, *Letters from Attica*, 45–79, at 57.

90. See William Kunstler's "Foreword" to Melville's *Letters from Attica*, vii–x, at ix.

91. Cohen, "Introduction," 67.

92. Ibid., 74–75.

93. Grandin, *Empire of Necessity*, 92.

94. Ibid. *Radical America*, the journal of the Students for a Democratic Society, published a special issue on the work of the great black Melville scholar C. L. R. James in May 1970. Here would be another possible source for a "subversive" reappropriation of Melville.

95. See Tom Robbins, "A Brutal Beating Wakes Attica's Ghosts," *New York Times*, March 1, 2014.

96. "Push to Close Notorious Attica Prison as Brutal Conditions Continue 40 Years after Uprising: Interview with Amy Goodman, Nermeen Shaikh and Tom Robbins," by Antonio Yarbough, Democracy Now, March 5, 2015, http://www.democracynow.org/blog/2015/3/5/part_2_push_to_close_notorious.

Part 2

✦

Audiovisual Melville

"A Sound Not Easily to Be Verbally Rendered": The Literary Acoustic of *Billy Budd*

David Copenhafer

> To end is to repeat, and to repeat is to be ungovernably open to revision, displacement, and reversal.
> —Barbara Johnson, "Melville's Fist: The Execution of *Billy Budd*"

On December 1, 1842, three sailors—Philip Spencer, Elisha Small, and Samuel Cromwell—were executed on board the USS *Somers* for allegedly plotting a mutiny. Two weeks later, after the ship docked in New York harbor and word of the incident began to spread, public opinion quickly divided into those who supported the decision of the *Somers*'s captain—Alexander Slidell Mackenzie—to execute and those who did not.[1] The incident clearly attracted the attention of Herman Melville, who mentions the *Somers* directly in two fictions separated by nearly forty years—the novel *White-Jacket* (1851) and the novella *Billy Budd* (started in 1886, unfinished at Melville's death in 1891).

The narrator of *White-Jacket*—an unnamed sailor aboard the USS *Neversink*, known only as "White Jacket"—is somewhat more explicit than the narrator of *Billy Budd* in criticizing naval discipline. No doubt because he himself comes close to facing the scourge, White Jacket is appalled by the frequent use of the whip to keep sailors obedient. He states that shipboard discipline, though it must be more stringent than the practice of the police on land, nevertheless "should not convert into slaves some of the citizens of a nation of freemen."[2] The reference to slaves seems particularly charged given the moment at which the novel appears—the era of U.S. slavery. *White-Jacket*'s narrator appears poised to raise the question of the impropriety of slavery whether on land or at sea, but he ultimately shies away from such an analysis.[3]

The issue of flogging also arises in *Billy Budd* (Billy is terrified it could happen to him), although it could be said that the story raises the stakes on questioning state power by considering capital, not just corporal, punishment. Indeed, *Billy Budd* addresses a fairly unique form of state power (unique owing to the potential isolation of ships)—the apparent right of a ship's captain to execute a sailor in summary fashion and without having granted the

141

accused an extended trial or due process (like the sailors aboard the *Somers*, Billy receives no legal counsel). Just as the public was divided in its interpretation of Mackenzie's actions, readers of *Billy Budd* have traditionally been split in their interpretation of the decision of the *Bellipotent*'s captain, Vere, to execute Billy. As Barbara Johnson notes in "Melville's Fist: The Execution of *Billy Budd*," readers tend to belong to one of two parties—either to the "acceptance" camp, those who see Melville, or at least his narrator, as acknowledging the necessity of state violence—or to the "irony" camp, those who read defiance or even rebellion into the story's pessimistic plotline.[4]

While my own sympathies and judgment veer toward the ironic, I agree with Johnson that the point of the story is likely not so much to provoke judgment but, instead, to inspire critical reflection on the act of judging itself ("Judgment is clearly the central preoccupation of Melville's text, whether it be the judgment pronounced *by* Vere or *upon* him").[5] Subtitled "An Inside Narrative," *Billy Budd* does indeed reveal "secret facts," such as Claggart's inscrutable hatred for Billy and effort to provoke him, which would have been unknown to Vere. And while this inside information does tend to frame a certain reading, if not judgment, of Vere, the narrative nevertheless tends to remain sphinxlike as to the propriety of the state's power to kill one of its citizens. That is, it could be argued that despite its preoccupation with judgment, the story nevertheless *suspends* judgment on Vere's exercise of power.

There is, however, one pathway to exploring what the text has to say about power which has gone relatively unexamined. This is the pathway of sound, or what I call the "literary acoustic" of *Billy Budd*, its careful presentation of sonic events as signs for the distribution of power both on the ship but also across time. The "pathway of sound" or "literary acoustic" comprises both sonic events *as well as their potential to re-sound in the future*. In different historical eras, sounds leave traces of various sorts—written description, musical notation, traumatic memory, audio recording, and so on. With *Billy Budd* as well as with the *Somers* affair, we have to do with sounds—the crack of a whip, for example—that are either entirely fictional or that long ago ceased to agitate the air. Nevertheless, the written traces of these sounds continue to agitate a reader and to call for re-signification. In this way, sounds re-sound.

The importance of sound to *Billy Budd* becomes especially prominent after Billy dies, although sound is very much at issue when Billy strikes his superior, Claggart, in a violent paroxysm which follows hard upon his inability to produce intelligible sound with his voice.[6] Despite the attention previous critics have paid to power relations aboard the ship, it has yet to be shown in detail how sound functions as an index of political power, as well as what might be called an ongoing sign of discontent with that power.

In what follows, I aim to give an account of the "radiophonic" or highly acoustic manner in which Billy's death is narrated. I will show how sound, along with music, reveal the depth of the narrator's ambivalence over Billy's death and form the basis of the story's faint but audible protest. *Billy Budd* closes with a poem—"Billy in the Darbies"—supposedly authored by one of his shipmates. If "Billy in the Darbies" had given voice to a sharper critique of state power and of Billy's execution, one might have been able to conclude that the narrator wished to align his voice with a popular refrain, one that had the potential to be picked up and chanted by successive generations. But the conclusion of *Billy Budd* seems to be a dead end—a somewhat melancholy indication that Billy's death was not, in fact, commemorated by means of a protest song and that the modest tribute to the sailor was relatively short-lived. If an "audible protest" is to be discerned in the story, it must be sought elsewhere, at the moment of Billy's execution. In other words, not *Billy Budd*'s end but the end of Billy Budd should be scanned for signs of resistance.

Ironically, a possible source for "Billy in the Darbies"—a ballad composed on the death of the *Somers*'s mutineers—does inveigh against the deadly power of the ship's captain. "The Somers Tragedy" was printed as a broadside and also appeared in the *New York Herald*, a large-circulation daily, shortly after the *Somers*'s captain was cleared by a naval court martial of having committed any offense. Like *Billy Budd*, the text of the ballad expresses a keen interest in the soundscape of the ship just before and right after the execution of the sailors. At the end of this essay, I will address the different rhetorics of sound and of commemoration to be found in the novella and the broadside ballad. But we begin by attending to what is set well before the events on board the *Somers,* though it was written nearly fifty years after that real-life incident, the text of *Billy Budd*.

Executing Music

The execution of Billy Budd represents a tour de force of narrated sound, one organized around relatively few sonic events: a cry, an echo, a murmur, and the piercing sound of a whistle. Earlier in the story, there is some attention given to acoustic phenomena, especially to Billy's voice. While Billy sometimes stutters, he is nevertheless described as being musical: "he was illiterate; he could not read, but he could sing, and like the illiterate nightingale was sometimes the composer of his own song."[7] Though singing while on duty is generally forbidden, Billy is a foretopman, one who works high above deck in the rigging, and thus may possess a greater freedom, along with his mates, to sing without disciplinary consequences, which is not to say that unchecked musicality may not have been one of the many unfathomable sources of Claggart's enmity for Billy. It is just possible that Billy's spontaneous improvisations were a little too "gay" for the master-at-arms, Claggart, to handle.[8]

The description of Billy's penchant for singing comes early in the tale and anticipates its end, for just prior to being hanged he calls out to those assembled:

"God bless Captain Vere!" Syllables so unanticipated coming from one with the ignominious hemp about his neck—a conventional felon's benediction directed aft towards the quarters of honor; *syllables too delivered in the clear melody of a singing bird on the point of launching from the twig*—had a phenomenal effect, not unenhanced by the rare personal beauty of the young sailor.[9]

Although he is formerly compared to a nightingale (a joyous bird, at least in Keats's depiction), this cry is Billy's swansong or *Todeslied*. It forms a remarkable counterpart with another of Billy's efforts to address a ship's company, his farewell address to the merchant ship from which he was removed to be impressed into the British navy. During his transfer from the merchant ship to the naval vessel, Billy shouts out: "And good-bye to you too, old *Rights-of-Man*."[10] And though it is said he lacked the "sinister dexterity" to make of this exclamation any sort of "sly slur," yet there are several among his new shipmates, including Vere, who take this valediction to be a rueful comment on his loss of a right to self-determination, the right to decide for himself on what ship and under whose command he will serve.

Unlike the address to the *Rights-of-Man*, Billy's cry out to Vere seems to be taken at face value by all who hear it, that is, it seems to be understood as a genuine pardon of the one who has ordered his execution. No doubt the singing tone of Billy's voice discourages an ironic reading of his benediction. For at least one critic, a member of the "ironist" camp—appalled by Billy's seemingly doglike obedience at the moment of execution—Billy's address is unpalatable: "'God bless Captain Vere!' Is this not piercing irony? As innocent Billy utters these words, does not the reader gag?"[11] Nevertheless, the story alleges that Billy's shipmates are able to repeat the phrase without altering it or changing its meaning. This "phenomenal effect" is worth lingering on: "Without volition, as it were, as if indeed the ship's populace were but the vehicles of some vocal current electric, with one voice from alow and aloft came a resonant sympathetic echo: 'God bless Captain Vere!'"[12] The slightly anachronistic reference to a "vocal current electric" is striking, given the difference between the years in which *Billy Budd* was composed and most likely narrated (1886–91) and the year in which it is set (1797). The simile suggests that the collective voice of the sailors is a unified natural phenomenon.

In 1797, the power of electricity had yet to be used in the great inventions of nineteenth-century modernity such as the telegraph, the telephone, and the radio, and the scientific understanding of "electric current" was still somewhat in its infancy.[13] But the biologist Galvani had used static electricity to move a dead frog's legs, a phenomenon likely to have inspired Mary Shelley in writing *Frankenstein*. Billy's shipmates are said to respond "without volition" as if they, too, have been animated by an electric current, though the "spark" in this case is none other than Billy's dying voice. Perhaps the narrator of *Billy Budd* has this "animatronic" meaning of electricity in mind when describing the involuntary reaction of the crew, or, in a mode more suited to the late nineteenth century, the narrator may mean that the "electrified" crew is functioning somewhat like a telephone (invented in 1876), relaying Billy's voice in the manner of a wire.[14]

The involuntary, as well as unitary, response of the crew seems to mark them as somehow "dead" in their initial reaction to Billy's execution. Vere appears to want to execute the law faithfully and without any willful interference; to execute, that is, as if he, Vere, were not quite alive insofar as he is incapable of acting otherwise. Vere states:

> When war is declared are we the commissioned fighters previously consulted? We fight at command. If our judgments approve the war, that is but coincidence. So in other particulars. So now. For suppose condemnation to follow these present proceedings. Would it be so much we ourselves that would condemn as it would be martial law operating through us? For that law and the rigor of it, we are not responsible. Our vowed responsibility is in this: That however pitilessly that law may operate in any instances, we nevertheless adhere to it and administer it.[15]

In its lack of volition, the crew's initial echo of Billy's cry seems almost a parody of Vere's decision to execute Billy—a decision that would pretend not to be a decision at all, but a mere carrying-out of what the law requires. But if the crew is indeed, in some remote sense, parodying Vere, they may also be said to be parodying (dying alongside) Billy, that is, not repeating his meaning but adducing new ones.[16] Put differently, one might ask: do the sailors actually repeat Billy's apparent wish to absolve Vere of any wrongdoing, or does not their unthinking echo hold other possibilities? Spoken in a certain tone of voice, could not one transform the sentence into a question: "'God bless Captain Vere!' (Did he really just say that?)" Or perhaps into an expression of disbelief: "'God bless Captain Vere!' (I can't believe he just said that!)" The narrator's "electrified" description seeks to unify the crew's response and to flatten any possible tonal differences, but this should be read, I believe, as an effort at containment and not as the "last word" on the meaning of the echo.[17]

After the "shock" of Billy's benediction registers as a kind of electric current, the narrator seeks a different metaphorical register—water—to indicate the sailors' return to life and something like the possibility of protest. This occurs in the extended set of sonic reflections the narrator makes on the sounds which immediately follow Billy's death, a virtuosic passage—not unlike a script for a radio play—which rewards careful attention and deserves to be reproduced in full:

> The silence at the moment of execution and for a moment or two continuing thereafter, a silence but emphasized by the regular wash of the

sea against the hull or the flutter of a sail caused by the helmsman's eyes being tempted astray, this emphasized silence was gradually disturbed by a sound not easily to be verbally rendered. Whoever has heard the freshet-wave of a torrent suddenly swelled by pouring however in tropical mountains, showers not shared by the plain; whoever has heard the first muffled murmur of its sloping advance through precipitous woods may form some conception of the sound now heard. The seeming remoteness of its source was because of its murmurous indistinctness, since it came from close by, even from the men passed on the ship's open deck. Being inarticulate, it was dubious in significance further than it seemed to indicate some capricious revulsion of thought or feeling such as mobs ashore are liable to, in the present instance possibly implying a sullen revocation on the men's part of their involuntary echoing of Billy's benediction. But ere the murmur had time to wax into clamor it was met by a strategic command, the more telling that it came with abrupt unexpectedness: "Pipe down the starboard watch, Boatswain, and see that they go."

Shrill as the shriek of the sea hawk, the silver whistles of the boatswain and his mates pierced that ominous low sound, dissipating it; and yielding to the mechanism of discipline the throng was thinned by one half.[18]

This extended example of a "literary acoustic"—writing which employs figurative language to try to capture the uniqueness of sound while at the same time calling attention to the difficulty, if not impossibility, of figuring sound ("a sound not easily to be verbally rendered")—is inflected at several points: a silence is interrupted first by nonhuman sounds of sea and wind (although, interestingly, the wind sound is interpreted as having a human cause—the helmsman's inattention);[19] it then gives way to a growing murmur comparable to a flash flood forming after a downpour in a tropical mountain; finally, this rising tide of rumor is interrupted by a voice commanding that the shrill sound of pipes send the assembled sailors to their stations. The pipes are compared to the cries of hawks, but they are of human origin. With the exception of the one spoken order, the sequence is a miniature symphony of "inarticulate" sounds whose meanings range from inscrutable to brutally clear. But it is the middle sound, the murmur, that is most difficult to assess and to interpret.

Anyone who has heard a large assembly make noise in such a way as to indicate its displeasure knows that individual words need not be audible for the dissatisfaction nevertheless to be communicated. Other factors, such as register—the murmur is described as an "ominous low sound"—or rising volume, indicating rising discontent, do the work of signification. It is remarkable how Melville slows the pace of the story down, to insist, as it were, that the reader tarry in the acoustic space and time opened just after the hanging of Budd—the time of the literary acoustic.[20] Yet the narrator appears to strike a reluctant stance toward the interpreted sound and is careful not to speak too authoritatively on what the murmur may mean.

The "muffled murmur" is described as "inarticulate," "dubious in significance further than it seemed to indicate some *capricious* revulsion of thought or feeling such as *mobs ashore* are liable to." In other words, the narrator would claim it is a fleeting sound, as likely to dissipate as quickly as it arises. And the reference to "mobs ashore" would seem to imply that while such a sound might gain traction with another mob, might "wax into clamor" among an undisciplined group of landsmen, this will not be the case with this particular group of sailors. It appears that the narrator does not wish to impute to them a mutinous thought or intention. But why not? They have just seen their favorite shipmate hanged right above them. Why wouldn't they be thinking in terms of possible rebellion, or at least protest, if they thought this killing was unjust? But the narrator seems reluctant to entertain this possibility. Perhaps he wishes to protect them, in some sense, from the accusation of mutinous intent. Or perhaps the narrator's interpretation of the murmur marks an ideological stance, one which favors the captain's action in this case and would downplay the risk of open defiance. To echo a previous point, *Billy Budd* is "about" judgment, but it is also about how the selection and framing of events, in this case sonic events, enables judgment to occur.[21]

According to the narrator, there is, at most, a possibility that the growing murmur indicates a "revocation . . . of their involuntary echoing of Billy's benediction." But the revocation of a benediction is not quite the same thing as an openly rebellious statement. And "before the murmur ha[s] time to become a clamor" it is piped down by strategic command, the shrill whistles of the secondary officers, hawks to the sailors' doves. The reference to "clamor" suggests that the crew's discontent was on its way to getting out of hand, but before this can happen, it is ruthlessly neutralized by the whistles and by Vere's order. Shrill sound pierces its low-pitched target and disperses the increasingly unruly mass. Here, sound is deployed as a means of careful crowd control and of shrewd executive management. The narrator quotes Vere on the need for such piercing, orderly sound: "'With mankind,' he [Vere] would say, 'forms, measured forms, are everything; and this is the import couched in the story of Orpheus with his lyre spellbinding the wild citizens of the wood.' And this he once applied to the disruption of forms going on across the Channel and the consequences thereof." Billy's ship, it should be recalled, is involved in a war with France, a war that has arisen, at least in part, because of the violence unleashed by the 1789 Revolution—the "disruption of forms" to which Vere alludes. Moreover, mutinies had occurred on board British ships in the first half of 1797 at the Nore and Spithead anchorages. War and mutiny are used to justify the violent treatment of sailors to maintain discipline, and Vere would enlist music—the lyre of Orpheus—in the effort to impose orderly form. Vere orders Billy Budd to be put to death less for his act of killing a superior officer and more for the way that act, if unpunished, might be interpreted by the crew as a license to commit further acts of potentially deadly insurrection. Vere states:

> To the people the foretopman's deed, however it be worded in the announcement, will be plain homicide committed in a flagrant act of mutiny. What penalty for that should follow, they know. But it does not follow. *Why?* they will ruminate. You know what sailors are. Will they not revert to the recent outbreak at the Nore? Ay. They know the well-founded alarm—the panic it struck throughout England. Your clement sentence they would account pusillanimous.[22]

The rising murmur after Billy's death hints at the possibility of insurrection and thus provokes strong countermeasures. Sound is the vehicle in and through which the mass of sailors threatens to transform itself into something dangerous to the shipboard hierarchy. But sound is also the agent whereby Vere and his officers reassert control over the crew. To stifle possible rebellion, Vere not only executes Billy, he executes his music, which is to say, he executes its playfulness, both its spontaneity and its potential to mean more than one thing if not to re-sound over time. In its place he substitutes his own scarcely musical sound—the whistle—which would make of music a mere signal, a pure imperative, rather than another form of address, such as a valediction or a benediction. It says simply: "Get back to work!"[23]

Commemorating Billy

In concluding his account of the deliberations of the officers who sentence Billy Budd to death, the narrator allows himself to speculate on their mental state:

> Not unlikely they were brought to something more or less akin to that harassed frame of mind which in the year 1842 actuated the commander of the U.S. brig-of-war *Somers* to resolve, under the so-called Articles of War, Articles modeled upon the English Mutiny Act, to resolve upon the execution at sea of a midshipman and two sailors as mutineers designing the seizure of the brig. Which resolution was carried out though in a time of peace and within not many days' sail of home. An act vindicated by a naval court of inquiry subsequently convened ashore. History, and here cited without comment.[24]

The narrator's terse "History, and here cited without comment" seems a heavy bit of irony, for one could take the entire text of *Billy Budd* as an extended "comment" on the *Somers* affair. In *White-Jacket*, Melville deals at length with the sovereign power of naval commanders and the mistreatment of sailors on board the fictional U.S. ship *Neversink* at sea in the 1840s. The narrator of *White-Jacket* is driven nearly to kill his captain after he commands that the narrator should be whipped for a minor infraction; only through a stroke of luck—the kind word of an officer—does White Jacket perhaps escape a fate not unlike Billy's. It is as if, many years later, having left something unfinished or unspoken in *White-Jacket*—and still haunted by the story of the *Somers* as well as his own experience on board the USS *United States* in 1843—Melville wished to return in *Billy Budd* to the theme of naval discipline (and to the more general issue of state power) by writing an odd sort of genealogical story, one that seeks to locate an origin for the deadly action of the *Somers*'s commanders in the actions of British naval officers attempting to quell rebellion on British ships (both real and fictional) in 1797. Although, discursively, it is the later event (the *Somers*'s mutiny) that the narrator brings to bear on the earlier event (the execution of Billy Budd) in order to illuminate the frame of mind of the officers, one could say that, in quasi-genealogical fashion, Melville seeks to frame the historical event by setting his fiction as its antecedent. In other words, he may be just as interested, if not more interested, in how the actions and intentions of nineteenth-century American naval officers can be derived from their understanding of the possibility for mutiny as it played out aboard British ships at the close of the eighteenth century. Such, then, would be his elaborate "comment."[25]

The final chapters of *Billy Budd* are concerned with how events are documented and transmitted in both official and unofficial forms. They thus speak to the narrator's own genealogical project. The narrator's reference to the "so-called" Articles of War, coupled with his pointed observation that the sailors on board the *Somers* were executed in a "time of peace and within not many days' sail of home," registers an unease over the killing—a discontent that remains, however, muted and not unlike the grumbling discontent of Billy Budd's shipmates. By juxtaposing, in the final two chapters of *Billy Budd*, the two ways in which Billy Budd's death has been previously remembered, the narrator provides the implicit justification for his own genealogical project—the insufficiency of the historical record leading up to his time.

The first mode of faulty documentation is the official naval record of what occurred on board the *Bellipotent*. The narrator cites "an authorized weekly publication" as saying:

> On the tenth of the last month a deplorable occurrence took place on board H.M.S. *Bellipotent*. John Claggart, the ship's master-at-arms, discovering that some sort of plot was incipient among an inferior section of the ship's company, and that the ringleader was one William Budd; he, Claggart, in the act of arraigning the man before the captain, was vindictively stabbed to the heart by the suddenly drawn sheath knife of Budd.[26]

About this account, which seemingly credits the false notion that Billy was the "ringleader" of a potential rebellion and which exaggerates Billy's violence by misreporting the cause of Claggart's death—Billy strikes Claggart with his bare fist and with no other weapon—the narrator goes on to say: "The above, appearing in a publication now long ago superannuated and forgotten, is all that hitherto has stood in human record to attest what manner of men respectively were John Claggart and Billy Budd."[27] Striking in its solemnity, this statement reinforces the notion that the narrator is somehow attempting to repair the historical record, to recast the official account of Billy as the "vindictive" evildoer and Claggart as the innocent accuser. But the narrator is too subtle to indicate that this is, in fact, his express intention. Instead, he complicates the question of how Budd might be remembered by almost immediately contradicting his statement that the official account is all that has "stood in human record" concerning the death of Billy Budd. He goes on to cite a poem of some thirty-two lines that commemorates Billy's death.

"Billy in the Darbies" is the ballad supposedly composed by one of Billy's fellow foretopmen. Here is the second half:

> Heaven knows who will have the running of me up!
> No pipe to those halyards.—But aren't it all sham?
> A blur's in my eyes; it is dreaming I am.
> A hatchet to my hawser? All adrift to go?
> The drum roll to grog, and Billy never know?
> But Donald he has promised to stand by the plank
> So I'll shake a friendly hand ere I sink.
> But—no! It is dead then I'll be, come to think.
> I remember Taff the Welshman when he sank.
> And his cheek it was like the budding pink.
> But me they'll lash in hammock, drop me deep.
> Fathoms down, fathoms down, how I'll dream fast asleep
> I feel it stealing now. Sentry, are you there?
> Just ease these darbies at the wrist,
> And roll me over fair!
> I am sleepy, and the oozy weeds about me twist.

Insofar as the poem gives voice to Billy moments before his death (if not, in a kind of prosopopoetic turn, giving voice to the dead Billy already at rest among the "oozy weeds"), it tends to evoke a certain sympathy for him and his plight. But the poem cannot be called a defense of Billy Budd.[28] It does not address the reason for his execution, and it registers only the barest protest over his sentence. Only the phrase "aren't it all sham?" hints at dissent, but this line may simply refer to the speaker's insistence that he is dreaming. As such a *quiet* poem, it conforms to the narrator's description of how the sailors who knew Billy eventually came to think of his execution: "Ignorant though they were of the secret facts of the tragedy, *and not thinking but that the penalty was somehow unavoidably inflicted from the naval point of view*, for all that, they instinctively felt that Billy was a sort of man incapable of mutiny as of willful murder."[29]

In other words, the narrator imputes to the crew a type of begrudging acceptance of the necessity "from the naval point of view" of putting Billy Budd to death. This acceptance is, of course, nearly impossible to contradict, given the events of the story and the narrator's presentation of them. The sailors do indeed return to their stations, their tasks, and not even the delayed, poetic commemoration of Billy, it would seem, raises any real objection to the actions of Vere and his officers. But here it is necessary to point out the narrator's role both in repeating and in defying the disciplinary actions of Vere and of the British navy. On the one hand, we have seen how the narrator is careful not to give voice to a mutinous intention among the crew. That intention remains, at best, an indistinct murmur. But the narrator is also not willing to let either the official story of Billy's attack or the ballad "Billy in the Darbies" stand as the only records of his life. On the contrary, the "inside narrative" reports the "secret facts" of Billy's life and death and shows to what extent Billy is abused by more than one disciplinary regime (impressed by the navy, harassed by Claggart, executed by Vere). The narrator hesitates to amplify the "vocal current electric" of the crew and its rising tide of mutinous murmur, but simply by reporting on these vocal effects, the narrator becomes a kind of "human microphone," relaying across what is imagined to be nearly a century the possibility of another type of reaction to Billy's death other than simple acquiescence.[30] The narrator is no revolutionary, but in laying bare the inside story (which is, quite literally, the story of Billy's death and not its subsequent commemoration), he restores a political potential to the scene of Billy's demise. Where previously the matter had been "settled," it now has the potential to re-sound, to echo into the future, and to pose the question of the origin of the justification of naval, that is to say, of state and of military execution, whether it should occur in 1797, 1842, or another year.

The Ballad of the *Somers*

Just as Billy Budd is remembered in two divergent ways, so were the alleged mutineers executed on board the USS *Somers* remembered by both official and unofficial organs. In February and March 1843, Captain Mackenzie stood trial for murder. In the transcript of the court martial, Melville's cousin, Guert Gansvoort, who had been first lieutenant on board the *Somers*, testified that just prior to being executed, nineteen-year-old Philip Spencer, believed to be the leader of the incipient mutiny, stated his wish to exonerate Captain Mackenzie of any wrongdoing. In court, Mackenzie asked Gansvoort: "Do you know what passed at the time of the execution?" To this, Gansvoort replied:

152   David Copenhafer

Just before Mr. Spencer went forward under the main yard, I took leave of him; he took my hand in both of his, and in the most earnest manner asked me to forgive him the great injuries he had done me; he said he deserved to be punished, that he did not object to his sentence; he deserved to die, but he did not like the way the commander chose to put him to death; he said he should like to have had a little longer time to prepare, or words to that effect.[31]

This "hearsay" evidence—testimony as to what a third party said—is perhaps the model for Billy's songlike benediction, although that phrase—"God bless Captain Vere!"—is clearly more affirmative than Gansvoort's account of Spencer's "words to that effect." Interestingly, Spencer is supposed to have objected only to the manner and timing, but not to the substance, of the proceeding.

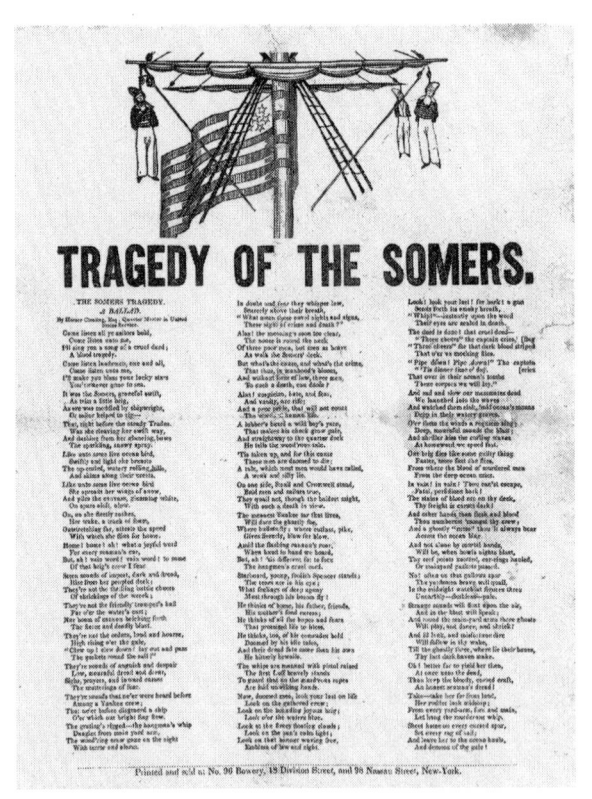

"Tragedy of the Somers" ballad illustration, 1843.

On April 1, the court found Mackenzie not guilty. A little over a month later—on May 11, 1843—the *New York Herald* published "The Somers

Tragedy: A Ballad" by Horser Clenling. The songlike text was also reprinted as a 9-by-12-inch "broadside" and sold out of a shop on the Bowery. The broadside featured at its head a somewhat crude drawing of the three executed sailors (Spencer, alone on the left, Small and Cromwell, his accomplices, to the right) and the ballad underneath the words "Tragedy of the Somers" in bold (see illustration). In a manner not unlike the climactic scene of *Billy Budd*, though perhaps in less self-consciously literary fashion, the speaker in "The Somers Tragedy" directs the listener/reader's attention to the soundscape of the ship just prior to the execution of the sailors:

> Home! Home! Ah! what a joyful word
> For every seaman's ear,
> But, ah! vain word! Vain word! To some
> Of that brig's crew I fear.
>
> Stern sounds of import, dark and dread,
> Rise from her peopled deck;
> They're not the thrilling battle cheers
> Of shriekings of the wreck;
>
> They're not the friendly trumpet's hail
> Far o'er the water's cast;
> Nor boom of cannon belching forth
> The fierce and deadly blast.
>
> They're not the orders, loud and hoarse,
> High rising o'er the gale,
> "Clew up! clew down! lay out and pass
> The gaskets round the sail!"
>
> They're sounds of anguish and despair
> Low, mournful dread and drear,
> Sighs, prayers, and inward curses
> The mutterings of fear.
>
> They're sounds that ne'er were heard before
> Among a Yankee crew;
> That ne'er before disgraced a ship
> O'er which our bright flag flew.
>
> The grating's rigged—the hangman's whip
> Dangles from main yard arm,
> The wond'ring crew gaze on the sight
> With terror and alarm.

In doubt and fear they whisper low,
Scarcely above their breath,
"What mean these novel sights and signs,
These signs of crime and death?"[32]

Neither sounds of victory nor of everyday command, these "stern sounds of import" turn out to be the "mutterings of fear." They no doubt resemble the murmur the narrator attributes to the crowd that watches Billy hang. Here, however, the poet attributes to the sailors a more interrogative and, ultimately, more accusatory response. After the crew poses its question—"What mean these novel sights and signs / These signs of crime and death?"—the poet responds:

Alas! the meaning's soon too clear,
The noose is round the neck
Of three poor men, but men as brave
As walk the Somers deck

But what's the cause and what's the crime
That thus, in manhood's bloom,
And *without form of law*, three men,
To such a death, can doom?[33]

With this, the ballad directly challenges the legality of the execution, a far cry from the noiseless plunge Billy makes both in the narrator's description of his death as well as in "Billy in the Darbies." The "signs of crime" alluded to previously appear to have been converted into evidence that the captain and his officers, and not those suspended above, have committed an offense.

Detail, "Tragedy of the Somers" ballad illustration, 1843.

Whereas the rhetorical strategy of "Billy in the Darbies" could be described as an effort to elicit sympathy by allowing the condemned one to speak at some length, in "The Somers Tragedy" the accused are notably silent, offering no last-minute benediction or other token of acquiescence. Instead, the voice of the ballad is that of an aggrieved fellow sailor who does not shy away, by the end of the poem, from referring to his shipmates' death as a murder:

> Our brig flies like some guilty thing
> Faster, more fast she flies,
> From where the blood of murdered men
> From the deep ocean cries.

In the manner of Billy's shipmates, however, the poet does not issue an open call to rebellion. Rather, he trusts that the ship will not be able to outrun the curse laid on it by the dead sailors whose blood, according to the poem, cries from the depths. One could say, however, that it is the poem itself, rather than the sailors' blood, which curses the ship.

If Melville drew inspiration for "Billy in the Darbies" from "The Somers Tragedy," it is worth noting to what extent he toned down its inflammatory rhetoric, giving voice to the dead or dying sailor rather than to a witness to the execution. Arguably, the position of the witness constitutes a greater threat to the power of the state, for his statement opens the possibility that others, beside the accused, are dissatisfied with the killing. The witness, the speaker in "The Somers Tragedy," accuses the captain, and by extension the state, of extralegal murder. And while the ballad does not call for the punishment of any individual in connection with the killings, it does recommend that the ship be destroyed as a fitting resolution to the violence that has happened on board it.

The narrator of *Billy Budd* strikes a more ambivalent tone concerning the propriety of Vere's action and of state-sanctioned execution. It seems likely that, having lived through the violence of the American Civil War, Melville would have been even more cautious than he was when he wrote *White-Jacket* about devising a sympathetic fictional character or narrator who would advocate rebellion. And yet, toward the end of his life and while writing *Billy Budd*, Melville's ear remained attuned to the sound of lingering discontent with the naked exercise of the state's power to kill. He did not sing out in response, but he amplified a distant and watery murmur.

Notes

Epigraph: Barbara Johnson, "Melville's Fist: The Execution of *Billy Budd*," in *The Critical Difference: Essays in the Contemporary Rhetoric of Reading* (Baltimore, Md.: Johns Hopkins University Press, 1992), 79–109, at 81.

1. For reactions to the execution, see part 1 of *The Somers Mutiny Affair*, ed. Harrison Hayford (New Jersey: Prentice Hall, 1959), 1–19.

2. Herman Melville, *White-Jacket*, in *Redburn, White-Jacket, Moby-Dick* (New York: Library of America, 1983), 341–770, at 498.

3. On slavery, see Michael Rogin's *Subversive Genealogy: The Politics and Art of Herman Melville* (Berkeley: University of California Press, 1985). Rogin writes: "It was politically provocative, in the middle of the debate over slavery, to identify shipboard with slave masters, and condemn the use of the whip. Antislavery forces led the campaign against naval flogging; slave-state congressmen opposed them" (ibid., 90).

4. Johnson, "Melville's Fist," 79–80.

5. Ibid., 101.

6. On whether to speak or kill, see Ann Smock, "*Speak or Kill*: Blanchot, Melville," in *What Is There to Say?* (Lincoln: University of Nebraska Press), 45–72. For a reading which emphasizes Billy's silence and relationship to the stateless, see Munia Bhaumik, "Literary Arendt: The Right to Political Allegory," *The Yearbook of Comparative Literature* 61 (2015): 11–34.

7. Herman Melville, *Billy Budd, Sailor*, in *Billy Budd and Other Stories* (New York: Penguin, 1986), 287–385, at 301.

8. On the importance of homosexuality to the text, see Eve Kosofsky Sedgwick's "Billy Budd: *After the Homosexual*," in *Epistemology of the Closet* (Berkeley: University of California Press, 1990), 91–130.

9. Melville, *Billy Budd*, 375 (emphasis added).

10. Ibid., 297.

11. Joseph Shiffman, "Melville's Final Stage: Irony," *American Literature* 22, no. 2 (May 1950): 128–36.

12. Melville, *Billy Budd*, 375.

13. In 1800 Alessandro Volta invented the first battery.

14. On the structure of telephony, see Avital Ronell, *The Telephone Book* (Lincoln: University of Nebraska Press, 1989), 252.

15. Melville, *Billy Budd*, 362.

16. The idea of "parody" as "dying alongside" is, of course, based on a false etymology, "parody" deriving from "para" + "ode" and not "para" + "to die." Yet there is something in this falsehood that rings true. In witnessing Budd's execution, the assembled sailors are being told, in no uncertain terms, that their lives are just as expendable as Budd's; that is, that they, too, can be killed in summary fashion aboard ship should similar circumstances arise. In identifying with Budd, a sailor is thus encouraged to renounce the value of his own life relative to the ongoing safety and operation of the ship. Furthermore, the sailors who echo Budd's cry are, arguably, repeating a one-line song or poem, and the question at hand is whether or not their repetition introduces, in the manner of a parody, any sort of difference, or if it remains a morbid, albeit "electric," copy of the original.

17. In seeking to restore potential to Billy's dying utterance, my work owes something to Giorgio Agamben's thought concerning the potential to be found in Bartleby's cryptic phrase, "I would prefer not to." But the illiterate Billy is no Bartleby. He would no doubt like nothing more than to return to his work in the foretop, whereas Bartleby places the work of copying in indefinite suspension. It could be said that Bartleby refuses writing in order to take up a passive mode of resistance marked by long silences and the occasional repetition of his famous phrase. He operates on a very different tempo from Billy, who leans toward

violence when speech or other action is checked. The tempo of the assembled sailors, however, and of the narrator who amplifies their fitful protest, is closer to the temporality of Bartleby's deferral. See Giorgio Agamben, "Bartleby, or On Contingency," in *Potentialities* (Stanford, Calif.: Stanford University Press, 1999), 243–76.

18. Melville, *Billy Budd*, 377–78.

19. The film critic Michel Chion would refer to these everyday sounds of the sea and the sail as "anaempathetic." They intensify the emotion of the scene in that they continue to occur as if nothing significant has taken place. In their "indifference" to Billy's death, they augment the emotional character of the situation for both the crew and for the reader. See Michel Chion, *Audio-Vision* (New York: Columbia University Press, 1994), 8–9.

20. More precisely, *at* the very moment of execution and just after. Curiously, the narrative does not relay the sounds one might expect to be associated with the hanging itself—a bit of flooring giving way, or a body catching at the end of a rope. This could be a bit of modesty on the narrator's part, but it also conforms to the extraordinary modesty of Billy himself who, it is implied, after crying out dies soundlessly.

21. A number of the essays in this volume are concerned with how Melville's text is reappropriated by later artists and generations. My contribution differs, perhaps, in its emphasis on how Melville himself reflects on the notion of ongoing mediation (*la dissémination*) by highlighting the way in which *Billy Budd* is a particular type of intervention (with its own frames and emphases) in a long history of commemoration and of forgetting.

22. Melville, *Billy Budd*, 364.

23. While a reader can only imagine, with difficulty, the sound-world conjured by Melville's language, a listener to Benjamin Britten's *Billy Budd* can hear the struggle between officers and crew transposed into a dynamic and impressive musical setting. With a fine ear, John Neufeld describes the moment just after Billy's execution in the following terms: "The crew's indistinct and inarticulate response to Billy's death is expressed with broken, short, almost shouted fragments of the work song [previously sung by them in the opera . . .]. The effect is a rippling, unsettling, indistinct sound that threatens violence. As the officers attempt to restore discipline, the crew's murmur rises and becomes more musically coherent, ultimately converging into the figure of the work song, now sung together in harmony" ("Billy Budd's Song: Authority and Music in the Public Sphere," *The Opera Quarterly* 28, no. 3–4 [2013]: 172–91, at 188). While I find much to like about Neufeld's interpretation, I do think he underplays the extent to which, in the opera, the officers are represented as having to do relatively little in terms of sonic production to disrupt the incipient rebellion. Their whistles and cries do not have the piercing quality Melville ascribes to them ("Shrill as the shriek of the sea hawk the silver whistles . . . pierced that ominous low sound, dissipating it"). Instead, the sailors' song seems *to organize itself* and to represent an accommodation or perhaps capitulation to the rhythms and protocols of their habitual labor aboard ship. In other words, the scene arguably enacts, in musical form, self-censorship rather than externally imposed discipline. Of course, the two go hand in hand, but the accent, in Melville's text, is, to my ear, slightly more on the latter, that is, on the imposition.

24. Melville, *Billy Budd*, 365.

25. William Spanos addresses the "genealogical" nature of Melville's fiction, as well as the peculiar figure of the narrator, in chapter 3 of *The Exceptionalist State and the State of Exception* (Baltimore, Md.: Johns Hopkins University Press, 2011), 75–140.

26. Melville, *Billy Budd*, 382.

27. Ibid., 383.

28. Though his first name is in the title, the ballad does not refer to Billy Budd by his full name. It seems, however, to register a kind of anxiety over this in the line: "I remember the Welshman when he sank / And his cheek it was like the *budd*ing pink."

29. Melville, *Billy Budd*, 384 (emphasis added).

30. On the human microphone, see Homay King's "Antiphon: Notes on the People's Microphone," *Journal of Popular Music Studies* 24, no. 2 (2012): 238–46.

31. *Proceedings of the Naval Court Martial in the Case of Alexander Slidell Mackenzie, A Commander in the Navy of the United States, etc., Including the Charges and Specifications of Charges, Preferred against Him by the Secretary of the Navy* (New York: Henry G. Langley, 1844), 39.

32. Horser Clenling, "The Somers Tragedy," *The New York Herald*, May 11, 1843, 2.

33. Ibid. (emphasis added).

Necrophilology

Jacques Lezra

> Which is more reasonable, to stop the machine when the works have done the task demanded of them, or to let it run on until it stands still of its own accord—in other words, is destroyed?
> —Nietzsche, *Human, All Too Human* II

> How it is that we still refuse to be comforted for those who we nevertheless maintain are dwelling in unspeakable bliss; why all the living so strive to hush all the dead; wherefore but the rumor of a knocking in a tomb will terrify a whole city. All these things are not without their meanings.
> —Melville, *Moby-Dick*

The problem that the general equivalent poses to Marx's theory of value stems from two sources. The first is the theory's first moment, preceding and setting under way what Alfred Sohn-Rethel called Marx's "commodity abstraction," and specifically from the requirement that *any commodity whatever* may pass from the field of relative valuation (of value that pertains to its use, here and now, to a concrete end) into the role of coin-of-the-realm in a circuit of exchange, of general equivalent, of money.[1] Whatever-commodity steps uncertainly into the abstract, general shape that awaits it, there to lose every particular relation to other commodities in use, but to gain correspondingly—a retroactive sense of having-been-destined for that waiting shape and role, value *as* the general form of value through which all things, made and unmade, thought and unthought, must pass henceforth. The messianism of the commodity: when it is touched with the golden hand of abstraction, whatever-commodity reveals itself to have been, always and already, the *singular* bearer of universality.[2]

The second is to be found in the theory's last moment: the requirement that whatever-commodity, in its abstract form and shorn of its relations to a moment, a place, and a use, *must* translate its ghostly universality back into any-other-particular commodity and indeed into *all* commodities inasmuch as they are such, rendering them recognizable to themselves, to each other, and to markets because they are likewise bearers of that ghostly annunciation. General equivalence rests upon this general analogy and upon a consequent, generalized principle of *translatability*—this much is well enough known.

It rests also upon a theology of universal incarnation and universal resurrection (every man, Messiah; every commodity the bearer of the abstract form of value).[3] Every negation, every limit, every little death imagined as the sacrificial step toward abstract life.[4] The philosophy of general equivalence is necrophilic, and trails with it the cluster of customary necrophilological concepts and techniques: prosopography, prosopopoeia, apostrophe ("Ah Bartleby! Ah humanity!").[5]

Four questions take shape around this contradiction. My purpose in this essay is to show how the strange, silent soundscape of Melville's "Bartleby, the Scrivener" allows us to tack toward them.

The first question. Not only may any commodity step into the abstract role of the general equivalent, but because any object may, in principle, reveal itself over the course of time to be value-carrying, and thus to work like and as a commodity (or rather: like a commodity and as a commodity does, did, or will do, at a time and under specific historic conditions), *any object* at hand may step, according to laws not given in the object and not given necessarily just now, at this moment when I am considering it, into the role of commodity, thence into the role of general equivalent.

This ontological uncertainty has obvious consequences for the domains of ethics and politics, bearing on how we conceive of ethical singularity on the one hand, and of political sovereignty on the other.

So, second. Any other stands before me, and my responsibility pertains to that singular subject and to that particular state of affairs, to that particular stance—who and which, however, may well come to stand in for a class or a generality, and to whom I should thus also respond as I would, not to *this* singular subject or state of affairs alone, but to these inasmuch as my response might obtain generally, or prove regulative with regard to many other subjects and states of affairs to whom these singular ones stand in a relation of exemplary equivalence: the general *ethical* equivalent. (We experience the discomfort of this situation analytically as well as phenomenologically: that's what the awkward marriage of contingency and necessity in my phrase expresses, that because any-other *may* come to be part of a class, I *must* or *should* respond to him or her with that possibility before me, *as if*.)

Third. As for the political domain, consider the minimal properties typically attributed to a democratic regime. A majority expresses the will to invest this-or-that political agent or institution with authority to act in certain domains, in its place, in its interests—with the understanding that another agent or institution may replace this first, under conditions that are not intrinsic to this moment, to the current definition of this majority's interests, or to the agent or institution. And: *any* interest, or *any* holder of interest, has access formally to the delegation of his or her interest to another, who will have standing to act for him or her. Conditions obtaining (consideration of merit, history, formal procedures felicitously followed, and so on: these conditions are not fully given at any historical moment), any political agent or institution could be invested with such authority; any one could *lose* it or be shorn of it. Neither of these properties obtains in aristocracies, in charismatic movements of a populist stripe, in regimes of force: in *tyrannies*. That this-or-that individual or institution can stand for my interest, on my act; that any-interest and any-holder of such an interest rises to the grace of representability: these are the general *political* equivalents on which we balance the concept of democracy. The characteristic, almost thermodynamic, drift toward identifying the ephemeral authority-to-act with the actor standing in that place; and toward defining an "interest" and the "holder of an interest" in terms of representativity (an "interest" in this or that situation is what another can represent, to another, in my place: here Rancière's advocacy for the "part of those who have no part" becomes pertinent), are on this account more than accidental defects of procedural and representative democracy. ("Accidental defects" explain, as a matter of historical circumstance, say, a circumstance we could call decolonization or its failure, the difficulty of establishing genuinely ephemeral, technical bureaucracies; of evading charismatic or demagogic populism; and the nonrecognition of individuals and groups as even potential bearers of representable interests.) These defects in the domain of politics, like the modal discomforts pertaining to the ethical situation, like the problem of the general equivalent on which I opened, are not only accidental.

Fourth and finally: precisely the nature of this "thermodynamic drift," this entropism. Before us, again: the asymmetry between the humility, the abjection, of whatever-commodity, whatever-object, whatever-other, whatever-interest; and the sovereign position of the general equivalent. And also: the means, forces, rules, tropisms or entropisms by which whatever-commodity, object, other, or interest steps into, and can then step or be brought out of, its sovereign role.

The abjection of whatever-commodity; the sublimity of the general equivalent. The messianism of the commodity; of *every* commodity. How do we approach the transformation of one into the other? And why does it matter, today? As to the first, the languages of strategy, hydraulics, contingency and necessity, of translation, of exemplarity, even of aesthetic equilibrium, suggest themselves, their number and difference an indication of general, productive failure, of a lack of terms, of missing concepts perhaps. And as to the second: the matter of value—whether it's imagined as relative, intrinsic, or general; whether it's determined by demand or indexed to an abstract term; whether it's taken to wax and wane with small local desires or global trends—is inseparable today, in the era of equity and of cognitive capital, not just from epistemological, but also from *ethical* and *political* concepts. Lacking the terms, concepts, even the storylines to understand the way value accrues, we find ourselves unable to consider classically ethical or classically political questions: what it means to hold an interest in common, or to agree in common on the value of this or that object, commodity, disposition, or institution; whether forms of association or of institutionalization may be found or built that entertain a relation to markets, but are or may be, or may be made to be, antagonistic to the verticalization of wealth and political capital that seems inseparable from capitalist economics generally, and from equity and cognitive capitalism in particular.

Let's return for now to the field of political economy, allowing the cognate epistemological and ethical matters to remain close to hand, never letting their murmuring voices out of our hearing entirely. How we should think of the "general" and the "index," of the relation between these two terms (which are not quite synonyms), of the becoming-general and becoming-sovereign of the value of an abject whatever-commodity—these seem to me the most pressing tasks today, whether our field is axiology, literary criticism, political philosophy, or the economics of globalization.

The difficulties I've raised briefly disable us: the problem of the general equivalent remains untouched. That these difficulties arise on such different levels suggests that the way we've analyzed the fading of the problem of the general equivalent or of the value-index conceals a conceptually much more problematical node. It is to this node that I now turn. Recall Melville's mysterious and immensely provocative story "Bartleby, the Scrivener." It narrates the imaginary birth, the emergence in the imaginary, of modern equity and cognitive capitalism.

Here is a section from the very end of the story. The narrator searches for Bartleby:

> I again obtained admission to the Tombs, and went through the corridors in quest of Bartleby; but without finding him. "I saw him coming from his cell not long ago," said a turnkey, "maybe he's gone to loiter in the yards." So I went in that direction. "Are you looking for the silent man?" said another turnkey, passing me.
>
> "Yonder he lies—sleeping in the yard there. 'Tis not twenty minutes since I saw him lie down."
>
> The yard was entirely quiet. It was not accessible to the common prisoners. The surrounding walls, of amazing thickness, kept off all sounds behind them. The Egyptian character of the masonry weighed upon me with its gloom. But a soft imprisoned turf grew underfoot. The heart of the eternal pyramids, it seemed, wherein, by some strange magic, through the clefts, grass-seed, dropped by birds, had sprung.[6]

It's next to impossible to say anything that is both new and interesting about this work, or indeed about these terrible, devastating lines. The story has been the subject of a great number of subtle and rigorous interpretations—I remind you of Giorgio Agamben's essay on potentiality in "Bartleby"; of Maurice Blanchot's remarkable analysis of Bartleby's passivity in *The Writing of the Disaster*; of Gilles Deleuze's magnificent analysis of Bartleby's "formula" collected in *Critique et clinique*; and many others.[7] In many ways, "Bartleby" is the standard against which a particular strain of political philosophy measures itself, a text that is enigmatic, among other things, in being written by an *American*, and in being set at the very heart of the monstrous engine of American capitalism: a story of Wall Street. One could put it more provocatively: "Bartleby, the Scrivener" operates as a sort of mute general equivalent allowing the fields of literary history, political philosophy, American studies, ethics, epistemology, rhetorical reading, and so on to be brought into contact with one another, their relative value assessed, indexed, compared, translated.

My remarks then join a river of glosses on "Bartleby." I'll be hoping to draw your attention to a peculiarity that has, I think, gone unremarked about the story—and which concerns the way in which and by what means the conception of value intrinsic to equity and cognitive capitalism is established *in* the text and *for* the work. Relative value in "Bartleby" gives way to a general standard of value found in the apparent silence of the debtor's prison, in the Tombs, where Bartleby meets his end, which is of course the end we will all meet. Of course; it goes without saying; it hardly merits speaking or writing; it's barely worth a whisper to insist that Bartleby's end is also our own, every human's end. In this respect, "Bartleby, the Scrivener" follows a sketchy arc leading from the value of words—the controlled value of the sound of certain words, for instance, the call of a certain lawyer's voice: "Bartleby! quick, I am waiting"[8]—to the value, as a general index, of "silence." Neither of these end points will be quite what it appears to be, and Melville takes a different path between them than we might expect—but in outline the story might be said to move stylistically from the rather involuted prose in which the narrator opens, through to the austere sentences in which he describes Bartleby's body almost at the end of the story, and to the silence to which his last words consign Bartleby and humanity. "Bartleby" might then move from focusing on individual, even individuated experience, to setting before its reader a concept of the general or the collective life; it might be understood to move *from* expressing value in the explicit, definitive, and decisive language indicated by a legally attested signature (on a bond, a mortgage, a contract, a will, and so on), *to* expressing it in the doubly lost "dead letters" the clerk is said, perhaps, to have sorted in the Dead Letter Office. The architecture and the dynamics of Melville's story furnish his readers with models for thinking how an abject whatever-commodity, an everyman, a whatever-scrivener, can, under the most singular of circumstances, become the clamorous, sovereign tongue that speaks in the heart of Wall Street: its index, its principle of general equivalence. What all humanity shares—death, conceived as the silence of the tomb and of the Tombs—becomes the device prompting and allowing us to transform a particular identity and a particular, even singular, value, the identity of whatever-scrivener and his value, the value of his life, into a stand-in for humanity. But just how?

I'll return in brief to the great and awful lines in which Bartleby's body reenters the narrator's prose at the end of the story, but let me remind you here of the ringing tones in which the narrator describes himself at the story's opening. "I am," the story begins,

> a rather elderly man ... The late John Jacob Astor, a personage little given to poetic enthusiasm, had no hesitation in pronouncing my first grand point to be prudence, my next, method. I do not speak it in vanity, but simply record the fact that I was not unemployed in my profession by the late John Jacob Astor, a name which, I admit, I love to repeat, for it hath a rounded and orbicular sound to it, and rings like unto bullion. I will freely add that I was not insensible to the late John Jacob Astor's good opinion.

The sketchy architecture that I laid out for you above in the register of value (passing *from* the relative or particular interest one singular scrivener, whatever-scrivener, might have to a quiet and conservative lawyer on a moody Manhattan morning, *to* the claim that this interest or value characterizes the universal, the human: is general; our general equivalent) can now be approached from a slightly different perspective. The narrator's round, Cartesian assertion of identity shifts by the story's end to become a comment regarding the general class to which the narrator belongs, alongside Bartleby, the narrator and the other inmates in the law practice, and the buzzing masses on Broadway and Wall Street. We step from "I" to the story's last word, "humanity"; from a singular to a collective identity; from the narrator's "I am," "My first grand point *is*," "I do not speak," "I was not," "I admit," "I love," "I add," to the subjectless, general exclamations that close the story. It reads as though Melville's narrator were opening by rehearsing the logical table of a school primer in elementary logic, enumerating first-person statements and claims (affirmations whose subject is what one famous primer of the time, Richard Whately's *Elements of Logic* of 1826, calls "a Singular-term [that] stands for *one* individual, as 'Caesar,' 'the Thames'") before passing in the story to the register of the universal, or at least the generically general, or to what Whately's primer calls "Common-terms ... that may stand for any of an indefinite number of individuals, which are called its *significates, ie.*, can be *applied* to any of them, as comprehending them in its *single signification*; as 'man,' 'river,' 'great.'"[9] "Ah Bartleby! Ah humanity!": Singular-term, Common-term. The story moves from a single or singular predicate of existence, as in "I am," to a class or common term, whether it is "a man" or "humanity," through various seemingly complementary ways of asserting identity (by negation, including the famous double negatives in which the narrator expresses himself—and which become, or seem to become, affirmations that do not affirm; simple predications; performative speech acts like commands, which set in place a subject, an object, and their relation; and then "preferences," which turn out to be something quite other than speech-acts establishing subjective positions or identities).

The class term, when it arrives at last, when it arrives in the form, not of "man" but of "humanity," only steps on stage when the singular existential predicator, the copulative "is," has passed out of the story. From the overproduction of logical operators that we find in the narrator's opening lines, then, to an ascetic elimination of the copula: "Ah Bartleby! Ah humanity!" Bartleby has passed from the story; so has the copulative "is" that links his name, as a singular example, to the class term: Bartleby is (not) humanity. What the fiction achieves, we suspect at this stage, is to transfer the simple assertion of "is" into our imagination: it is the reader, faced with the mute parataxis of the narrator's last exclamation, who supplies the yoking, the linking of the whatever-scrivener to the universal human. "Ah Bartleby! Ah humanity!" the narrator exclaims, and we don't at first know whether Melville's narrator is asserting the identity of the particular name "Bartleby" and the general term "Humanity"; or whether he is contrasting them; or whether he is establishing their equivalence with regard to a separate standard of value (Bartleby, like all humans, is mortal); or what, indeed, the logical form is that underlies that exclamation. "Is," the basic assertion of existence, has passed from the story, as Bartleby himself has done, and into our imagination. (Whately: "The *copula* . . . indicates the act of Judgment, as by it the Predicate is affirmed or denied of the Subject.")[10] An elided or a silenced copula hovers, ghostly, in the narrator's exclamation, and it is resurrected or voiced in our imagination, which will confess to us, silently, that yes, indeed, "Bartleby" *is* (a stand-in for) "humanity." As is the narrator who witnesses his passion, as are we who read this tale of Wall Street. Yes, we say, silently assenting, copying silently the narrator's implied assertion. Yes: death, conceived as silence, the silence of the tomb and of the Tombs, becomes the device that transforms a particular identity, the identity of whichever-scrivener and also the identity of whichever-narrator, into stand-ins for humanity.

Of course, the movements I've just traced, the story's production of silence as the index-commodity and its production of logical universals out of first-person, indexical statements, don't always proceed in hand or in time.[11] But let me firm up this architectural scheme, before suggesting its limits and passing to Melville's alternative: to *necrophilology*.

Let's say, for now, that "Bartleby," that "Story of Wall Street," is concerned not only to show its readers the costs of displacing a singular identity by the abstract class term, but also to establish, and to set out the moral, conceptual, and aesthetic limits of, what I've been calling equity and cognitive capitalism—forms of capitalism structured by the messianic contradictions of general equivalence. Melville achieves this description-critique of the poetics of equity capital by describing a different kind of poetics, a poetics related to sound. I have in mind, of course, the hustle and bustle of urban space and of Wall Street in particular, and on the other side the silence of the Tombs to which Bartleby is consigned at the end of "Bartleby, the Scrivener." Between the noise of Wall Street and all that it implies, and the silence of pure debt and pure death, as the Tombs appear to symbolize, stands the aural figure that most interests Melville, and where he locates the most searching definition of necrophilology: the figure of rumor.

Let me return to Bartleby. Our narrator has tried to chase the recalcitrant scrivener out of the offices because Bartleby has not only ceased scrivening, but has begun to scare off clients. Desperate at Bartleby's strange, and strangely effective, form of passive resistance, the narrator charges out of the office debating with himself:

> After breakfast, I walked down town, arguing the probabilities *pro* and *con*. One moment I thought it would prove a miserable failure, and Bartleby would be found all alive at my office as usual; the next moment it seemed certain that I should find his chair empty. And so I kept veering about. At the corner of Broadway and Canal Street, I saw quite an excited group of people standing in earnest conversation.
> "I'll take odds he doesn't," said a voice as I passed.
> "Doesn't go?—done!" said I, "put up your money."
> I was instinctively putting my hand in my pocket to produce my own, when I remembered that this was an election day. The words I had overheard bore no reference to Bartleby but to the success or nonsuccess of some candidate for the mayoralty. In my intent frame of mind, I had, as it were, imagined that all Broadway shared in my excitement, and were debating the same question with me. I passed on, very thankful that the uproar of the street screened my momentary absent-mindedness.[12]

This is a wonderful description, in a comic key, of the way in which the mind can be both excessively present and "intent," and somehow missing ("absent-mindedness"): this double condition, for Melville's narrator, constituting the *imagination*, supplying an imaginary collective identity ("*all* Broadway . . . debating . . . with me") and an imaginary collective economic space, the space of the bet. It anticipates the way the matter is taken up in the story's last lines, if my account of them is right, if indeed they serve to translate to the reader the burden of imagining a copula linking singular to collective identities, of translating notions of particular value into abstract general equivalents. There, at the end, a "rumor," and not the "uproar of the street," awakens the narrator's speculative imagination, and apparently his readers' as well. We add another architectural determination to the cluster we have noted already—not just the movement from "uproar" and noise to the silence of tomb and Tombs, from the proper name to the common, from a particular value to a general equivalence, but the movement from a comic to a tragic prompt for our imagination. The argument that Bartleby, translated, becomes a figure, a metonym, for "humanity" stands on the "rumor" the narrator offers in conclusion—the "rumor" concerning Bartleby's occupation as a clerk in the Dead Letter Office. But it is suggested already on the street, at the corner of Broadway and Canal, when our narrator too quickly translates what he hears a voice utter into the register of his internal preoccupations, as if every voice on Broadway echoed his thoughts, and every "person" he passed were, potentially, Bartleby, the representative reduction of "person" to "voice" anticipating and hanging over the story's close, the subsumption of a singular voice in the clamorously general concept of "humanity."

But perhaps this is too wonderful: perhaps our narrator's prose is too good; perhaps neither a comic, nor a tragic imagination will succeed in translating entirely, and hence "screening," whatever it is about the "mind" that is at once excessively present and quite absent when we try to follow the story's dynamics. So in order to supply the alternative figure that Melville sketches for us, let me route my argument *through* translation, and take up a different language than Melville's, a different moment, and a different set of concerns.

It's now 1944. The European war grinds to its disastrous close. Jorge Luis Borges publishes his translation of Melville's story, "Bartleby, el escribiente," with a brief, principally biographical preface that also treats *Moby-Dick*, and which has the main critical merit of linking "Bartleby" to Kafka's *The Trial*. In "Bartleby," Borges says, "the incredible lies in the way characters act, rather than in the events of the story," whereas, "In *The Trial*, the protagonist is judged and executed by a tribunal with no authority whatsoever, whose rigorous sentence he obeys without any protest. More than half a century before, Melville gave us the strange case of Bartleby, who not only acts against all logic, but forces others to be his accomplices as well."[13] This is not, perhaps, the best analysis of "Bartleby," but it has a few suggestive features—among others, the stress Borges will place upon the illogicality of the character's actions, as well as the appeal to the "incredible." When Borges follows Melville's narrator to the corner of Canal and Broadway, a number of curious things happen. This is how he translates the lines I just cited in English.

> Después del almuerzo, me fui al centro, discutiendo las probabilidades pro y contra. A ratos pensaba que sería un fracaso miserable y que encontraría a Bartleby en mi oficina como de costumbre; y en seguida tenía la seguridad de encontrar su silla vacía. Y así seguí titubeando. En la esquina de Broadway y Canal, vi a un grupo de gente muy excitada, conversando seriamente.
> —Apuesto a que . . .—oí decir al pasar.
> —¿A que no se va?, ¡ya está!—dije—: ponga su dinero. Instintivamente metí la mano en el bolsillo para vaciar el mío, cuando me acordé que era día de elecciones. Las palabras que había oído no tenían nada que ver con Bartleby, sino con el éxito o fracaso de algún

candidato para intendente. En mi obsesión, yo había imaginado que todo Broadway compartía mi excitación y discutía el mismo problema. Seguí, agradecido al bullicio de la calle, que protegía mi distracción.[14]

Borges's translation is not entirely accurate, though what might seem immediately to be errors turn out to be examples of idiomatic difference—for instance, the substitution of the word that Castilian Spanish uses for "lunch," *almuerzo*, for Melville's "breakfast," or the (again to the speaker of Castilian Spanish) equally perplexing translation of "mayor" by "intendente," when the word *alcalde* lies at hand and is in current use. Argentine Spanish rather than Castilian, though; and coupled words, *intendente, alcalde,* and *desayuno, almuerzo,* in which the rumor of languages sounds confusedly—Latin, Arabic, even the chimeric *almuerzo*, composed of both: the Arabic particle *al-* and the Latin *morsus*, a "bite." It is unexpected, of course, to hear a small clamor of languages break out where a silent protagonist ("Are you looking for the silent man?" asks one of the Tombs' turnkeys as the story closes—but the word "silent" attaches from the story's opening to the scrivener) is being translated—but of just what might this incongruity be a symptom?

Borges's translation is critically different from Melville's text in three ways. Each bears on the story's meditation on the *costs* of translation, in the domains we have been touching upon: logical, philological, characterological, economic. And, of course, political—the translation of a proper name into a class term telling, also, the story of the politicization of singular identities.

Recall. Our "veering," baffled narrator sees a group of excited people, and when he passes them, "'I'll take odds he doesn't,' sa[ys] a voice." Borges's narrator, in contrast, hears no "voice." Borges's "—Apuesto a que . . .—oí decir al pasar.—¿A que no se va?, ¡ya está!—dije" turns "a voice" into "I heard say in passing," *oí decir al pasar*. It's a small difference, but not a trivial one: for Melville's narrator, the pressure of thought and uncertainty, the comic imagination poised between intent over-presence and absence, converts "people" into "voices" alone. The metonym substituting the voice for the person who articulates a phrase by means of the voice is conventional, not just in English and in Spanish, but of course in other traditions as well. It is, indeed, a substitution foundational for a conception of participatory politics of the sort the scene represents—the civic discussion of candidates for elected office, carried out by "people" whose interests are manifested in voice and vote: *vox populi*, the ancient phrase goes, *vox Dei*.[15] But this substitution of voice for person has, in the context of the story, a peculiar shape. We remember that the hustle and bustle of Wall Street has the effect of taking from Bartleby his voice. In the Tombs, in the tomb, Bartleby becomes "the silent man"; there, the "voice" that his silence is granted, the symbolic register in which it is articulated, is seemingly not "voiced" in the register of politics, participatory or not, but of religious allegory. But *here*, on the corner of Canal and Broadway, matters are different. Here, Melville's English tells a story about the social, the explicitly *political*, context in which a singular figure (Bartleby, or a candidate for the mayoralty) becomes the occasion for a collective transaction—a bet, a vote, the call of a voice, an image produced and held collectively. That this social translation of the preference expressed by a voice into its abstract condition or its general equivalent involves the death of one singular scrivener speaks to the classically tragic genre in which the story appears to belong. And Borges's translation, perhaps because it is too "intent" or too "absent-minded," drops Melville's "voice" and thus screens from its readers the tragic translation into the political domain that the scene stages in Melville's prose.

So, at any rate, it would appear. Matters, however, are not this simple. Here is the second thing that Borges's translation of "Bartleby" shows us, by getting wrong what Melville's narrator says.

We're back on the street. Our "veering" narrator speaks up to take a bet whose object he misunderstood—only to realize his mistake as his hand reaches into his pocket to pull out his stake in the bet. Abashed, he "passe[s] on, very thankful that the uproar of the street screened [his] momentary absent-mindedness." We are used to screens in "Bartleby, the Scrivener." A screen separates our narrator from his employee, who sits behind it, palely writing or not, depending on whether we are at the beginning or toward the end of the story. The screen becomes, partway, Bartleby's screen; it stands in for him when the narrator turns toward it to address, to it, words intended for the pale scrivener concealed behind it. The uproar of the street not only screens our narrator's error, in confusing the object of the voices' bet with the clamor of thoughts within his head: this uproar places him, like Bartleby, behind a screen. The topology is elegantly and subtly sketched: the narrator's hand, arrested at the pocket; the object of the narrator's thought, arrested in its externalization, arrested before becoming the object of the public, even civic bet. The narrator, identified with the scrivener who was moving out, from behind the screen of the narrator's imagination and out onto the street, now moves back within his own imagination. The screen that stood between thought and its object has slipped: thought thinks itself within itself: the narrator's "absent-mindedness" is something more—it is, simultaneously, the record of the mind's presence to itself, unscreened, immediate.

This is not what Borges hears, however, or at any rate it is not what his Spanish renders for us, as if on a screen. Where Melville's narrator "passe[s] on, very thankful that the uproar of the street screened [his] momentary absent-mindedness," Borges's narrator says that he "Seguí, agradecido al bullicio de la calle, que protegía mi distracción." Spanish cannot make the word for screen, *biombo*, into a verb, "to screen"—Spanish does not have *biombar*—so Borges chooses instead one of the possible functions of the screen, and substitutes that in place of the screen itself: the narrator is grateful that the uproar protects, *protege*, his distraction or absent-mindedness. This is a very good compromise indeed, inasmuch as it allows Borges to place before his reader an important ambiguity that can seem to stand in for Melville's demanding topology, simultaneously internal and external, a mind and an imagination both absent from and excessively present to itself, the screen between thought and object impassable as well as absent. "Proteger mi distracción" in this case can mean that the narrator's absent-mindedness, his *distracción*, is protected from discovery by others, that it is hidden behind a screen, like a shameful secret; and it can mean that his absent-mindedness, his *distracción*, is preserved and protected, as if absent-mindedness were the kernel of the narrator's being, the genuine and definitive, but ephemeral and vulnerable, core of his subjectivity. Absent-mindedness, *distracción*, may be screened from sight out of shame, or protected out of solicitude. The epistemological register on which Melville's complex topology operates has been replaced by an affective one. It is no longer knowledge, the mind's knowledge of its objects and itself, that is at issue, but love: self-love, the narcissistic screening of one's ego-ideal. Philanthropy. Philology.

Finally, and perhaps most revealingly, there is something that Borges's translation manages to bring out from behind the screen of the narrator's self-love. Here is Melville again:

> After breakfast, I walked downtown, arguing the probabilities *pro* and *con*. One moment I thought it would prove a miserable failure, and Bartleby would be found all alive at my office as usual; the next moment it seemed certain that I should find his chair empty. And so I kept veering about. At the corner of Broadway and Canal Street, I saw quite an excited group of people standing in earnest conversation.
> "I'll take odds he doesn't," said a voice as I passed.
> "Doesn't go?—done!" said I, "put up your money."[16]

When Borges translates this minimal exchange of exclamations—the "voice's" "I'll take odds he doesn't" and our narrator's answering "Doesn't go?—done!" said I, "put up your money"—he writes "En la esquina de Broadway y Canal, vi a un grupo de gente muy excitada, conversando seriamente.—Apuesto a que . . .—oí decir al pasar. —¿A que no se va?, ¡ya está!—dije—: ponga su dinero." Now the difference is remarkable: the "voice" that Melville's narrator overhears bets on the negative, and it is left for the narrator to supply the object—the "going" of the scrivener. But Borges's voice says much less: his translation subtracts the negative, and leaves merely the naked *bet*: "Apuesto a que . . . ," "I bet that . . ." Here Borges has heard something that Melville's narrator hasn't quite made out, not here, not yet. For the hustle and bustle, the "uproar," the aural confusion of Wall Street that our narrator is evoking on election day is also the hustle and bustle, the aural environment, of what we should call early equity capitalism—an environment in which information circulates not only as sanctioned, legitimated, verifiable, and *secured* articulations, but also in the form of the promise, the

Necrophilology 171

tip, the bid, the secret, the rumor, all affecting the sorts of controlled bets we call the equities market—the former eventuating in the sorts of "bonds, and mortgages, and title deeds" in which our narrator's practice specializes, the latter in risky, speculative, and exposed commitments. Rumor—what the voice, unattached to the utterer of the statement—conveys, that supplement to the formal structure of information-delivery, is the great fear and the great resource of equity capitalism.[17] Let us recall Marx's column about "The Charter of the East India Company," published in the *New-York Daily Tribune* in June 1853, just a few months before "Bartleby" appeared:

> The charter of the East India Company expires in 1854. Lord John Russell has given notice in the House of Commons, that the Government will be enabled to state, through Sir Charles Wood, their views respecting the future Government of India, on the 3d of June. A hint has been thrown out in some ministerial papers, in support of *the already credited public rumor*, that the Coalition have found the means of reducing even this colossal Indian question to almost Lilliputian dimensions.[18]

Or consider this bit of news about "the firm Marshall & Self—better known to the vulgar as the 'Original Butter-Cake Dick's'," reported on November 1, 1854, in the *New York Daily Times* under the heading "Another Painful Rumor—Wall Street Again Alarmed." I turn to it for its *general*, exemplary value: it is precisely not a *singular* case or expression. My argument about singular terms and class terms is also an argument about historiography. "There was," the *Daily Times* columnist reports,

> another of those disagreeable—in fact, painful—rumors which have of late so much perplexed the moneyed interest of the country, afloat in Wall street yesterday . . . Notwithstanding appearances last night were calculated to excite the worst fears, we trust the rumor will yet be shown to have had, if at all, at least but a temporary foundation. And yet trusting is the very poorest ground for hope in mercantile affairs. In fact, it is stated that trusting, without discrimination and too much, was one of the main causes of the suspension of the House which we chronicle in deep sorrow.

A droll version of the "foundations" of mercantile affairs in Wall Street: the dialectic of *rumor* and *trust*, of unlicensed excitation and wild trade on the one hand, and "trust," belief, and credit on the other. Both unsecured and as-yet uncredited—*rumor*, unsecured by any authoritative, credible name standing behind the wild voice; *trust*, excessive trust, unsecured by any collateral, only made tolerable, predictable, useful to the machinery of Wall Street by the formal and formalizing instruments at the disposal of an "eminently *safe* man" like Melville's narrator: "bonds and mortgages and title-deeds." Rumor "perplexes" Wall Street because it adds or subtracts value mysteriously to the matter traded on the Street, commodities, institutions, what have you—and this perplexity will generate compensatory, formalizing offices and institutions, "avocations" (the narrator's play on words is fine), as well as sinecures like the "good old offices . . . of a Master of Chancery" serving to regulate that mysterious instability, among other things. Rumor *also* "perplexes" the street much more profoundly, however, and it is to this that Borges's translation attends just here, before Melville's English-speaking narrator can quite hear, in the uproar of the street, the ring of what's at stake. As if the translator reads from the story's conclusion backward, with the benefit of the end before him. The claim, in Borges's Spanish, is now stronger: rumor cannot, on firm formal grounds, really be distinguished from statements of fact, signed statements remitting to a legitimate and sanctioned authority. The efforts made by "trust," by trustees, advocates, lawyers pursuing avocations, and others to master, or formalize, regulate, render predictable, or disarm the vagaries introduced in capital's value-system by rumor are not to be trusted, or no more than a rumor might be. "Notwithstanding appearances . . ." runs the *Daily News* article that I cited above, "we trust the rumor will yet be shown to have had, if at all, at least but a temporary foundation. And yet trusting is the very poorest ground for hope in mercantile affairs." And it is this ungrounding of trust, of the device and logic intended to regulate the contingencies of rumor, that Borges's translation hears and repeats for his readers, on the corner of Broadway and Canal. His phrase, "Apuesto a que . . . ," shorn (as Spanish does routinely) of the subject pronoun but also of the predicate, of the content of the bet (an elision no more common in Spanish than in English), profits from and defines, tremblingly, the indefinite syntax of rumor. This sort of rumor, the rumor that Borges's translation (and not yet Melville's narrator) hears on the street corner, is more than "perplexing" to the emergent logic of equity and cognitive capitalism. In Spanish, our narrator's imagination is solicited by a subjectless, objectless, occurring—an overhearing, an event that seems to crop up headlessly. We add, in our imagination and according to the logic of the "intent" and "absent" mind, both the subject (the subject of the bet, of the tip; the identity of the person in possession of the information that the rumor provides; but also my own, your own, subjectivity, our own capacity to act so as to add to, to posit, predicate, or imagine anything in the first place) and the object (whatever it is that is the object of our assertion, or holds our imagination in thrall: ourself, our mind, screened to you and to me, a screen before us). What appeared to us the burden of the imagination—the task of producing, in compensation for the silencing of Bartleby himself, the copula allowing the story to translate his singular sacrifice into the general condition of humanity—shifts now. On rumor's paradoxical wings, the imaginary translation of general equivalency fatally fails, with a fatality we can no longer convert, or

Necrophilology

translate, into a general attribute reigning sovereign over the class to which we belong.

This, then, is the rumor on which "Bartleby, the Scrivener" closes, and which rings in Borges's ear as he translates the scene that Melville's narrator, still caught in the diegesis of his story, still trusting to the step-by-step path he takes on Broadway and in his narrative, has not yet learned to hear.[19] Melville's narrator has closed his former employee's sightless eyes. Some time has passed; in these few months, Melville's narrator has at last heard what Borges's translation voices a century after the story was published. He tells us this:

> Yet here I hardly know whether I should divulge one little item of rumor which came to my ear a few months after the scrivener's decease. Upon what basis it rested, I could never ascertain, and hence how true it is I cannot now tell. But, inasmuch as this vague report has not been without a certain suggestive interest to me, however sad, it may prove the same with some others, and so I will briefly mention it. The report was this: that Bartleby had been a subordinate clerk in the Dead Letter Office at Washington, from which he had been suddenly removed by a change in the administration. When I think over this rumor, I cannot adequately express the emotions which seize me.[20] Dead letters! does it not sound like dead men? Conceive a man by nature and misfortune prone to a pallid hopelessness, can any business seem more fitted to heighten it than that of continually handling these dead letters, and assorting them for the flames? For by the cartload they are annually burned. Sometimes from out the folded paper the pale clerk takes a ring:—the finger it was meant for, perhaps, moulders in the grave; a bank note sent in swiftest charity:—he whom it would relieve, nor eats nor hungers any more; pardon for those who died despairing; hope for those who died unhoping; good tidings for those who died stifled by unrelieved calamities. On errands of life, these letters speed to death. Ah Bartleby! Ah humanity![21]

Our English-speaking narrator's closing lines now bring into a systematic relation the themes of rumor and contingency, and the syntactic, economic problem of *indexicality*. This last has kept us quiet company throughout our reading of "Bartleby, the Scrivener": How do we assess the value of the "singular"? How do we understand what something "singular" means? (Everything seems to hang on the narrator's reticent, if not straight-out contradictory expression, in the story's second line: "an interesting and somewhat singular set of men." Is not the term "singular" categorical? Can something, some "set of men," be "*somewhat* singular" in the same way that a hand, the narrator's, is "somewhat nervously extended with the copy" of a document presented for Bartleby to proofread?) Against what is the narrator's "somewhat singularity" to be measured? How do we compare it, and to what? What sort of "set" *is* "somewhat singular"? Is a "somewhat singular" set the set of individuals who are themselves "somewhat singular," that is, only "somewhat" individuals? Melville's return to the question of indexicality at the story's conclusion is carried, as has often been remarked, by the exquisite ambivalence in the deictic expression "these letters," by means of which Melville's narrator indicates not only the letters sorted by the clerks in the Dead Letter Office, but the letters that comprise his story, "these letters" of "Bartleby, the Scrivener," or at any rate the letters offered us in the rumor, by the rumor, as the rumor that closes the story. This is well-enough known; it's hard to miss, singularly hard to miss. By means of the metonym linking the English "letters," epistles, to the graphemes of his story, our (English-language) narrator turns the "temporary foundation" of rumor into a base as solid as the single word "letter," which stands at the point of intersection, at the urban corner, of both registers (Canal, Broadway . . .): the internal, diegetic register of the "Dead Letter Office," and the extra-diegetical, self-referential register in which "Bartleby, the Scrivener's" *letters* are the object of "Bartleby, the Scrivener's" indication. At least *this* rumor we can trust, since "these letters" speed at once to us (they are what we are reading) and to the work itself (they are elements in the work). On this minimal, but definitive, point of suture economies can be built, translations accomplished, communities imagined—communities built on *trust* in *rumor*'s "temporary foundations": suturing, universal terms like "humanity," or indeed like "singularity." Communities (including the sorts of communities we call "markets") that emerge and persist on the condition that the mode of their actualization as well as their constituting index-values are contingent, precarious. Communities possessed of the definitive properties of their members, and thus, in a strange way, parts or elements or members of themselves: like "somewhat singular sets" composed of "somewhat singular" elements.

But we are trusting blindly. For consider: just how are we to determine on what register to read the last lines of "Bartleby, the Scrivener"? According to which standard—one in which the deictic "These" does indeed fold the narrator's words back upon themselves, inviting us to see his "rumor," or the whole story, as "speeding to death"? Or is our (English) narrator's last phrase working contrastively, and distinguishing between "these letters" you are reading and "these other letters," the ones in the Dead Letter Office, the ones we can keep in the tomb of rumor itself, closed away? Is our narrator saying that *those* letters, the ones the Dead Letter Office collects, sorts, and consigns to flame, *those letters* speed toward death, while *these* letters, the ones that you are reading, tell, with the lively and enlivening morality of the tragic tale, the sad but valuable allegory of that tragic destination? Sometimes, headless, rumorously, the index-function switches, and these letters you are reading acquire the surplus-value of the literary work; perhaps out of them you will derive a message—hope, despair, wealth, value. It may be that these letters that speed to death are indeed the ones you are reading. Sometimes they sound like "dead men," but sometimes not. In short—the figure of rumor, long associated with the nameless and unattributable mobility of the field of language, the dissecting of the letter from its intent, "somewhat singularly" wandering outside from the circuit faithfully linking the sender of the letter to its recipient—rumor reenters Melville's story here not only to firm up the foundation of "trust," but also in its more perplexing, strong, Borgesian sense.

Yes, a poetics of regulated rumor—ambivalent, undecidable, overdetermined—at first *seems* to supply these closing lines with a "temporary foundation" and index permitting us to translate between the proper, singular name and the class name, and to make possible the representation of the general equivalent as the "human" (and vice versa). Yes, this translation is the moral, economic, even political charge of the narrator's ideology, the conversion of the mad contingencies of rumor into the universal condition on which equity capitalism and its many communities will prove to operate. And yes, on the back of our (English-language) narrator's "letters" we may, in our imaginary tongue, give voice to the hidden copula linking Bartleby to humanity, the most singular of the "somewhat singular" "set of men" to the "somewhat singular set" of humans.

This is not, or not only, what Melville's story stages for its readers.

I titled this essay "Necrophilology," and by this I intend to evoke the singular set of necrophilological concepts and techniques that make up the poetics of equity and cognitive capitalism: prosopography, prosopopoeia, apostrophe, the rhetorical arsenal of commodity abstraction and general equivalence. I intend to evoke the love of dead letters, and also the study of the love of the dead, the death of the study of language, and the love of the study of the dead. But I also mean something more precise, to which I turn in conclusion. "Bartleby, the Scrivener" is a work of necrophilology inasmuch as it *resists* substantializing, or elevating to the ontological level, or translating into even a "temporary foundation," the indeterminacy of the relative value or of the relative sense of its letters. It holds the mind to its contradictory determination: too "intent," always also "absent." To catch Melville at work, let's return in closing to Borges's translation. Here too his Spanish seems a little off in trivial ways, but it's where it departs most substantially from Melville's text that "Bartleby, el escribiente" shows us, I think, what's at work when Melville's narrator moves to embrace a substantialized, moralized political economy of contingency. Here is Borges's translation of the story's last lines:

> El rumor es éste: que Bartleby había sido un empleado subalterno en la Oficina de Cartas Muertas de Wáshington, del que fue bruscamente despedido por un cambio en la administración. Cuando pienso en este rumor, apenas puedo expresar la emoción que me embargó. ¡Cartas

muertas!, ¿no se parece a hombres muertos? Conciban un hombre por naturaleza y por desdicha propenso a una pálida desesperanza. ¿Qué ejercicio puede aumentar esa desesperanza como el de manejar continuamente esas cartas muertas y clasificarlas para las llamas? Pues a carradas las queman todos los años. A veces, el pálido funcionario saca de los dobleces del papel un anillo —el dedo al que iba destinado, tal vez ya se corrompe en la tumba— ; un billete de Banco remitido en urgente caridad a quien ya no come, ni puede ya sentir hambre; perdón para quienes murieron desesperados; esperanza para los que murieron sin esperanza, buenas noticias para quienes murieron sofocados por insoportables calamidades. Con mensajes de vida, estas cartas se apresuran hacia la muerte. ¡Oh Bartleby! ¡Oh humanidad!

Notice just two things. My argument to this point has stressed that Melville's (English-language) narrator universalizes the figure of rumor, and makes it the device for moving between the story's levels—hence the operating verb on which the affect is carried, "When I think over this rumor, hardly can I express the emotions which seize me. Dead letters! does it not sound like dead men?" Here "this rumor" indicates the story our narrator has just relayed to his reader, and the expression "sounding like dead men" is the device on which the narrator's allegorical impulse will operate. Rumor and sound work in hand—*this* rumor, the rumor concerning the Dead Letter Office, is what sounds like "dead men." Spanish can easily capture this turn of phrase: all we would have to say is something like "¡Cartas muertas!, ¿no suena a hombres muertos?" But Borges does not choose to do so—he translates the English narrator's "sounds like" as "parece," the verb meaning *to resemble, to appear like something else*. He broadens the frame—resemblance in general, in the abstract, is at work to close "Bartleby, el escribiente," and not just "sound." But when Borges disengages the movement between the singular name and the class term from the phonic register on which Melville's narrator has been building it, we lose the (English) story's intervening device, its specific organ, but also the device linking the story's formal architecture to the moment and setting it seeks to evoke (Wall Street's "uproar," the Tombs' and the protagonist's "silence").

This process of abstraction is at work where the Spanish of Borges's translation makes its specificity felt most starkly. Here are two examples, at different levels. The word "letters," in English and in the French *lettres*, and in other languages as well, has the useful, immensely rich peculiarity that it can refer to the missive that you and I might exchange by mail, and the grapheme we write out in order to compose the words of such a letter. All the indexical ambiguity of Melville's conclusion turns on this metonymous peculiarity: Bartleby's dead letters are, or could be, the letters in which the story "Bartleby, the Scrivener" is written. But this is not an ambivalence that Spanish permits. Borges's prose cannot make this pun: the difference between "carta" and "letra" is unbridgeable; there is no way for Spanish to move, literally, from the letter to the letter, from "letra" to "carta." A letter, in Spanish, may be composed of letters, *una carta se puede escribir en letras* or *se puede componer de letras*, but the metonym substituting the letter for the letter is foreclosed. And notice also something strange—something that Spanish does permit, indeed, something that Borges's translation should have caught, surely an error rather than the manifestation of an irreducible linguistic particularity. Melville's narrator tells us that "When I think over this rumor, hardly can I express the emotions which seize me." This is wonderful—it places the relation to rumor, and also to this literary work, "Bartleby, the Scrivener," in its proper temporal frame: a rumor or a story comes to one's attention, and at any time, whenever one thinks it over, it produces an affect, an emotion. Thought and affect coincide; the self can hardly express the seizure it experiences when emotion follows on thought in this way, necessarily, correlatively. This is the governing fantasy of the aesthetic of equity capital, one might say—the generality of value is like the chronological universality of the affect elicited by the work, by the letter: whenever you think about a rumor, about *this* rumor, an emotion seizes you, hard to express but universal, a definitively *human* emotion: "When I think over this rumor, hardly can I express the emotions which seize me."

Borges has at his disposal precisely the same tense form for rendering this governing fantasy—the present tense, intended to convey that the emotion seizes you now and here, at any time indicated by the moment in which you think: I think, therefore I feel. But Borges chooses instead to translate Melville's "When I think over this rumor, hardly can I express the emotions which seize me" as "Cuando pienso en este rumor, apenas puedo expresar la emoción que me *embargó*." This would be in English: "When I think over this rumor, hardly can I express the emotions which *seized me*," "seized me" *then*, "seized me" at the moment when I first heard the rumor, presumably, but not necessarily just now, not at this moment when I think about the rumor and seek, with difficulty, in English or in Spanish, to express what I feel. Borges's Spanish seizes on something that Melville's narrator lets slip. Whether Borges's narrator intends it or not, whether it is a mark of the structural specificity of Spanish (the lack of a metonym in Spanish linking *carta* and *letra*) or the expression of the translator's decision (the shift in tenses affecting the relation between reason and emotion), Borges's translation achieves precisely what Melville's narrator seeks to displace: the de-substantialization of contingency as the general equivalent or index. Borges's translation is profoundly anti-indexical and anti-copulative—but the alternative it provides to Melville's necrophilology is not a sort of abstraction that lends itself to the setting-into-circulation, for exchange and general valuation, of whatever-commodities, identities, or letters. The abstraction that Borges's translation performs on and discloses in "Bartleby, the Scrivener" unlinks Melville's "letters" from themselves, and disjoins the time of thought from the time of affect. His translation, in short, seizes and guards—*embarga*: the play on the term's economico-juridical sense, which we hear in English's "embargo," is much stronger in Spanish than in English—in its apparent failures, the ideological bases on which Melville's narrator seeks to make a story of Wall Street into the story of "humanity," the insistence of whatever-commodity into the general form of value, of whatever-scrivener into the chronicler of emergent modern subjectivity and subjection.

Notes

An earlier version of this essay appeared in *On the Nature of Marx's Things* (New York: Fordham University Press, 2018).

1. Alfred Sohn-Rethel, *Intellectual and Manual Labor: A Critique of Epistemology*, trans. Martin Sohn-Rethel (London: Macmillan, 1978). Sohn-Rethel's early work has been amply discussed and substantially revised—including by Sohn-Rethel himself, in his 1989 revised edition of *Geistige und körperliche Arbeit* (1970; repr. Weinhem: VCH, 1989). Useful, more recent accounts of the problem of the value-form are Alberto Toscano, "The Open Secret of Real Abstraction," *Rethinking Marxism* 20, no. 2 (2008): 273–87; Geert Reuten and Michael Williams, *Value-Form and the State: The Tendencies of Accumulation and the Determination of Economic Policy in Capitalist Society* (London: Routledge, 1988); Fred Moseley, ed., *Marx's Method in "Capital": A Reexamination* (Atlantic Highlands, N.J.: Humanities, 1993); and, especially, Hans-Georg Backhaus, *Dialektik der Wertform: Untersuchungen zur Marxschen Ökonomiekritik* (Freiburg: Çaira, 1997).

2. This is how Sohn-Rethel puts it—in terms just slightly different from the ones I am using. He is discussing the way in which the exchange abstraction arises in societies and in individuals. He is characteristically precise—and as a result builds into his analysis a symptomatic hesitation that we catch in the story's odd dynamics: the exchange abstraction both develops socially with the gradual consolidation of commodity production, and occurs, for the individual consciousness, as the result of external accidents that "befall" consciousness: "As commodity production develops and becomes the typical form of production, man's imagination grows more and more separate from his actions and becomes increasingly individualized, eventually assuming the dimensions of a private consciousness . . . The individualized consciousness also is beset by abstractness, but this is not the abstractness of the act of exchange at its source. The abstractness of [the act of exchange] cannot be noted when it happens, since it only happens because the consciousness of its agents is taken up with their business and with the empirical appearance of things which pertains to their use. One could say that the abstractness of their action is beyond realization by the actors because their very consciousness stands in the way. Were the abstractness to catch their minds, their action would cease to be exchange and the abstraction would not arise. Nevertheless the abstractness of exchange does enter their minds, but only after the event, when they are faced with the completed result of the circulation of the commodities" (*Intellectual and Manual Labor*, 26–27).

3. I have tried to formalize the relation between the economic value-form and the principles of translatability and untranslatability, in Jacques Lezra, "Translation,"

Political Concepts: A Critical Lexicon, http://www.politicalconcepts.org/translation-jacques-lezra/; and in Jacques Lezra, "This Untranslatability which Is Not One," *Paragraph* 38, no. 2 (2015): 174–88.

4. Sacrifice—sacrificiality, the preference for sacrifice, the refusal of sacrifice: these are the terms in which and through which Jacques Derrida approaches "Bartleby, the Scrivener" in *Donner la mort* (Paris: Transition, 1992), 106ff.; Jacques Derrida, *The Gift of Death*, trans. David Wills (Chicago: University of Chicago Press, 1995), 76. See, among others, Giselle Berkman, *L'Effet Bartleby: Philosophes lecteurs* (Paris: Hermann, 2011), 53–75.

5. An approach to apostrophe in "Bartleby," in Tom Cohen, "The Letters of the Law: Bartleby as Hypogrammatic Romance (Letters)," in *Antimimesis from Plato to Hitchcock* (Cambridge: Cambridge University Press, 1994), 152–178, esp. 165–69.

6. Herman Melville, "Bartleby, The Scrivener," in *Melville's Short Novels*, ed. Dan McCall (New York: Norton, 2002), 3–34, at 33.

7. Giorgio Agamben, "Bartleby, or On Contingency," in *Potentialities*, trans. Daniel Heller-Roazen (Stanford, Calif.: Stanford University Press, 1997), 243–74; Maurice Blanchot, *L'Écriture du désastre* (Paris: Gallimard, 1980); Gilles Deleuze, "Bartleby; or, The Formula," in *Essays Critical and Clinical*, trans. Daniel W. Smith and Michael A. Greco (Minneapolis: University of Minnesota Press, 1997), 68–90. An excellent reading of the story is in Branka Arsić, *Passive Constitutions: or, 7½ Times Bartleby* (Stanford, Calif.: Stanford University Press, 2007).

8. Melville, "Bartleby, The Scrivener," 11.

9. Richard Whately, *Elements of Logic: New Edition* (New York: Sheldon, 1871), 67–68.

10. Ibid., 64

11. For one account of how the story tends to disaggregate itself, see Kevin McLaughlin, "Transatlantic Connections: 'Paper Language' in Melville," in *Paperwork: Fiction and Mass Mediacy in the Paper Age* (Philadelphia: University of Pennsylvania Press, 2005), 69–79, at 76: "Bartleby's 'paper language' marks the spot where the literary medium of Melville's tale is exposed to a mass mediacy that cannot be integrated into a national literary movement conceptualized in terms of a reflexive self-consciousness. This exposure is dramatized in the tale on the level of the individual subject by the narrator's encounter with Bartleby—or, more precisely—with the disintegrating force that Bartleby supports and that the clerks and in turn the narrator himself come involuntarily to support, as they discover when they display the impression the disarticulating formula has made on them. The impression is disarticulating in that it disintegrates grammatically and syntactically—it is not a self-consistent linguistic unit—and in that it disintegrates the self-consistency of its support—in this case, the self-conscious and self-contained subjectivity of supposedly individual subjects."

12. Melville, "Bartleby, The Scrivener," 23.

13. Herman Melville, *Bartleby, el escribiente*, Prólogo y traducción de Jorge Luis Borges (Buenos Aires: Emecé and Cuadernos de la quimera, 1944).

14. Melville, *Bartleby, el escribiente*, 57–58.

15. The principle *vox populi, vox dei* is not uncontroversial. Francis Lieber's *On Civil Liberty and Self-Government,* published in London in the same year that Melville published "Bartleby" in *Putnam's Monthly*, in New York, closes a

chapter sharply critical of the principle with these words: "Whatever meaning men may choose, then, to give to *Vox populi vox Dei*, in other spheres, or, if applied to the long tenor of the history of a people, in active politics and in the province of practical liberty, it either implies political levity, which is one of the most mordant corrosives of liberty, or else it is a political heresy, as much so as *Vox regis vox Dei* would be. If it be meant to convey the idea that the people can do no wrong, it is as grievous an untruth as would be conveyed by the maxim, the king can do no wrong, if it really were meant to be taken literally . . . Individuality is destroyed, manly character is lost, and the salutary effect of parties is forfeited. He that clings to his conviction is put in ban as unnational, and as an enemy to the people. Then arises a man of personal popularity. He ruins the institutions; he bears down everything before him; yet he receives the popular acclaim, and the voice of the people being the voice of God, it is deemed equally unnational and unpatriotic to oppose him" (Francis Lieber, *Civil Liberty and Self-Government* [London: Richard Bentley, 1853], 370–71).

16. Melville, "Bartleby, The Scrivener," 23.

17. On rumor, panics, and markets, consult David Zimmerman, *Panic! Markets, Crises, & Crowds in American Fiction* (Chapel Hill: University of North Carolina Press, 2006). Zimmerman's focus is a little later than my own. Here is how he describes the logic of markets: "The stock market is constituted and sustained by . . . acts of reading. The market is composed of readers who are intensely aware that other investors are reading the same material at the same time and that their collective interpretations and predictions will have an effect on the market. Because price fluctuations, especially when the market is most volatile and unpredictable, are tied to collective interpretations, investors react to 'what they believe will be the probable effect of facts or rumor on the minds of other traders,' as one early market psychologist put it" (ibid., 25).

18. First printed as Karl Marx, "The Charter of the East India Company," *New-York Daily Tribune*, June 9, 1853; reprinted in the *New-York Semi-Weekly Tribune*, June 10, 1853. Collected in Karl Marx and Friedrich Engels, *Collected Works: 1853–1854*, vol. 12 (New York: International Publishers, 1979), 103. My emphasis.

19. Some reports of the possible sources for Melville's Dead Letter Office can be found in Dan McCall, "The Reliable Narrator," in *The Silence of Bartleby* (Ithaca, N.Y.: Cornell University Press, 1989), 99–154, reprinted in Herman Melville, *Melville's Short Novels*, ed. Dan McCall (New York: Norton, 2002), 266–86, at 277–78.

20. The phrase as I cite it, "When I think over this rumor, I cannot adequately express the emotions which seize me," and as it appears in McCall's edition, comes from the version Melville published in *Putnam's* in December 1853. The version that Melville revised and had printed in *The Piazza Tales* (New York: Dix and Edwards, 1856), reads instead: "When I think over this rumor, hardly can I express the emotions which seize me" (107).

21. Melville, "Bartleby, The Scrivener," 34.

Whaling in the Abyss between Melville and Zeppelin: Alex Itin's *Orson Whales*

John T. Hamilton

In 2008, the multimedia artist Alex Itin published *Orson Whales*, a four-minute animated video that provocatively combines Orson Welles's reading of Melville's *Moby-Dick* with Led Zeppelin's "Moby Dick," an instrumental number that centers on an extended drum solo by the band's drummer, John Bonham.[1] In a clearly playful fashion, Itin's piece constitutes a striking and highly entertaining conglomeration of materials that may at first appear random or disparate, yet which in fact unleash an array of surprising resonances and suggestive correlations, which together form a sustained interpretation of entangled complexity. In adducing three distinct sources—Melville, Welles, and Bonham—Itin allows a critical response to develop out of embedded reactions, whereby each element mutually mirrors the others, collectively reflecting the whole, which in turn imparts new meanings for each part. Precisely in this regard, the presentation's structure may be best understood as a *mise en abyme*—a reduplicating form that is frequently achieved in visual art by placing a figure between two mirrors. As Itin's title and approach already imply, Orson Welles is the protagonist who is placed between Melville and Bonham, between two works that perfectly mirror each other, at least in terms of name: *Moby-Dick* / "Moby Dick." Underscoring and further intensifying this reduplicative effect is the double meaning of the verb "to whale" ("to engage in whale-hunting" and "to beat vigorously"). The viewer's expectation, then, is that "Orson whales" in a way that somehow mirrors, but also disturbs and distorts, Ahab's lust for whaling and Bonham's approach to percussive whaling.

The term *mise en abyme* originally stems from heraldic iconography, where the *abyme* or "abyss" refers to the shield's center. It describes examples in which the shield contains a miniature, replicating version of the design "placed in the center." First identified as a narrative technique by André Gide, the *mise en abyme* became an important term in literary analysis to address instances where representations embedded within a work are regarded as reflecting the work itself.[2] As attested throughout the Western literary tradition, the *mise en abyme* is a formal device that consistently involves various media, for example, when a literary description of a painting or a piece of music introduces motifs or themes that relate to the narrative as a whole. Itin's innovative *multimedia* endeavor, therefore, is perfectly consonant with this tradition, in addition to participating in the commonly accepted filmic usage of the device, noted above, whereby a figure is caught between two mirrors. The technique of incorporating a series of reflections may be—and indeed, has been—evaluated as constructing an internally consistent and coherent system of representation, where each part contributes to the meaning of the whole without remainder, without excess. The heraldic provenance of the *mise en abyme*, its evident links to nobility, indicates the power that strives to contain all parts within a sovereign whole, or—to speak with Hobbes— within a great Leviathan created by art. Yet, as Melville's epic work loudly demonstrates, this whale-like whole—this Common Weal—is more elusive than one might imagine.[3]

By boldly synthesizing text, image, spoken word, and music, Itin's video lodges a radical critique of any system of containment. The proliferating multiplicity of embedded, mirroring responses complicates Itin's own reflexive response, which gestures toward interpreting two very different interpretations of Melville's text: Welles's dramatic recitations and Zeppelin's musical performances. A close examination of *Orson Whales* will demonstrate that Itin not only shapes his piece by means of *mise en abyme* devices, but does so by promoting this specular, abysmal form as a principal and ultimately uncontrollable theme of the work. The *mise en abyme*, in other words, is the key to it all. To be sure, multimedia approaches almost invariably redefine form as content. Yet, what makes this particular piece a critical response is that it suggests, rather compellingly, that Melville's novel, Bonham's drum solo, and Welles's identity likewise involve recursive forms to the point where recursivity itself becomes the dominant theme. The ultimate result is a thorough exacerbation of identity, insofar as the specular imago, reduplicated ad infinitum, shatters any attempt at establishing a firm, singular ground for the subject, aggravating sameness to the point of difference. Rather than achieving the terra firma of personal identity, the subject finds itself lost at sea, drowning in the mirroring abyss.

To begin, in order to appreciate some of the major ramifications of Itin's interpretive attempt, it is worthwhile describing the general nature of his animated images and then explicating some of the details and contexts of his source materials. The animation consists nearly entirely of a fast-paced montage of simple, rough images, alluding generally to Melville's plot and drawn on printed pages of the novel, which also appear rapidly in sequence, from the opening "Extracts" to the "Epilogue." The pictures, painted with a broad brush primarily in black ink, focus on ideas of viewing, mirroring, and engulfment. Images of disembodied eyes predominate, which already posit the specular structure: eyes that both see and are seen. In the first sequence, Ishmael's head, then the heads of Queequeg and others, all viewed from multiple angles, yield to a single, large eye (fig. 1), which stares directly at the viewer, while also exposing itself to view. The rapidity of the shots, however, further propelled by the intoxicating soundtrack, prevents scrutiny and frustrates visual mastery. In very quick succession, the large eye suddenly dissolves into a tiny fish, which is then swallowed by a whale. The theme of reflection becomes explicit in the subsequent scene, where a figure gazes into a handheld mirror that turns into a standing, cheval mirror, out of which another man emerges (figs. 2 and 3). Waves then rise up, until the entire field is saturated in black, before images of single eyes return, now with heads occupying the place of the pupil (fig. 4). With a flare for imaginative reflection, Itin has the eye subsequently metamorphose into the eye of the whale, whose shape is made to resemble the eye itself. The shape of the eye, in turn, expands into a whale-shaped zeppelin, which bears the *Citizen Kane* inscription "Rosebud." Finally, when Ahab harpoons the great white whale, the beast morphs into the *Hindenburg*, which bursts into flames (fig. 5).

The overall effect is one of frantic excitement, propelled by the hurried force of each medial component. The printed pages, which serve as the background field of the animation, flash by in such a rush that they defy reading or even general recognition, thus transforming the ground into an *Abgrund* or abyss, incapable of providing any steady support, textual or visual. The images, which are placed on this abyss, further contribute to the frenetic pulse as each figure hastily dissolves into another. Both figure and field therefore provide little for the viewer to grasp cognitively. Instead, one is assaulted by a nearly dizzying impermanence. The quick and frequent splices of Welles's dramatic delivery reflect this sweeping sense of speed. Snippets of text are intoned in stylized phrasing before being brusquely interrupted, constituting a rhythmic counterpoint to Bonham's percussive flourishes and syncopations. Itin's heavily manipulated soundtrack relentlessly matches the quickness of the audio edits to the velocity of the animation. All in all, a feeling of energetic precipitation, at once exhilarating and frightening, electrifying and bewildering, drives the presentation throughout—again, abysmally.

The piece opens starkly with Welles's resounding "Call me Ishmael," which is immediately punctuated by Bonham's cymbal crash and pumping hi-hat. The voice-over edits continue to accelerate, buffeted along by the rolling, sixteenth-note and triplet patterns on the drums. For the music, Itin creates a vigorous composite mix of Led Zeppelin's "Moby Dick," lifted from the 1969 studio recording (*Led Zeppelin II*) and the live album, *The Song Remains the Same* (1976).[4] For the narration, assembled mostly from the first chapter ("Loomings") and the concluding three chapters ("The Chase") of Melville's text, Itin uses a 1971 recording of Welles, who intended it for a film project that would, however, never be completed. This recitation is further interspersed with additional audial material, including outtakes of Welles's evidently inebriated performance, advertising Paul Masson Champagne for a television commercial in 1978—a recording that features an idiosyncratic, warbling exclamation ("Ahhhhh, the French Champagne . . . !"), which provides Itin with a chilling sample of Welles's wailing.[5]

(1)

(2)

(3)

Figures 1–5. Stills from Alex Itin, *Orson Whales* (2008). Images courtesy of Alex Itin.

Figure 6. Still from *Citizen Kane*, dir. Orson Welles, 1941.

After a climactic fanfare, the video abruptly quiets down, to conclude with the famous "mirror" or "*mise en abyme*" scene from Welles's *Citizen Kane* (1941). The shot shows the aged protagonist's repeated image in multiple facing mirrors as he walks slowly across a grandly ornate hall at Xanadu (fig. 6). Played over this sequence, which Itin presents in slow motion, one listens to Welles's somber reflections on transience from his last production, *F Is for Fake* (1974): "Our works in stone, in paint, in print, are spared, some of them, for a few decades or a millennium or two, but everything must finally fall in war, or wear away into the ultimate and universal ash—the triumphs, the frauds, the treasures and the fakes. A fact of life: we're going to die."[6] In the film, Welles stands before the Chartres Cathedral, eulogizing the fate of anonymous craftsmen, whose aspirations are reflected in monumental works of art. For the video, Itin pairs the older Welles and his dark musings on ephemerality with the younger Welles and his portrayal of the aged Kane. The audio and the video thus comment on each other: comments reflecting comments, identity colliding with identity, at least until all "wears away into the ultimate and universal ash." Referring to the scene from *Citizen Kane*, one recalls that the newspaper tycoon here clutches the snow globe, which encapsulates the film's generative mystery. In this film, of course, the snow globe is a central *mise en abyme* motif, reflecting in miniature a biographical plot composed of various and often conflicting reports. This mass-produced piece of kitsch, this cheap souvenir, is present in the very first and the very last shots of Kane, and shatters to bits as Kane passes away.[7] The journalist Thompson, who sets out to research the meaning of Kane's enigmatic last word ("Rosebud"), essentially needs to put together the fragmented pieces—to reassemble the globe—while the film resists any definitive unified account.[8] As the passage from *F Is for Fake* underscores, a man's identity, including the works of art in which that identity is reflected, may be spared "for a few decades or a millennium or two," but like ephemeral kitsch, all must "finally fall" into oblivion, into the abyss.

The closing voice-over of Itin's video gives the phrase, "This is the key to it all," which is spliced to the end of the *F Is for Fake* quotation: "A fact of life: we're going to die.... This is the key to it all." The latter line was heard before, as Welles recited the Narcissus passage from Melville's first chapter: "And still deeper the meaning of that story of Narcissus, who because he could not grasp the tormenting, mild image he saw in the fountain, plunged into it and was drowned. But that same image, we ourselves see in all rivers and oceans. It is the image of the ungraspable phantom of life; and this is the key to it all."[9] When Welles recites these sentences earlier in Itin's piece, the animated waves grow in volume until the entire screen goes black; and it is against this pure blackness that we hear "This is to the key to it all"—a fitting foreshadowing of the phrase's recurrence, which brings the video to an end.

As noted, foreshadowing is the primary role of the *mise en abyme* device in literature; and in Melville's novel, Ishmael's allusion to the Narcissus myth clearly constitutes a figurative mirror that prefigures the demise of Ahab. It is Ahab who was haunted by an "ungraspable phantom" and who ended his life by plunging into the sea and drowning. That said, the story of Narcissus, and by extension the story of Ahab, also prefigures the fate of every one of us ("But that same image, we ourselves see in all rivers and oceans"). From the very first imperative ("Call me Ishmael"), we the readers are imperiously implicated. The mirroring myth of Narcissus mirrors Ahab, who ultimately mirrors us.

Within the logic of Melville's novel, the narrative demand that Ishmael imposes on himself, namely, to bear witness to Ahab's death and the wreck of the *Pequod*, leads him to emend the traditional version of the story and have Narcissus drown. To be sure, in Ovid's classic account from book 3 of the *Metamorphoses*, the beautiful youth does not drown, but rather transmutes into a flower. Ishmael, a learned man, must knowingly revise and expand the mythical topos in order to have it work as a directly reflective device. Similarly, Melville's narrator is careful to stress that "*he* [Narcissus] could not grasp the tormenting, mild image," an emphasis that diverges from Ovid's description, where the image does not allow itself to be grasped:

quisquis es, huc exi! quid me, puer unice, fallis,
   quove petitus abis?[10]

Whoever you are, come out! Why me, singular boy, why do you deceive?
Why do you leave when I reach for you?

Whereas Ovid defines the longed-for image as ungraspable, Ishmael portrays Narcissus himself as incapable of grasping. This slight but important aspectual shift aligns the Narcissus story even more closely to the fate of Ahab, who deliberately chooses to hunt the whale and, failing to capture it, willfully dives into the waters.[11] Finally and above all, in addition to causing Narcissus to drown and underlining his incapacity, the import of the narrator's digression is to suggest that the object of the Captain's mad pursuit is none other than himself, and that this identification, if and when it is achieved, will be fatal. Here, Ishmael borrows wholesale from Ovid: when the mother of Narcissus asks Tiresias if her child will live to an old age, the prophet assures her that he will, "unless he should come to know himself."[12] Specular identification is but an exposure to the abyss.

Itin accentuates this insight by incorporating Welles's reading from "The Symphony" chapter:

> That glad, happy air, that winsome sky, did at last stroke and caress him; the step-mother world, so long cruel—forbidding—now threw affectionate arms around [Ahab's] stubborn neck, and did seem to joyously sob over him, as if over one, that however wilful and erring, she could yet find it in her heart to save and to bless. From beneath his slouched hat Ahab dropped a tear into the sea; nor did all the Pacific contain such wealth as that one wee drop.[13]

This moment of tranquil respite, which in fact is the calm beginning of Ahab's stormy end, is produced by a pause for quiet reflection. The paragraph opens with a barely veiled reference to Narcissus: "Slowly crossing the deck from the scuttle, Ahab leaned over the side, and watched how his shadow in the water sank and sank to his gaze, the more and the more that he strove to pierce the profundity."[14] Although Itin does not use this sentence, it is fair to say that his presentation invites the viewer to return to the novel, which is precisely what a critical response should aim to do. The faint echoes of this passage ("sank and sank," "the more and the more") again recall Ovid's poetic treatment, which innovatively introduces the figure of Echo into the traditional tale.[15] Of course, Ovid's addition of Echo is entirely justified: the one whose relation to the other is in fact a relation to the same finds a perfect companion in the other who is only capable of returning the same. For Echo is a nymph condemned to utter nothing but those words that are given to her. She produces language by listening to language, by permitting it to reverberate, by putting forth a repetition with a difference. Although chronologically posterior, the nymph's responses, precisely as echoes, must already be present in Narcissus's question. Immediately upon pronunciation, Narcissus's phrases already belong to the other; they therefore evade subjective intention and are open to incalculable usages.[16] In large measure, Itin's work in image and sound is but an unfurling of this core idea.

The implicit narcissism in the myth of Narcissus is not without relevance for Orson Welles's biography. In addition to the persistent employment of mirroring in his films, Welles's personally reflective identifications are often quite evident. The actor-filmmaker was clearly fascinated with Melville and his epic work. In the 1940s, besides producing a radio broadcast of *Moby-Dick* and then considering a film version of Bernhard Herrmann's 1938 *Moby-Dick* oratorio, there are many motifs and allusions that link Captain Ahab to the megalomaniacal Kane. It may even be the case that Kane's notoriously enigmatic last whisper, "Rosebud," makes reference to Captain Vere's deathbed scene in *Billy Budd*: "He was heard to murmur words inexplicable to his attendant: 'Billy Budd, Billy Budd.'"[17] In 1954, Welles was given the small but powerful role of Father Mapple in John Huston's ambitious film adaptation of the novel; and Welles used the earnings for this cameo appearance to fund his own two-act drama, *Moby Dick—Rehearsed*, which premiered in London the following year. The theatrical piece exploits and complicates the traditional *mise en abyme* device of the play-within-a-play by portraying a nineteenth-century troupe of actors, who are coerced by the stage-manager named Ahab—played by Welles himself—into improvising a performance of the novel, rather than continuing their rehearsal of *King Lear*.[18] Lear mirrors Ahab, and both mirror Welles (just like Narcissus mirrors Ahab, and both mirror us).[19] According to Welles's initial intention, he had the London performances filmed, to be used in a television film for the *Omnibus* series produced by CBS. Welles was confident that the film would be accepted, given his success with *King Lear*, which had appeared in the CBS series two years prior. The plot of *Moby Dick—Rehearsed* therefore replicates precisely Welles's master plan. This figurative mirroring, moreover, was literally executed for the stage production. As Welles's lighting director relates, "[Welles] had me get a two-thousand-foot film can from Chabrol's production company. He had me buy a mirror and hammer, smash the mirror to pieces, and put the mirror in the film can, then pour water in that. Then he'd read off the cue-cards for *Moby-Dick*, and with both hands he'd wash the water back and forth over the broken mirrors, which gave the impression of being at sea."[20] The broken mirror may serve as an allegory for Welles's fantasies of identity, readily recalling the shattered snow globe of *Citizen Kane*. Gestures of self-reference, tightly controlled, inevitably self-implode or crash to the ground, like a zeppelin made out of lead.

As suggested above, Itin's *Orson Whales* capitalizes on these strategies of identification and excessive, self-defeating reduplication by placing Welles in the midst of mirrored works: Melville's *Moby-Dick* and Zeppelin's "Moby Dick." Set in this specular abyss, Orson whales, hunting after the enormous monstrosity that is in fact a projection of his own image multiplied over and over until it threatens fatal engulfment.

Beyond the explicit allusion in the title, Led Zeppelin's "Moby Dick" ostensibly evokes the ambition, will power, and adventurousness attributed to Ahab. Since its very first concert tours, Zeppelin had included a drum solo number; but it was only after Jimmy Page, the band's guitarist and producer, edited together recordings of Bonham's improvisations, that "Moby Dick" was created and released on the band's second album. From that point forward, "Moby Dick" was set as Bonham's showcase, with solos ranging anywhere from six to thirty minutes, as the other musicians remained offstage—a move that would come to be imitated by many other bands afterwards. Typically, Bonham would begin playing the drums with his bare hands, exploiting the acoustic qualities but also, no doubt, indulging in the dramatic spectacle, exhibiting vigorous exertion as he pounded the drumheads, frequently to the point of bleeding. The effect was one of greater immediacy and ritualistic proximity, staging a hand-to-hand combat with the drums. Thus, as the song's title promises, the whaling Bonham is cast as the whaling Ahab, offering a relentless performance on an epic scale, pitting his imperious will against a mighty foe, recalcitrant yet responsive.[21]

As already noted, the two distinct meanings of the English verb "to whale"—an ambiguity that clearly motivates the title, *Orson Whales*—is still another example of repetition with a difference. Moreover, the possible derivations of this usage may indicate a further instance of the identification of Ahab and the Whale, the identification, that is, of the hunter and the hunted. "Whaling" as denoting the act of beating, flogging, or thrashing is first attested in 1790 in the second edition of Francis Grose's *Provincial Glossary*, where the definition reads: "to beat with a horsewhip or pliant stick."[22] Some historians of the language have conjectured that the verb's meaning may stem from the punitive practice of thrashing a person with a whalebone whip. Here, the instrument of pain would metonymically stand for the act of inflicting pain, just as the noun "flail," which names the wooden rod used to thresh corn, becomes the verb "to flail," just as the nouns "scourge," "whip," and "lash" are employed to describe the acts of scourging, whipping, and lashing. In all these related instances, cognate constructions readily come to hand: to whip with a whip, to flail with a flail, to whale with a whale's bone.

Cognate metonymies also account for an alternative explanation, which derives the verb of whaling from the "weal" or "welt" that is caused by such assaults. The Old English *walu* denotes "the mark or ridge raised on the flesh by the blow of a rod, lash or the like";[23] so that the act of whaling is named after the wound it produces. The two variant etymologies are distinguished by their temporal and hence causal position in the narrative that motivates the figure: whereas the whalebone is the *terminus a quo* for whaling, the weal is its *terminus ad quem*. On the one hand, it is the perpetrator's instrument that defines the act, while on the other hand it is the victim's bruises. Whaling refers potentially to both aspects—the active and the passive, the effective and the affected, the violent and the vulnerable—which all come to be curiously fused together through the contingent vagaries of confused etymology. Melville, who places "Etymology" at the head of his work, before the story begins, would arguably endorse the verbal reversibility that correlates the pursuer and the pursued. Itin's closing sequence, in which the Ahab figure harpoons the whale that suddenly dissolves into the exploding *Hindenburg*, suggestively involves the chiasmus that structures the novel's plot: the whaling ship that aims to destroy the whale is ultimately destroyed by the ship-sized beast. The song remains the same in Itin's animation: the harpooned whale turns out to be the hunter's vessel that bursts into flames. Both are figures of the leviathan; both constitute, and suffer from, the shared or Common *Weal*.

In the nineteenth century, "whaling" goes on to convey the relentlessness and vehemence that are commonly associated with this method of corporal punishment. Quotations from the *Oxford English Dictionary* include this line from Frances M. Whitcher's *Widow Bedott Papers* (1883): "You remember that one that come round a spell ago a whalin' away about human rights," in addition to the definition from Albert Barrère and Charles G. Leland's *Dictionary of Slang, Jargon & Cant* (1897): "*To whale away* (Amer.), to preach, talk, or lecture away continuously or vehemently."[24] In this figurative use of the figure of whaling, the same ambiguity applies: a fervent speaker's unremitting harangue is likened to a whale bone that bashes his listeners, who consequently suffer as though they had welts on their ears. As Itin's video suggests, Orson whales in pursuit of his imagined identity, while Orson whales, assaulting his audience with histrionic flair.

Poised between Ahab's whaling and Bonham's whaling, Orson certainly does whale, searching for an identity in mirror after mirror, until the quest shatters the image altogether, beating out his lines, until the lines beat him down. "A fact of life: we're going to die. . . . This is the key to it all." Itin's fanciful conglomeration of text, image, and music picks up on this key, compelling a consideration of how each component reflects the others and how fresh readings thereby open up. This process, which taps into the excess latent in the multiple sources that Itin gathers, is already at work in the addition of a silent "H" to the protagonist's name: *Orson Whales*. This change by addition may recall the very first quotation that Melville prints before the narrative begins:

Etymology

While you take in hand to school others, and to teach them by what name a whale-fish is to be called in our tongue leaving out, through ignorance, the letter H, which almost alone maketh up the signification of the word, you deliver that which is not true.[25]

This leading citation from Richard Hakluyt suggests that it is the silent letter "H" that conveys the sublime power of the whale, as though it were an inaudible mark of what Hegel identified as the experience of "absolute negativity" in the sovereign creation of the world ex nihilo.[26] For Hakluyt, and presumably for Melville, this silent letter, "H," this slight nothingness, transmits the enormous sublimity of the whale and, following Itin, the massive force of Bonham's whaling. Accordingly, this negative presentation of heaviness, which is nonetheless lighter than air, serves as a figure of coincident extremes and merging polarities, very much like a floating dirigible made out of heavy metal.

As a vociferous, whaling figure, Welles, whose career obstinately spanned the Atlantic, is well positioned between the mutual reflection of Melville's American novel and Zeppelin's British performance. Melville, who explicitly called for the liberation of American literature from European models ("No American writer should write like an Englishman"),[27] would have marveled at the explosion of the *Hindenburg* over New Jersey—an appropriate and much-used image for Zeppelin's explosive effect on American culture, which has much to do with the band's tireless obsession with African American blues and soul. Whereas Melville insisted that American writers should break with the specular allure of their counterparts in Europe, *Moby-Dick*, like *Orson Whales*, demonstrates the futility of trying to avoid the mirrors, which at any rate ultimately shatter of their own accord. This kind of mirroring comes down to little more and nothing less than the transmedial events tracked here—events driven by the creative energy that is all too often overlooked in aesthetic experiences, particularly those that are eager, in their very modes of speculation, to flee the captivation ascribed to the mirror stage. Welles as Kane, Welles as Ahab, Welles as the aged melancholic and the embarrassing drunk—is a figure ideally suited to be "placed in the center" and thereby to stand for us. To be placed thus in the center, amidst these waves or *Wellen* of excessive reflection, is little more than to be "placed in the abyss"—to be *mise en abyme*.

Notes

1. Alex Itin, *Orson Whales* (January 13, 2008), 3:55, https://vimeo.com/604918.

2. For a comprehensive account of this formal device, see Lucien Dällenbach, *Le Récit spéculaire: Essai sur la mise en abyme* (Paris: Seuil, 1977).

3. For some reflections on Hobbes's *Leviathan* and *Moby-Dick*, see Peter Szendy, *Prophecies of Leviathan: Reading Past Melville*, trans. Gil Anidjar (New York: Fordham University Press, 2010), esp. 86–93.

4. Led Zeppelin, *Led Zeppelin II*, Los Angeles: Mirror Sound, 1969, LP; and Led Zeppelin, *The Song Remains the Same*, Swan Song, 1976, LP.

5. The Paul Masson commercial outtakes can be viewed at http://www.willtheblogger.com/post/23420208855/the-sad-case-of-orson-welles-paul-masson.

6. Orson Welles, "Orson Welles—*F Is for Fake*," YouTube video, 2:32, posted by "TheMusicStalker," August 9, 2010, https://www.youtube.com/watch?v=oB3tj1c1Itg.

7. See Jeffrey Knapp, "'Throw That Junk!' The Art of the Movie in *Citizen Kane*," *Representations* 122 (2013): 110–43, at 135.

8. On the significance of the snow globe in the film, see Robert Carringer, "Rosebud, Dead or Alive: Narrative and Symbolic Structure in *Citizen Kane*," *Papers of the Modern Language Association* 91 (1976): 185–93.

9. Herman Melville, *Moby-Dick; or, The Whale, Norton Critical Edition*, ed. Hershel Parker and Harrison Hayford (New York: Norton, 2002), 20.

10. Ovid, *Metamorphoses*, 3.454–55.

11. On the central significance of the Narcissus story in Melville's novel, see Suzanne Stein, *The Pusher and the Sufferer: An Unsentimental Reading of "Moby-Dick"* (New York: Garland, 2000), 29–52.

12. "si se non noverit" (Ovid, *Metamorphoses*, 3.346).

13. Melville, *Moby-Dick*, 405.

14. Ibid.

15. Most scholars understand the addition of Echo to be Ovid's innovation, although the possibility of a Hellenistic source cannot be entirely dismissed. Generally, as in the Homeric *Hymn to Dionysus*, Echo is associated with Pan. See Franz Bömer, *Metamorphosen: Kommentar, Buch I–III* (Heidelberg: Winter, 1969), 537–38.

16. In this regard, Echo's role is far from the function ascribed to it by John Brenkman, who reads Echo's presence as a narrative device aimed at reducing textual incalculability. See John Brenkman, "Narcissus in the Text," *The Georgia Review* 30, no. 2 (1976): 293–327.

17. Herman Melville, *Billy Budd*, in *Billy Budd, Sailor, and Other Stories* (New York: Bantam, 1982), 82. Thanks to Daniel Hoffman-Schwartz for this suggestion.

18. Orson Welles, *Moby Dick—Rehearsed: A Drama in Two Acts* (New York: French, 1965).

19. Charles Olson offers many fruitful reflections on the comparison of Ahab and Lear in *Call Me Ishmael* (New York: Harcourt, Brace, 1947), 47–51.

20. Cited in John McBride, *What Ever Happened to Orson Welles? A Portrait of an Independent Career* (Lexington: University of Kentucky Press, 2006), 232–33.

21. George Cotkin likens Bonham to Ahab in *Dive Deeper: Journeys with "Moby-Dick"* (Oxford: Oxford University Press, 2012), 55–56.

22. Francis Grose, *A Provincial Glossary, with a Collection of Local Proverbs, and Popular Superstitions*, 2nd ed. (London: Hooper, 1790), s.v. "whale."

23. *Oxford English Dictionary*, 2nd ed., s.v. "weal."
24. Ibid., s.v. "whale, *v.* 2"
25. Melville, *Moby-Dick*, 7.
26. G. W. F. Hegel, *Lectures on the Philosophy of Religion*, trans. E. B. Spiers and J. B. Sanderson, 3 vols. (London: Routledge, 1974), 2:424.
27. Herman Melville, "Hawthorne and His Mosses," cited in Eyal Peretz, *Literature, Disaster & the Enigma of Power: A Reading of "Moby-Dick"* (Stanford, Calif.: Stanford University Press, 2003), 23. Peretz provides an excellent analysis of the significance of "America" for Melville's project and its reception, 19–25.

The Confidence-Image
(Melville, Godard, Deleuze)

Peter Szendy

Melville ceaselessly collected images, above all, engravings.[1] As if the number of reproductions, the very quantity that he possessed, would in the end have the task of making up for a striking rarity: that of the *word*—the rarity, that is, of the word "image" and its equivalents.

When I went back to *The Confidence-Man* after having seen the Godard film adapted from it—*Le Grand Escroc*, produced in 1964—I couldn't believe my eyes. Assuming I could find some stable value or solid anchoring there, I looked in the text for tangible occurrences—that is to say, occurrences worthy of confidence—of the signifiers "image" or "picture"; I did this with the vague hope that I would perhaps be able to exhume in Melville's story a thinking (however implicit) of the visual, a thinking on the basis of which Godard, anachronically, could in his turn be *read*, the same Godard who had filmed his reading of Melville. In other words, I sought the possibility, however delicate it might be, of a reading of the one by the other *and of the other by the one*—such a reading implying however no mutuality, reciprocity, or symmetry.

I was thus confident as I dove into the text, pursuing explicit occurrences of the lexemes "image" or "picture" in *The Confidence-Man*. I counted on the countability of words, as if my reading should compute and calculate their value in advance, on the sole basis of their frequency and quantitative repetition. With the seriousness of a veritable accountant of reading, scrupulously and precisely navigating my textual data bank (*banque de données textuelles*), I gave myself over to the intoxication of calculation and calculability. (To be sure, counting words and being able to count *on* them do not amount to the same thing; but the compulsion governing lexical counting necessarily brings along with it a confidence in the fiduciary stability of a lexicon.)

So you can imagine my surprise upon discovering that, in place of the intriguing lexical fluctuations I expected to encounter, there was instead a great silence, a near-total absence. "Picture" was in fact completely absent (save for the occurrence twice of "picturesque" and once of "picturesqueness"), while "image" appeared a mere three times.[2] I had imagined a number of complications following from my attempt to count (for instance: the variability of meaning according to context rendering the investigated lexeme quasi-unrecognizable), but certainly not this remarkable rarity.

195

I therefore didn't believe my eyes, or for that matter, my fingers (because I count with them as well). At first I thought that this was no doubt an error of calculation. Nevertheless, I had to admit it, without any possible doubt: the word "image"—that word so common and so banal that one thinks one will find it everywhere and on every page—stands out for its quasi-absence from the last novel that Melville published in his lifetime, *The Confidence-Man*.

Among its three occurrences, there were two that proved rather quickly to be of little interest. Thus, when it appears in chapter 45, the book's final chapter, the word "image" designates a graphic reproduction: "In the middle of the gentleman's cabin burned a solar lamp, swung from the ceiling, and whose shade of ground glass was all round fancifully variegated, in transparency, with the image of a horned altar, from which flames rose, alternate with the figure of a robed man, his head encircled by a halo."[3] Here the word "image" empties itself out into its supposed referent: the image says nothing of itself as an image, says nothing of its own image-character, which is to say that it effaces itself in what it represents, giving way to a description, a brief *ekphrasis* of what is painted on the lamp. The image is reduced to an "image of."

I thus move back to the preceding occurrence, in chapter 22. There "image" does not designate an image properly speaking (if there is a "proper" of the image—I will return to this question), but a comparison or metaphor:[4] "The man-child not only possesses these present points, small though they are, but, likewise—now our horticultural image comes into play—like the bud of the lily, he contains concealed rudiments of others; that is, points at present invisible, with beauties at present dormant."[5] The character (I leave it deliberately undetermined) who utters this phrase uses the word "image" in the middle of an interpolated clause circumscribed by long dashes that open the space of a metalinguistic fold: with this supplementary mark, he remarks that he speaks figuratively, with tropes. In short, he indicates that his language is imagistic, rhetorically "flowered" or florid, guided by the horticultural comparison. Here the image names not only discourse's capacity to be figurative, but also its capacity to designate itself as such, to indicate its own figurality.

I thus move backwards again, toward the beginning of the novel, to the first occurrence, in chapter 4. In relation to the two other occurrences, it appears to have an intermediary status: it is neither a question of the image as it is inscribed on a material support like the glass, nor a question of the image as an immaterial phenomenon demonstrating (to put it simply) the metaphorical power of language; it is, rather, a question of the impression of images *in the mind*, as if the mind were composed of malleable clay: "You see, sir, the mind is ductile, very much so: but images, ductilely received into it, need a certain time to harden and bake in their impressions, otherwise such a casualty as I speak of will in an instant obliterate them, as though they had never been. We are but clay, sir, potter's clay, as the good book says."[6] It's the elusive and shifty protagonist of the story—dressed here in mourning clothes—who speaks, addressing himself to a merchant who he insists he knows, even as this merchant, for his part, does not recognize him. The former slyly attributes this situation to a hypothetical accident, which is to say a head wound or cranial trauma that the latter would have suffered without remembering it. Their incongruous and unexpected encounter therefore takes place under the sign of a radical dissymmetry, as if the supposed recognition of the shopkeeper by the man in mourning would open between them the abyss of an infinite debt. Or better: as if in being called to recognize that other who he nonetheless does not know, the shopkeeper must put his signature to an *acknowledgment of debt*, an IOU.

But perhaps—or no doubt—it is already to say too much to attribute the words that we just read, in particular the word "image"—in this way and with all certainty—to such a "protagonist." For just like his dubious interlocutor, we readers never have the full assurance that the character who ceaselessly returns under new guises is truly *the same*. Behind his perpetually changing appearance, everything takes place as if he lacked what one could call an "archi-image"—some core imago that would remain constant and firm, thus conferring a stable identity upon him.

No doubt—I insist on using this syntagm ("no doubt") for reasons that will soon be made apparent—it would be more accurate to suppose that the character in question—if he is one, and who would be precisely *one*—already begins, in his bereavement-costume, to perform the mourning (or to make us perform the mourning) of his identification, of his possible recognition. Impossible to recognize or to pin down, he is no doubt nothing other than and will be nothing other than that endless debt of recognition (because we *owe* this recognition without ever being able to fully perform it), which is translated into countless IOUs (in fact, the "confidence-man" manages to take money from most of those who cross his path on the deck of the *Fidèle*).

Incidentally, it is he who pronounces the word "image" for the first time in the novel: an image, he argues, is above all the time of crystallization; an image, one understands him to say, is above all the time that it takes (*le temps qu'il faut*)—and the time that is therefore taken away (*fait défaut*)—for it to be solidified *as an image*. But, as he adds immediately, the image is always ready to unburden itself of this freshly acquired and always provisional consistency; it is always on the verge of losing its stability and rediscovering its malleability, the formless plasticity of clay in which it molds and shapes itself—the clay that "we" are, we who are always indebted to images.

I must pause here, interrupting the reading of the *The Confidence-Man* that we have just barely begun, in order to supply without further delay a first series of reasons justifying my inelegant and insistent recourse to that remarkable expression which I perhaps have been abusing: "no doubt." "At sunrise on a first of April"; these are the first words, the incipit, of the novel entitled *The Confidence-Man*. In Melville's time, the "first of April" was no doubt already *April Fool's Day*, that day, whose origin is lost to memory, in which precisely credulity or "confidence" is put to the test. I at least attempted to verify it, scanning yet one more time the textual data banks. "Whence proceeds the custom of making April Fools?" One already finds this question posed in 1708 in the pages of the *British Apollo*, one of those periodicals that in the England of this era asked its readers to send in questions to which its "experts" would respond.[7]

To the extent that I can confirm it with all of the necessary credit or credibility, believe me: in 1708, someone, an inquisitive reader of the journal, requested that an expert inform the readership of the history of the longrunning custom that was (and is) April 1st. What interests me, nevertheless, is not this history per se, which remains largely a matter of conjecture (the journal in question traced the custom back to the foundation of Rome), but the simple fact, indubitably affirmed, that this tradition which consists of testing "confidence" was already in effect during the period in which Melville put this incipit into writing: "at sunrise on a first of April." Everything that follows is thus placed under the sign of this certitude: the knowledge that the novel's very first words render the rest uncertain, as if it were a matter of a vast April's Fool's Day prank. In short, we know for sure, without any doubt, that we will no doubt be absolutely certain of nothing at all.

If I therefore use and abuse the expression "no doubt" (*sans doute*), it is in order to mark its singular ambivalence, its remarkable double-value or double-valence, the fact that it indicates at the same time certitude *and* probability. This duplicity is even greater in English than in French: whereas *sans doute* in the sense of certitude is generally considered to be obsolete, an English dictionary like the *Pocket Oxford Dictionary*, to cite a relatively typical reference work, juxtaposes the two significations of the syntagm without any periodization; "no doubt" signifies "certainly" just as much as "probably."

Flipping through successive editions of the *Dictionnaire de l'Académie Française*, however, one can in a way witness the emergence of the new value of this locution. Up to and including the 1762 edition, one in effect finds only the following mention: "SANS DOUTE, se dit adverbialement pour Assurément. *Il arrivera sans doute aujourd'hui*" ("NO DOUBT, used adverbially for Definitely. *He will no doubt arrive today*"). Then, with the edition of 1798, an addition appears, an insertion that introduces into the preceding mention the trembling of a doubt on the subject of the absence of doubt: "SANS DOUTE, se dit adverbialement pour Assurément. *Viendrez-vous demain? Sans doute*. Il signifie aussi, Selon toutes les apparences. *Il arrivera sans doute aujourd'hui*" ("NO DOUBT, used adverbially for Definitely. *Are you coming tomorrow? No doubt*. It also means, To all appearances. *He will no doubt arrive today*").

In that other reserve of textual data that is the recent digital version of the *Trésor de la langue française*, the emergence of the new meaning is described in terms of "value."[8] The first and oldest usage is defined as the "affirmative value" ("valeur affirmative") of the locution, which therefore signifies "definitely, certainly" ("assurément, certainement"). And the authors of this *Trésor* or treasury add: "This value of *sans doute* is attenuated to the point that, in order to express the affirmation, one reinforces it with *aucun, nul*." These attenuations—"*sans aucun doute*" or "*sans nul doute*"—find their equivalents in the English expressions "without the *slightest* doubt" or "without any doubt." If there has been attenuation, it is because the second usage has carried the day, thus rendering prevalent what the same dictionary describes as the "dubitative value" ("valeur dubitative") of the locution, thus signifying "probably" ("probablement").

There is therefore no doubt that "no doubt" is itself caught up in a problem of value that leads to what one could thus call its devaluation or discredit. But are we so sure? Can we affirm, without the slightest doubt, that the loss of credit or confidence in the force of this syntagm affects it simply in the manner of an accident that comes from the exterior, from the outside of a historical or linguistic becoming in which it would be caught up as if in spite of itself? What if, in other words, this devaluation or discredit were instead already inscribed in the logical structure of what is at stake here?

Before returning to Melville's novel, let's try to formalize what's at work in these vicissitudes, in the turns and returns of the English locution "no doubt" and its French equivalent "sans doute." Everything takes place as if this formula were its own opposite, in that the absence of doubt (what the *Trésor* refers to as the syntagm's "affirmative value") is equivalent to doubt (what the *Trésor* refers to as its "dubitative value"). But if "no doubt" is its own proper contrary, this also means, without any doubt, that "no doubt" has no contrary. On the subject of this singular structure, one could thus repeat the hypothesis that Derrida, commenting upon a passage from the second chapter of the *Genealogy of Morals*, advances concerning belief or credit in general:

> To believe is this strange divided state or this strange divided movement . . . in which I do not know what I know . . . in which I doubt the very thing I believe or in which I believe. Believing, in sum, is not believing; to believe is not to believe. And the whole origin of religion, like that of society, culture, the contract in general has to do with this non-belief at the heart of belief . . . Believing is its own contrary and thus it has no contrary. Not believing in it is not the contrary of believing, of trusting, of crediting, of having faith. This is the essence of the fiduciary and of interest. And the market, exchange, the social contract, the promise, the whole system of assumed equivalences that ground money just as much [as] language . . . all of this presupposes that trafficking in the act of faith, in believing, which is also believing without believing as condition of trafficking.[9]

When it comes to such a trafficking in belief or credit, Melville's novel is the most rigorous and most abyssal exploration of which I know.

Why? And what does this novelistic staging of the "(no-)doubt" have to do with the image? And, moreover, with film?

The first character who appears in the novel is the protagonist who is not one; we never know with certainty if he in fact remains the same underneath what seems to be a series of disguises, his pallor and whiteness seemingly destined to be confused with that of the white page: "At sunrise on a first of April, there appeared, suddenly as Manco Capac at the lake Titicaca, a man in cream-colors, at the water-side in the city of St. Louis."[10] The ensuing description emphasizes the absolute novelty and freshness of the character: "His cheek was fair, his chin downy, his hair flaxen, his hat a white fur one, with a long fleecy nap. He had neither trunk, valise, carpet-bag, nor parcel. No porter followed him. He was unaccompanied by friends. From the shrugged shoulders, titters, whispers, wonderings of the crowd, it was plain that he was, in the extremest sense of the word, a stranger." Without any baggage, past, or history to drag along with him, this a-character at the limit appears to be nothing more than the virginity of a surface of inscription, on which written signs acquire value or credit purely through reference (*renvoi*) to and among themselves, as is hinted by several of the chapters that follow.[11] Chapter 33, bearing the remarkable title "Which May Pass for Whatever It May Prove to Be Worth," explicitly poses the problem of the coherence or credibility of the (non-)protagonist, of whom one cannot not assume that, in spite of all of his guises and disguises ("his masquerade," to cite Melville's subtitle), he would have been the same since the beginning, since the incipit in which he emerges out of a pure self-positing.[12] On the topic of this character who one must at the same time believe and not believe, Melville writes the following, echoing the objections that readers no doubt will have formulated in the course of reading: "How unreal all this is! Who did ever dress or act like your cosmopolitan?"[13] And the end of chapter 33 brings the response, the following justification or accreditation: "All such readers as may think they perceive something inharmonious between the boisterous hilarity of the cosmopolitan with the bristling cynic, and his restrained good-nature with the boon-companion, are now referred to that chapter where some similar apparent inconsistency in another character is, on general principles, modestly endeavored to be apologized for."[14] The chapter in question is chapter 14, equipped with a title every bit as remarkable as the one which just sent us here in the attempt to fix its value: "Worth the Consideration of Those to Whom It May Prove Worth Considering."[15] This chapter (*capitulum*) which aims to confer upon the other chapter what in contemporary French is sometimes called *capital confiance*—a kind of capital of trust akin to "consumer confidence" or "brand loyalty"—this chapter which thus must dispel doubts and give credibility to the character, no doubt ultimately does nothing other than lay bare the structure of every positing of value: in the last instance, a value can only be referred to other values, which themselves require fiduciary credit in turn—and so on, to infinity.

But how exactly does this incessant rerouting from relative value to relative value, this *différance* of every absolute value or narrative "gold standard," concern (or *trouble*) the image? How does it enter into a system with the *undoing* of the image, with its instability, which is also to say with its movement, its kinetics, and its cinematography *avant la lettre*?

To attempt to respond to these questions (the stakes of which are nothing other than the very hypothesis of a potential Melville who would be the thinker of something like a proto-cinema), we must turn towards an outside. We leave the novel behind, breaking the supposed textual boundaries of *The Confidence-Man*. Not in order to seek firm grounding in a supposed *hors-texte*, nor in order to stabilize anything by recourse to an absolute reference, but because the Melvillean theory of the image itself does not escape the rule, the economic law that begins to emerge out of our readings and our lexical account-keeping: our quest after or inquiry into the Melvillean image is itself on the verge of being caught up in an infinite movement of referral (and referral of referral and . . .).

Preserving as well as possible in the clay of our memory the images of the "masquerade" that is *The Confidence-Man* and promising to return to them—this is a promise or acknowledgment of debt that we will have to honor—let's take a look at some other Melvillean scenes that take place elsewhere, in other texts.

Which ones?

One is of course tempted to look in the direction of *Moby-Dick*. First, because Melville's most famous work devotes considerable space to images of whales; Ishmael devotes three chapters to them: "Monstrous Pictures of Whales," then "Less Erroneous Pictures of Whales, and the True Pictures of Whales," and finally "Whales in Paint; in Teeth; in Wood; in Sheet-Iron; in Stone; in Mountains; in Stars." And second, because, no doubt, "no other American literary text can rival *Moby-Dick* in having so many reproductions."[16]

It is, however, not in this whale- or leviathan-text that I will look for images or discourse on the image—which definitely can be found in *Moby-Dick*—since as I have suggested elsewhere, one *necessarily* finds everything there. Rather, it is by investigating some of Melville's (slightly) less well-known writings that I want to try to give consistency to the hypothesis that one can find in Melville's writings the premises of a theory that could be qualified as "proto-cinematographic" (as one could say that in Baudelaire, for example, there are premonitions, portents, or even prophecies of cinema).[17]

In the short story titled "The Two Temples," submitted in May 1854 to *Putnam's Monthly*—the publication refused it and the piece was only published posthumously—one thus finds a scene in the course of which the narrator is imprisoned in what he himself refers to as a "huge magic-lantern." "I seemed inside some magic-lantern. On three sides, three gigantic Gothic windows of richly dyed glass, filled the otherwise meager place with all sorts of sun-rises and sun-sets, lunar and solar rainbows, falling stars, and other flaming fire-works and pyrotechnics."[18] What the narrator sees from the little tower of the church, to whose summit he climbs after having been refused entry, is thus a phantasmagoria created with the help of magic lanterns, in the manner of those produced from the end of the eighteenth century on.[19]

However, two years before that story, in 1852, in *Pierre: or, The Ambiguities*, the eponymous protagonist already undergoes a similar experience of visual magic, not thanks to the *dispositif* of stained glass filtering natural light in a luminous tower, but on the interior screen of the soul. And the light producing the phantasmagoria—a revelatory phantasmagoria, a bearer of reality-effects—is a light at once electrifying and electrified, produced by the shock of a spark, an electric discharge within the psyche. In book 5 of *Pierre* ("Misgivings and Preparations") one reads the description of a veritable electrical illumination, which, out of the intimacy of the soul, transfigures the entire field of the visible:

> It is the magical effect of the admission into man's inmost spirit of a before unexperienced and wholly inexplicable element, which like electricity suddenly received into any sultry atmosphere of the dark, in all directions splits itself into nimble lances of purifying light ; which at one and the same instant discharge all the air of sluggishness and inform it with an illuminating property; so that objects which before, in the uncertainty of the dark, assumed shadowy and romantic outlines, now are lighted up in their substantial realities. . . . Thus with Pierre. . . . every other image in his mind attested the universality of that electral light which had darted into his soul. . . . and now, when the electrical storm had gone by, he retained in his mind, that so suddenly revealed image, with an infinite mournfulness.[20]

The sudden and irruptive magic of the electrical image, with a fantastical or phantasmagoric realism that goes straight to the heart of things, disrupts visibility and reconfigures the visible as such. But it remains, depositing itself there, as if the illumination of the electrifying spark engraved itself in the malleable clay of the soul, in the time of its provisional crystallization.

Disseminated between bits of texts that silently refer to each other—lighting each other up under the electric lantern of a reading crisscrossing the back-projected screens of our Melvillean textual data banks—there are something like the unfinished fragments of a discourse on archi-cinema.[21]

The consequence that must be drawn, at the moment when we prepare finally to turn to Godard's *Le Grand Escroc*, is that Melville reads Godard every bit as much as Godard reads Melville.

Le Grand Escroc does not have a good reputation among cinephiles or film critics. In his monumental biography of the director, Antoine de Baecque thus writes: "This twenty-five-minute black-and-white film is absolutely charmless. There are perhaps two redeemable images in it: Godard himself at the opening of the film, sporting a fez and saying 'Action!' ["Moteur!"] in front of Patricia Leacock's camera and the same camera turning back towards [Raoul] Coutard's camera [*objectif*] at the film's end."[22] But the judgment is immediately nuanced by the following remark: "It's thus a film about cinema, just before *Contempt*—which is its apotheosis; the *cinéaste* films cinema in the process of its production [*en train de se faire*]. It is the virtue of Godard's short-format experimental films that he is able to try things in them that he then takes to their conclusions in his 'great' films." One finds a somewhat similar position in Deleuze's *Cinema Two*: "*Le grand escroc*," Deleuze writes, is "a film [that is] . . . minor, but nonetheless fundamental."[23] As for Godard himself, a year after *Le Grand Escroc* (which made up the last part of an omnibus film that appeared in 1964 under the name *Les plus grandes escroqueries du monde* [*The World's Greatest Swindles*]), he took the trouble to cite it—to "redeem" it, as Antoine de Baecque writes—in at least one scene from *Pierrot le fou* (1965): Ferdinand (Jean-Paul Belmondo) is in a movie theater; after sleeping through news and images of the current events in Vietnam, he then wakes up and reads through the *Modern Art* volume of Élie Faure's *History of Art*, occasionally also lending his attention, with a mixture of distraction and excitement, to a brief sequence from *Le Grand Escroc*. What is it about *Le Grand Escroc*—not unlike *The Confidence-Man*—that has incited such radically contrasting critical evaluations?

After the title, accompanied by an original Gainsbourg song, we see Patricia Leacock (incarnated onscreen by Jean Seberg), a reporter working for the American television chain WXYZ;[24] she reads Melville's novel in a hotel room in Marrakech, with some serene jazz in the background (bearing the signature of Michel Legrand). The telephone rings; Patricia responds while continuing to gaze upon the novel she holds in her hand. Cut. Close-up on a page of the novel (in the French translation by Henri Thomas), in which the following phrase from the first chapter stands out: "La charité ne pense pas le mal" ("Charity thinketh no evil"). Middle Eastern music briefly cuts in over the jazz. Return to Patricia on the telephone, with jazz in the background. Another cut and a close-up on another phrase from the first chapter, also accompanied by a surge of Middle Eastern music: "La charité endure toute chose" ("Charity endureth all things"). Etc.

The film seems to stutter, hesitating between image and text. Or perhaps it is a strange telephony that takes possession of the editing table, producing an alternation between the diegetic present and another temporality pulsing through the line, that of the novel.

Before putting the receiver down, Patricia says to her interlocutor that before their *rendez-vous* in two hours she will go to the Medina quarter to "finish off" the roll of film she still has in her camera. She begins filming immediately, even though she has yet to leave her hotel room. Sitting on the bed, she turns towards the camera, with her own camera rolling; the face-off between the two cameras (*objectifs*) is briefly interrupted by an insert that shows Godard himself, wearing his fez, pronouncing the word "Action!" ("Moteur!").

Later, Patricia is arrested in the Medina as she purchases a djellaba with counterfeit money. Driven to the police station, she is interrogated but says she knows nothing of the false bills that inundate Marrakech. In passing, speaking with the commissioner (László Szabó) who asks what she means by "*reportage*," she responds "it means filming"—and with these words, she in effect films the commissioner, who adjusts his tie—"ça veut dire filmer les choses, les endroits et les gens tels qu'ils sont" ("that is to say, filming things, people, and places as they are").

The commissioner: "That's it, I've got it; you make documentary films, like Monsieur Rouch." Patricia, stopping filming and rewinding the motor of her camera: "Yes, that's exactly it. These are images taken from life [*prises sur le vif*]—*cinéma-vérité*." The commissioner: "I too seek the truth, but in a different way. But we will never find it, neither you nor I."

Patricia thus takes or borrows images that she then sells, images thus restituted with interest—the profit of truth. She traffics in images, just as she traffics (without knowing it) in counterfeit money. And these two trades have the same "condition," what Derrida terms "belief without belief," which is to say the "(no-)doubt."

While the commissioner accompanies Patricia in the car so that she won't be late for her date, she tells him that she was previously in Poland for her reporting: "I got to know a rather strange character in Warsaw. He purchased photos of Karl Marx from the government, drew a different beard onto them, and then resold them to the peasants, telling them it was the portrait of Christ." Patricia traffics in images, which may themselves be trafficked, in the manner of photos retouched in order to become articles of faith subject to fiduciary exchange.

Still later, stumbling upon a conversation, Patricia discovers the counterfeiter: she follows him, wanting to film him: "Okay, it's alright with you if I film you and ask you some questions?" The Moroccan con-man responds with lines borrowed from the same pages of *The Confidence-Man* that we already looked at ("Charity endureth all things"), then with lines taken from the end of chapter 16: "Du mal vient le bien. La méfiance est une étape vers la confiance" ("From evil comes good. Distrust is a stage to confidence"). The con-man, as if he is being ventriloquized by the voice of Melville's novel, asks Patricia if she's not having an amnesiac episode; what one thus hears from his mouth is a paragraph from chapter 14: "Dites-moi, . . . ne vous est-il pas arrivé . . . un accident, une blessure à la tête ?" ("Pray, sir, . . . did it happen to you to receive any injury on the head?"). In the novel, this passage immediately precedes the passage concerning the impressions of the image upon the clay of the mind. Godard pauses at the threshold of the Melvillean theory of the malleability or plasticity of the image; he occults it, seeming to forget it, as if performatively putting the theory to work through this very forgetting. The lines from the novel on the accidental effacement of images are themselves effaced.

When Patricia remarks that giving false bills to the poor is "presque du vol" ("almost theft"), the con-man boasts, with words borrowed from chapter 7, of being "un philanthrope doublé d'un financier" ("a philanthropist and a financier"), in distinction from Fourier and "promoteurs de plans impossibles" ("projectors of impossible schemes"). He then speaks of establishing "un projet philanthropique et financier réalisable" ("a philanthropy and a finance which are practicable"), of "organiser méthodiquement la bienfaisance universelle" ("the methodization of the world's benevolence"), and of "lever annuellement un grand impôt de bienfaisance sur l'humanité entière, comme du temps de César-Auguste" ("levy[ing] annually, one grand benevolence tax upon all mankind . . . as in Augustus Cæsar's time").

"Pourquoi vous me filmez comme ça?" ("Why do you film me?"), he asks Patricia, who then responds: "Je ne sais pas. Parce que je cherche quelque chose de . . . la vérité" ("I don't know. Because I'm seeking some . . . truth"). He responds: "Pour faire quoi?" ("In order to do what?"). Patricia: "Pour montrer aux gens" ("To show to people"). The con-man: "Donc vous me volez quelque chose. Et vous aussi, vous le donnez aux autres" ("So you steal something from me. And you too give it to others.").

The truth of cinema—and of cinema vérité as the cipher or allegory of cinema in general—is thus theft: the theft of capture and appropriation (*c'est le vol de la captation, de la prise*), a kind of tax levied on the visible. And this seizure of the real demands restitution, as if cinema amounted to the honoring of a certain debt.

Patricia, at the end of the film, recounts her strange encounter to the commissioner, with whom she meets up again. Whereas Patricia avows herself to be perplexed, not knowing "à quel moment on avait abandonné le personnage fictif pour reprendre le vrai, si tant est qu'il existe" ("at what moment he abandoned the fictional character for the true one, to the degree that there is such a thing"), Godard himself recites in voice-over the famous speech from Shakespeare: "Le monde entier est un théâtre . . ." ("All the world's a stage . . ."). The words are declaimed over the final image, that of Patricia in close-up, filming all the while.

So: where are we, in the end, with the theory of the image articulated in Melville's novel? And what does it become in Godard's *Le Grand Escroc*?

This theory bears upon the plasticity and malleability of the image, which is to say, on the time in which it consists, insists, and desists. As it is enunciated, it is immediately translated into the economic register, as an acknowledgment of debt. "You must recognize me, your recognition is due, and you owe me all the more, a debt all the more indebting to the degree that you are the basis of an incessant effacement, a constant forgetting"; this, in sum, is what the strange mournful character—seeming to mourn the stability of his own image—says to the merchant.

This image that is always on the verge of being effaced is the fiduciary image, which, from the iconic register to the economic one, immediately translates the debt of recognition into the recognition of debt. "You are no doubt the same, because you never cease to be other"; this is what the merchant, constantly referred back to an irreducible exchange-value of the image that can never be stabilized as an absolute value, is forced to recognize in the face of the character who incarnates the mourning of every fixed or stable photogram. And this is why, on the fluctuating market in which the cinema vérité of identifications dissolves itself in the floating economy of the fiduciary, the distinction that Patricia desperately seeks between the fictive character and the true one finally gives way.

In this sense, the Melvillean series of *renvois* and the Godardian one—each referring image to image and character to character—can be superimposed on one another, as Deleuze so nicely suggests in *The Time-Image*:

> [Melville] presents a series of forgers that includes a mute albino, a legless negro, a man in mourning, a man in grey, a man in a cap, a man with an account book, a herbal doctor, up to the Cosmpolitan with the colorful clothes, the great hypnotist, the "metaphysical scoundrel," each metamorphosing into the other, all confronting "truthful men" who are no less false than they are. Godard outlines a similar series whose characters will be the representatives of *cinéma-vérité*, the police-man, the confidence-man himself, and finally the *auteur*, the portrait of the artist in a fez.[25]

Each of the two series consists of a *renvoi* from term to term. Each of the two series is a becoming and can be so only by way of what Deleuze calls the "the power of the false," namely the fiduciary necessity that returns the value of one term towards an other and so on, no doubt endlessly (*sans doute sans fin*). And just as the logic of the series is on the verge of appearing, the series itself is then rerouted: Melville's series is referred to that of Godard, or vice versa. Each series is in its turn a becoming that does not cease to open onto other becomings.

This is why Deleuze, more Nietzschean than ever, can legitimately draw the following conclusion: "If becoming is the power of the false, the good, the generous, the noble is that which raises the false to the Nth power."[26]

There must be the false (*il faut du faux*), up to infinity, in order for there to be becoming. This is because becoming, as masquerade, is *no doubt* the image that never really solidifies itself, that does nothing other than refer or reroute its capture, that unburdens itself of its consistency so as to insist in its referral to the other image or the image of the other.

Becoming *is* the indebted image, the fiduciary image. But this is a matter, however, of a debt that is also the condition of possibility of all generosity or all philanthropy, because the acknowledgment of this debt is finally in the hands of no one: as open as their becoming itself, the debt of images or words with respect to images and words to come is a debt that is incessantly deferred; it is always "to come."

More than an instrument of power or of a control exercised over us, the eternal debtors who we are, these image-debts are the token of what—in these images and for us—holds open the power or potentiality of the false. Which is to say: they remain in default of the future, the future that is thus at once lacking and demanded (*en défaut de cet avenir que donc il faut*).

Notes

1. In "'Unlike Things Must Meet and Mate': Melville and the Visual Arts," in *A Companion to Herman Melville*, ed. Wyn Kelley (Malden, Mass.: Blackwell, 2006), 342–62, Robert K. Wallace writes: "Melville's interest in the visual arts began in the family home in New York City in the 1820s, grew as he became a reader of illustrated books in Albany in the 1830s, diversified on his voyages to Liverpool and the South Seas in 1839 and the early 1840s, found expression in his novels of the later 1840s, reached an epiphany during his voyage to London and the Continent in 1849, and achieved artistic and psychological integration in *Moby-Dick* in 1851, at the age of thirty-two. During the remaining forty years of Melville's life—in spite of vicissitudes that took him from being a famous fiction writer to a writer of unread poetry, from a professional author to a customs inspector, and from a sociable youth to a reclusive elderly man—his interest in the visual arts continued to grow. . . . The print collection . . . in his own New York house was a work of art itself. More than four hundred prints have now been discovered and documented from his personal collection of art. Their geographical, temporal, and stylistic range—including Italian, French, Dutch, German, English, and American artists from the early Renaissance up through the modern painters of his own day—reflects the catholicity of his taste and the acuity of his eye" (342). Article translated by Daniel Hoffman-Schwartz.

2. In the final paragraph of chapter 2, the "varieties of mortals" embarked on the steamship *Fidèle* that follows the course of the Mississippi (as the novel follows the course of its own narration) are described as a "cosmopolitan tide" characterized by "a Tartar-like picturesqueness." At the beginning of chapter 36, when he has just encountered the protean and loquacious cosmopolitan who occupies the place of protagonist in the story, a "stranger" observes "the picturesque speaker, as if he were a statue in the Pitti Palace." Later on in the same chapter, the beggar who interrupts the scene is described as having a "look of picturesque Italian ruin" (Herman Melville, *The Confidence-Man: His Masquerade*, ed. Harrison Hayford, Hershel Parker, and G. Thomas Tanselle [Evanston, Ill.: Northwestern University Press and Newberry Library, 1984], 8, 131, and 135, respectively).

3. Melville, *Confidence-Man*, 238.
4. Ibid., 126.
5. Ibid.
6. Ibid., 28.

7. The complete title of the journal, which appeared between 1708 and 1711, is the following: *The British Apollo or, Curious Amusements for the Ingenious: To Which Are Added the Most Material Occurrences Foreign and Domestick, Perform'd by a Society of Gentlemen*. The first journal using the format of question and response was *The Athenian Gazette of Casuistical Method Resolving All the Most Nice and Curious Questions*, founded by John Dunton (4 volumes, 1691–97). It appears that it was the deliverers of the *Apollo* who, at the same time, also collected the questions of the readers; see William F. Belcher, "The Sale and Distribution of the *British Apollo*," in *Studies in the Early English Periodicals*, ed. Richmond Pugh Bond (Chapel Hill: University of North Carolina Press, 1957), 75–101.

8. *Trésor de la langue française* (*Treasury of the French Language*) was completed in 2002; the digitized version can be accessed at atilf.atilf.fr/.

9. Jacques Derrida, *La Peine de mort, vol. I (1999–2000)* (Paris: Galilée, 2012), 219–20; Jacques Derrida, *The Death Penalty, Vol. 1*, trans. Peggy Kamuf (Chicago: University of Chicago Press, 2013). The passage in question is from the sixth session of the seminar, that of February 2, 2000. I give my warmest thanks to Laura Odello, author of an as-yet unpublished thesis on this seminar, for drawing my attention to this passage and its strange logic—that of Derridean *différance* or autoimmunity, which as it were short-circuits the oppositionality of a contrary term. She argues for the importance of this logic in Derrida's work before rigorously working out its consequences for another thinking of the drive(s) of sovereignty and cruelty. See Laura Odello, "*Walten*, ou l'hypersouveraineté," in *Appels de Jacques Derrida,* ed. Danielle Cohen-Lévinas and Ginette Michaud (Paris: Hermann, 2014), 135–46.

10. Manco Capac was the founder of the Inca empire, sent to earth by his father the Sun.

11. Translator's note: "*Renvoi*," elevated to the status of a *terminus technicus* by Jacques Derrida, is used throughout in the French original text; I have usually rendered it as "referral" or "rerouting."

12. Melville, *Confidence-Man*, 186. In his French translation, Henri Thomas rather strikingly inserts "sans doute" ("no doubt") into the chapter title: "Dont la valeur dépend sans doute de ce que le lecteur y trouvera"—literally, "The value of which no doubt depends on what the reader finds there"; *Le Grand Escroc*, trans. Henri Thomas (Paris: Editions de Minuit, 1950), 288.

13. Melville, *Confidence-Man*, 186.

14. Ibid., 187.

15. Ibid., 107; id., *Le Grand Escroc*, 74.

16. See Elizabeth Schulz, "Creating Icons: Melville in Visual Media and Popular Culture," in *A Companion to Herman Melville*, ed. Wyn Kelley (Malden, Mass.: Blackwell, 2006), 533.

17. Prophecy or auto-prophecy is a Melvillean gesture par excellence. In *Les Prophéties du texte-Léviathan: Lire selon Melville* (Paris: Minuit, 2004), and the English *Prophecies of Leviathan: Reading past Melville*, trans. Gil Anidjar (New York: Fordham, 2010), I proposed an interpretation of Ishmael's abyssal phrase "Leviathan is the text." If it is true, as I have attempted to show, that this phrase implies that there is no outside-the-text (*il n'y a pas de hors-texte*) and thus no outside-of-*Moby-Dick*, could one go then so far as to think that this novel-world

already contains all "its" images—which is to say, *all* images? I leave the question open. The fact remains that I am neither the first person nor the only person to seek a prefiguration of cinema in Melville. Although he does so from a different perspective, see Alberto Gabriele, "Traces and Origins, Signs and Meanings: Analogy and the Pre-Cinematic Imagination in Melville's *Pierre, or the Ambiguities*," *Leviathan: A Journal of Melville Studies* 15, no. 1 (March 2013): 46–62. See also Laura Rigal, "Pulled by the Line: Speed and Photography in *Moby-Dick*," in *Melville and Aesthetics,* ed. Samuel Otter and Geoffrey Sanborn (New York: Palgrave Macmillan, 2011), 103–16. As for Baudelaire, it is in his 1853 essay "The Philosophy of Toys" that he describes the proto-cinematographic *dispositif* of the phenakistiscope: Charles Baudelaire, "The Philosophy of Toys," in *The Painter of Modern Life and Other Essays,* ed. and trans. Jonathan Mayne (New York: Garland, 1978), 197–203, at 201; Charles Baudelaire, "Le Morale du joujou," in *Curiosités esthétiques, L'Art romantique, et autres oeuvres critiques,* ed. Henri Lemaitre (Paris: Garnier, 1962), 201–8, at 205. In a famous passage from "The Painter of Modern Life," Baudelaire also writes of the artist as a "kaleidoscope endowed with consciousness" ("The Painter of Modern Life," in *The Painter of Modern Life and Other Essays,* 1–40, at 9). In *The World Viewed,* Stanley Cavell sees in "The Painter of Modern Life" nothing less than "an anticipation of film" (*The World Viewed* [Cambridge, Mass.: Harvard University Press, 1979], 43).

18. Herman Melville, "The Two Temples," in *The Writings of Herman Melville,* vol. 9 (Evanston, Ill: Northwestern University Press, 1987), 303–15, at 304–5.

19. Étienne Gaspard Robertson was the first to use the term "phantasmagoria" (*fantasmagorie*), for the magic lantern shows that he put on in Paris starting in 1799. See Theodore Barber, "Phantasmagorical Wonders: The Magic Lantern Ghost Show in Nineteenth Century America," *Film History* 3, no. 2 (1989): 73–86.

20. Herman Melville, *Pierre: or, The Ambiguities* (New York: Harper and Brothers, 1852), 119. *Pierre* was adapted for the cinema by Leos Carax in 1999 as *Pola X.*

21. In *Technics and Time 3: Cinematic Time and the Question of Malaise,* Bernard Stiegler uses the term "arche-cinema" to name "the cinema of consciousness," which is to say consciousness *as* cinema (Bernard Stiegler, *Technics and Time 3: Cinematic Time and the Question of Malaise,* trans. Stephen Barker [Stanford, Calif.: Stanford University Press, 2010], 6). In *Apocalypse-Cinema,* it is also with such an arche-filmic texture of the world in mind that I propose "there is no outside-of-film" (*il n'y a pas de hors-film*); see Peter Szendy, *Apocalypse-Cinema: 2012 and Other Ends of the World,* trans. Will Bishop (New York: Fordham University Press, 2015); Peter Szendy, *L'Apocalypse-cinéma: 2012 et autres fins du monde* (n.p.: Capricci, 2012).

22. Antoine de Baecque, *Godard, biographie* (Paris: Grasset, 2010), 224.

23. Gilles Deleuze, *L'Image-temps* (Paris: Minuit, 1985), 173; Gilles Deleuze, *Cinema Two: The Time-Image,* trans. Hugh Tomlinson (Minneapolis: University of Minnesota Press, 1989), 128.

24. The character's name is an allusion to Richard Leacock, the pioneer of cinema vérité who directed *Primary* (1960).

25. Deleuze, *Cinema Two,* 130.

26. Ibid., 137.

Belle Trouvaille: Between Aesthetics and Philology in *Billy Budd* (after *Beau Travail*)

Daniel Hoffman-Schwartz

The following reflections set out from the question of "*Billy Budd* and aesthetics." Why aesthetics? *Billy Budd* is famously a novella highly concerned with beauty, as embodied above all by the neoclassical male beauty of its protagonist. Moreover, it is also the case that the historical setting of the novella—"toward the close of the last decade of the eighteenth century," in the words of the narrator—is the moment when philosophical aesthetics, in the double-wake of Kant's *Critique of Judgment* and the French Revolution, takes on a new political urgency.[1] What would it mean to read *Billy Budd* as the anachronic contemporary of the *Critique of Judgment* and its postrevolutionary reception in the likes of Schiller, Hölderlin, or Schlegel?[2] What if *Billy Budd* were a meditation on the philosophical (aesthetic, political) "moment" of the 1790s?

The story of the *Bellipotent*, the British man-of-war upon which Billy finds himself at the beginning of the novella, is, among other things, that of a struggle over the aesthetic constitution of community, a struggle over the *sensus communis*, and indeed, the very sense of *sensus communis*. If Billy is described as the "peacemaker" of the *Bellipotent*, the novella nonetheless poses the question of whether his beautiful form—and by extension, the aesthetic in general—will work to preserve political order, to catalyze political insurrection, or indeed to suspend the political altogether.[3] But any rigorous attempt to think about aesthetics in *Billy Budd* necessarily encounters a difficulty as soon as it moves beyond merely narrative and thematic considerations and attempts to account for the "aesthetic" dimensions of the novella itself. In Melville, the signifier, no longer or not only given over to "signification," begins to tell its own story, a story that is perhaps no story at all, or at most an allegory. Paradoxically, it is this material dimension of language, the dimension irreducible to reference and to any phenomenal *aisthesis*, that gives the key to the "aesthetics" of *Billy Budd*.[4] The discourse *on* aesthetics that the novella presents is consistently interrupted by effects of the signifier that can only be reassimilated to "aesthetics" at the cost of pushing "aesthetics" to a limit, rendering it a paleonym (an old name for a new or refashioned concept) or a catachresis (an irreducibly figurative but nonetheless necessary term).[5] The present essay thus takes a decidedly paratactic shape, organized as much around individual words, signifiers, and shards of sense as it is around scenes, themes, or characters. Following a cue from Werner Hamacher, we might say that *Billy Budd* gives us an example of literature as "first philology," *prima philologia*;[6] Melville is a philologist in the literal sense, a "lover of language" or a "lover of words." In *Billy Budd* the imperatives of *aisthesis* repeatedly collide with those of *philia* and philology, the fascination with language in its materiality thus interfering with any disinterested apprehension of "mere form."

One "reading" of *Billy Budd* that has recognized this tension between *aisthesis* and materiality is Claire Denis's 1998 film *Beau Travail*, an adaptation of Melville's novella that transposes the story to postcolonial Djibouti, replacing Melville's British naval men with members of the French Foreign Legion.[7] The very title *Beau Travail* frames *Billy Budd* as the story of aesthetics, and indeed, the film bearing this title if anything heightens the aesthetic engagement of its source-text. At the same time, there is a paradox lurking in the relation between adaptation and source: if *Billy Budd*'s concern with aesthetics is continually shadowed by an emphatically material literary-linguistic dimension, *Beau Travail* is an intensively cinematic film, a film that presents a veritable *ars poetica* of cinema, an exploration of film's constitutive possibilities and limits. Where *Billy Budd* is "philological," *Beau Travail* is—to bend the usual sense of the word somewhat—"cinephilic." What is at issue, then, is a mode of disjunctive translation, a translation of one material intensity—that is, exactly what usually escapes translation—by another. But I am getting ahead of myself. Though this essay is primarily engaged with *Billy Budd*, the question of the aesthetic motivates recurrent detours through *Beau Travail*, an adaptation which—not without a certain risk—seems to reflect and deepen this dimension of its source.

Aldebaran

Billy Budd begins with a scene of aesthetic judgment situated in historical time:

> In the time before steamships or then more frequently than now, a stroller along the docks of any considerable seaport would occasionally have his attention arrested by a group of bronzed mariners, man-of-war's men or merchant sailors in holiday attire, ashore on liberty. In certain instances they would flank, or like a bodyguard quite surround, some superior figure of their own class, moving along with them like Aldebaran, among the lesser lights of his constellation. That signal object was the "Handsome Sailor" of the less prosaic time alike of the military and merchant navies. With no perceptible trace of the vainglorious about him, rather with the off-hand unaffectedness of natural regality, he seemed to accept the spontaneous homage of his shipmates.[8]

The tone of the passage is elegiac, nostalgic: the narrator laments an almost lost aesthetic experience, an experience whose seeming disappearance coincides with the invention of the steamship and thus the onset of industrial modernity. (To get our historical bearings: the first steamship took to sea in 1813; by the following decade, the steamship was widespread.) The spectator in this scene is nonetheless that exemplary modern subject, "the stroller" or flâneur. The scene of *flânerie* is also a scene of judgment with a subtle but unmistakable political implication: "with the off-hand unaffectedness of natural regality, he seemed to accept *the spontaneous homage of his shipmates*." This "spontaneous homage" is a form of judgment that presents a miniature social order in which the aesthetic coordinates freedom with lawfulness: in place of the artificial conventions of kingship, we have "natural regality"; in the place of coerced subjection, "spontaneous homage." But this "spontaneity" can only be dubious, precisely to the extent that it aligns itself with nature: freedom negates itself by expressing itself as the mere *recognition* of an ostensibly natural model, in this case the "natural regality" of the Handsome Sailor.[9] For such a "nature" is never simply natural, but always an overdetermined cultural form, a fetish—in this case, the classicistic fetish of athletic male beauty, one of the preferred fetishes of an allegedly disenchanted Enlightenment. Such a repressive, restrictive classicism haunts Enlightenment aesthetics from within. It is this model of aesthetic judgment as producing an allegedly spontaneous community through what is in fact the recognition of culturally legitimated forms that Melville's novella will call into question in different ways.[10] With Kant, we might write of the distinction between "free" and "adherent" beauty, *pulchritudo vaga* and *pulchritudo adherens*, the "pure" and the "ideal." Whereas beauty in its "pure" form is without concept, adherent beauty—which is therefore also *im*pure—smuggles in a degree of conceptuality; it judges under a type or model, as in precisely "the Handsome Sailor."[11] While "free beauty" in this sense is more radical, the critical interest of *pulchritudo adherens* resides in its avowal of impurity, the entanglement of beauty in concepts (and therefore: culture, ideology, and politics).

A loanword from Arabic, "Aldebaran" (*al-dabarān*) *designates* the "eye" of the Taurus constellation, even as its *meaning* is in fact "the follower," exactly what the Handsome Sailor *is not*, according to the narrator's description.[12] Aldebaran the eye is reversed into the object of the gaze, the Handsome Sailor. A philological-political speculation: Melville's literally alpha-betical predilection for names like Ahab, Aldebaran, Bartleby, or indeed Billy Budd seems always to be bound up with issues of command. Following the model of the Greek *archē* (and its verbal form *archēin*), order in the sense of sequence—alpha precedes beta—slides into order in the sense of command—alpha commands beta. These Melvillean alphabetical-allegorical orderings turn out of course to be misleading or volatile: just as *Billy Budd* and *Bartleby* come to exemplify a *resistance* to command, Ahab's orders lead towards madness.

Street-Wall

Though *Billy Budd* will have been the story of *one* Handsome Sailor in particular—the eponymous Billy—his entrance onto the scene of the novella is in fact preceded by the very brief appearance of another example of the type, as if to fulfill a mere logical (or ontological) exigency: in order for an example to be an example, rather than an abstract form or generality, there must be more than one; an example always belongs to a series of examples, some "better" than others. In literary terms, however, this example, at once the first example *and* an extra example, can appear only as digression or distraction, a moment of inoperativity (or *désoeuvrement*), an unmotivated stalling that suspends the teleology of narrative without therefore producing any suspense:[13] "A somewhat remarkable instance recurs to me. In Liverpool, now half a century ago, I saw under the shadow of the great dingy street-wall of Prince's Dock (an obstruction long since removed) a common sailor so intensely black that he must needs have been a native African of the unadulterate blood of Ham—a symmetric figure much above the average height."[14] The example is shot through with the language of mediation, as if the very conditions of memory and unconscious desire were embedded in the scene itself: this Handsome Sailor is seen "under the shadow" of a wall itself qualified as an "obstruction." This mediation serves in turn to emphasize the sailor's blackness, a blackness so "intense" that it is visible even through the shadow cast by a large wall.[15] The interaction between racialization and *aisthesis* is complexly overdetermined: intense blackness is presented as negativity, a remainder or excess materiality that must be bracketed in the experience of beautiful form—here, "a symmetric figure much above the average height"—even as, at the very same time, this excess holds its own sublime appeal; it is the very play between form and materiality—"symmetric figure" and "intense blackness"—that makes *this* "instance" so "remarkable" (or indeed "insistent," to play off the etymology of "instance") to the narrator. But this tensional play is itself ambiguous in its constitution; the pulsation between form and matter cannot itself remain purely formal; the material supplement to form, which by rights should be a-semantic or unreadable, slides immediately into racial discourse: "so intensely black . . . that he must needs have been a native African of the unadulterate blood of Ham." The allusion is to the Noah story, in its interpretation as a justification for slavery: Ham, whose name resembles a Hebrew word for "black" or "burnt," is punished for seeing his father Noah drunk and naked in his tent with the placement of a curse upon his son Canaan; people of African descent are thus imagined as Ham's descendants, bearing the "black" stigma of his misdeeds. If the Handsome Sailor as such is a kind of sovereign, this Handsome Sailor is nonetheless a slave as well. The oscillation thus turns out to be double, between beautiful form and material intensity, but also between blackness *as* material intensity and blackness as racialized semiosis;[16] the degree of intensity ("*so* intensely black") finds its index or measure in racial language ("that he must needs have been a native African of the unadulterate blood of Ham"), and this operation itself goes unremarked; the link between blackness and racialized subjection thus comes to appear as necessary or at least inevitable. At the same time, according to the logic of the "captive king" outlined by Jonathan Elmer, blackness as non-being appears at certain moments—in an inversion that may not fundamentally alter the inverted terms—as more or otherwise than (mere) being, which is to say, precisely, sovereignty.[17] In this regard, blackness is the supplement that supplies the sovereign difference of *this* Handsome Sailor. We might speak here as well of a splitting and doubling of the body, since form and matter do not quite seem to cohere into *one* body, but persist in a strange relation of mutual exteriority or disjunction; this splitting and doubling is no less the signature of sovereignty—the king's body spiritual doubles the king's body's natural—than that of the commodity, famously described by Marx as a "sensuously supersensible thing."[18]

The duality of the sovereign-slave double-body[19] echoes the various other antithetical juxtapositions in the passage: "a *somewhat remarkable* instance," "a *great dingy* street-wall," and finally, "a *common* sailor" at the "*Prince's* Dock." There can be no doubt, according to the dream-logic of the scene, that this uncommon "common sailor" is the sovereign prince of the "Prince's Dock." A similar logic compels us to hear an echo of "Wall-Street" in "street-wall."[20] This syntactical inversion affirms the dreamlike character of the tableau, with each element in it a potential signifier, susceptible to shifting and displacement like so many building-blocks or modular walls. The distance from the "street-wall" at the Prince's Docks, erected in order to protect transported commodities from theft, to the "Wall-Street" of capital accumulation and finance is perhaps not so great.

What to do with this "somewhat remarkable instance," which is left aside just as quickly as it surfaces? Here, one is tempted to invoke the narrator of Melville's famous Wall Street tale, when he says of Bartleby: "no materials exist for a full and satisfactory biography of this man. It is an irreparable loss to literature."[21] Even more than in the case of Bartleby, who is at least the topic of an enigmatic short story, these words apply here; Melville inscribes the trace of an unwritten story into *Billy Budd* as a cryptic prelude or epigraph.[22] To some extent, this scene anticipates the story of Billy, whose own strange sovereignty is doubled by the secret of impressment, which renders him as well a kind of commodity-body, a "king's bargain" or a "capital investment," to cite the terms used later on in the novella.[23] But what is lost in this analogy is the specifically racialized aesthetic logic of the passage. Billy's story *translates* the story of this ostensible "native African of the unadulterate blood of Ham"; race is the untranslated (or *encrypted*) remainder of this conversion.[24] It is as though the story proper cannot begin until this other story—perhaps the story of what the story proper excludes or includes *in exclusion*—has been told, however cursorily.[25]

Aesthetic

The word "aesthetic" occurs once in *Billy Budd*, in a description of Claggart, the enigmatic evildoer whose envy of Billy sets the novella's plot in motion:

> One person excepted, the master-at-arms was perhaps the only man in the ship intellectually capable of adequately appreciating the moral phenomenon presented in Billy Budd. And the insight but intensified his passion, which assuming various secret forms within him, at times assumed that of cynic disdain, disdain of innocence—to be nothing more than innocent! Yet in an *aesthetic* way he saw the charm of it, the courageous free-and-easy temper of it, and fain would have shared it, but he despaired of it.[26]

In a more or less Kantian manner, Claggart is caught between interest and disinterest or indeed nature and freedom; it is not that Claggart is incapable of the aesthetic disposition whereby the subject of judgment suspends his own interests and appetites in order to apprehend the object as pure form, but rather that this disposition coexists with another disposition, that of pathological self-interest.[27] In a curious redoubling of the Kantian conflict, the two dispositions are interlaced with one another here; to the very extent that Claggart "adequately appreciat[es] the moral phenomenon presented in Billy Budd," he turns against him. The very capacity to elicit disinterested admiration thus triggers jealousy, the self-interested disposition par excellence.

Later in the novella, the narrator, seeming to channel Billy's perplexity at Claggart's emergent antipathy, asks, with a characteristic flourish, "What was the matter with the master-at-arms?"[28] We must read this phrase literally: "matter" is precisely what is at issue in the phenomenon of self-interest, the inability to grasp the object as form. On this level, the matter with the master-at-arms might be said to be matter itself, the answer already contained in the question. But we must also read the phrase more than literally or super-literally, as a matter of letters—that is, as the material transformation, through the trope of paronomasia ("the name besides the name"), of "*matter*" into "*master*." Such a moment of self-reflexivity further calls attention to the literal sense of "matter," even as it is in fact predicated on the undoing of this literal sense; in showing the material dimension of language, the word "matter" comes to lose its sense, its status as a non-signifying signifier winning out over the movement of signification itself. Cutting against the strict distinction between form and matter of Kantian aesthetics—the notorious stumbling block of Kant's enterprise (as readers from Heidegger and Adorno through de Man and Derrida have argued in different ways)—this movement on the level of the material signifier could be said to have its own kind of "aesthetic" dimension, insofar as it is irreducible to meaning or conceptuality.[29] Indeed, to the degree that this tendency towards paronomasia affects the signifier from (before) the very beginning, its "materiality" starts to come into conflict with the classical Kantian understanding of matter in terms of nature, causality, and determination; in this sense, the "materiality" of language is what frees language from its determination as mere matter and endows it with a peculiar freedom not to be confused with any mastery.

Beauty

Billy Budd is referred to throughout the novella by various other names, most pointedly "Baby Budd" and "Beauty Budd." How can we make sense of this odd tendency for the eponymous protagonist to be renamed again and again, as if the very name of the character and therefore of the novella itself were errant or insufficient? Here too the aesthetic trajectory crosses the philological one. Like a proper name, aesthetic reflective judgment is "applied" to singularities. But at the same time, one cannot say that the predicate "beautiful"—as in "this is beautiful"—is quite proper, insofar as it has no cognitive content and ultimately applies as much to the "sensation" of the one who utters it as it does to the "object" in question. The uncertainty concerning the propriety of the proper name figures the peculiar relation between the quasi-predicate "beautiful" and its object. It is as if each *renam*ing yearns to retain the time of reflection and the accompanying uncertainty in the name itself, only to finally call forth yet another, supplementary name. Thus at one crucial juncture in the story, when Billy encounters a forecastleman immediately after the thwarted attempt to entrap Billy in a conspiracy of "impressed men," the name "Beauty Budd" is abbreviated in an allegorically pointed manner: "'Hallo, what's the matter?' here came growling from a forecastleman awakened from his deck-doze by Billy's raised voice. And as the foretopman reappeared and was recognized by him: '*Ah, Beauty, is it you?*'"[30] The (im)proper name thus converges with the aesthetic judgment, "Beauty Budd" contracting simply into "Beauty," the propositional demand "this is beautiful" recoiling into a version of the reflective question that it implicitly retains within it, "Beauty, is it you?"[31] What unifies the demand and the question, in spite of their differing or even seemingly opposed tonalities, is their shared non-apophantic character. Neither assumes the being of what it names; whereas the former tries to bring about that which it speaks of, the latter suspends its subject.[32] The question in this sense is its own answer; beauty resists embodiment in any "you" and is instead provisionally "embodied" in the question and the time of the question. The question thus betrays the (un)truth of the "you"; if beauty is to be narrated—extended in time—its subject can only be an allegorical one, one that names the non-persistence of what it "narrates."

Cynosure

The Handsome Sailor is a figure of the unity of the moral and the aesthetic, a figure of morality made sensible. The narrator can thus write the following: "The moral nature was seldom out of keeping with the physical make. Indeed, except as toned by the former, the comeliness and power, always attractive in masculine conjunction, hardly could have drawn the sort of honest homage the Handsome Sailor in some examples received from his less gifted associates."[33] "The moral nature" tones the "comeliness and power" of the Handsome Sailor, thus transforming what could be a merely sensible (or erotic) "attraction" into an "honest homage."[34] The metaphor of "tone," itself situated at the threshold of the sensible, hints at the precariousness of this distinction between sensible attraction and the "honest homage" associated with morality. Put slightly differently, we are in the realm of the instrumentalization of the aesthetic or indeed of "aesthetic ideology." The narrator lingers on this problematic relation between the moral and the aesthetic, beginning with the proposal of the somewhat unusual word "cynosure" to further qualify the type of the Handsome Sailor in general and Billy Budd in particular. The sentence runs as follows:

> Such a cynosure, at least in aspect, and something such too in nature, though with important variations made apparent as the story proceeds, was welkin-eyed Billy Budd—or Baby Budd, as more familiarly, under circumstances hereafter to be given, he at last came to be called—aged twenty-one, a foretopman of the British fleet toward the close of the last decade of the eighteenth century.[35]

"Cynosure" derives from the Greek *kynos-oura*, literally "a dog's tail." The primary definition of "cynosure," according to the *Oxford English Dictionary*, is "the northern constellation *Ursa Minor*, which contains in its tail the Pole-star"; it is "also applied to the Pole-star itself."[36] There is thus already a displacement at work within this primary definition: the name "cynosure" is transferred from the "tail" of the constellation to the pole-star that this "tail" contains, thus leaving the etymology of the term behind. According again to the *Oxford English Dictionary*, there is a second, figurative definition of the term, itself ambiguously divided in two: "a. Something that serves for guidance or direction; a 'guiding star' "; "b. Something that attracts attention by its brilliancy or beauty; a centre of attraction, interest, or admiration."[37] While the former definition generalizes the pole-star contained in the "dog's tail" into the metaphor of the "guiding star" in the sense of an exemplar, the latter one generalizes the term on the basis not of the star's guiding quality, but of its "brilliancy or beauty." The narrator is thus quite precise in suggesting that the equivocal character of the protagonist's relation to the concept "cynosure" corresponds to an equivocation in the concept itself: "Such a cynosure, at least in *aspect*, and something such too in *nature* ... was welkin-eyed Billy Budd." What is at issue—and this is confirmed in a way by the fact that the *Oxford English Dictionary* classes these two definitions together—is the tendency, written into the word itself, to treat the "brilliant or beautiful" as a (moral or ethical) guide or exemplar. The signifier "cynosure" thus arrests the forward movement of the narrative, becoming in its own peculiar way "a center of attraction or attention," albeit not on the basis of any "brilliancy" or phenomenality; in its own allegorical operation, it puts the lie to the collapsing of phenomenal beauty and ethical exemplarity. The narrator's invocation of "important variations" between the general concept of "cynosure" and the singular proper name "Billy Budd" point to a troubling of the movement of subsumption and of the copula that would achieve it ("such a cynosure ... though *with important variations* ... was welkin-eyed Billy Budd"). The question implicitly posed is that of the limits of "variation": at what point does variation become "important" enough to qualify as deviation from a type? Where is the limit between the adherent and the free? Not only do these "variations" indicate that what is named cannot really be subsumed under the concept, but the name itself is subject to further variation; as the sentence unfurls itself, "welkin-eyed Billy Budd" is transformed into "Baby Budd"—"as more familiarly, under circumstances hereafter to be given, he at last came to be called." In a radicalization of the singularity of beauty, the name resists itself, generating variations. Late in the text, when Vere explains to Billy that he will be judged on the basis of his actions rather than his intentions and thus be sentenced to death for the fatal blow to Claggart, the cynosure becomes a mere *cynos*, as if to confirm the unraveling of the metaphor and the philological decomposition of the allegorical signifier:[38] "This utterance ... caused him to turn a wistful interrogative look toward the speaker, a look in its dumb expressiveness not unlike that which a *dog* of generous breed might turn upon his master, seeking in his face some elucidation of a previous gesture ambiguous to the canine intelligence."[39]

Vere

The *Bellipotent*'s captain Edward Fairfax "Starry" Vere is a man of letters: "he loved books, never going to sea without a newly replenished library, compact but of the best." His theory of literature, as it turns out, is inseparable from his practical authority; the hinge between reading and practical authority turns out to be the capacity to resist the seductions of the mere "vehicle" (or signifier) in order to get to the "realities" presented by the text:

> With nothing of the literary taste which less heeds the thing conveyed than the vehicle, his bias was towards those books to which every serious mind of superior order occupying any active post of authority in

the world naturally inclines: books treating of actual men and events no matter of what era—history, biography, and unconventional writers like Montaigne, who, free from cant and convention, honestly and in the spirit of common sense philosophize upon realities.[40]

Authority is maintained by the willed erasure of any specifically literary or aesthetic moment of reading; the hierarchy of command—the superiority of the superior mind—corresponds to the imposition of a hierarchy of sign ("the vehicle") over sense ("the thing conveyed"). Here philosophy, insofar as it is understood as "philosophiz[ing] upon realities," could not be more opposed to philology in the strict etymological sense; rather than being the object of love or *philia*, words are a mere means to an extralinguistic reality.[41] The irony is difficult to miss, inasmuch as Melville, however much he liked to write "upon realities" or read "books treating of actual men and events," is also a writer famously and exceptionally attentive to "the vehicle," a writer for whom "the vehicle" can never simply be separated from "the thing conveyed." (If Melville frequently writes of command and insurrection, insurrection is also always an insurrection against the instrumentalization of the signifier in command.)

In this regard, it is significant that Vere's own nickname, *Starry* Vere, the name by which he is referred to on the ship, derives from poetry—traditionally the form of writing in which the "vehicle" can least be separated from the "thing conveyed." Vere is given the name by a relative who stumbles upon the following lines in Andrew Marvell's "Appleton House," a bit of seventeenth-century topographical poetry named after the estate of Marvell's patron Thomas Fairfax:

> This 'tis to have been from the first
> In a domestic heaven nursed,
> Under the discipline severe
> Of Fairfax and the starry Vere.[42]

At first glance, the lines are clearly appropriate to the captain; the reference to "nursing" within a "domestic heaven" recalls the pastoral power Vere exercises in the space of the ship. But the details of this name and this story of nomination tell a somewhat different story. There is potential for scandal here, in the question of who names the captain-father charged with holding together the symbolic order and in the question of how exactly this nomination come about. A relative of Vere's, a certain Lord Denton, having recently reread the Marvell poem, spontaneously interpolates a fragment of the line from the poem into his greeting of the captain: "Give ye joy, Ed; give ye joy, my starry Vere!" The interpolation utterly alters the sense of the phrase, not least of all because the "starry Vere" in question is in fact Fairfax's wife, *Anne* Vere, whose maiden name has the added poetic value of rhyming with *severe* and thus carrying along the rhyme-scheme of the poem. The referential aberration is thus double: not only does the one Vere, in a kind of metalepsis, acquire the nickname of the other Vere solely on the basis of their shared surname, but the mention of this surname in the first place results only from the arbitrary formal structure that is the rhyme-scheme. The transformation of the lowercase adjective "starry" into the capitalized name "Starry" thus amounts to a fetishistic freezing, as Melville's language attests: "it remain[s] permanently attached to the surname."[43] The descriptive infelicity of the name only underscores the arbitrariness of the moment of nomination: "whatever his sterling qualities, [Vere] was," in the narrator's words, "without any brilliant ones." In truth, Vere is not so starry. "Starry Vere": the name lies not only about truth—Vere's verity—but about appearance or *Schein* as well—Vere's starriness. Indeed, according to the terms of the novella, the metaphor of starriness would be better suited to the "cynosure" or "pole-star" Billy Budd; this mismatching of name and attribute, as if through a kind of surreptitious communication, adds to the sense of queer intimacy aboard the *Bellipotent*, the peculiar affinity between the foundling Billy and his would-be father Vere.[44] And yet, this moment also exemplifies and anticipates the logic of Vere's own mode of authority, an authority grounded not in truth or adequation so much as in formalization and the pure signifier. If Vere "philosophize[s] upon realities," the "realist" lesson he seems to draw is that of the necessity of fiction.

Skipping ahead to the novella's final episodes, the spontaneous verdict proclaimed by Vere upon the confirmation of Claggart's death at the hand of Billy is conspicuously oriented toward the linguistic "vehicle," as if the law were going mad or indeed becoming *literature* at the very moment of its instantiation: "Struck dead by an angel of god! Yet the angel must hang!"[45] The madness of these words resides not merely in their somewhat odd grammar (a would-be passive construction, lacking its passive grammatical subject) nor their far from "commonsensical" or "realist" recourse to theology, but in the virtual collision and combination of signifiers: "the *ang*el must h*ang*!" The rhyme hides in plain sight, obscured only by phonetic difference. Like all rhymes, it hints at a pun or neologism, compelling the hallucination of a "new word" even as it also calls into question the unity and integrity of "words" as self-contained entities.[46] The "hanging angel" is therefore, inevitably, an "*hangel*." *Ascension* is canceled, converted into *suspension*; the resolutely material, more or less unpronounceable barbarism *hangel* figures such an annulled transcendence.

Usage

One deceptively simple term, employed repeatedly throughout the novella, best describes what we might think of as the *linguistic* political theology of the *Bellipotent*: "usage." (The term recurs throughout "Bartleby, the Scrivener" as well.)[47] It refers to the rigidly naturalized conventionality of the world of the ship, a world of what is described at the outset of the story as "continuous martial discipline"; tellingly, this term crosses over from the semantic field of language to that of law. The ship is a lexical utopia, a space with its own idiosyncratic codes and jargon, all of which seem to acquire an absolute intelligibility and absolute regularity. For all of Melville's evident pleasure in linguistic aberration and transgression, the novella conveys as well a fascination with the arbitrariness and rigidity of jargon. More to the point: with jargon, aberration becomes the law. "Usage" implies that names have a theological-political weight, as the paradigms of baptism (and christening) imply. The relation between "usage" and "christening" is nonetheless rather paradoxical: once a name has been given, it is as though it has always been the name and could not have been otherwise. In this regard it is significant that Vere's nomination, the nomination of the one who represents usage itself, takes place ashore. Against the backdrop of the paradigm of usage and the "permanent attachment" of the name, we can return to the curious plurality of names that characterizes the novella's eponymous protagonist; in this anomalous case, it is as though the very investment in the signifier generates the series of alliterative variations (transformations, deformations) on the name—Billy Budd, Baby Budd, Beauty Budd—as if he were perpetually escaping and being recaptured by usage, as if the aesthetic pleasure in usage were constantly on the verge of undoing usage itself.[48]

When Billy is brought to trial for his fatal blow, the dimension of usage becomes ever more pronounced, as though the latently juridical essence of life aboard the *Bellipotent* were meant finally to come to the surface;[49] for example: "The thing to do, [Vere] thought, was to place Billy Budd in confinement, and in a way dictated by *usage*";[50] "so thinking, [Vere] was glad it would not be at variance with *usage* to turn the matter over to a summary court of his own officers";[51] or in Vere's address to the ship's jury, "the people have native sense; most of them are familiar with our naval usage and tradition";[52] or finally: "In this proceeding as in every public one growing out of the tragedy strict adherence to usage was observed; nor in any point could it have been at all deviated from, either with respect to Claggart or Billy Budd, without begetting undesirable speculations in the ship's company, sailors, and more particularly men-of-war's men, being of all men the greatest sticklers for usage."[53] Like Marx's commodity, there's something "sticky" about "usage"; once the name is attached or affixed, it is so permanently; it sticks or adheres.

Galoup

If *Beau Travail* is a more radically "aesthetic" text than *Billy Budd*, to the degree that it "subtracts" much of the narrative scaffolding of the story, leaving the viewer either to fill it in or not, depending on her knowledge of the source-text, there is nonetheless one way in which *Beau Travail* would seem—at least on the surface—to *diminish* the enigma of *Billy Budd*: the formal mechanism of the voice-over, which in cinema tends to signify "consciousness" or "interiority"—both of which Melville rigorously avoids in *Billy Budd*. This is all the more striking given the fact that voice-over is the formal strategy most frequently used to "translate" literary inner-monologue in film adaptation, the literary inner-monologue that is missing in *Billy Budd*. In this peculiar regard, *Beau Travail* would seem to be more "novelistic" than the novella from which it is adapted. More pointedly still, the voice-over is given to arguably the most enigmatic character in the story. Near the end of the novella, Captain Vere is explicit that Claggart, having been killed by Billy, is fated to remain radically enigmatic—"there is a mystery . . . to use scriptural phrasing, a 'mystery of iniquity' . . . for us any possible investigation of it is cut off by the lasting tongue-tie of—him—in yonder."[54] The narrator specifies that this "yonder" "designat[es] the mortuary stateroom." It is as though Claire Denis returns to this mortuary stateroom, to the very crypt of Claggart, who will be reborn—translated—as "Galoup."

And yet the unexpected turn to a voice-over does not dissolve the enigma, but effectively deepens it. In the first occurrence of voice-over, Galoup gives a vague and minimalist retrospective recounting of the story that is about to unfold for the viewer. The narration oscillates between the first-person and the third, as though his identification with his own story were hesitant, uncertain—as if his grasp on his own subjectivity were precarious—only introducing his name at the end of this narration: "My story is simple. It is the story of a man who left France for too long, a soldier who left the army with the rank of officer, chief officer Galoup. Galoup is me [*Galoup, c'est moi*]."[55] "*Galoup, c'est moi*"—the phrasing is detached and highly conventional, an impersonal and mechanical way of announcing one's identity, an identity with which one may not identify, a non-identification with one's own subjectivity and story. Thus, in this same voice-over, Galoup's "confession" of his secret arrives at a radical limit, which ultimately only points back to the "mystery" named by Captain Vere; speaking of Forestier, the Vere-figure in *Beau Travail*, he says "je l'admirais profondément, sans comprendre pourquoi" ("I admired him profoundly, without understanding why"); the voice-over thus entails no privileged moment of self-consciousness, no disclosure of a withheld secret. The "profundity" in question is abyssal. In classic triangular fashion, this admiration for Forestier motivates Galoup's resentment of Sentain, who is the object of *Forestier*'s admiration; but the motivation of this initial admiration, the ur-cause of the antipathy or resentment towards Sentain, remains opaque even to Galoup.

The name "Galoup" is itself hardly innocent; this may bear on the peculiar disjunction inhabiting the phrase "Galoup, c'est moi." With its embedding of the word "loup" ("wolf"), "Galoup" recalls the Hobbesian motif of *homo homini lupus* ("man is a wolf to man").[56] The allusion is apt, as Galoup is undoubtedly a "wolf" to his fellow man, particularly to the decidedly lamb-like Sentain (who, like Billy, is something of a Christ-figure). Galoup is so wolfish that part of his strategy is to impute wolfishness to the lamb, to sow suspicion that (seeming) innocence is the best ruse of all. Thus, while engaged in a game of chess with Forestier, Galoup warns of Sentain's subterfuge: "il cache bien son jeu" ("he hides his trickery well"), he says—as though the wolfish rationality of the game (*jeu*) of chess were in fact to underlie all of *Sentain*'s actions.[57]

But this Hobbesian allusion is not the only significance of the name "Galoup"; it alludes as well to another signifier, this one named rather more explicitly in the film. As Galoup attempts to explain his own animosity towards Sentain, again in voice-over, he approaches but does not quite utter his own proper name, as if repeating and revising the initial scene of self-nomination: "he [Sentain] had seduced everyone, attracting everyone's attention by his calm and by his availability. At bottom, I felt in myself a kind of rancor, a sort of rage. I was *jealous* [*j'étais jaloux*]."[58] Instead of "Galoup, c'est moi," "j'étais jaloux." "Jaloux" as (barely) distinct from "Galoup," "g" as (barely) distinct from "j," the exemplary minimal difference that distinguishes and constitutes the phoneme. The implication is not exactly that we hear the echo of *jaloux* in *Galoup* and thus recognize jealousy as the defining trait of Galoup or take Galoup as the allegorical embodiment of Jealousy itself; rather, what is indicated by the minimal difference of the signifier—"g" as distinct from "j," "Galoup" as distinct from "jaloux"—is the fragility of the name and the fragility of the identification with it, and ultimately the lack of substance in subjectivity as what compels *jealousy*. "J'étais jaloux" is the ironic truth of the disjunctive identification "Galoup, c'est moi": the comma produces an interval; the subject becomes the impersonal object *of* predication; "jaloux" becomes the properly improper name of the "subject" riven by this interval.

Handsome

Though the term "handsome" and its variants proliferate throughout *Billy Budd*, starting with the novella's opening lines, the precise sense and functioning of this concept and word has received relatively little attention in the criticism, perhaps because it is taken to be banal or transparent, unworthy of conceptual reflection or philological scrutiny. Apparently, everyone knows what it means to be "handsome." Ordinary use places it at the threshold between the aesthetic and the erotic, as a term for physical beauty, usually but not always in reference to a human being, most often a male human being. Taking etymology into account, the "handsome" is "literally" that which one would like to *handle* or lay hands upon, that which looks worthy of use; the "handsome" thus implies haptic seeing, virtual touch at a distance. This etymological register of "handsome" is at least as much *technical* as it is erotic or aesthetic. The paradigmatic handsome object, in this primitive, etymological sense is the *tool*, albeit not as an object of use so much as an object of potential or suspended use.

Reading for the handsome puts a decidedly different spin on the lines from Claggart that follow Billy's famous soup-spilling stumble: "Handsomely done, my lad! And handsome is as handsome did it, too!" In Barbara Johnson's classic reading, what is at issue in these famously ironic lines is the continuity or lack thereof between the order of being and the order of doing.[59] Moving from the question of being and doing to that of the hand, we might note that it is Billy's hands that fail him here, yielding to the humbling—or stumbling— prerogatives of the feet, which are linked to tragedy and tragic falls going all the way back to the swollen feet of the Oedi*pus* who famously solves the riddle of sphinx. (While Oedipus is adept at figurative thinking and misses the literal sense, Billy remains all too tied to the literal.)[60] Moving from the hand back to the specifically hand*some*, we reencounter the question of being and doing, albeit differently; if the handsome is above all a figure for potentiality, it is located at the very threshold of the order of being and is entirely foreign to the other of doing. That which is hand-some remains untouched (or only virtually touched). According to this logic, "handsomely done" (or "handsome did it") would be a kind of category-mistake or impossible utterance; to say "handsomely done" is to describe that which must remain strictly potential according to the logic of the achieved act. It is thus perhaps the fate of all that is "handsomely done" to negate itself and become ironic; the handsome is what remains other to the order of doing, what remains undone but also what is undone by any act or actualization.[61]

Nonetheless, the reference to the handsome here is not entirely infelicitous, insofar as it tacitly introduces a technical register and connects it, via Billy's fall, to a certain failure or dysfunction; once one lays hands upon the tool, it is defined by its capacity to *not work*. The latent technical register of the handsome recalls Heidegger's famous analysis in *Being and Time* of "equipment" (*Zeug*) in terms of the distinction between *Zuhandenheit*, usually rendered as "ready-at-hand," and *Vorhandenheit*, usually rendered as "presence-at-hand."[62] From this point of view, though the handsome is not *zuhanden*—which for Heidegger indicates a state of practical use governed by a non-thematic, non-thematizable knowing, it is not simply *vorhanden* either, in the sense of being merely given or available. The "handsome," which in this literal sense would be almost as untranslatable in German as *Zuhandenheit* and *Vorhandenheit* are in English, seems to name a kind of hesitation between the two, reducible to neither detached objectivity nor tactile immediacy. We might even describe it as an eroticized *Vorhandenheit*, a *Vorhandenheit* that is no longer certain of itself, even a queer *Vorhandenheit*—in the sense that it mixes sexuality into the existential analytic and confuses the relation between the human and the technical. For Heidegger, we only become aware of *Zuhandenheit* in its disruption, by way of the dysfunction of the tool and thus the interruption of the nontheoretical immersion characteristic of use. Perhaps such a disposition resembles that of philology, which disrupts the flow and functionality of language by attending to words, such as, for example, "hand" and "handsome" and their derivatives. In the light of *Billy Budd*, Heidegger's tool-analysis comes to look like nothing other than a theory of literature and literary language, a language in which dysfunction is the proper mode of functioning.

Stutter

Billy's famous stutter too comes to look somewhat different in light of the handsome. For stuttering—if that is indeed what Billy does—takes place at the precise threshold between sheer potentiality and technical dysfunction; stuttering can be construed as either speech that has gone awry or the active withdrawal from actual speech, a tracing out of potentiality within actuality.[63] Here is the still-baffling exposition of Billy's stutter: "Though in the hour of elemental uproar or peril he was everything that a sailor should be, yet under sudden provocation of strong heart-feeling his voice, otherwise singularly musical, as if expressive of the harmony within, was apt to develop an organic hesitancy, in fact more or less of a stutter or even worse." The narrator acquires some of Billy's "hesitancy," as if this not quite properly nameable "vocal defect"—this "in fact more or less of a stutter or even worse"—itself withdraws from linguistic comprehension and mimetically incites inarticulateness; the narrator cannot quite speak of this not-quite stuttering. The unnamed fear, this "even worse"—which resembles the circumlocutions and elisions that arise throughout the novella in relation to the event of the Nore Mutiny—is that of the sliding or slipping of the signifier, the non-fixation that both compels and threatens the theological-political operations of linguistic ordering and designation that define "usage" on the *Bellipotent*.

Hand

A further political-theological explanation immediately follows upon this moment of abyssal freedom or indetermination. It is at this point that the motif of the hand, a notably prosthetic or inorganic hand, (again) intervenes: "In this particular Billy was a striking instance that the arch interferer, the envious marplot of Eden, still has more or less to do with every human consignment to this planet of Earth. In every case, one way or another he is sure to slip in his little card, as much to remind us—*I too have a hand here.*"[64] In the theological language that Melville's narrator deploys here, Billy's flaw is evidence of original sin. From the point of view of sovereignty, it is original sin that justifies political theology;[65] only because of this finitude, expressed by the signifier's tendency to slide, to "stutter or even worse," that the name must be made to "stick"; there must be a *point de capiton*—or indeed a *point de capitaine*, as it is Captain Vere who oversees the work of nomination aboard the *Bellipotent*.[66] The line "I too have a hand here" recalls the motif of *Et in arcadia ego* ("I am in Arcadia too"), best known from Poussin's paintings of that name, though Melville may become aware of the topos through Schiller.[67] There, the "I" (or "I am"—*ego*) is spoken by death. As Erwin Panofsky has argued in a now-classic analysis, the essential point is a temporal one: not the lament for a lost Arcadia, but the presence of death within Arcadia itself.[68] Billy no doubt is a kind of Arcadian figure; the "singularly musical" quality of Billy's voice affirms this, given the status of mythical Arcadia as a realm of song. The shift in localization from "*in Arcadia*" simply to "*here*" is pointed: not only have we left behind the idyll of the *Rights-of-Man*, but the delegate and survivor of this Arcadia of enlightened humanism must, like everyone else, bear the marks of finitude. Whereas in Poussin's version the inscription is written on a tomb and thus directly channels the pathos of death, Melville's inscription is written on that most disenchanted and generic of modern supports, a "little card," presumably on the model of a business card or calling card. The card attests to the absence (or virtual presence via writing) of the hand whose presence it announces. It is as if the hand wants to point to itself in an act of impossible deixis—"I too have a hand *here*"—but can only do so via the prosthesis of the "little card."

And yet if Melville's version of the inscription ties finitude not to death so much as to errancy and thus a certain freedom that is not reducible to free will, this is perhaps the lesson of Enlightenment or indeed some Enlightenment *about* Enlightenment itself: if there is to be freedom, it must not be—cannot be—Arcadian; freedom as finitude is inseparable from the possibility of "evil." This freedom starts when the *Rights-of-Man* sails off into the distance. The movement of the signifier from the Arcadian "Handsome Sailor" to the fallen, worldly "I too have a hand here" performs the drift aligned with this odd freedom.[69] This discreet wordplay is arguably a Melvillean signature, the displaced trace of the author's own hand. Even (or perhaps *especially*) the handsome is touched by the hand of finitude.

Trouvaille

Beau Travail does not dare to depict the soup-spilling scene, perhaps in fear of a descent into slapstick; auteurism in this sense takes priority over the imperative to radical fidelity. In Claire Denis's own words: "Renverser la soupe, dans le livre, on l'accepte parce qu'il y a l'écriture de Melville, mais il fallait dépasser ça" ("To knock over soup, you can accept it in the book, because there is Melville's writing, but we had to go beyond that").[70] In other words, Denis's fidelity at this level is to cinema; instead of following Melville's text faithfully, beyond the boundaries of cinematic "good form" or "good style," Melville's text is transformed by cinematic adaptation.

Similarly, though *Beau Travail* is concerned with nothing if not male beauty and homoeroticism, the semantic network around the signifier "handsome" would seem to be absent or untranslated, perhaps untranslatable. And yet, the very title of the film subtly recalls the scene and signifier that are otherwise excluded: "beau travail" is in fact the translation offered for "handsomely done" in Pierre Leyris's 1980 Gallimard translation of the novella.[71] Though the title certainly alludes to the question of beauty, its ironic exclamation also must be taken in reference to the work of adaptation itself, as a commentary on everything that is lost in translation, everything that the adaptation excludes—beginning with the tragicomic scene of the soup-spill and the enigmatic workings of the concept-signifier "handsome." "Nice try!"—the adaptation chides itself. The allusion is nothing if not discreet; the titular phrase "*beau travail*" goes through the film unuttered. And yet in spite of this encryption, the emphasis is not entirely upon what is lost in translation; though the phrase "*beau travail*" goes unspoken, its near-double *is* spoken in the film, namely "*belle trouvaille*," which in the Leyris translation renders Captain Vere's characterization of the foundling Billy as a "pretty good find."[72] We move from encrypted loss to what is found, *une trouvaille*.[73] In a stroke of philological (or cine-philological) brilliance, Denis notices the translator's most likely unconscious rhyme between two disconnected phrases, separated by some eight chapters in the novella; this, in other words, is her *trouvaille*. The feminine echo of *trouvaille* in *travail* affirms the undoing of the work; it is handsomely (or perhaps beautifully) *un*done, the achieved act reimagined as a feminine foundling without author or intention.

Haptic

Early on in *Beau Travail*, we see Legionnaires training on an obstacle course; they shimmy under trip-wires, vault over various hurdles and bars, and leap into and then climb back out of a pit.[74] At each station of the course, we see a series of Legionnaires performing the required task; the effect is that of a survey of gestural styles. The cuts between the stations are rapid and syncopated, seeming to come in "early," that is, just before the final Legionnaire in each series completes the depicted act, the highly formalized camera-work just out of sync with the highly formalized choreography of the Legionnaires; here *cinema* seems to fulfill its etymologically prescribed task of showing *kinesis*. The effect produced by the very slight disjunction between the movements of bodies and the movements of the camera is that of a glitch or indeed a *stutter*.

The camera-work is frontal and stiflingly close, with the effect that the Legionnaires constantly seem on the verge of colliding with the spectator. The mode is "haptic" or precisely "handsome," proximate vision and touch at a distance, as if this thwarted contact or "touch without touch" were the cinematic translation of Melville's seemingly untranslatable concept-figure. If anything, the haptic cinephilia of *Beau Travail* intensifies the experience of "the handsome" that the film cannot name. This is to say that it is perhaps here where *Beau Travail* and *Billy Budd* touch. Cinematic intensity (*cinephilia*) indirectly translates literary intensity (*philology*); it as if the encounter between the two objects discloses the ontological specificity of each medium *and* their virtual crossover—the haptic cinema of *Billy Budd* and the cinephilology of *Beau Travail*.

Orpheus

If Vere himself "philosophizes upon [what he takes to be] realities," the lesson he takes away from these "realities" is in fact that of the prevalence of form, which is to say, fashioning or fiction. Vere is a political aesthetician. Thus the narrator recounts Vere's distinctly aesthetic explanation for the execution of Billy Budd and, by extension, the privileging of the maintenance of the rule of law over justice or morality: "'With mankind,' [Vere] would say, 'forms, measured forms, are everything; and that is the import couched in the story of Orpheus with his lyre spellbinding the wild denizens of the wood.' And this he once applied to the disruption of forms going on across the Channel and the consequences thereof."[75] Form is aligned with a fiction or noble lie; in the absence of any transparent metaphysical truth or ontological certainty, "forms, measured forms" offer a fictive security. Vere's familiar suggestion is thus that men should recognize themselves within an aesthetic-political order, on the premise that the absence of such an order would lead to chaos or even apocalypse. But there is something odd in the precise formulation of this Platonic-Hobbesian scenario: the example of Orpheus.[76] Though it is unthematized in the narrator's blank, neutral reporting of speech, the relation between the example and the principle it is meant to exemplify seems to be fraught at best. This appears to be a deliberate, unmarked irony, a play of perspective. To cite one well-known example from the history of aesthetics: in the *Critique of Judgment*, music more than any other art troubles the distinction between form and matter upon which aesthetics is founded.[77] Irreducibly durational and sensible, music cannot be grasped as form without losing what makes it what it is. Whatever is going on in the story of Orpheus and the lyre—here redescribed as that which brings the "wild denizens of the woods" to order—it is difficult to understand it simply as a story of *form*. Indeed, the "spellbinding" described by Vere follows from a necessary *incapacity* to grasp music as abstract form rather than as material sensation;

music is spellbinding—which is to say, effective as music—to the degree that it is *not* simply form, to the degree that it does not allow contemplative detachment or distance. Orpheus's own fate, unmentioned here, makes clear the limits of this identification of music with form and, by extension, with the law. The narrative of Billy doubles that of Orpheus: the aesthetic supplement to the law, the sensible materialization of its form, ultimately leads to the crisis of the legal order.

Syllables

Usage has its limits: Billy Budd must be executed, the form must be followed, but law nonetheless cannot saturate existence. Again, it is only because of this irreducible freedom or contingency that there must be law or "measured forms" in the first place. Thus, the scene of Billy's execution is characterized by a distinctly aesthetic surplus, a break with "usage," or perhaps more accurately, a moment when "usage" slides into shadow-concepts like "abuse" or "usury." In a moment that recalls and doubles the excessive deference of Billy's initial "goodbye to you too, old Rights-of-Man," Billy uses his last opportunity to speak to visit a benediction upon Captain Vere:

> At the penultimate moment, [Billy's] words, his only ones, wholly unobstructed in the utterance, were these: "God bless Captain Vere!" Syllables so unanticipated coming from one with the ignominious hemp about his neck—a conventional felon's benediction directed aft towards the quarters of honor; syllables too delivered in the clear melody of a singing bird on the point of launching from the twig— had a phenomenal effect, not unenhanced by the rare personal beauty of the young sailor, spiritualized now through late experiences so poignantly profound.[78]

Though the narrator emphasizes that Billy does not stutter—his "utterance" is "wholly unobstructed"—the articulate and musical exclamation is in fact not so distant from the stutter: where the stutter is characterized by a deficiency of articulation, the benediction is excessively articulate; not only is the exclamation as much a breach of decorum as the stutter, it may be equally involuntary; just as Billy *cannot* speak at certain moments, he seemingly *cannot not* speak at other moments. The paradox of the utterance is that the love of authority that it expresses exceeds this authority and the laws that it dictates; the blessing of the captain by the one the captain has sentenced to death can only be aberrant with regard to "usage." Billy's words are in turn repeated by the other sailors; this time, the involuntary character of the utterance is explicit: "Without volition, as it were, as indeed the ship's populace were but the vehicles of some vocal current electric, with one voice from alow and aloft came a resonant sympathetic echo: 'God bless Captain Vere!' And yet at that instant Billy alone must have been in their hearts, even as in their eyes."[79] If Billy's initial utterance is paradoxical in its implication and effect, that of transgression by excessive obedience, its repetition by the crew is characterized by the maximal degree of tension between semantic content and performative force: while the *énoncé* would seem to express a kind of obedience to Vere, the *énonciation* pledges loyalty to Billy, against Vere and "usage," by echoing Billy's words; as the hierarchy of authority breaks down, words become mere "syllables," a language divorced from its sense, stripped down to the force of its utterance. This breakdown uneasily coexists alongside the classicistic appeal to "the rare personal beauty of the young sailor"; the latter threatens to absorb and neutralize the former, even as the former may render the latter a mere pretense. This echo is at once a repetition and an affirmation, a judgment; in its light, Billy's benediction retroactively appears as an act of *poeisis*. In the interaction of exclamation and echo, there is the demand of and for a new *sensus communis*, a "redistribution of the sensible" tied to the most fragile sensible *minima*—"syllables" trembling at the edge of language.[80]

Notes

1. Herman Melville, *Billy Budd, Sailor*, in *Melville's Short Novels*, ed. Dan McCall (New York: Norton, 2002), 103–70, at 104.

2. Though my reading here is not constrained by the question of what exactly Melville read, it is clear that he had some knowledge of Kant and the post-Kantian German philosophical tradition. For a classic account, see Henry Pochmann, *German Culture in America: Philosophical and Literary Influences, 1600–1900* (Madison: University of Wisconsin Press, 1961), 436–40, 755–60. Pochmann argues that Melville had at least some familiarity with Kant's own texts and definitely knew something of (post-)Kantianism from acquaintances, as well as from popularizer-translators like Coleridge and Carlyle. For more recent assessments of Melville's relation to the German philosophical tradition, see Paul Hurh, *American Terror: The Feeling of Thinking in Edwards, Poe, and Melville* (Stanford, Calif.: Stanford University Press, 2015); and Birgit Mara Kaiser, *Figures of Simplicity: Sensation and Thinking in Kleist and Melville* (Albany: State University of New York Press, 2010).

3. Melville, *Billy Budd*, 127.

4. I am alluding here to the reading of the aesthetic tradition developed by Paul de Man in the essays collected in *Aesthetic Ideology* (Minneapolis: University of Minnesota Press, 1996); see in particular "Phenomenality and Materiality in Kant," 70–90.

5. A paleonym, following Jacques Derrida, is an old term that is put to new conceptual work, even as it can never transcend the history in which it is embedded. A catachresis is a term that is at once proper *and* figurative, that is, an originally metaphorical term like the legs of a table or the face of a mountain. On paleonymy, see Jacques Derrida, *Dissemination*, trans. Barbara Johnson (Chicago: University of Chicago Press, 1981), 3. On catachresis, see Quintilian, *Institutes of Oratory*, 8:6.

6. Werner Hamacher, "95 Theses on Philology," in *Minima Philologica*, trans. Catharine Diehl and Jason Groves (New York: Fordham University Press, 2015), 17.

7. *Beau Travail*, dir. Claire Denis, 1999.

8. Melville, *Billy Budd*, 103.

9. For "the short-circuit between freedom and nature [as] the inaugural antinomy of revolutionary modernity," see Rebecca Comay, *Mourning Sickness* (Stanford, Calif.: Stanford University Press, 2011), 18, following Hannah Arendt, *On Revolution* (London: Penguin Book, 1990), 47–51.

10. For Kant's pointed criticism of any aesthetics based on notions of perfection (and thus of conformity to a recognizable model), see Immanuel Kant, *The Critique of the Power of Judgment*, ed. Paul Guyer, trans. Paul Guyer and Eric Matthews (Cambridge: Cambridge University Press, 2000), 111–13.

11. For this distinction, see ibid., 114–16.

12. Insofar as the relative alphabetical primacy of "Aldebaran" is dependent on a prior act of translation or transliteration—from Arabic to English—it makes particularly clear the arbitrary character of the alphabetical allegory. On commandment, see the unpublished lecture by Giorgio Agamben, "What Is a Commandment?" A transcript can be found at https://waltendegewalt.wordpress.com/2011/04/01/giorgio-agamben-what-is-a-commandment-απομαγνητοφώνηση/.

13. On "inoperativity" or *désoeuvrement*, see Maurice Blanchot, *The Space of Literature*, trans. Ann Smock (Lincoln: University of Nebraska Press, 1989); as well as Jean-Luc Nancy, *The Inoperative Community*, ed. Peter Connor (Minneapolis: University of Minnesota Press, 1991). The example is a major question in Giorgio Agamben, *The Coming Community*, trans. Michael Hardt (Minneapolis: University of Minnesota Press, 1993), esp. 9–11.

14. Melville, *Billy Budd*, 103.

15. For an insightful recent reading of this scene with many points of overlap with my own, see Jonathan Elmer, "Was Billy Black? Herman Melville and the Captive-King," in *On Lingering and Being Last: Race and Sovereignty in the New World* (New York: Fordham University Press, 2008), 78–117.

16. I draw on Fred Moten for the argument concerning blackness as the remainder of the aesthetic and the freedom associated with the aesthetic. Though Moten privileges sound in this formulation, it applies well here as well: "the reduction of (phonic) materiality is modern thought's most fundamental protocol, an ordinance that protects the exclusionary universality of a totality that cannot stand, in its orderedness, in the face of the rough non-sense or extra-sense—the non-reduction of sense that is more than sense—of the surface in its ordinary serrations. It is not accident that irruptions on the surface of the event, that irruption as (the surface of) the event, will have constituted the severest challenge to that Kantian notion of freedom that depends upon smooth containment. The romanticism of the black radical tradition, if you will, is at issue here." See Fred Moten, "Knowledge of Freedom," *CR: The New Centennial Review* 4, no. 2 (2004): 269–310, at 272–73. See also Fred Moten, *In the Break: The Aesthetics of the Black Radical Tradition* (Minneapolis: University of Minnesota Press, 2003).

17. In Elmer's perceptive words: "The problem of the modern sovereign subject emerges for Melville from a matrix in which slave and sovereign, despot and pirate, trade places with confounding frequency . . . Any account of this theme

will fall short if it does not recognize the shadow of race in Melville's imaginative horizon" (Elmer, "Was Billy Black?" 79). For a meditation on the question of the possible affirmation of blackness *as* nothingness, see Fred Moten's brilliant "Blackness and Nothingness: Mysticism in the Flesh," *South Atlantic Quarterly* 112, no. 4 (2013): 737–80.

18. See Ernst Kantorowicz, *The King's Two Bodies* (1957; repr. Princeton, N.J.: Princeton University Press, 1985); Karl Marx, "The Fetishism of Commodities and Its Secret," in *Capital: A Critique of Political Economy*, trans. Samuel Moore and Edward Aveling (New York: Random House, 1906), 83.

19. A few lines later, reinforcing the reversible logic of the inhuman—at once more and less than human—this sovereign is aligned with the animal as well: "At each spontaneous tribute rendered by the wayfarers to this black pagod of a fellow . . . the motley retinue showed that they took that sort of pride in the evoker of it which the Assyrian priests doubtless showed for their grand sculptured Bull when the faithful prostrated themselves" (Melville, *Billy Budd*, 104).

20. As Branka Arsić has argued in relation to "Bartleby," Melville's walls are figures for thinking, understood in the architectonic terms of construction and assembly, but also in terms of the radical stupidity and opacity that is inseparable from thinking. See Branka Arsić, *Passive Constitutions, or 7½ Times Bartleby* (Stanford, Calif.: Stanford University Press, 2007), 2–3, 60–63, 90.

21. Herman Melville, "Bartleby, the Scrivener: A Story of Wall Street," in *Melville's Short Novels*, ed. Dan McCall (New York: Norton, 2002), 3–33, at 4.

22. The reference to Anacharsis Cloots later in the passage makes explicit the revolutionary humanist universalism the narrator associates with this scene, even as it also cannot be fully separated from a certain spectacle governed by the logic of exoticism: "[His shipmates] were made up of such an assortment of tribes and complexions as would have well fitted them to be marched up by Anacharsis Cloots before the bar of the First French Assembly as Representatives of the Human Race." In a peculiar *mise en abyme* of the structure of the example, *this* example itself contains a proliferation of singular yet ultimately equivalent or interchangeable examples, in this case, examples of humanity as such. The example, which is by definition an element in a virtual series, itself includes a virtual series within it.

23. Melville, *Billy Budd*, 142: "In sum, Captain Vere had from the beginning deemed Billy Budd to be what in the naval parlance of the time was called a 'King's bargain': that is to say, for his Brittanic Majesty's navy a capital investment at small outlay or none at all."

24. For a classic analysis of race as the absence-presence at the center of American literature, see Toni Morrison, *Playing in the Dark* (Cambridge, Mass.: Harvard University Press, 1992). This point resonates as well with Morrison's account elsewhere of Melville's "deliberate misdirections": "Since my earliest readings of *Moby-Dick*, I always sensed Melville's deliberate misdirections: that he was telling some other story underneath the obvious one" (Toni Morrison, "Melville and the Language of Denial," *The Nation*, January 7, 2014, https://www.thenation.com/article/melville-and-language-denial/). As Elmer emphasizes, this seemingly unmotivated or digressive scene, the scene of the "extra example," was a late addition to the text and indeed one of the last things Melville ever wrote. The question of its motivation, which may have remained obscure to

Melville himself, must remain open; see Elmer, "Was Billy Black?" 83, note on 230. Elmer bases this assessment on Herman Melville, *Billy Budd, Sailor (An Inside Narrative), Reading Text and Genetic Text, Edited from the Manuscript with Introduction and Notes*, ed. Harrison Hayford and Merton M. Sealts Jr. (Chicago: University of Chicago Press, 1962), 7.

25. In transferring the story of *Billy Budd* to the postcolonial milieu of Djibouti, *Beau Travail* picks up, however indirectly, on this "other story" of racialized violence; indeed, in an interview Denis goes so far as to remark without further explanation that this enigmatic, shadowy scene "clarifies the whole novella" ("cette scène éclaire toute la nouvelle"); see "The Weight of the Here and Now: Conversation with Claire Denis, 2001," by Jean-Philippe Renouard and Lise Wajeman, trans. Julia Borossa, *Journal of European Studies* 34, no. 1–2 (2004): 19–33, at 22; "'Ce poids d'ici-bas,' entretien avec Claire Denis," by Jean-Philippe Renouard and Lise Wajeman, *Vacarme* 14 (2001), http://www.vacarme.org/article84.html.

26. Melville, *Billy Budd*, 130.

27. On the various forms of interest that negatively define the aesthetic, see Kant, *Critique of the Power of Judgment*, 98; on the distinction between form and "charm" and other appeals to empirical sensation, see ibid., 107–10.

28. Ibid., 126.

29. See, respectively, Martin Heidegger, "The Origin of the Work of Art," in *Basic Writings: From "Being and Time" (1927) to "The Task of Thinking" (1964)*, ed. David Farrell Krell (New York: Harper Perennial, 2008), 139–212; Theodor Adorno, *Aesthetic Theory*, trans. Robert Hullot-Kentor (Minneapolis: University of Minnesota Press, 1997); Jacques Derrida, *The Truth in Painting*, trans. Geoffrey Bennington and Ian Macleod (Chicago: University of Chicago Press, 1987); and Paul de Man, "Kant's Materialism," in *Aesthetic Ideology* (Minneapolis: University of Minnesota Press, 1996), 119–28.

30. Melville, *Billy Budd*, 133. For an important recent attempt to grapple with the strange relation between Kantian "mere form" and textually oriented forms of literary criticism (or "philology" in my terminology), see Robert Lehman, "Formalism, Mere Form, and Judgment," *New Literary History* 48, no. 2 (2017): 245–63.

31. On the presumption of universal assent to what must nonetheless be a subjective judgment—that is, the paradox of subjective universality—see Kant, *Critique of the Power of Judgment*, 121–24; on reflective judgment, see ibid., 15–20.

32. On this point, see Hamacher, "95 Theses," 10–11.

33. Ibid., 104.

34. For an important commentary on this passage, see Barbara Johnson, "Melville's Fist: The Execution of *Billy Budd*," in *The Critical Difference: Essays in the Contemporary Rhetoric of Reading* (Baltimore, Md.: Johns Hopkins University Press, 1980), 79–109, at 84.

35. Melville, *Billy Budd*, 104.

36. *Oxford English Dictionary*, 2nd ed., s.v. "cynosure."

37. Ibid.

38. For a related understanding of allegory as narrative grounded in the signifier, see Maureen Quilligan, *The Language of Allegory: Defining the Genre* (Ithaca,

N.Y.: Cornell University Press, 1979); Quilligan addresses *The Confidence-Man* in this regard, but does not take up *Billy Budd*. On this point, see also Jonathan Culler, "The Call of the Phoneme: Introduction," in *On Puns: The Foundations of Letters*, ed. Jonathan Culler (Oxford: Basil Blackwell, 1988), 1–16, at 9.

39. Melville, *Billy Budd*, 151.

40. Ibid., 118.

41. On this point, see Hamacher, "95 Theses," 9–15.

42. Andrew Marvell, "Upon Appleton House," in *The Complete Poems*, ed. Elizabeth Story Donno (New York: Penguin, 2005), 75–99, at 78.

43. Melville, *Billy Budd*, 117.

44. For an important queer reading of *Billy Budd*, see Eve Sedgwick's now-classic essay "Some Binarisms (1): *Billy Budd*; After the Homosexual," in *Epistemology of the Closet* (Berkeley: University of California Press, 1990), 91–130.

45. Melville, *Billy Budd*, 146.

46. On this relation of pun and rhyme, see Geoffrey Hartman, "The Voice of the Shuttle: Language from the Point of View of Literature," *Journal of Metaphysics* 23, no. 2 (December 1969): 240–58, at 250.

47. See Melville, "Bartleby, the Scrivener," 12, 20.

48. For a different approach to the question of naming in the novella, see Stuart Burrows, "Billy Budd, Billy Budd," in *Melville's Philosophies*, ed. Branka Arsić and K. L. Evans (London: Bloomsbury, 2017), 39–60.

49. The domination of law over life is the theme of Giorgio Agamben's *Homo Sacer: Sovereign Power and Bare Life*, trans. Daniel Heller-Roazen (Stanford, Calif.: Stanford University Press, 1996). For an important recent reading of *Billy Budd* that is indebted to *Homo Sacer*, but which (unlike Agamben) largely neglects the relation of language to law and life, see William Spanos, *The Exceptionalist State and the State of Exception: Herman Melville's "Billy Budd, Sailor"* (Baltimore, Md.: Johns Hopkins University Press, 2010).

50. Melville, *Billy Budd*, 147.

51. Ibid., 149.

52. Ibid., 155.

53. Ibid., 158.

54. Ibid., 151–52. The phrase "lasting tongue-tie" draws an implicit contrast with Billy's intermittent and occasional "tongue-tie," which was in fact its cause. Just as Billy the "cynosure" is linked to "Starry Vere" through his seeming misnaming, certain attributes (or signifiers) are transferred from Billy to Claggart. This system of floating attributes works against usage, constituting something of a counter-system.

55. Denis, *Beau Travail*, 5:30–5:40.

56. For Hobbes's version of this motif, see *De Cive*, collected in *Man and Citizen: De Homine and De Cive* (Indianapolis, Ind.: Hackett, 1991), 89.

57. Denis, *Beau Travail*, 40:08.

58. Ibid., 32:00

59. Johnson, "Melville's Fist," 83–84.

60. As Hölderlin puts it in his "Anmerkungen zum Oedipus," Oedipus reads "too infinitely" (Friedrich Hölderlin, "Anmerkungen zum Oedipus," in *Theoretische Schriften*, ed. Johann Kreuzer [Hamburg: Felix Meiner, 1998], 94–101,

at 96). For the broader point, I'm indebted to John T. Hamilton, *Security: Politics, Humanity, and the Philology of Care* (Princeton, N.J.: Princeton University Press, 2013), 57–58. See also Michael Dillon, "Otherwise Than Self-Determination: The Mortal Freedom of *Oedipus Asphaleos*," in *Violence, Identity, and Self-Determination*, ed. Hent de Vries and Samuel Weber (Stanford, Calif.: Stanford University Press, 1997), 162–85.

61. I am in conversation here with Giorgio Agamben's essays "On Potentiality" and "Bartleby: or, On Contingency," both collected in *Potentialities*, ed. and trans. Daniel Heller-Roazen (Stanford, Calif.: Stanford University Press, 1999): "On Potentiality," 177–84, and "Bartleby: or, On Contingency," 243–71.

62. Martin Heidegger, *Being and Time*, trans. Joan Stambaugh (Albany: State University of New York Press, 1996), 62–71; Martin Heidegger., *Sein und Zeit* (1927; repr. Tübingen: Max Niemeyer Verlag, 2006), 66–76. See also Martin Heidegger, *What Is Called Thinking?* trans. J. Glenn Gray (1954; repr. New York: Harper and Row 1968); Jacques Derrida, "*Geschlecht II*: Heidegger's Hand," in *Deconstruction and Philosophy*, ed. John Sallis, trans. John. P. Leavey Jr. (Chicago: University of Chicago Press, 1987), 161–96. For one of the few other attempts to make sense of the "handsome"—or in this case, the "unhandsome"—see, also with reference to Derrida's *Geschlecht* (though without any reference to Melville), Stanley Cavell, *Conditions Handsome and Unhandsome: The Constitution of Emersonian Perfectionism* (Chicago: University of Chicago Press, 1990), 38–41.

63. For powerful recent readings of Billy's stutter, see Ann Smock, *What Is There to Say? Blanchot, Melville, des Forêts, Beckett* (Lincoln: University of Nebraska Press, 2003), 57–62; and Nancy Ruttenburg, *The Democratic Personality* (Stanford, Calif.: Stanford University Press), 350–70.

64. Melville, *Billy Budd*, 111. Italics mine.

65. For this argument, see Carl Schmitt, *The Concept of the Political*, trans. George Schwab (1932; repr. Chicago: University of Chicago Press, 1996), 58–60; Carl Schmitt, *Political Theology*, trans. George Schwab (1922; repr. Chicago: University of Chicago Press, 1985), 56–58.

66. The term derives from Jacques Lacan, *The Seminar, Book III: The Psychoses, 1955–1956*, trans. Russell Grigg (London: Routledge, 1993), 268–69.

67. See Erwin Panofsky, "*Et in Arcadia Ego*: Poussin and the Elegiac Tradition," in *Meaning in the Visual Arts* (Chicago: University of Chicago Press), 295–320. Panofsky offers a list of variations on the topos, including Schiller's "Auch ich war in Arcadia geboren" ("I too was born in Arcadia"), from the poem "Resignation"; see ibid., 296. Melville owned a copy of *The Poems and Ballads of Schiller* (translated by Sir Edward Bulwer-Lytton) and alludes to "The Diver" in *Moby-Dick*; see Merton M. Sealts, *Melville's Reading, Revised and Enlarged Edition* (Columbia: University of South Carolina Press, 1988), 50, 71, 210–11. Melville also kept a quotation from Schiller's *Don Carlos* at his writing desk ("Keep true to the dreams of thy youth"); see Nathaniel Philbrick, *Why Read "Moby-Dick"?* (New York: Viking, 2011), 126.

68. Panofsky, "*Et in Arcadia Ego*."

69. For an argument tying non-voluntaristic freedom to the contingency of the signifier via a reading of atomism, see Jacques Derrida, "*Mes Chances/My Chances: A Rendezvous with Some Epicurean Stereophonies*," in *Psyche:*

Inventions of the Other, Vol. 1, ed. Peggy Kamuf and Elizabeth G. Rottenberg (Stanford, Calif.: Stanford University Press, 2007), 344–76. For a related argument, see Jacques Lezra, *Unspeakable Subjects: The Genealogy of the Event in Early Modern Europe* (Stanford, Calif.: Stanford University Press, 1997), 1–34. See also Jean-Luc Nancy, *The Experience of Freedom*, trans. Bridget McDonald (1988; repr. Stanford, Calif.: Stanford University Press, 1993).

70. Renouard and Wajeman, "Ce poids d'ici-bas;" Renouard and Wajeman, "The Weight of the Here and Now," 26.

71. Herman Melville, *Billy Budd, marin (récit interne), suivi de Daniel Orme,* ed. and trans. Pierre Leyris (Paris: Gallimard, 1980).

72. Ibid.

73. This seems to be what Claire Denis is referring to when she says, in the interview with Renouard and Wajeman, that "much of the film is in that 'nice find' [*belle trouvaille*]" (Renouard and Wajeman, "The Weight of the Here and Now," 28).

74. Denis, *Beau Travail,* 10:45–13:00.

75. Melville, *Billy Budd,* 166–67.

76. For a highly insightful recent essay that takes its point of departure from this passage, see Jason Frank, "The Lyre of Orpheus: Aesthetics and Authority in *Billy Budd,*" in *A Political Companion to Herman Melville,* ed. Jason Frank (Lexington: University Press of Kentucky, 2013), 358–85; though I largely agree with Frank's essay, Frank does not consider the possibility that Vere himself has misread the example of Orpheus and that the passage might thus constitute an ironic commentary on Vere's aesthetic theory and conceptualization of reading.

77. See Kant, *Critique of the Power of Judgment,* 201–2. For an important reading of Kant on music, see John Hamilton, *Music, Madness, and the Unworking of Language* (New York: Columbia University Press, 2008), 109–14.

78. Melville, *Billy Budd,* 163.

79. Ibid.

80. On the *sensus communis,* see Kant, *Critique of the Power of Judgment,* 122–24, 173–76; on the "distribution of the sensible," see Jacques Rancière's reworking of Kant (and much else) in *The Politics of Aesthetics,* ed. and trans. Gabriel Rockhill (London: Bloomsbury, 2006).

A-religion

Jean-Luc Nancy

Should we wish to praise Claire Denis's latest film, *Beau Travail* (good work, handsomely done), it would not be advisable to direct its title back at it, as a compliment. For this title should be understood as an exclamation uttered in front of a disaster: "Good work, handsomely done," as one might say "Congratulations!" in order to lash out with irony at a stupid act or a clumsy gesture. So that no doubt should remain as to the correct tone of the title, one need only look up the expression in the short story from which the film was adapted, Melville's *Billy Budd, Sailor*. "Handsomely done" is an expression uttered by Claggart (Budd's sworn enemy) when Billy knocks over his bowl of soup. Melville prolongs it by "And handsome is as handsome did it, too,"[1] going on to comment on this allusion to Billy's particular, angelic type of beauty, by noting that it was the deep-seated reason for Claggart's hatred of him. "Handsomely done!" not only takes "handsome" against the grain: beauty in itself is mocked. This is the effect of the "perverse nature" of Billy's tormentor.

This "handsomely done" or "beau travail" echoes in the book as in the film the expression "pretty good find" or "belle trouvaille,"[2] also directed at Billy (Gilles Sentain in the film), this time by the commander whose desire for the beautiful young man is alluded to both by Melville and by Claire Denis. If he is a "pretty good find," it is because he is a foundling. This is one of the characteristics that make him into a Christic figure—into this victim offered up to the "mystery of iniquity," as Melville puts it, following Saint Paul. Melville's tale is a tale of a Christic passion whose iniquity leads to no salvation, other than the salvation of sailor's poetry, which at the end of the story makes the writing self-referential (Melville was a poet as well). A ship called the *Athée* (the *Atheist*) leaves no room for doubt: the tragedy of Billy is that of Christ in a world without God—and perhaps, by that token, the tragedy of an art whose very art abandons it to the hatred of the world. But it is in the very power of that hatred, in the "depravity according to nature" which attacks beauty, innocence, and goodness, that this art finds its springboard: it is "the point of the present story," as Melville puts it.[3] Claire Denis is less explicit. As she hides the precise meaning of "beau travail"—at least during the film, since the film itself invites a rereading of Melville—so she uses the markers of a Christic allegory differently, paradoxically, in a more insidious and more showy manner. She does not cite the scriptures, does not name "the Atheist," but she does show the cross (as does Melville) and the Madonna (to which Melville alludes). Mainly, she makes Gilles overtly into a savior (he saves a soldier during an explosion) whose sin in the eyes of his enemy is not a cup which is knocked over, but a flask which is proffered to a torture victim; he utters "Lost" as he lies dying (perhaps—but perhaps he will also be resurrected at the end of the film?).

A lost savior then; and the one who lost him, like a Satan leading him astray in the desert, is equally lost, banished from the Legion and committing suicide, but only in order to live again in the film's final scene, this time without any ambiguity, in the intense life of a precise and feverish dance, executed in a disco with the lights dimmed, to a song whose title (no secret title to decipher here) is "Rhythm of the Night."[4]

A paradox, which belongs to Claire Denis and owes little to Melville, or that Melville exploits little, is that he who loses a savior belongs to an impeccable order—quite the thing to say!—symbolized here by the Legion: the order of the army, or a monastic order (the equivalence is raised in Melville), ritual order (the entire film is scanned on the figures of ritual, its songs, its marches, its observances); the order finally of an accomplished, powerful, and harmonious beauty, incarnated in this instance in the bodies of the men. This order, this religion, is posited in the face of religion—the Christian one, but also the Muslim one (present in the fact that it is Ramadan with the prayers at the mosque, in a marked complicity and solidarity with the "savior"). In the face of, and also against, just like the two men who closely confront one another: another religion, or rather, and more strangely, an a-religion—an a-religion that defines itself in closely similar terms to the Christian one ("I am the guardian of your flock, commander," the cross of the Legionnaires' cemetery). This a-religion is made up of a body of observances closed upon itself, referring only to itself, and in this it is similar to the corps of underemployed Legionnaires on the fringes of the desert, on the fringes of the South, on the fringes of misery, on the fringes of possible conflicts, suspended between idleness and guard duty, preoccupied with its appearance: body, clothing, virile gestures of combat simulated in an empty building. It is this order that the "savior" troubles ("a guy who had nothing to do with us"), says his enemy, who also acts as the narrator.

But this order of a-religion: what is it after all, to what does it refer after all, other than the film itself, its image, the process of its filming? At least it is at this point that I risk an interpretation of this film which calls so ostentatiously for the interpretation of the secret that it reveals. The secret it reveals is also the secret of the important transformations made to Melville's story: transformations that go far beyond the rationales of an "adaptation," that divert the topic fundamentally while remaining secret, beginning by this title which does not say where it comes from and where it leads.

This interpretation, among other possible ones, would start precisely with the title. "Beau travail" substituted for the name of a character means that it is not the story of that character which is at stake. It is the film itself that is: here is good work. Consequently, it is a work on beauty: body, light, appearance, harmony, majesty, stark rhythm of editing, which holds the narrative at bay, in favor of an ostentation of the image through which the camera signals or signs itself. Image signifies itself from the opening images of the film (the insignia of the Legion in extreme close-up on a wall). Image signifies itself in its prestige, in its power, to the extent that it proposes a cult of itself to the point of turning the film into a kind of icon of the image and of cinema: an icon in the strong sense of the term—in other words, an image which in itself gives birth to the image it represents. Everything in the film indicates something of a nonrepresentational, nonfigurative affirmation of the image: the power, the intensity, the fire even of a self-presentation. (One can add to this the pattern according to which the sexes are divided upon this stage entirely peopled by unusually virile men, traversed by homosexual allusion, and where the few women are situated on the side of rest, of relaxation, or of compassion for the lost savior.)

Melville's tale can be read as the parable of an art which would be the substitute for redemption in a world without redemption: the torment of the "handsome sailor" subjected to a terrible but necessary law of the world opens up on its own history and its own poetry. Denis's film can be understood as a sustained, nervous inquiry into what could be called Melville's religion (and which holds true for any kind of religion or mystique of art). Can beauty save itself? Should it not, rather, save itself from itself? What is an absolute order of self-presentation, a form which finds completion in its representation of itself?

I have heard it said that there is in this film an "unbearable literalness." In fact, it is the literalness of hieratic and hierarchical ordering in the proper sense of both terms: sacred power, the sacrality of power and the power of the sacred making up a full, autonomous, and exclusive order, representing for itself the immanence of its own transcendence, appropriating it in its self-image. It is none other than fascism as the fascination of auto-sacrality and of auto-figuration. (This does not mean that Claire Denis reduces the Legion to that category; the internal complexity of the film shows it sufficiently.) But the use of the term "fascism" can lead us astray if I do not take the time here for the digressions it necessitates. I will only say that the "unbearable literalness" of the film is that of an image, an art, a beauty which is worried for itself, which is worried precisely by what one might mistake for self-satisfaction. "Beau travail, handsomely done"; can a work of beauty be a fine mess? But without beauty, can we even begin to pose the question? Or, also, if art finds itself in charge of something which is none other than the escheating of the theologico-political order, what does "art" then mean? To the fascinating and perverse sufficiency of an "a-religion," what affirmation can we oppose? What atheist art which would neither be closed on itself, nor submitted to injunctions of meaning? The astonishing strength of this philosophical film—the strength of its work—is to produce no less than such questions: and its *beauty* is that of such *work* (or indeed the opposite).

Notes

This essay was originally published as Jean-Luc Nancy, "L'areligion (*Beau travail* de Claire Denis)," *Vacarme* 14 (Winter 2000): 69–70, http://www.vacarme.eu.org/article81.html. Translated by Julia Borossa.

1. Herman Melville, *Billy Budd, Sailor,* in *Billy Budd, Sailor and Other Stories* (Harmondsworth, Eng.: Penguin, 1986), 287–385, at 350.

2. Ibid., 330.

3. Ibid., 326.

4. Corona, vocal performance of "The Rhythm of the Night," by Francesco Bontempi et al., on *The Rhythm of the Night,* Warner Music, ZYX, 1995.

CONTRIBUTORS

Emily Apter is Silver Professor of French and Comparative Literature at New York University. She is the author of many books, including *Continental Drift*, *Against World Literature*, *The Translation Zone*, and *Unexceptional Politics: On Obstruction, Impasse, and the Impolitic*. She is also an editor of the *Dictionary of Untranslatables*.

David Copenhafer is an assistant professor at Bard Early College Queens. His work has appeared in *Camera Obscura*, *Qui Parle*, and *Sound Studies*, as well as in nonacademic settings. He is at work on a book about "the literary acoustic."

Sorin Radu Cucu is an associate professor of English at Laguardia Community College, City University of New York. He is the author of *The Underside of Politics: Global Fictions in the Fog of the Cold War*. His recent work explores the intersections of media philosophy, aesthetics, and globalization.

Paul Downes is an associate professor of English at the University of Toronto. He is the author of *Democracy, Monarchism, and Revolution in Early American Literature* and *Hobbes, Sovereignty, and Early American Literature*. His next book project focuses on representations of political resistance in Melville's fiction.

John T. Hamilton is a professor of comparative literature and German at Harvard University. He is the author of *Soliciting Darkness* and *Music, Madness, and the Unworking of Language*, as well as, most recently, *Security* and *Philology of the Flesh*. He has published articles on authors ranging from Ovid to Hölderlin to Pascal Quignard.

Daniel Hoffman-Schwartz is a lecturer in comparative literature at Princeton University. He is the coeditor of *Flirtations: Rhetoric and Aesthetics This Side of Seduction* with Barbara Natalie Nagel and Laurel Shizuko Stone. His writings have appeared in venues such as the *Oxford Literary Review*, *Derrida Today*, and *The Dictionary of Untranslatables*. He is currently at work on a monograph entitled *Infinite Reflection on the Revolution in France*.

Walter A. Johnston is a visiting assistant professor of English at Williams College. His current manuscript traces contemporary debates bearing on the politics of judgment back to the unresolved problem of political Romanticism. An excerpt of this larger project, a critique of Ernesto Laclau's *On Populist Reason*, recently appeared in *Diacritics*.

Jacques Lezra is professor and chair of Hispanic studies at the University of California at Riverside. He is the author of many books, including *Wild Materialism*, *Untranslating Machines*, and *On the Nature of Marx's Things*. He is the coeditor of *Lucretius and Modernity* with Liza Blake and of the English version of *The Dictionary of Untranslatables* with Emily Apter and Michael Wood, as well as the cotranslator, with Hugo Rodríguez Vecchini, of the Spanish edition of Paul de Man's *Blindness and Insight*.

Barbara N. Nagel is an assistant professor of German at Princeton University. She is the author of *Der Skandal der Literalen* and has just finished a manuscript on *Ambiguous Aggressions*, as well as the coeditor of *Flirtations: Rhetoric and Aesthetics This Side of Seduction*. Her writings have appeared in *Law and Literature*, *Weimarer Beiträge*, and *Critical Inquiry*.

Jean-Luc Nancy is professor emeritus of philosophy at the University of Strasbourg. He is the author of more than twenty books, including *The Inoperative Community*, *The Experience of Freedom*, *The Sense of the World*, *Being Singular Plural*, and (with Philippe Lacoue-Labarthe) *The Literary Absolute* and *The Title of the Letter*.

Peter Szendy is a professor of humanities and comparative literature at Brown University. He is the author of many books, including *Of Stigmatology*, *Le Supermarché du visible*, *All Ears*, *Phantom Limbs*, *Apocalypse-Cinema*, and *Kant in the Land of Extraterrestrials*.

Roland Végső is an associate professor of English at the University of Nebraska-Lincoln. He is the author of *The Naked Communist: Cold War Modernism and Popular Culture*. His articles and translations have appeared in journals such as *Cultural Critique*, *The New Centennial Review*, *Epoché*, and *Parallax*.

INDEX

Adorno, Theodor W., 53n52, 110n77, 216
aesthetics, 5; *aisthesis*, 9, 211–12, 214; in *Billy Budd*, 9, 211–13, 216–18, 222, 230; Kant and, 229, 232n10; "recessionary," 47; transcendental aesthetic, 61
Agamben, Giorgio, 37, 42, 45, 46, 156n17, 162, 235n49
Alexander, Michelle, 116, 135n50
April Fool's Day, 197–98, 200
"a-religion," 9, 240
Arsić, Branka, 5, 7, 68, 233n20
Attica Liberation Front, 117, 125, 130, 135n55
Attica Prison riot, 5, 115–21, 123–25, 129, 131n11, 132nn20–21, 133n23, 134n40, 135n57, 136n58, 136n68
Atwater, Lee, 118–19
Aust, Stefan, 15–16
Austin, J. L., 37

Baecque, Antoine de, 202–3
"Bartleby, the Scrivener," 36–47, 156n17, 160, 162–78, 213, 215; acoustics in, 8, 160, 163, 165–66; Borges's translation of, 8, 167–70, 172–73, 175–78; cognitive capitalism and, 161–62, 163, 165, 175; interpretations of, 39–41, 45, 162–63; necrophilology and, 175; obstinacy in, 6, 38, 45; Occupy movement and, 5, 38–39; rumor in, 166–67, 171–73, 176–77
Baudelaire, Charles, 201
Beau Travail (Denis), 3–4, 5, 9, 212, 222–24, 227–29, 234n25, 237n73, 239–42
Benito Cereno, 55–57, 62, 64–82, 85n52, 113–16, 119–24, 127–30; atmosphere in, 67–70, 82; historical basis for, 56–57, 113, 115; interpretations of, 115, 130; theatricality in, 7, 56, 57, 71–72, 75
Benjamin, Walter, 3, 4, 86n52
Bennett, Jane, 53n52
Bergson, Henri, 103–4
Bhabha, Homi, 85n52
Billy Budd, 3–5, 114, 141–55, 189, 211–31, 239–42; acoustics in, 7–8, 142–48, 154, 157nn19–20, 157n23; aesthetics and, 9, 211–13, 216–18, 222, 230; beauty (and handsomeness) in, 211, 213–14, 217–19, 224–25, 228–29, 239; "Billy in the Darbies," 8, 143, 150–51, 154–55; French translation of, 3, 228; "handsomely done" phrase in, 3, 225, 228, 239; historical basis for, 141–42, 147, 148–49; interpretations of, 142; Montaigne in, 92, 220; theology and, 9, 226–27, 239–41; Vere's name in, 220–21. *See also Beau Travail*; translatability
Billy Budd (Britten opera), 157n23
Black Lives Matter, 5, 6, 49, 129. *See also* police violence against African Americans
blackness, 214–15, 232n16
Blanchot, Maurice, 162
Blum, Hester, 40
Bonham, John. *See* "Moby Dick" (Led Zeppelin instrumental)
Borges, Jorge Luis, 8, 167–70, 172–73, 175–78
Boulainvilliers, Henri de, 24
Brodtkorb, Paul, Jr., 109n65
Brown, Sterling, 7, 130, 131n9
Brown, Wendy, 42, 45
Buchanan, James M., 44

245

Butler, Judith, 35, 42, 45
Butterfield, Alexander, 126

capitalism, 14, 50n10, 89, 115, 118–19, 121, 128, 129, 172; "Bartleby" and, 8, 36, 39, 41, 163, 165, 170; *Benito Cereno* and, 114, 118–19; *Billy Budd* and, 215, 233n23; "*capital confiance*," 200; "cognitive capitalism," 162–63, 165, 172, 175; "disaster capitalism," 134n33; "equity capitalism," 8, 165, 170–71, 172, 175, 177; *Moby-Dick* and, 16, 21–22. *See also* commodities
Castronovo, Russ, 39
Chase, Richard, 14
Chion, Michel, 157n19
Clausewitz, Carl von, 13, 19
Clenling, Horser, 152–54
Clinton, Hillary, 128, 137n79
Cloots, Anacharsis, 233n22
Coates, Ta-Nehisi, 105
Cohen, John, 130
colonialism, 5, 51n27, 67, 75, 114
Comay, Rebecca, 35, 38
commodities, 159–63, 165, 172, 175, 177, 178, 178n2, 215, 222
community, 36, 42, 90, 102, 174–75, 211, 213. *See also sensus communis*
Confidence-Man, The, 8–9, 90–91, 195–97, 199–207; Godard's film adaptation of, 8–9, 195, 202–6; "image" scarcity in, 195–97
Conrad, Joseph, 90, 97, 107n40
cowardice, 7, 89–105, 106n18, 106n33
Cox, Brandon Coley, 53n56
Currie, Elliott, 122
Curtis, Adam, 44, 51n35

Dante Alighieri, 90, 94, 100, 107n47
Davis, Angela, 113, 116, 121–22
Davis, Kim, 6, 35–36
Deepwater Horizon oil spill, 13
Delano, Amasa, memoir by, 56, 57, 64, 72, 76, 113–14, 119, 120–22, 124, 127, 134n33, 137n73, 137n78
Deleuze, Gilles, 8, 33n32, 37–38, 53n52, 91; on "Bartleby, the Scrivener," 42–43, 47, 162–63; on Godard's *Le Grand Escroc*, 203, 206

de Man, Paul, 216, 231n4
Denis, Claire. *See Beau Travail*
Derrida, Jacques, 3, 37, 47, 53n52, 96, 127, 131n5, 208n9, 216; on belief, 199, 204; on Melville, 8, 179n4; on Nixon, 113; on paleonymy, 231n5
Descartes, René, 68, 70
des Forêts, Louis-René, 6, 35, 45–49
Dimock, Wai Chee, 105

Echo and Narcissus myth, 8, 187–89, 193nn15–16
Elmer, Jonathan, 215, 232n17, 233n24
"Encantadas, The," 70
Esposito, Roberto, 42

Force Majeure (Östlund film), 107n40
Fore, Devin, 50
Forman, James, Jr., 128–29, 133n25, 137n82
Foucault, Michel, 24, 108n61, 135n47
French Revolution, 9, 43, 211

Galvani, Luigi, 144
general equivalent problem, 159–62, 163, 165
Genet, Jean, 108n55
Godard, Jean-Luc. *See Grand Escroc, Le*
Goffman, Alice, 110n76
Grand Escroc, Le (Godard film), 8, 195, 202–6
Grandin, Greg, 113, 119, 130
Greek mythology. *See* Echo and Narcissus; Oedipus; Orpheus
Grimstad, Paul, 5
Guattari, Félix, 33n32

Hakluyt, Richard, 192
Haldeman, H. R., 118, 126
Hamacher, Werner, 212
Harris, Aisha, 97
"Hawthorne and His Mosses," 99, 111n80
Hegel, Georg Wilhelm Friedrich, 19, 28, 50n10, 192
Heidegger, Martin, 96, 216, 225–26
Hemingway, Ernest, 20–21
Hobbes, Thomas, 24, 63, 182, 223–24

Index

Hölderlin, Friedrich, 7, 103, 211, 235n60
Hunt for Red October, The (novel and film), 33n26
Hurh, Paul, 5

image, 4, 8–9, 20, 49, 169; "Bartleby" and, 40; *Beau Travail* and, 240–41; *Benito Cereno* and, 66–67, 76; *The Confidence-Man* and, 195–97, 200, 201, 204, 205–7; in *Le Grand Escroc*, 203–5; *Moby-Dick* and, 8, 17, 99, 201; in *Orson Whales*, 182–92; *Pierre* and, 202; Schmitt and, 60–62, 66
imperialism, 16, 21, 67
Israel Potter, 92
Itin, Alex. *See Orson Whales*

James, C. L. R., 14–15, 17, 18, 22, 31n1, 32nn6–7, 90, 138n94; on *Benito Cereno*, 75; on Pip, 108n57, 109n64
Jameson, Fredric, 50n10
Jay, Antony, 44, 51n35
Johnson, Barbara, 141, 142, 225
Jonck, Michael, 40
Jünger, Ernst, 7, 55, 57, 62

Kafka, Franz, 167
Kaiser, Birgit Mara, 5
Kant, Immanuel, 33n28, 61, 74, 211, 213, 216–17, 229; Melville's familiarity with, 231n2
Kaphar, Titus, 49
Kapp, Ernst, 59
Keaton, Buster, 109n66
Keats, John, 144
Kelley, Win, 39
Kennedy, Randy, 13
Kierkegaard, Søren, 102
King, Martin Luther, Jr., 124

Lawrence, D. H., 13
Led Zeppelin. *See* "Moby Dick" (Led Zeppelin instrumental)
Levinas, Emmanuel, 105
Lewis, R. W. B., 14
Leyris, Pierre, 3, 228
Locke, John, 119–20, 121–22
Lordon, Frédéric, 45

Lyotard, Jean-François, 53n52

Mackenzie, Alexander Slidell. *See Somers* affair
Mardi, 91, 92
Markels, Julian, 100
Marvell, Andrew, 220–21
Marx, Karl, 8, 30n10, 125, 159, 171, 204, 215, 222
Marx, Leo, 40
Mastroianni, Dominic, 5
Mathiessen, F. O., 14, 17
McLaughlin, Kevin, 179n11
mediation (media, mediality), 4–5; *Benito Cereno* and, 113–15; *Billy Budd* and, 214; *Moby-Dick* and, 16, 17, 26–31; ontology of, 34n41
Melville, Herman: "-ability" (*-barkeit*) of, 4; abolitionism and, 39, 65, 75; art collection of, 195, 207n1; language (and philology) of, 4, 9, 212, 220, 222, 226
Melville, Samuel, 7, 129–30
Milner, Jean-Claude, 43, 45
mise en abyme, literary use of, 181–82, 187, 233n22
Moby-Dick, 13–31, 33n29, 55, 62, 67, 76, 89–105, 159, 181–82, 187–92; allegory and, 14, 21, 29–30; as anticapitalist parable, 16; Cold War discourse and, 14–20, 22, 26, 31, 32n10, 33n25; images in, 201, 208n17; mediation and, 16, 17, 26–31; Pip in, 6, 7, 89–90, 94–105, 108n57; war and, 16, 18–26, 28–29, 33nn31–32; Welles's reading of, 8, 182, 183, 188; "whiteness of the whale" in, 6, 27–28
Moby-Dick (Hermann oratorio), 189
Moby-Dick (Huston film), 6, 19–20, 189
"Moby Dick" (Led Zeppelin instrumental), 4, 8, 181, 182, 183, 190, 191–92
Moby Dick—Rehearsed (Welles drama), 189
modernity, 16, 21, 22, 24; war and, 6, 18, 26, 33n28
Montaigne, Michel de, 90, 92, 94, 102, 220

Morrison, Toni, 114, 115, 130, 233n24
Moten, Fred, 232n16
Murphy, Geraldine, 14

Nancy, Jean-Luc, 42
Naughton, John T., 45–46
necrophilology, 165, 166, 175, 177
Negt, Oskar, and Alexander Kluge, 6, 38, 49, 50n10, 53n58
Neufeld, John, 157n23
Nietzsche, Friedrich, 159, 199
Nixon, Richard M., 7, 113, 116–18, 123–28, 132n20, 133n23

obstinacy, 6, 35, 38, 45, 48–49, 50n10, 53n52
Occupy movement, 5, 6, 38–42
Odello, Laura, 208n9
Oedipus myth, 225
Oliver, Egbert, 40
Olson, Charles, 100–101, 193n19
Omoo, 90–91
Orpheus myth, 147, 229–30, 237n76
Orson Whales (Itin video), 8, 181–89, 190, 191–92
ostinato, 6, 35, 36, 47–49, 53n52
Oswald, Russell G., 117, 135n45
Otter, Samuel, 5
Ovid, 8, 187–88, 193n16

Panofsky, Erwin, 227
Pease, Donald, 14, 17, 31n4, 108n59
Peretz, Eyal, 194
philia, 9, 212, 220; cinephilia, 229
philology, 9, 170, 212, 220, 226, 229. See also necrophilology
"Piazza, The," 76–78
Piazza Tales, The, 56; title of, 76
Pierre, 79, 202
Plato, 70, 95–96, 127, 131n5. See also Socrates
Pochmann, Henry, 231
police violence against African Americans, 104–5, 109nn69–72, 110nn73–78, 118
Poore, Jonathan, 39–40
Povinelli, Elizabeth, 89

Queneau, Raymond, 46

racism, 118–19, 123–25, 128–29, 133n25, 134n28, 138n85, 215. See also police violence against African Americans; slavery
Rajan, Tilottama, 108n61
Rancière, Jacques, 40, 161
Rankine, Claudia, 49, 90, 105
Rebentisch, Juliane, 85
Red Army Faction (RAF), 5, 6, 15–17, 18
Redburn, 90–91
Robbins, Tom, 130
Robin, Cory, 118
Rockefeller, Nelson, 116–18, 123–24, 133n23, 135n57, 136n58
Rogin, Michael, 40, 156n3

Said, Edward, 5
Saint-Just, Louis Antoine de, 43
Sanborn, Geoffrey, 5, 85n52
Schiller, Friedrich, 211, 227, 236n67
Schlegel, Friedrich, 211
Schmitt, Carl, 7, 55–67, 69, 72–75, 79–82, 83n20; on political Romanticism, 73–75; theory of space, 58–61
sensus communis, 211, 231
Shakespeare, William, 55, 70, 78, 90, 97, 100–102, 189, 205
Shelley, Mary, 144
slavery: "Bartleby" and, 39; *Benito Cereno* and, 7, 56, 57, 62, 64–66, 68–73, 75–76, 81, 113–16, 119, 124, 129; *Billy Budd* and, 214–15, 232n17; as metaphor, 46, 70, 72, 81, 97–98, 115–16; *Moby-Dick* and, 96, 97–98; *White-Jacket* and, 141, 156n3
Sloterdijk, Peter, 28
Snediker, Michael, 101
Socrates, 39, 53n52
Sohn-Rethel, Alfred, 159, 178n2
Somers affair, 141–43, 148–49, 151–55
sound: in "Bartleby," 8, 160, 163, 165–66; in *Billy Budd*, 7–8, 142–48, 154, 157nn19–20, 157n23; "literary acoustic," 142, 146
sovereignty, 7, 25, 37, 38, 40, 42, 44, 45, 46, 57, 62, 72, 79, 93, 97, 128–28, 149, 160, 161–62, 163, 173, 182, 192, 208n9; in *Billy Budd*, 214, 215,

Index 249

227, 232n17, 233n19; Schmitt and, 7, 58, 81–82
space, 19, 33n25, 65, 79, 86n52; "Bartleby" and, 40; *Benito Cereno* and, 67, 73; *Billy Budd* and, 220, 222; economic, 166; Kant and, 61; public, 41, 165; Schmitt and, 58–61, 63–64, 73, 80–82
stasis, 6, 38, 45
Stephanson, Anders, 19, 33n25
Stirner, Max, 38
Sundquist, Eric, 67, 72
Szendy, Peter, 31, 89–90

Thomas, Brook, 40
Thompson, Heather Ann, 132n20, 133n25
Thoreau, Henry David, 39, 40
time (and temporality), 6, 48, 115, 177–78, 197, 203; *Billy Budd* and, 8, 142, 146–49, 212, 217; Kant and, 61; Schmitt and, 60
translatability, 159–60, 168; *Billy Budd* and, 3–5, 212, 215, 223
Trap, The (documentary), 44, 51n35
Trump, Donald, 137n83
Turner, J. M. W., 67
"Two Temples, The," 201–2

Wallace, Robert K., 207
Walser, Robert, 108n55
Walsh, Chris, 91, 104, 106n18, 106n33
war: *Billy Budd* and, 145; Clausewitz on, 13; cowardice during, 91; Deleuze and Guattari on, 33n32; *Moby-Dick* and, 16, 18–26, 28–29, 33nn31–32; perpetual, 6, 23–26; Schmitt on, 63
"War on Terror," 5, 17, 32n18, 37
Weber, Samuel, 4, 116
Welles, Orson, 8, 181, 182–83, 186–89, 191–92; *Citizen Kane*, 183, 186–87, 189, 192; *F Is for Fake*, 186–87
"whale" (verb), 8, 181, 190–91
Whately, Richard, 164, 165
White-Jacket, 21, 91, 92–94, 141, 148–49, 155
Wicker, Tom, 120, 124–25, 133n23
Williams, Stanley, 120
Wordsworth, William, 67, 84n38

Yes, Minister and *Yes, Prime Minister* (TV series), 43–44, 51n35, 52n36

Zakim, Michael, 42
Zimmerman, David, 180n17
Žižek, Slavoj, 40–41, 45